Y[illegible]’S

BI[illegible]AD

A Pictorial History

1860 to 1960

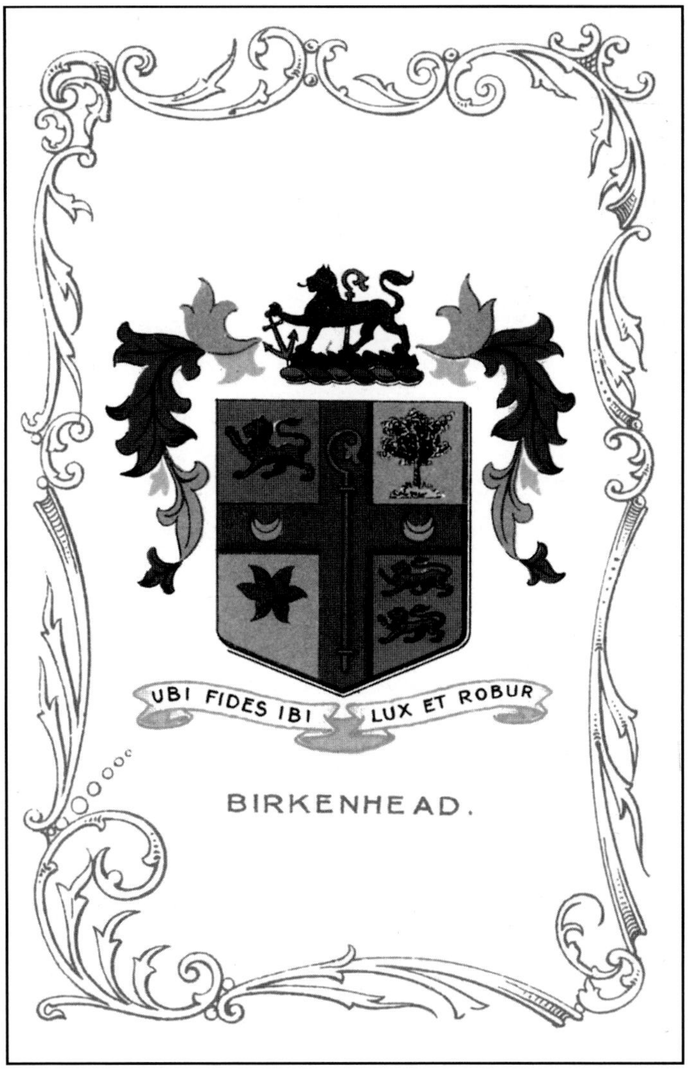

Design & Origination: Ian Boumphrey

Published by: Ian Boumphrey *The Nook* 7 Acrefield Road Prenton Wirral CH42 8LD
Tel/Fax: 0151 608 7611
E-mail: ian@Yesterdayswirral.co.uk
Website: www.yesterdayswirral.co.uk

Printed by: Vivapress, Barcelona

ISBN: **978-1-899241-26-2**

PRICE
£ 9.95

BIBLIOGRAPHY

These abbreviations are used in the text as a source reference guide

A	Arwe - The story of Arrowe, Pensby and the Liverpool Slave Trade	Greg Dawson	1994
AWSB	Inauguration of the Alwen Water Supply to Birkenhead	County Borough of Birkenhead	1921
BAW	Birkenhead at War 1939–45	Ian Boumphrey	2001
BB	The Birkenhead Brewery The First Hundred Years 1865-1965	Birkenhead Brewery	1965
BIW	Birkenhead Iron Works	Messrs Laird Brothers	1874
BET	Birkenhead Electric Tramways	Charles Rycroft	1993
BLTC	Birkenhead Lawn Tennis Club	K Clifford Cook	1992
BP	Birkenhead Park	Jean McInniss	1984
BPCC	Birkenhead Park Cricket Club 1846-1996	Chris Elston	1997
BSPH	Birkenhead School Pictorial History 1860-1960	Archives Department Birkenhead School	2006
4BCR	Story of the 4th Battallion the Cheshire Regiment 1859-1959	Lt Col JH McGuinness	1959
BW	Birkenhead Wasp - Theatrical & Athletic Gossip		1892
DoS	Diocese of Shrewsbury		1990
DRPB	Della Robbia Pottery Birkenhead 1894-1906	Williamson Art Gallery & Museum Birkenhead	
FB	Family Business - the story of Willmer Brothers & Haram Ltd	Wrayford Willmer	1961
FOBB	Festival of Britain - Birkenhead	Festival of Britain Committee	1951
FPH	Fire precaution Handbook	Birkenhead Borough Fire Brigade	1966
FVLB	A Free Village Library - Bebington	Reprinted from the *Standard*	1878
MMB	Murder & Mayhem in Birkenhead	David Malcolm	1994
MMMB	More Murder & Mayhem in Birkenhead	David Malcolm & Ian Boumphrey	1997
MOI	Men of Iron - The Study of Cammell Laird		1992
MQP	Maintaining The Queen's Peace	SP Thompson	1958
NEWS	Newspaper cuttings of the time		
OIH	One in Heart - History of Birkenhead School	WE Woodhouse	1967
OPB	Outline Plan for for the County Borough of Birkenhead		1947
OTT	On The Turf - The Origins of Horse Racing in the North West	Phil Thompson	1991
PROG	Information taken from booklet or programme issued at the time		
PWR	Portrait of Wirral Railways	Roger Jermy	1987
RF	Rock Ferry - New Ferry & Bebington	Dave Mitchelson	1989
ROB	Reminiscences of Birkenhead	Charles Grey Mott	1900
RSoW	Railway Stations of Wirral	Mersey Railway History Group	1994
SOT	Sidelights on Tranmere	JE Allison	1976
SOUV	Information taken from Souvenir booklet - not a book		
SSW1	Silver Screens of Wirral - Birkenhead & Bebington	PA Carson & CR Garner	1990
ST	The Storeton Tramway	RC Jermy	1981
SUAH	Set Upon A Hill	Ken Burnley	1993
TBB	The Birkenhead Bus	TB Maund	1994
TBW	Tramways of Birkenhead and Wallasey	TB Maund & M Jenkins	1987
TPG	The Peoples' Garden	Clifford E Thornton	
TR 1881	Tranmere Rovers 1881-1921 - A New History	Gilbert Upton	1991
TR 1921	Tranmere Rovers 1921-1997 - A Complete Record	Gilbert Upton and Steve Wilson	1997
TST	The Storeton Tramway	Roger Jermy	1981
TTM	The Tapestry Makers	Alan Johnston and Kevin Moore	1987
VS	The Birkenhead News Victory Souvenir of the Great War 1914-18	Birkenhead News	1919
WBD	Willmer's Birkenhead Directory 1915-16		1916
WCS	West Coast Steamers	CLD Duckworth & GE Langmuir	1953
WDFA	Wirral District Football Association 1885-1995		1995
WLGC	Wirral Ladies Golf Club 1894-1994	Betty Lloyd	1994
WRPS	Woodchurch Road Primary School	Joan C Nelson	1983
WTDW	Where to Drink in Wirral	Birkenhead Brewery	1961
WPPB	Wirral Past & Present - Bidston	Metropolitan Borough of Wirral	1982
YWPH	Yesterday's Wirral Pictorial History	Ian & Marilyn Boumphrey	2000

INTRODUCTION

This is my fifth "Pictorial History" publication, the others being "Yesterday's Wirral 1890 to 1953"; "Yesterday's Port Sunlight 1888 to 1953"; "Yesterday's Liverpool 1857 to 1957" and "Birkenhead - A Pictorial History" - the only one which, although I compiled it, was published by someone else - Phillimore. This is my fourth general book about Birkenhead and surrounding areas - although it is the first to include Rock Ferry, New Ferry and most of Tranmere and Bebington. I have used over 550 photographs and graphics, the majority of which have not been used in my other books on Birkenhead. I initially gleaned the information from the annals in *Kelly's Directories, Gore's Directories* and *Willmer's Birkenhead Postal Directory 1915-16* and then from local publications, booklets, guides etc and have acknowledged the source if possible through the Bibliography [see opposite page].

I chose 1860 as the starting point because this was the year Birkenhead 'came of age' in that it was the first place to recognise the American Francis Train's revolutionary tram system and opened the first public tram system in Europe. The trams ran from Woodside Ferry to the entrance of Birkenhead Park which was the first public park in the world, opening in 1847. I continue the book in chronological order for the next hundred years, with some years taking up two pages.

I have illustrated the book with postcards and photographs mainly from my own collection and have placed them in or as near to the year as possible. I apologise in advance for any photographs which I have used, where I have been unable to acknowledge details of the source. When compiling a book of this kind, it is difficult to include every aspect of Birkenhead's history - I hope you approve of my selection.

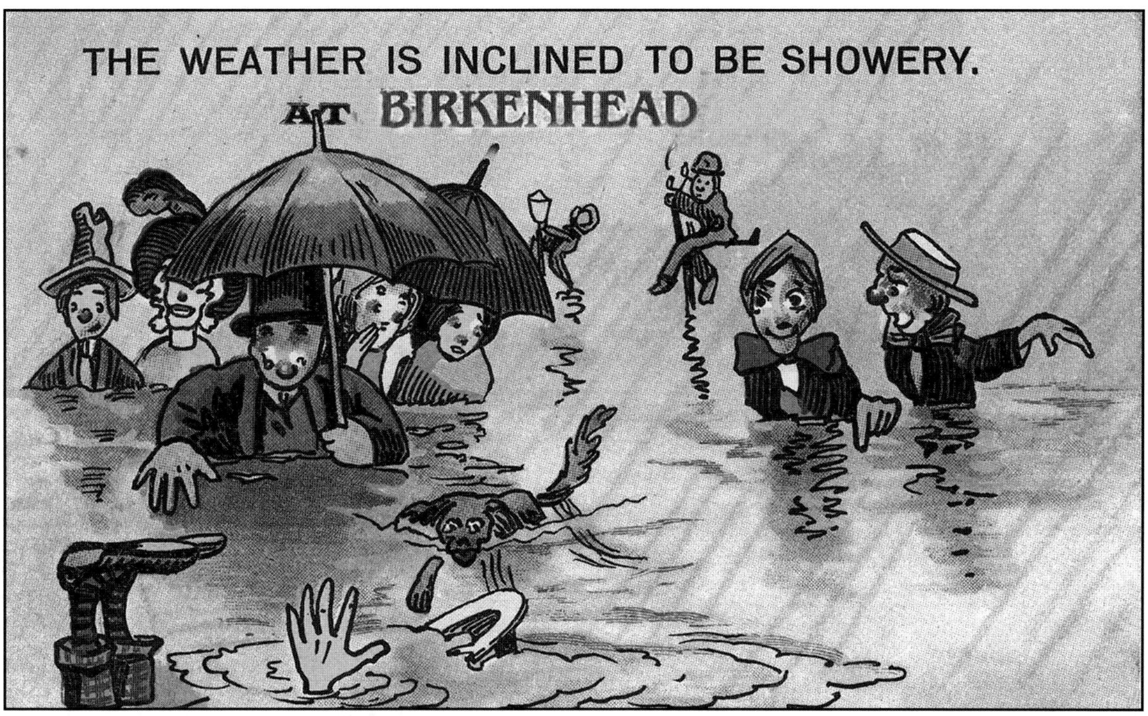

This was a comic postcard sent from Birkenhead in 1916

ACKNOWLEDGEMENTS

I would like to thank the following people who contributed towards the publication of this book:-
Doug Bastin, Birkenhead School Archives, James Boumphrey, Marilyn Boumphrey, Bromborough Society Archives, Peter Edwards, Ted Gerry, Mr Google, Anna Graham, Bill Johnstone, Len Kirkham, TB Maund, Susan Nicholson, Joseph Ruiz and Guy Woodland

1860

– The **Bidston** Signal Station now connected from Holyhead to Liverpool via Bidston with the aid of an electric telegraph. Originally signal flags were used from 1873, they were superceded in 1827 by a telegraphic system using eight semaphore stations, including Bidston, which could relay messages the 75 miles in just over 5 minutes[WPPB] [see 1871]

– St Paul's Presbyterian Church, Jackson Street **Birkenhead** opened - cost £2,500 seating for 780

– Completion of *Harefield House* at a cost of £20,000 built for the shipowner William Inman in Moreton Road **Upton** - it was described as 'a handsome stone residence in the Grecian style' - later named *Upton Manor* [see 1914]

– Holt Hill Convent Chapel **Tranmere** opened[DoS]

Jun 27 First cotton-loaded ship *William Singer* with over 3,000 bales, entered **Birkenhead** docks

Aug 9 **Birkenhead** Proprietory School [became Birkenhead School in 1871] opened with 18 boys - 30 by the end of the first term[BSPH]

Aug 17 **Birkenhead** Railway transferred to the London & North-Western and Great Western Railway companies

Aug 30 **Birkenhead** Street Railway opened - first public tram system in Europe - banquet given by George Francis Train[BET]

Nov 1 Great Float at **Birkenhead** completed and water admitted

Nov 13 Foundation stone laid for **Birkenhead** County Court in Chester Street

Dec John Laird retired from his company John Laird, Sons & Co, which was then continued by his three sons under the name Laird Brothers. He then went into politics, becoming the first Member of Parliament for **Birkenhead** [see 1861][ROB]

COWLEY (LATE GIBSON,)
TAILOR AND DRAPER,
No. 22, Market Cross Street,
BIRKENHEAD.

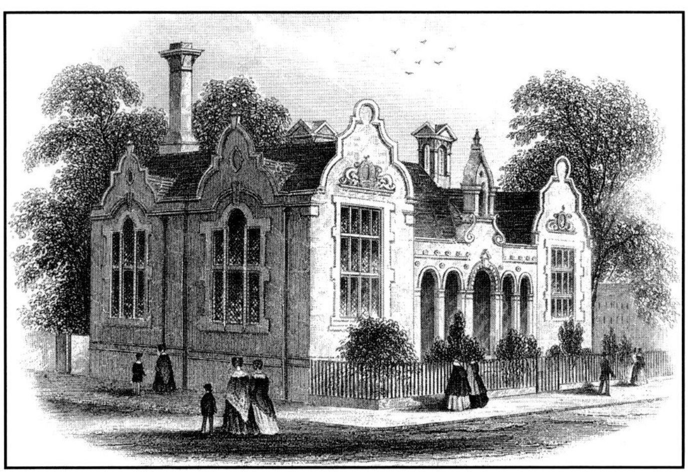

Above: *St Mary's Schools, 44 Priory Street* ***Birkenhead***

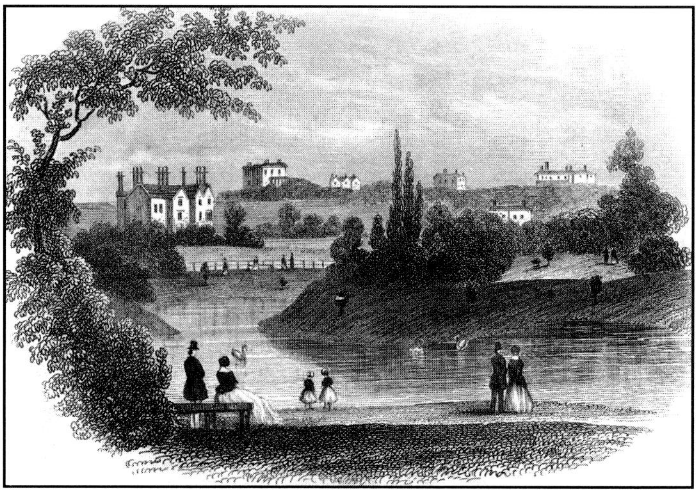

Above: ***Birkenhead*** *Park, which had opened over ten years previously has developed from the swamp-land that it was built on - opening in 1847 [see also 1865]*

THE YOUNG MAY DIE SOON, THE AGED MUST.

MR. JAMES CROMPTON,
8, PRINCE'S TERRACE, GRANGE LANE, BIRKENHEAD,
AND
16, SOUTH JOHN STREET, LIVERPOOL,
DISTRICT MANAGER, (LIVERPOOL BRANCH,) TO THE
English Widows' Fund Life Assurance Company.
PROSPECTUSES &c. WILL BE SENT, ON APPLICATION, TO ANY ADDRESS.
This Company offers Special Advantages to all Parties. POLICIES will be PAID DURING LIFE, by the appropriation of BONUSES, or at DEATH, whenever that may occur.

AGENT FOR THE ROYAL FIRE INSURANCE COMPANY.
" " AGRICULTURIST CATTLE INSURANCE CO.
" " ACCIDENTAL & MARINE INSURANCE CO.

LOANS GRANTED ON PERSONAL SECURITY.
ESTATE, HOUSE AND COMMISSION AGENT.

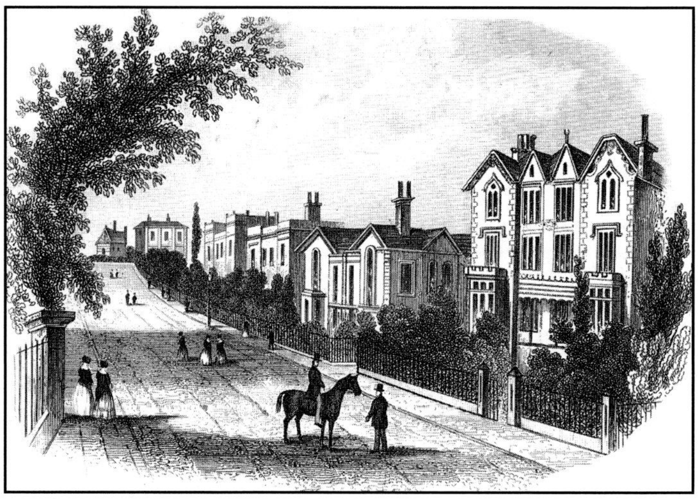

Above: *Clifton Road was within Clifton Park and is seen in this sketch of the time as a very desirable residential area. It seems that only half the scheme was completed. Although the villas were described as "the most beautiful construction in the whole of* ***Birkenhead****" it continued "would be most desireable but for the intolerable nuisance of a pestilence spreading odour from a pool by the gas works"*

GEORGE AGNEW,
HOUSE & ESTATE AGENT,
AND
COLLECTOR OF ACCOUNTS.
No. 46, RUSSELL STREET,
BIRKENHEAD.
AGENT FOR THE LANCASHIRE INSURANCE COMPANY.

1861

– **Birkenhead** became a Parliamentary Borough

– The Conway School wooden frigate HMS *Conway*, which was the school's first ship and had opened in the River Mersey off **Rock Ferry** in 1859, was replaced with the former HMS *Winchester* [see also 1953]

– Charles Willmer set up business at 64-66 Chester Street **Birkenhead** as a printer with his wife and seven children[FB] [see also 1877]

– Football had previously been prohibited in **Birkenhead** Park, but a small area was set aside for the game to be played in the park[TPG]

Apr 7 **Hoylake** fishing smack *Ben Bullbin* was recovered after a collision in the River Mersey with the steamship *African* where three out of the crew of five drowned - one of the bodies was taken to the Fire Engine House of the Main Bridewell in Hamilton Street **Birkenhead**[MMB]

Oct 30 Foundation stone laid for the Wesley Church, Church Road **Hr Tranmere**[souv] [see photo 1907]

Dec John Laird elected the First Member of Parliament for **Birkenhead** - he defeated the Liberal candidate, Thomas Brassey Jnr, son of the eminent railway contractor, by a majority of 347 votes [see cartoon below and photo]

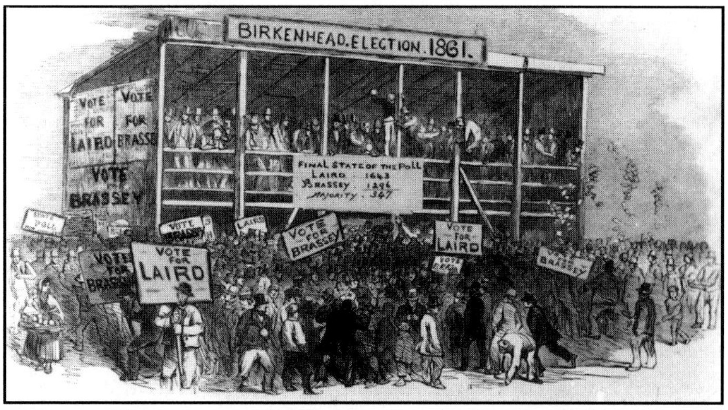

Above: *This cartoon highlights the election in* ***Birkenhead*** *for its first Member of Parliament. The contest was between John Laird, founder of John Laird Son & Co - shipbuilders and Thomas Brassey, son of the eminent railway contractor. John Laird won by a majority of 347 votes [he was re-elected in 1865, 1868 and 1874]*

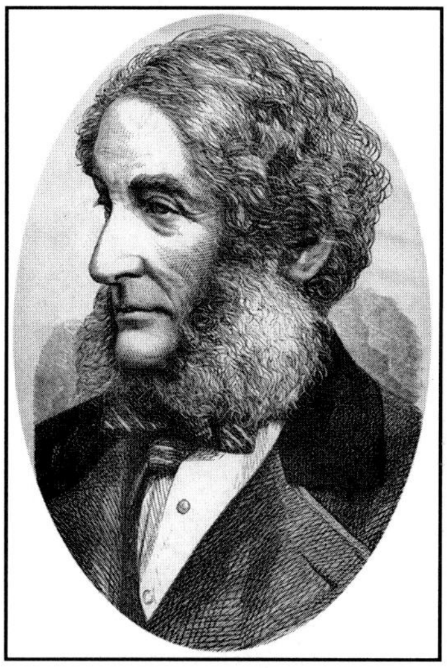

Right: *John Laird, founder of the shipbuilding company John Laird, Son & Company in* ***Birkenhead*** *1827 - he was elected first Member of Parliament for* ***Birkenhead*** *December 1861 [see cartoon]*

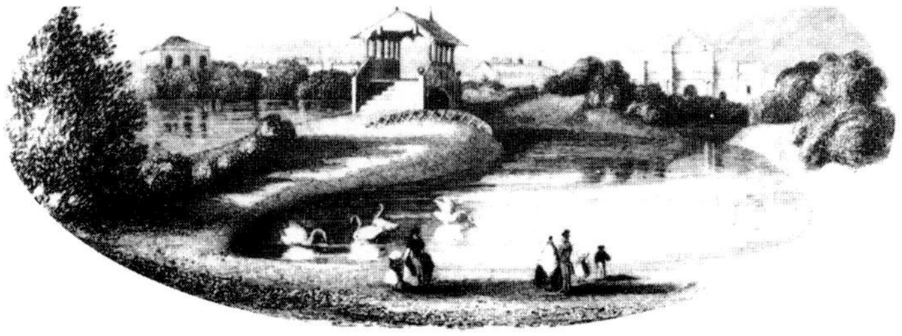

Above: *This sketch by Pinkey's of Birkenhead shows one of the lakes in* ***Birkenhead*** *Park overlooked by the Swiss Bridge. The park was designed by Sir Joseph Paxton and laid out on former waste swamps, opening in 1847. A crowd of some 10,000 people enjoyed the magnificent features of the park whilst listening to the many bands and watching games of cricket, football and 'old English sports'*

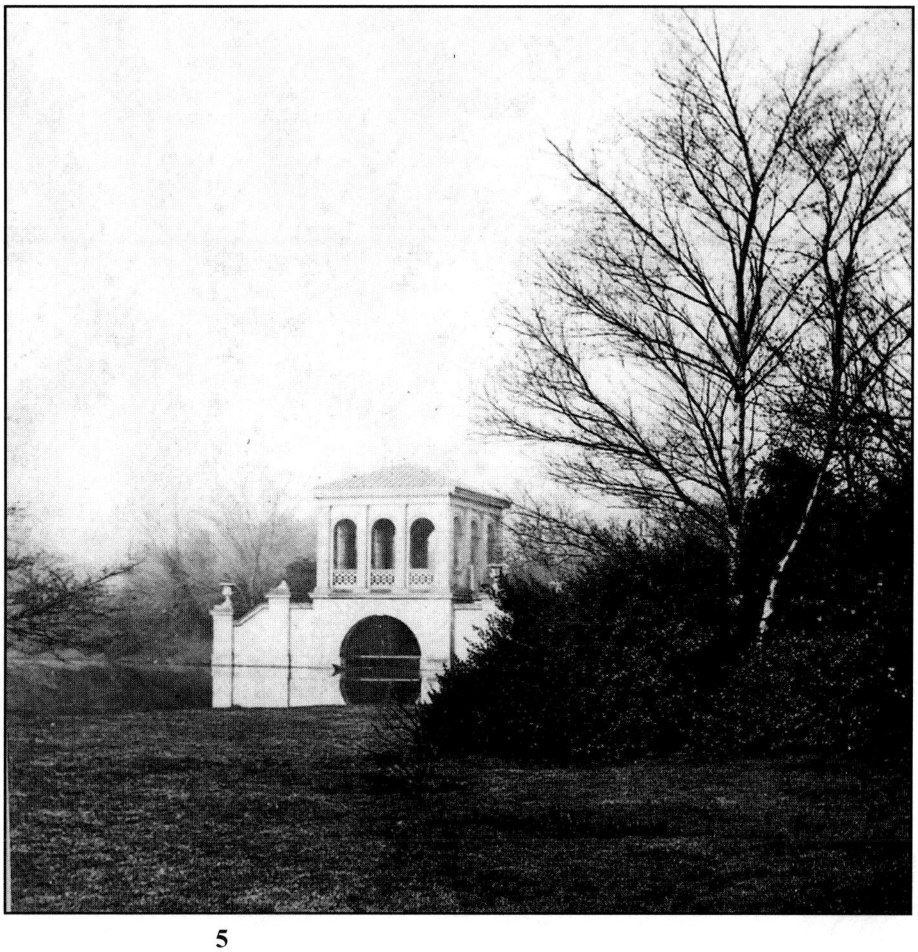

Right: Birkenhead *Park Boathouse is seen with its reflection in the lower park lake. The covered bandstand kept the musicians under cover but in later years it lost its balustrading and roof. This photo was a on a sterocard by an unknown photographer and dated 1865. The park was opened the same day as the Birkenhead Docks - the days events ended with a firework display*

1862

– **Tranmere** Old Hall demolished and Church Road straightened out [see image][souv]

– **Tranmere** Village Cross disappeared to be found over 70 years later [see 1935 & 1937][souv]

– The **Birkenhead** Commissioners advised the justices not to grant any more intoxicating liquor licences - "on account of the misery and crime drunkenness has brought into the township"

Jan 21 **Birkenhead** Music Hall, Claughton Road, inaugurated

Feb 10 South Bridge of **Birkenhead** Woodside Landing Stage opened

July 29 Celebrated US Confederate ship No. 290 *Alabama,* built at Laird's Shipyard, **Birkenhead**, left the Mersey [see article]

Aug 30 Opening service for the Wesley Church, Church Road **Hr Tranmere** (known as "The Pepperbox" due to its design) - total cost £4,786. The Sunday School opened beneath the Chapel[souv] [see 1907]

Nov 1 **Rock Ferry** Station, Bedford Road, opened on the Chester to Birkenhead Railway replacing station at Rock Lane[RSoW]

Nov 24 Foundation stone for the **Birkenhead** Borough Hospital laid by the Marquis of Westminster - on land paid for by Thomas Brassey and built at the expense of John Laird[souv] [see 1863]

ESTABLISHED 25 YEARS.

PARK HOTEL,

CHARING CROSS, OXTON ROAD,

BIRKENHEAD.

This Hotel has been remodelled and newly furnished, and offers first-class accommodation to Private Families, Commercial Gentlemen, Captains, &c. Its situation is central, being within a few minutes' walk of Claughton, Oxton, and Tranmere; three minutes' walk of the beautiful Birkenhead Park, and ten minutes' of Woodside Ferry. Omnibuses pass the door every 15 minutes.

CHARGES STRICTLY MODERATE. BAIT AND LIVERY STABLES.

CHARLES H. TAYLOR,

CHARING CROSS, OXTON ROAD, BIRKENHEAD.

Bass's Mild Ale		(4½ Gallon Cask)	9s 0d
Aspinall's Strong Ale		Ditto	8s 0d
Fine Mild Ale		Ditto	6s 6d
East India Pale		Ditto	8s & 9s
Combe, Delafield & Co's. Stout		(4½ Gallon Cask Imperial)	9s 6d
Ditto	ditto	ditto No. 3	8s 6d
Ditto	ditto	ditto No. 2	7s 6d

Dunville's Old Irish Whisky, 3s. 8d. per Bottle.

GLENLIVAT OLD SCOTCH WHISKY, 4s 6d per Quart.

Fine Old Cognac, 6 Years Old, 5s 4d per Bottle.

Port, 24s, 30s, 42s, 60s and 84s. Sherry, 30s, 42s and 60s.

GOODS DELIVERED FREE WITHIN 6 MILES. ORDERS BY POST PROMPTLY ATTENDED TO.

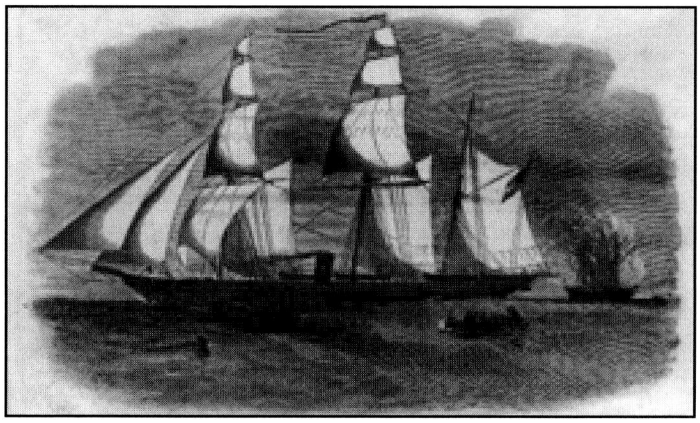

Above: *The '290', afterwards called the* Alabama, *left the River Mersey under the command of Captain Semmes, having been built at Laird's shipyard in Birkenhead. During the American Civil War she captured about 70 Northern vessels and was eventually sunk by gunfire off the French coast. Lairds had also built two iron rams, which were about to be launched from Laird's shipyard when the Government prevented them from putting to sea. The nation paid £3.25 million in compensation to the American Government for the damage the* Alabama *caused*

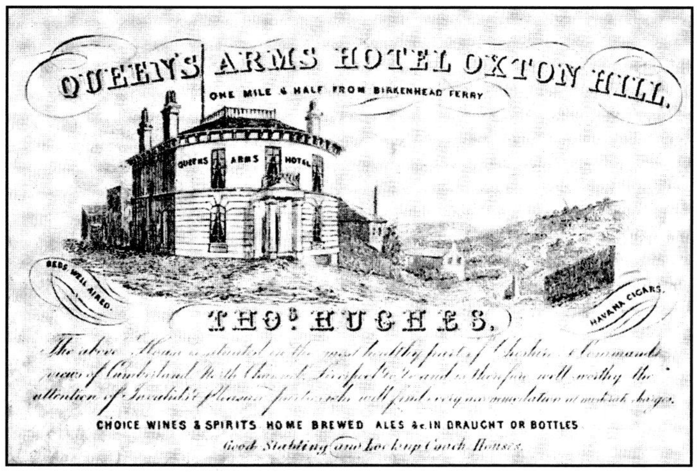

Above: *This advert for the* Queen's Arms Hotel ***Oxton*** *Hill tells us:- that this area around the top of Storeton Road used to be known as 'Oxton Hill' - the licensee was Thomas Hughes - the hotel was one mile and a half from Birkenhead Ferry - its beds were well aired - its ales were 'home brewed' - there was good stabling and lock up coach houses and the building is recognisable today about 150 years on*

Right: *Tranmere Old Hall was* ***Tranmere's*** *most striking building and is seen from Church Road. It stood in 1.5 acres of grounds at the junction of Church Road and Greenway Road Tranmere. The main entrance was through the archway in the wall the far side of the house which had a datestone of 1614 above and the initials GL - AL which were those of George and Ann Langford who were married that year. It was demolished in the early 1860s by 'an ignorant boor' (he was financially ruined by this venture) with Church Road being straightened out - shops and houses were built on the site with the foundations reputed to be under the Co-op store*

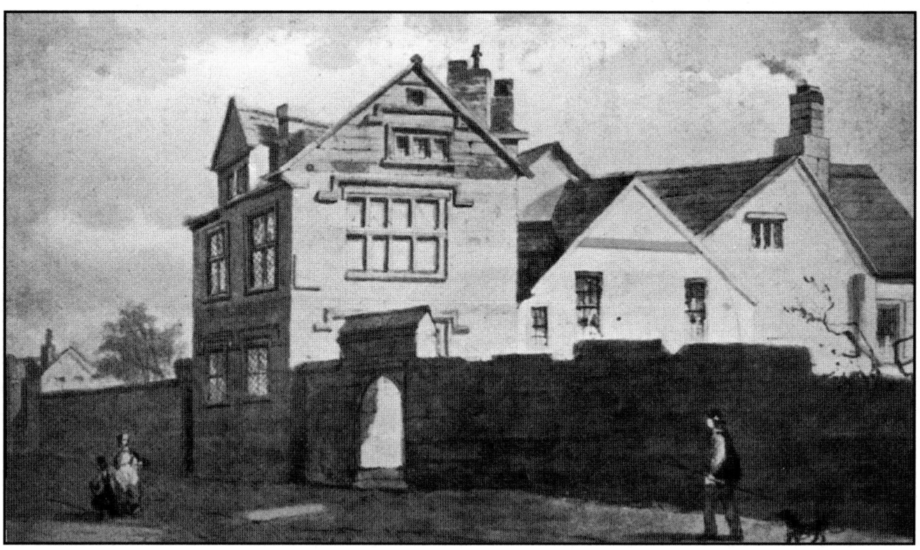

1863

– **Tranmere** Workhouse opened - later to become St Catherine's Hospital[souv] [see 1906]

– The first Chief Constable of **Birkenhead** Borough was appointed[souv]

– Drinking fountain in the centre of **Bebington** Village was a gift of Charles Hill [see 1903][YWPH]

– The Faithful Companions of Jesus bought ***Upton Hall***, built a new three-storey building and moved their boarding school for girls there from Lingdale House in Claughton - the beginnings of Upton Hall Convent

May 12 Trinity Presbyterian Church, **Claughton** formed [see 1866]

June 1 Foundation stone laid for the Wesleyan Chapel at junction of Laird Street/ Conway Street **Birkenhead**

Nov 21 The new **Birkenhead** Borough Hospital was completed and handed over to the committee [see photo]

J. GREEN,
PHARMACEUTICAL CHEMIST,
APOTHECARIES' HALL,
80, ARGYLE STREET,
(NEAR THE GENERAL POST-OFFICE.)
BIRKENHEAD, AND TRANMERE PARK.
ESTABLISHED 1846.
ESPECIAL ATTENTION DIRECTED TO THE DISPENSING DEPARTMENT.
ELASTIC AND SURGICAL BANDAGES, TRUSSES, &c.
A LARGE STOCK OF TURKEY AND HONEYCOMB SPONGES.
TOOTH, NAIL AND HAIR BRUSHES, WARRANTED.
FLESH GLOVES, SPONGE BAGS, &c.
RIMMELL'S PERFUMERY.
O'CONNELL'S PATENT SYPHONIA, THE ONLY PERFECT FEEDING BOTTLE.
FAMILY AND SHIPS' MEDICINE CHESTS SUPPLIED AND RE-FITTED.
SOLE AGENT FOR THIS DISTRICT FOR
HAMILTON & CO.'S PURE TEAS AND COFFEE, IN AIR-TIGHT PACKAGES.

JAMES CARROLL,
COAL ∵ MERCHANT,
25, IVY STREET, BIRKENHEAD.

1st QUALITY	..	17/6 PER TON.
2nd	"	16/ "
3rd	"	13/6 "

DELIVERIES IN LARGE OR SMALL QUANTITIES.
NO EXTRA CHARGE IN BAGS.
ORDERS PUNCTUALLY ATTENDED TO.

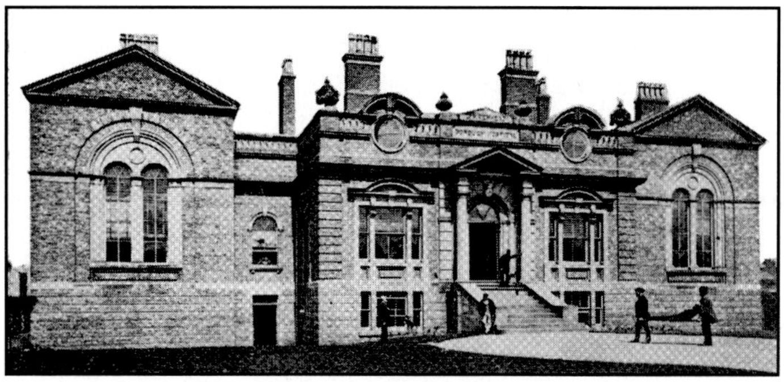

Above: *The land for the **Birkenhead** Borough Hospital in Conway Street (later Park Road North) had been provided by Thomas Brassey and John Laird paid for the building, which overlooked Birkenhead Park. The foundation stone had been laid 24 November 1862 . There was a successful public appeal for £2,000 to equip the hospital and when it was handed over to the committee on 21 November 1863, most of the latest equipment and furniture had been installed, ready for its opening to patients on 1 January 1864. It was two storeys high with a basement, built of brick and Storeton Stone. It consisted of three male wards and one female ward with accommodation for 50 beds*

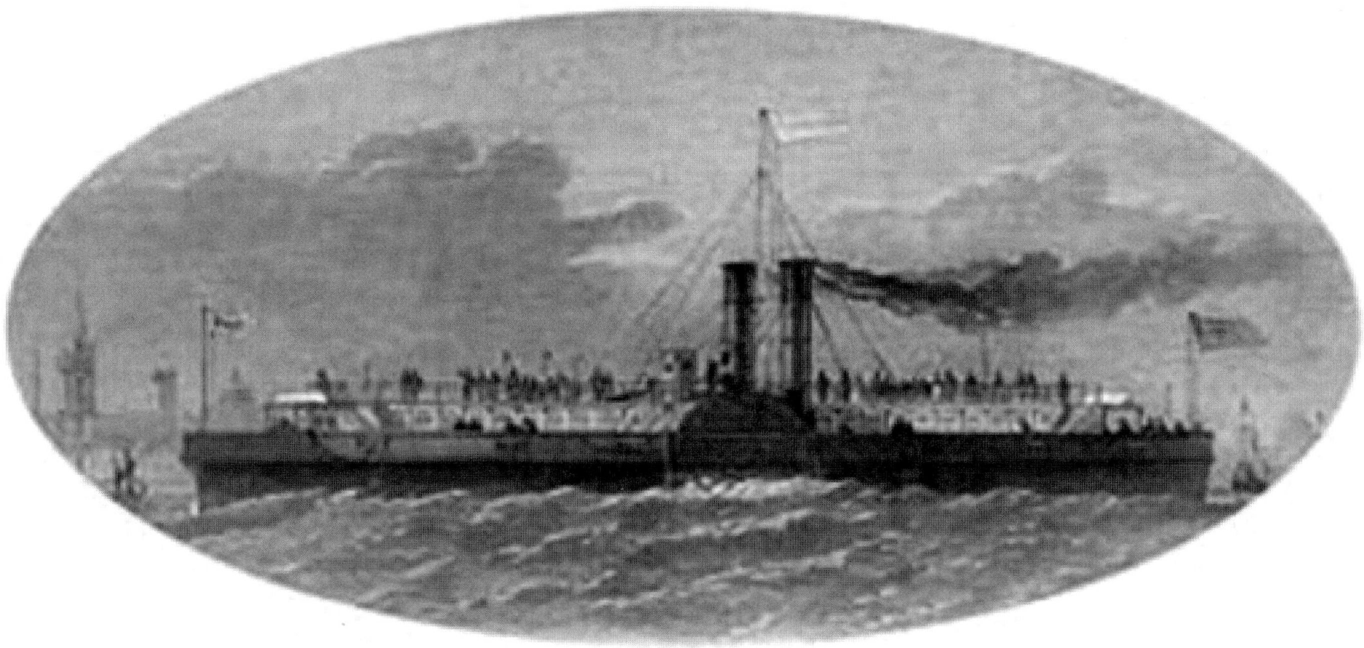

Above: ***Birkenhead** ferry boat* Cheshire *was built by HM Laurence & Co of **Liverpool** and launched in 1863 - making her first Mersey crossing in 1864. This iron paddle steamer, which weighed 420 tons and was 150 ft. long, was the first to have an enclosed saloon, offering passengers protection from the often inclement weather. However her length was found to be impracticable to berth expeditiously at **Liverpool**. She was sold in 1888 to the Liverpool Steam Tug Company and became the tug* **America**

1864

– *The Ring O'Bells Inn* - which once stood on the corner of School Lane **Bidston** - was forced to close due to drunken behaviour outside the Church on Sunday morning [see this page]

– Simon Croft died - the last publican of the *Ring O'Bells*, **Bidston** [reputed to be 'Simon The Cellarer' of the famous song]

– *Arudy* later to be renamed *The Towers* was built in what is now Victoria Park **Tranmere** [see 1957]

– **Birkenhead** Commissioners' first Saloon Ferry Boat, the two-funnelled *Cheshire*, made its appearance [see photo][SOUV]

– Flaybrick Hill Cemetery **Birkenhead** opened with an area of over 36 acres

– John Lee opened his first tailor's shop in **Birkenhead** [later to become Hope & Lee - see 1880]

Jan 1 The new **Birkenhead** Borough Hospital was opened for patients[SOUV]

Jan 15 A terrible explosion took place on board the *Lotty Sleigh*, bound for Africa, which had just taken on board 11 tons of gunpowder from the magazine boats lying off **Tranmere**. Damage caused both sides of the Mersey, especially in **Birkenhead** [see sketch]

Apr 23 **Birkenhead** Free Library opened to the public in Hamilton Street[souv]

Apr 23 Shakespeare's tercentenary was celebrated in **Birkenhead** - where a crowd of over 6,000 people in Birkenhead Park saw an oak tree planted and heard much speechmaking[TPG]

J. OLIVER,
PRINTER AND STATIONER,
"ADVERTISER" OFFICE,
9, MARKET CROSS STREET, BIRKENHEAD.
THE
"BIRKENHEAD AND CHESHIRE ADVERTISER,"
Published every Wednesday and Saturday, Price One Penny, and SATURDAY'S WEEKLY EDITIO Price Twopence.

Above: *The* Birkenhead and Cheshire Advertiser *was the first* ***Birkenhead*** *newspaper, founded in 1853. The first edition of the* Birkenhead News *was in 1877. In 1957 the two newspapers merged* [FB]

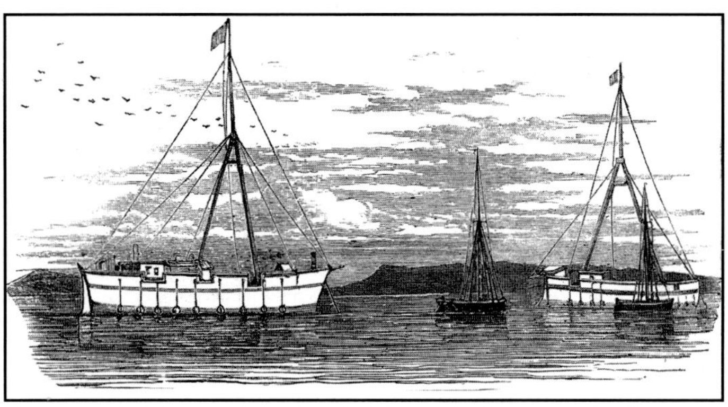

Above: *Two magazine ships are seen moored off* ***New Ferry****. Ships entering the River Mersey had to deposit any gunpowder they had on board, during their stay in port. From 1768 they were stored ashore at the Magazines in Egremont, but an Act of Parliament in 1851 stipulated they had to be stored offshore so they were moved to vessels moored off New Ferry. However, on 15 July 1864, the* Lotty Sleigh *had just taken on board 11 tons of gunpowder from a magazine ship, when it exploded causing damage to property ashore*

TRANMERE FOUNDRY, BIRKENHEAD.

WILLIAM AND MAXWELL SCOTT,
ENGINEERS, IRONFOUNDERS, AND MILLWRIGHTS,
ALL DESCRIPTION OF CASTINGS IN LOAM OR SAND,
SCREW PROPELLERS UP TO 10 TONS WEIGHT.
RANGES, PALISADING, TOMB RAILS, AND SMITH-WORK.
EXPANSION ENGINEERS,
MAKERS OF
SCHIELE'S PATENT VARIABLE EXPANSION GEAR,
And fitted by us to numerous land engines, has given entire satisfaction.
HUNTLEY'S PATENT EXPANSION GEAR,
Will cut off from any point down to 90 per cent. of the stroke, and fitted by us to the steamers "Great Conquest," and "Merry Andrew," has given the greatest satisfaction.
The saving of Coal by the use of the above has been in some instances 25 per cent., and in all cases the saving has more than compensated for the outlay, besides being a yearly gain.

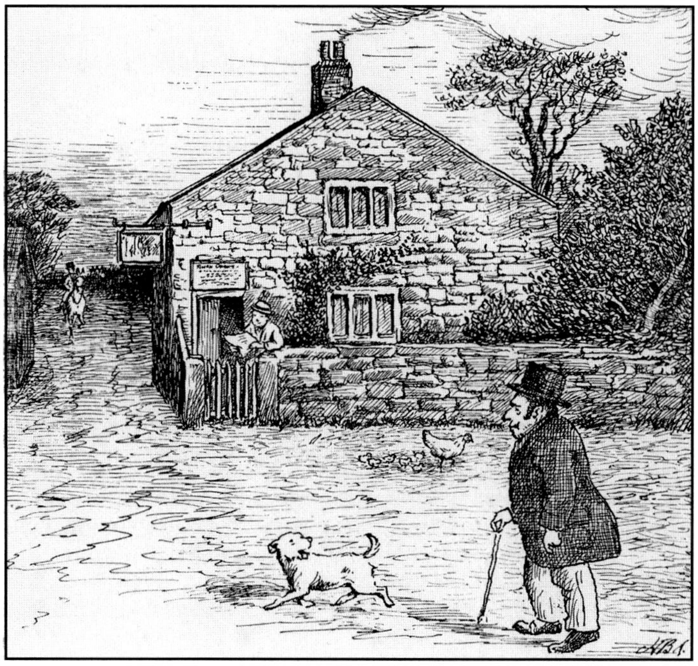

Above: *The* Ring O' Bells *was an inn standing at the top of School Lane* ***Bidston*** *on the opposite side to St Oswald's - the Parish Church of Bidston. The inn dates back to 1750 but its most famous landlord, Simon Croft, was also its last. He married the previous landlord's daughter, Mary Pendleton, for whom he had great affection. Unfortunately she died in 1847 and he remarried. The Ring O'Bells became famous for its Ham and Eggs, with customers travelling far and wide - the inn yard would be crowded with gigs, spring-carts and traps of every description. It was especially popular at certain holidays - one Easter Monday between 30 and 40 hams [Simon bred his own sows] and a proportionate number of eggs were consumed. The meals were served in long wooden sheds or 'arbours' which were on the Green at the back of the inn. It was said that a good deal of smuggled liquor found its way into the inn. Simon was a very large man and on his death in 1864, the coffin could not be carried down the steep and narrow inn stairs - so the window frame was removed and he was lowered from his bedroom window. Following complaints of drunkenness, the inn was closed in 1868. It then became known as* Stone Farm. *The hostelry was immortalised by Albert Smith in his book* Christopher Tadpole *- a journey around this country in the 1850s. He describes their meal of ham and eggs as "excellent and the ale as something beyond that"*

1865

– William Inman, the shipowner, is reputed to have bought the Lordship of the ***Upton*** *Manor* from his neighbour, Thomas Webster[SOUV]

– Trinity Presbyterian Church **Claughton** opened a Sunday School in a house in Patten Street **Birkenhead** which proved very successful[SOUV]

– The *Queen* was built at Laird Brothers shipyard **Birkenhead** for the National Steamship Company [see photo]

– **Birkenhead** Commissioners introduced two new Saloon Steamers - the *Lancashire* and *Woodside*[SOUV]

Mar 27 Launch of the armour-clad steam frigate *Agincourt* built for Her Majesty's Government at Laird Brothers' shipyard **Birkenhead**[BIW]

Aug 29 The **Birkenhead** Amalgamated Brewery Company Ltd was registered. It was formed by amalgamating two brewing firms: the Cook family of Oxton Road, **Birkenhead** and the Aspinall family of Cleveland Street, Birkenhead[SOUV]

JOSEPH RAY,
UMBRELLA AND PARASOL MANUFACTURER,
DOOR AND WINDOW-PLATE MAKER,
46, MARKET STREET,
N.B.—Engraving neatly executed, Jewellery Repaired, Cutlery Ground and Repaired, &c.

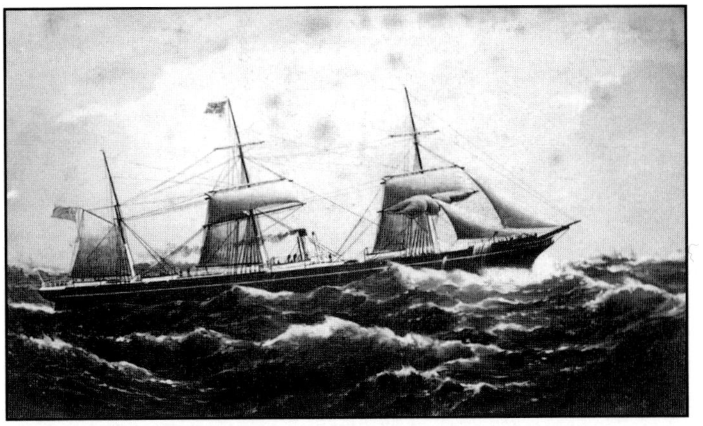

Above: In 1865, Messrs. Laird Brothers built the *Queen* of 3,253 tons, 368 ft. length, 42 ft. 3 in. breadth, and 29 ft. 5 in. depth of hold for the National Steamship Company. The beautiful symmetrical lines of this vessel made her the cynosure of the shipping world at the time she was launched. She was rigged as a barque, with square sails upon her fore and main masts. Her topsails were double, and she was fully supplied with every means of working them from the deck, and so to spread or shorten sail immediately. But even with all her beauties of construction, the *Queen* was fairly eclipsed by the *Spain*, another vessel launched for the same company by the Messrs. Laird, in May, 1871

Right: *This advert for the Mersey River Steam Boat Company appeared in the 1865 publication* The Liverpool Guide its Highways, Byeways and Thoroughfares, By Land and Water. *It highlighted the opening of the new ferry service between Prince's Landing Stage,* ***Liverpool*** *(opposite the bottom of Chapel Street) and* ***New Ferry*** *Pier - calling (except at low water Spring tides) at the Company's South-End Landing Stage (situate near the foot of Park Street* ***Toxteth****). The weekday service was every half hour from 7.45am to 8.45 pm - the fare was one penny*

MERSEY RIVER
Steam Boat Company, Limited.

THE NEW FERRY
BETWEEN
PRINCE'S LANDING STAGE
(Opposite bottom of Chapel Street),
AND
NEW FERRY PIER,
Calling (except at Low Water Spring Tides,) at the Company's
SOUTH-END LANDING STAGE,
(Situate near the Foot of Park Street,)
IS NOW OPEN.

FROM NEW FERRY PIER.
On Week Days—At 7 45 a.m. and every quarter before and quarter after each hour, until 8 45 p.m.
On Sundays—At 8 45 and 9 45, a.m.; after 1 15 p.m. the Boats will ply as on Week Days.

FROM PRINCE'S LANDING STAGE.
On Week Days—At 8 15 a.m., and every quarter before and quarter after each hour until 9 15 p.m.
On Sundays—At 8 15 and 9 15 a.m., after 1 15 p.m. the Boats will ply as on Week Days.

Fare—ONE PENNY.

ROBERT LAMONT,
Secretary and Manager.

Lancaster Buildings, Liverpool,
September, 1865.

TRANMERE PARK HOTEL,
CHURCH ROAD, HOLT HILL.
J. GRIFFITHS,
Begs to inform his Friends and the Public that he has taken the above Hotel, and Re-Opened it with a choice Stock of Wines and Spirits, Mild and Bitter Ale, London and Dublin Porter, &c., trusting by moderate charges to merit a share of their patronage. Bed and Breakfast, 2s. 6d. Dinners, Luncheons, Chops, Steaks, &c., in a few minutes. A new and excellent Billiard Table. Daily Papers kept and filed for reference. Bait and Livery Stables. Family Orders punctually attended to.

THOMPSON AND CAPPER'S
HOMŒOPATHIC COCOA.

This delicious Food is GUARANTEED FREE FROM ADULTERATION, and as a BREAKFAST or SUPPER beverage is UNSURPASSED, being infinitely more WHOLESOME and NUTRITIOUS than either Tea or Coffee, a fact acknowledged by those accustomed to its daily use.
Being peculiarly easy of digestion it is with confidence recommended to Invalids, and in the Sick room is found invaluable.
The increasing demand by the public for Cocoa during the last few years has created a supply of much that is worthless. Hence the Caution appended to this advertisement.

SOLD WHOLESALE AND RETAIL BY
THOMPSON AND CAPPER,
HOMŒOPATHIC CHEMISTS,
43, BOLD STREET, AND 4, LORD STREET, LIVERPOOL,
AND 32, HAMILTON STREET, BIRKENHEAD,
And may be procured of all respectable Grocers & Chemists. In 1lb., ½lb., & ¼lb. packages, at 1s 6d per lb.

CAUTION.—Purchasers desirous of obtaining GENUINE HOMŒOPATHIC COCOA, in perfection, should observe that the name of THOMPSON and CAPPER is on the label of each Package, there being many imitations of this excellent article of diet.

1866

– The Albert Memorial Industrial Schools in Corporation Road **Birkenhead** opened with accommodation for 180 children, which was erected at the expense of William Jackson and named after the late Prince Consort[MOB]

Jan 1 **Bebington** Library opened in a house at the bottom of Heath Road rented for the purpose by Joseph Mayer, a Liverpool jeweller and goldsmith who came to live in Bebington - it contained 1,500 books [see next page][PROG]

Apr 29 Foundation stone laid for St Mark's Church **New Ferry** by Mr Alfred Turner

June 21 Duke of Edinburgh visited HMS *Conway* and afterwards opened the new Northern entrances to the **Birkenhead** Docks

June 23 Duke of Edinburgh visited Laird Brothers shipyard, **Birkenhead**

July 2 **Hoylake** Railway to **Birkenhead** opened for traffic

July 23 **Birkenhead** Park Cricket Club played a two day match against Surrey CCC at Kennington Oval - Surrey won by 5 wickets[BPCC]

July 26 **Birkenhead** Park Cricket Club played a two day match against MCC at Lords. MCC won by an innings and 12 runs[BPCC]

Oct 11 Trinity Presbyterian Church Beresford Road **Claughton** opened at a total cost of £8,000 [see photo][SOUV]

1867

– The **Birkenhead** Commissioners were authorised to construct waterworks at Flaybrick Hill and **Upton** and a reservoir on **Bidston** Hill[SOUV] [see 1959]

– The Roman Catholic Church of Our Lady was erected in Price Street **Birkenhead** at a cost of £8,000 and had seats for 800 [see 1905]

– The *Great Eastern* was coated with McInnes Patent preservative at **New Ferry** to prevent the iron hull from rusting [see 1890]

Aug 22 **Birkenhead** Park CC beat an All England XI by seven runs[BPCC]

Aug 28 ***Arrowe Hall*** was put up for auction - however it was withdrawn when the final bid reached £50,000[A]

Sept 21 The One O'Clock Gun fired for the first time from Morpeth Pier **Birkenhead** [see photo]

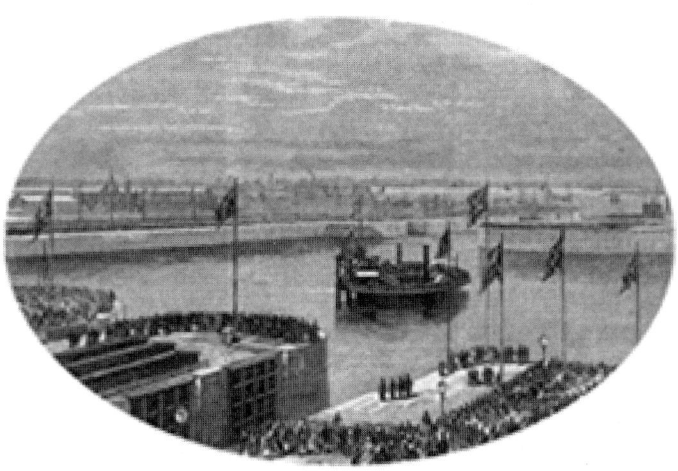

Above: *The Alfred Dock and Northern entrances to the system were opened by the Duke of Edinburgh, a son of Queen Victoria 21 June 1866. The construction of the Vittoria Dock came sometime later in 1909*

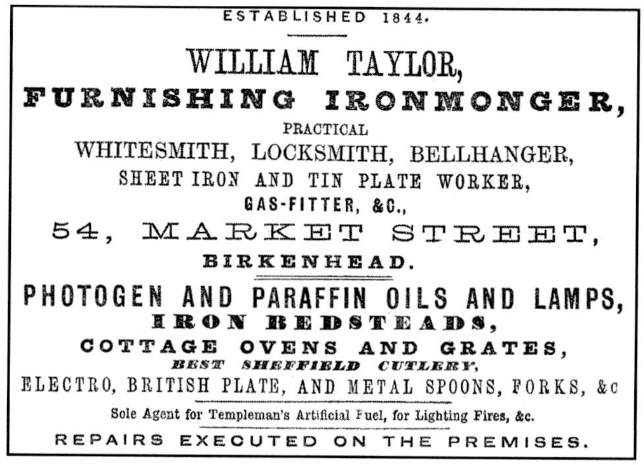

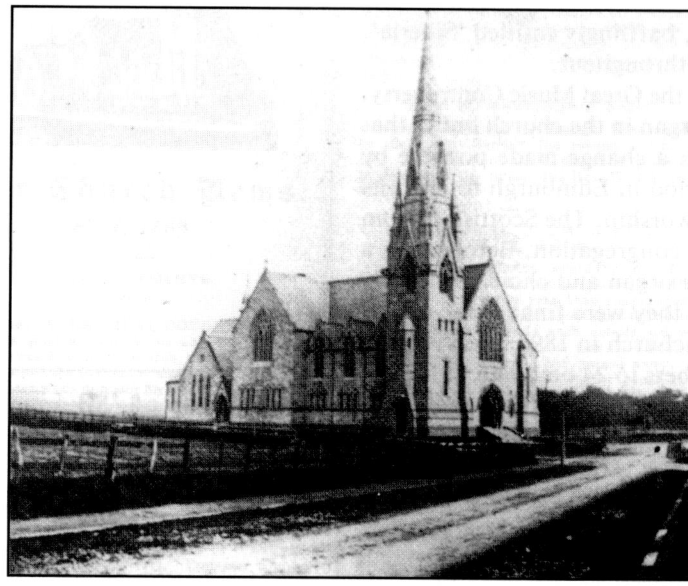

Above: *Trinity Presbyterian Church Beresford Road* ***Claughton*** *opened 11 October 1866 at a cost of £8,000. This large new Church, which had 800 seats, was built on land surrounded by fields. However, the Church's gamble paid off as over the next 25 years large houses were built on roads in the surrounding area with one big house supplying a dozen church-goers including servants. Over half of the Church's revenue came from rent paid on pews.*

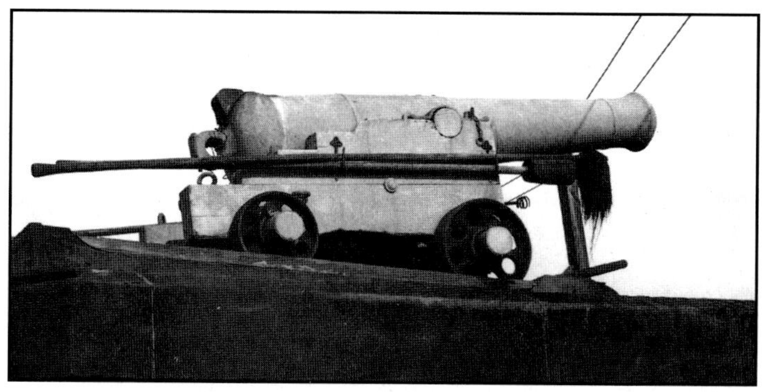

Above: *The One O'Clock Gun, is pictured standing on a plinth at Morpeth Pier* ***Birkenhead*** *facing the River Mersey. It was used as a time-check for shipping, first being fired electronically 21 September 1867 from* ***Bidston*** *Observatory. The first gun was a 34 pounder from the Crimean War and with the aid of the pole, seen resting on the side of the gun, seven pounds of powder were used. However, following complaints this was reduced to five pounds. This gun was used until 1932, then replaced with a 32 pounder. The gun ceased in Septemnber 1939, starting again in June 1946 with a replacement Hotchiss six-pounder - it was last fired 18 July 1969*

1868

– The 22.5 acre cemetery in Town Lane **Bebington** formed at a cost of £17,900

Mar 28 St Peter's Church Cathcart Street **Birkenhead** consecrated

Apr 26 Last service held at the second **Upton** Church in Greasby Road (opposite the Toll Bar Cottage) - the building demolished in 1887 [now the site of a Funeral Home]

Apr 28 The new St Mary's Church **Upton** was consecrated - as was the graveyard[SUAH]

Dec 21 *Argyle Theatre* opened in Argyle Street **Birkenhead** by Dennis Grannell

1869

– **Birkenhead** Park CC drew with an All England XI[BPCC]

– The Wirral Hospital and Dispensary for Sick Children was established at 24 Wilkinson Street **Birkenhead** with accommodation for five patients and one nurse[SOUV]

– The National School opened in Church Road **Upton** with about 60 children attending although it was built to hold 120[SUAH]

July 16 The foundresses of the Convent of The Sisters of The Holy Family took possession of a house in Highfield Road **Rock Ferry** - part of the building was later transformed into a private school which was eventually transferred to Woodland Road

Sept 28 Statue of Joseph Mayer, benefactor of **Bebington** was unveiled in St George's Hall **Liverpool** by his worship the Mayor, Alderman Dover. It was Joseph Mayer who gave **Bebington** its first Free Library [see article this page]

Oct 10 First service held of the Highfield Congregational Church **Rock Ferry** in the Albert Rooms near New Chester Road and Rock Lane[SOUV]

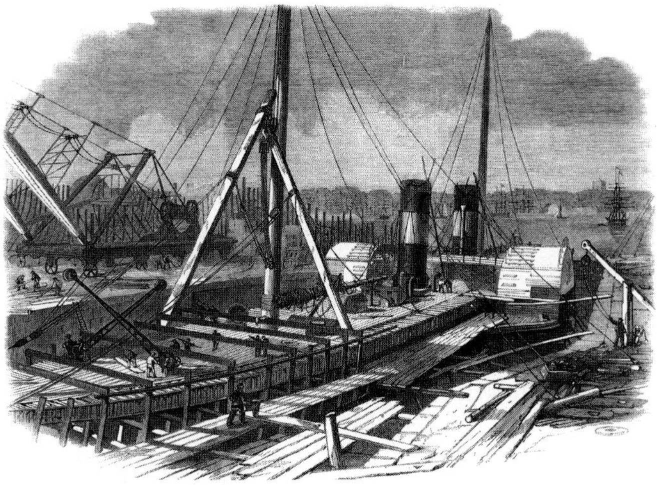

Above: The Hibernia, *a steamer operated by the Dundee, Perth and London Shipping Company which operated from Dundee to London is under repair at the Laird Brothers' Graving Docks* ***Birkenhead***

Below: ***Bebington*** *Free Library was established in a house in Lower Bebington which faced the bottom of Heath Road, rented at the expense of Joseph Mayer off the Bebington eccentric Thomas Francis [the sign for the library is seen in the middle of the building]. Due to the success of the library Thomas Mayer bought a farmhouse [see 1870]. Thomas Francis built in his garden the tower on the right and mounted it with two big wooden guns. He put a verandah along the front of the house and lay in wait for passers-by, inviting them to a dinner of roast sparrows, cockles and such unsubstancial food. He was a talented sculpturer - over his front door he raised a big figure of Britannia, with shield and spear. Beneath this, in the verandah, he set up a statue of himself, in knee breeches and shoes, striking a rock with a bricklayer's hammer, whence issued a stream of water. Under it ran the inscription:- "When the people of Bebington murmured for water, I cut the rock, and God gave them plenty - Thomas Francis" . He also sculptured a large dog standing in its kennel, which put off unwanted boys from approaching the house*[FVLB]

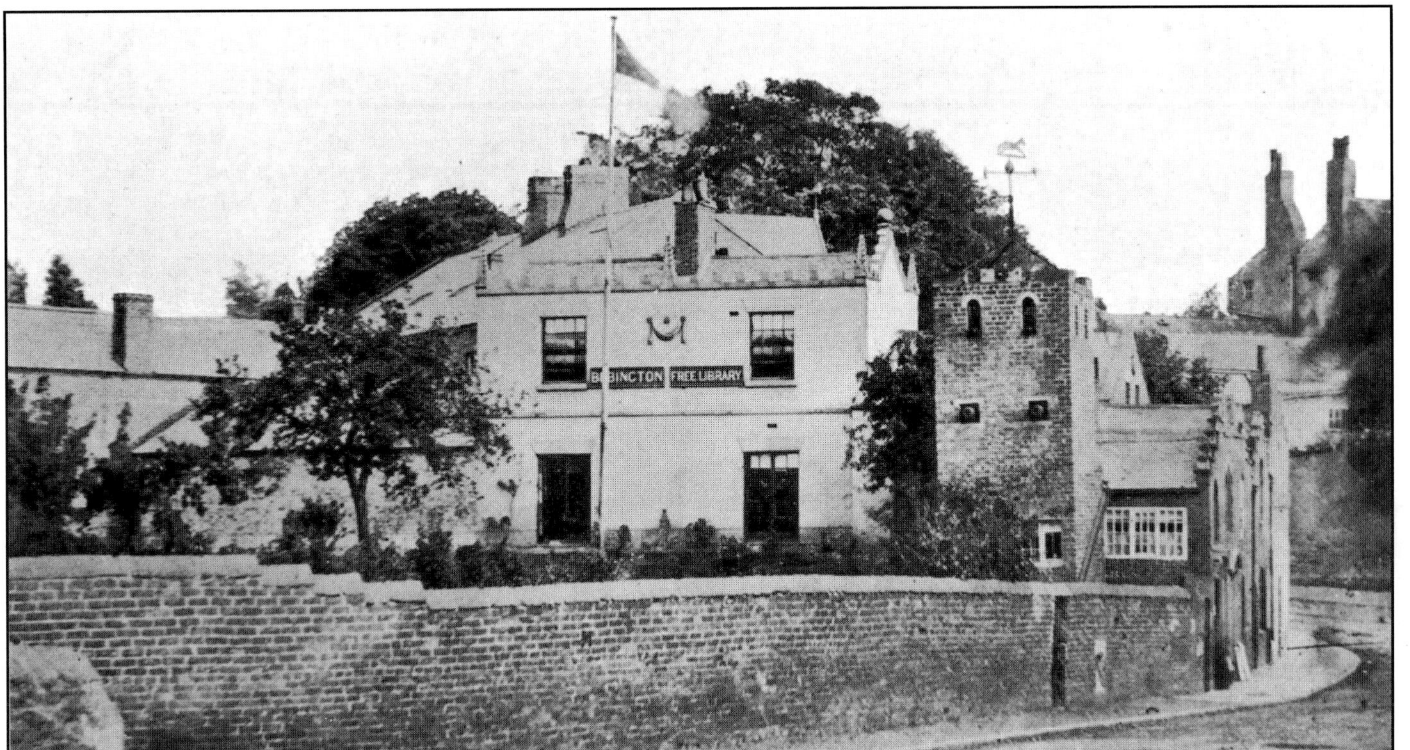

1870

– In their fourth match against the an England XI, **Birkenhead** Park CC won by 126 runs at Birkenhead Park. A local newspaper reported: "the Band of the 4th Dragoon Guards played 'war-like' music in glorious weather and here and there the tall masts of some big ships [in the Mersey] pierced the sky deeper than the highest trees"[BPCC]

Jan 1 The Free Library at **Bebington** proved so popular [see 1869] that it moved to bigger premises and was named the Mayer Library, after the man who bought the farmhouse and converted it for the purpose [see photos][FRVB]

Jan 13 Highfield Congregational Church was formed at **Rock Ferry**[SOUV]

July 8 **Hoylake** to **Birkenhead** Railway seized by bailiffs

Aug 8 John Laird offered land in Conway Street **Birkenhead** to erect a School of Art at his own cost

Aug 9 **Birkenhead** Ferry (Tranmere) offered for auction - no bids

Oct 15 Fire at Laird's Shipbuilding yard **Birkenhead** fully covered by insurance

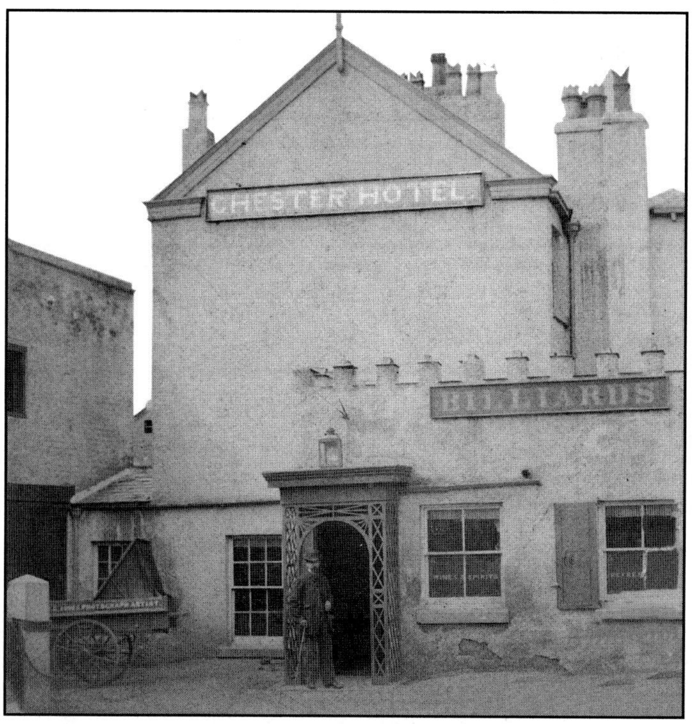

Above: *The man is standing in front of the* Chester Hotel *which was a public house in Park Street* ***Birkenhead.*** *At one time owned by Birkenhead brewery, it has long since gone. The cart on the left belonged to C Jones, Photographic Artist, who probably took this photograph*

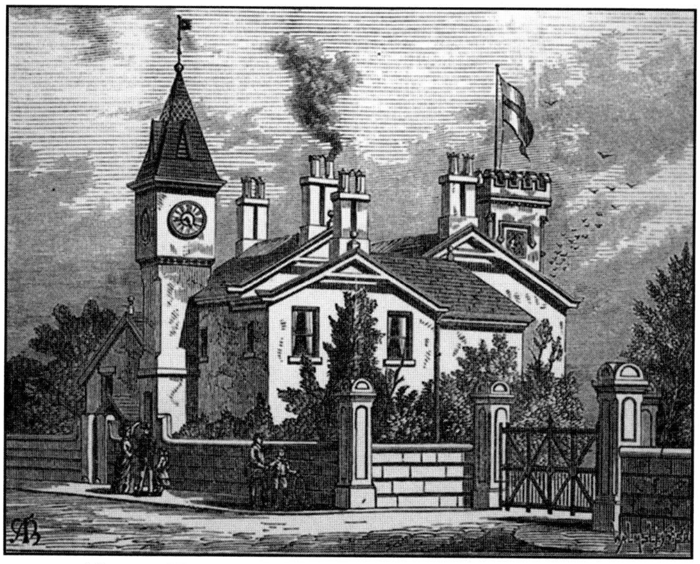

Above: *Having established a Free Library in Lower* ***Bebington*** *in 1866, [see photo 1869] in a rented house opposite the end of Heath Road, and proving very popular, Joseph Mayer purchased an old farm house with five and a half acres of land on the main street in Bebington. The date of 1716 was recorded over the door. He converted it into a commodious Library containing 22,000 books, built with a lofty tower and a sonorous clock [seen on the left]. On the right he built a tower with a viewing area on top. The scene is described thus:- "From the top one obtains a view of great breadth, not picturesque nor even pretty, but most curious and interesting. Under a cloud which never lifts, through a veil of smoke from the innumerable steamers, Liverpool is seen, bristling with masts and spires, and tall factory chimneys. Just opposite stands Aigburth. Gardens and shrubberies slope down to the river bank, and white walls glimmer against the dull horizon. One follows the winding Mersey, dotted with vessels, as far as Runcorn, where it spreads into a sheet of water five miles broad". The hours of opening were Monday and Friday evening 7pm to 8.30pm and Wednesdays from Noon to 1pm. The only charge was a penny for a personalised card. In 1870 there were 2,875 tickets borrowing 38,086 volumes.*

Below: *This is the view of the Mayer Free Library from the Gardens - described thus:- "The considerable space of land around the library is laid out in public walks, planted with trees and shrubs, adorned with flower beds, and furnished with seats. Both library and walks are without any charge to the inhabitants of the village*[FVLB]

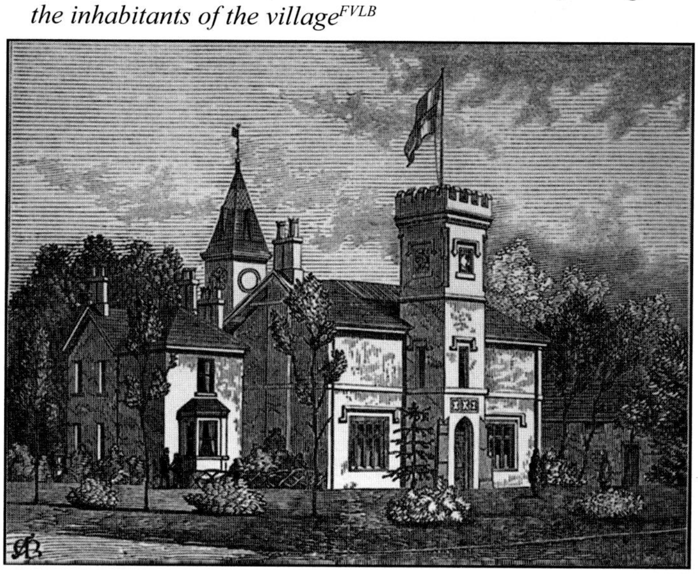

1871

–	**Birkenhead** Park Rugby Football Club founded
Mar 8	Foundation stone laid for a new Wesleyan Methodist Chapel in Palm Grove **Oxton** - the original transept took only a matter of months to complete - but the second phase took a further 16 years[SOUV]
Sept 27	New School of Art, gift of John Laird, opened in **Birkenhead**

1872

–	**Bidston** Lighthouse built - replaced the previous one which was erected in 1771[SOUV]
–	Approximately 1872, the **Bidston** Toll Bar abolished[WPPB]
–	The **Birkenhead** Amalgamated Brewery Co Ltd changed its name to the Birkenhead Brewery Co Ltd[BB]
Jan 1	Portrait of Joseph Mayer by JP Knight presented to the Mayer Free Library by the inhabitants of **Bebington**
Mar 22	The building of the Mersey Railway Tunnel commenced at **Birkenhead** near Morpeth Dock - at the same time as it was started in **Liverpool**
Apr 12	Large fire at Laird's shipbuilding yard **Birkenhead** caused great damage
June 26	Mr Goschen, First Lord of the Admiralty, distributed prizes aboard school-frigate HMS *Conway*, moored off **New Ferry**
June 29	**Tranmere** Ferry steamers (lease having expired) ceased plying
Aug 1	The **Hoylake** Railway re-opened from the Docks Station **Birkenhead** to Hoylake

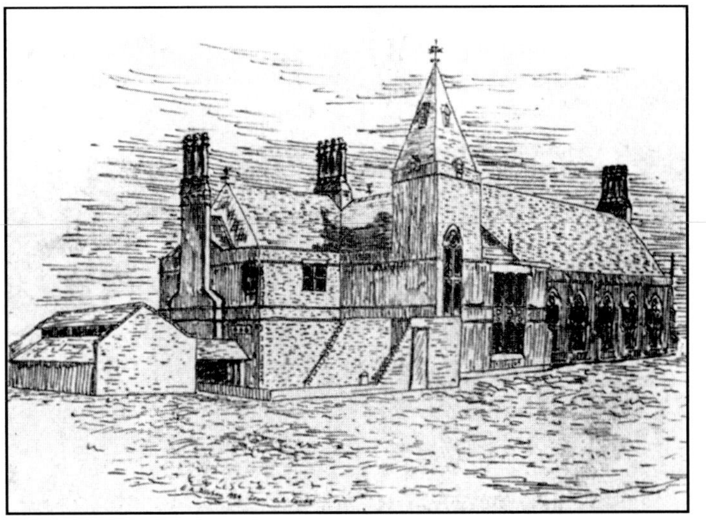

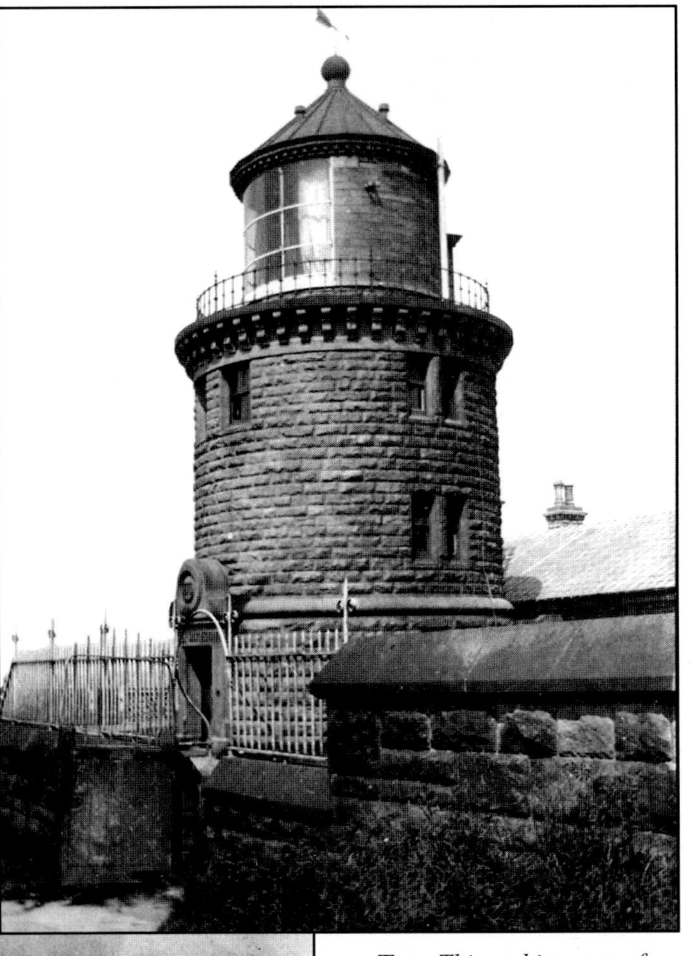

Right: ***Bidston*** *Lighthouse a few years after it was built in 1872, replacing the one built in 1771 [see below]*

Below: *The original Lighthouse pictured here at* ***Bidston*** *was built in 1771 - it was replaced in 1872 with the one pictured above right*

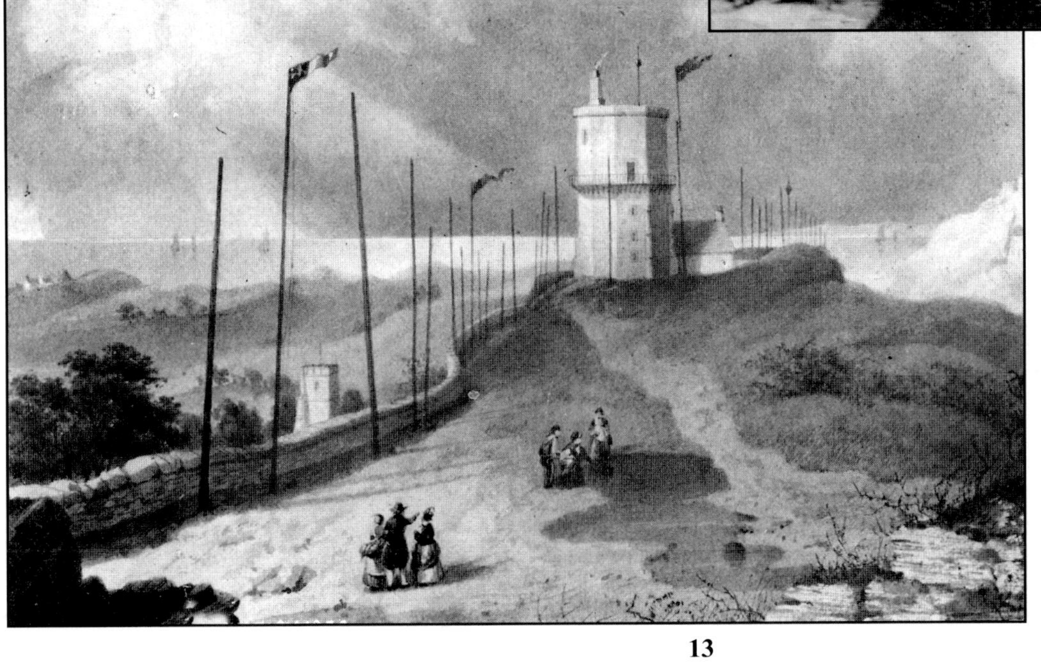

Top: *This etching was of the purpose built buildings at Birkenhead School in Shrewsbury Road* ***Oxton****, as they looked when they moved from Park Road North in 1871. The main buildings on the right are still there today including the building on the right which was the main teaching area with four classes being taught in the one big room simultaneously. However, the ceiling was very high which made the room difficult to heat. It was not until 1908 that this room was bisected with classrooms below and hall with stage above*[BSPH]

1873

– New National School (mixed) erected for 168 children at **Woodchurch** at a cost of £1,511 [see May 1941][SOUV]

– **Birkenhead** Park Cricket Club played their last of the matches against the All England XI, when a crowd of 10,000 saw a drawn match[BPCC]

– Brassey Street Mission **Birkenhead** Working Lads Society formed with a Bible class Monday evenings - attendance was necessary to participate in other events including an annual outing to **Brimstage**[PROG]

May 15 Fire at British Patent Lubricating Oil, Duke Street, **Birkenhead**, caused £5,000 worth of damage

May 20 **Tranmere** Ferry re-opened for passengers

Aug 7 The Mersey Docks & Harbour Board resolved to convert the low-water basin at **Birkenhead** into an additional wet dock

Sept 6 Tramway in **Birkenhead** connected with the **Hoylake** Railway at Birkenhead Docks station, opened[TBW]

Sept 10 Swimming bath for the training ship *Indefatigable*, moored off **New Ferry,** was launched

Oct 13 New station at Shore Road, **Birkenhead**, opened for goods traffic by Cheshire Lines Committee

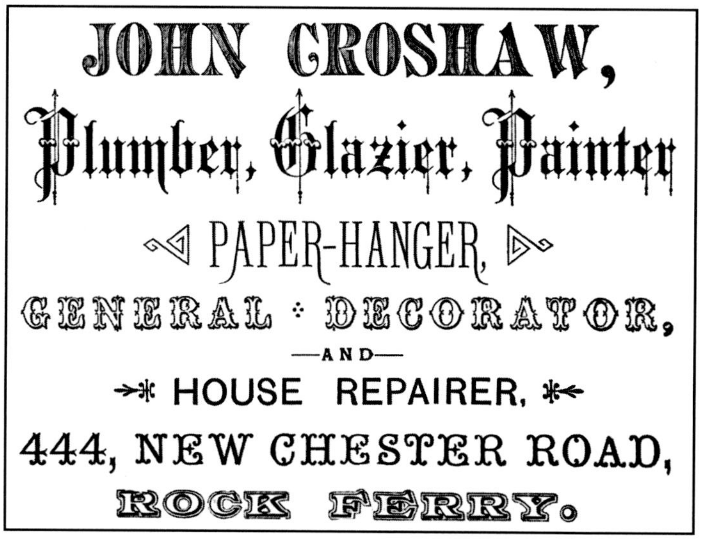

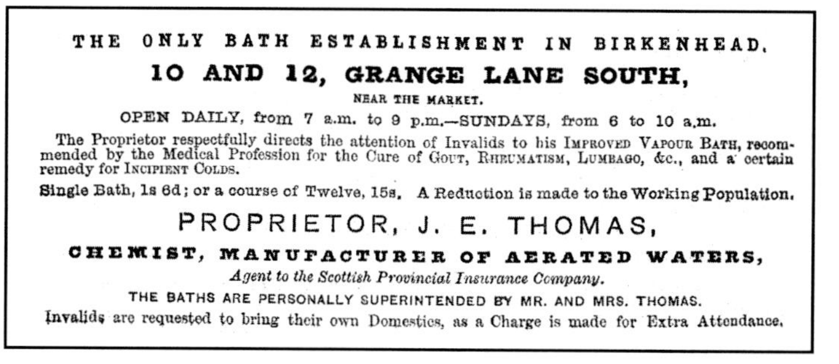

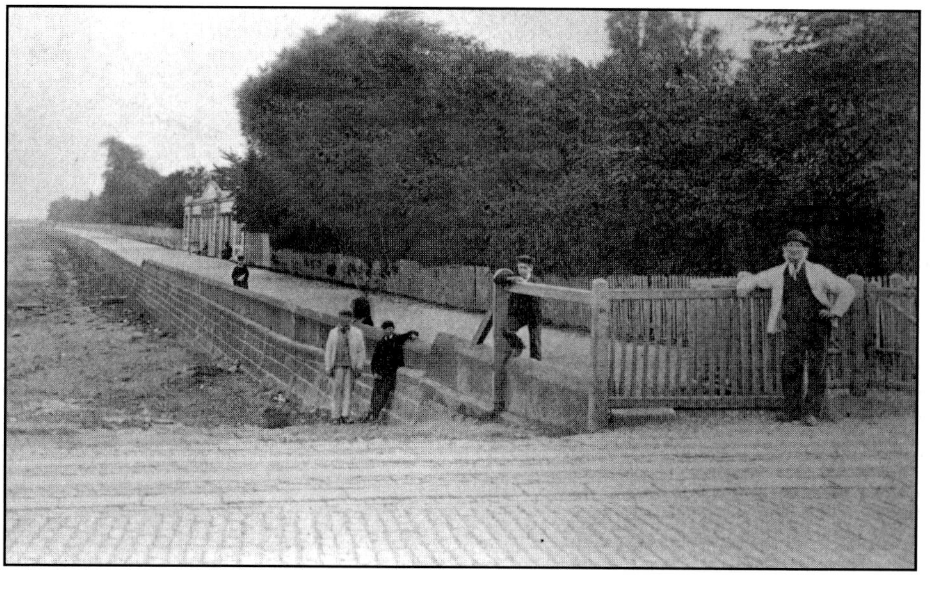

Right: *The Esplanade at* ***Rock Ferry*** *where promenaders could enjoy a stroll along this stretch fronting on to the River Mersey. It is interesting to note that the man on the right is leaning on a gated fence - which probably meant that access was restricted. The building behind the gentleman in the distance was Bath Cottages which dated back to at least 1836 and provided hot and cold baths for residents and visitors. The original plan was to have the keepers' quarters in the centre with a row of bathrooms either side. The building was later converted into cottages and being the oldest buildings in Rock Park were protected by being within the Rock Park Conservation Area. However, they have since been demolished.*

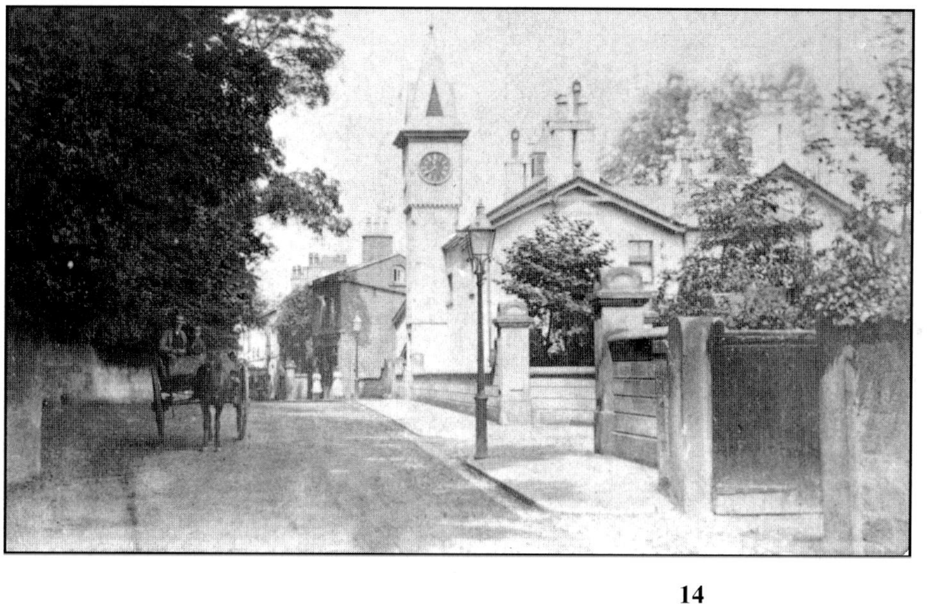

Left: *Mayer Free Library, which is seen to the right of the man in the pony and trap, was originally a farmhouse dating back to 1716 with five and a half acres of land. It was purchased by Joseph Mayer who converted it into the library in 1870. The stone pillars to the right of the gas lamp mark the entrance to Mayer Park, which Joseph Mayer laid out for the free use of the people of Bebington [see 1870]. The white building in the far distance was the* Rose and Crown Inn *which probably stood on the site of one of two inns in Bebington in 1561 - this being on the main road from Birkenhead to Chester*

1874

– The Wirral Tramway Company formed and obtained a Tramway Act authorising it to construct a line between Woodside **Birkenhead** and **New Ferry** [see 1877][BET]

1875

– Grange Road Presbyterian Church, Grange Road West, **Birkenhead** added a new vestry with classroom beneath

– **Bidston** Windmill last used - it could no longer compete with steam powered mills[WWPB]

– The 92 Gun Auxiliary Screw Battleship HMS *Nile* was handed over by the Navy to the Mercantile Marine Service Association as a training ship and replaced the second HMS *Conway* (founded in 1859) - to be based in the River Mersey, moored off **Rock Ferry**[BTCR]

Sept 16 Captain Webb (formerly a Conway Boy) was presented by the boys of the training ship HMS *Conway* with a handsome binocular field glass, to mark his feat of swimming the English Channel

Sept 27 **Oxton** Cricket Club formed

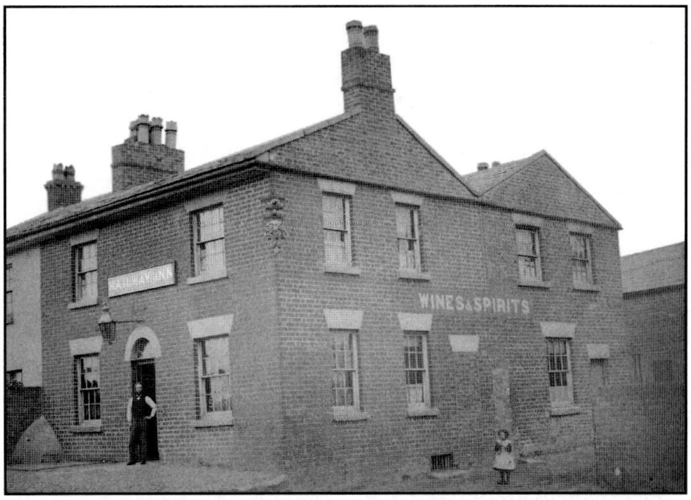

Above: *The* Railway Inn *is pictured in Bebington Road* ***New Ferry*** *with the publican standing in the doorway wearing a bow tie. Its proximity to Bebington Station probably gave it its name*

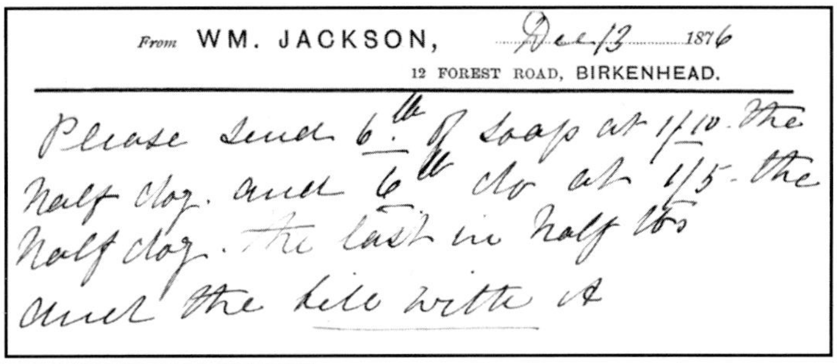

From WM. JACKSON, Dec 13 1876
12 FOREST ROAD, BIRKENHEAD.

Please send 6lb of soap at 1/10 the half doz. and 6lb do at 1/5 the half doz. the last in half lbs and the bill with it

Right: *This was a postcard order sent to Mr Graham - trading as a grocer at 13 Market Place South* ***Birkenhead*** *- from William Jackson of 12 Forest Road Birkenhead who ordered:- "6lb soap at 1/10d the half dozen; 6lb soap at 1/5d the half dozen, the last in half pounds - and the bill with it"*

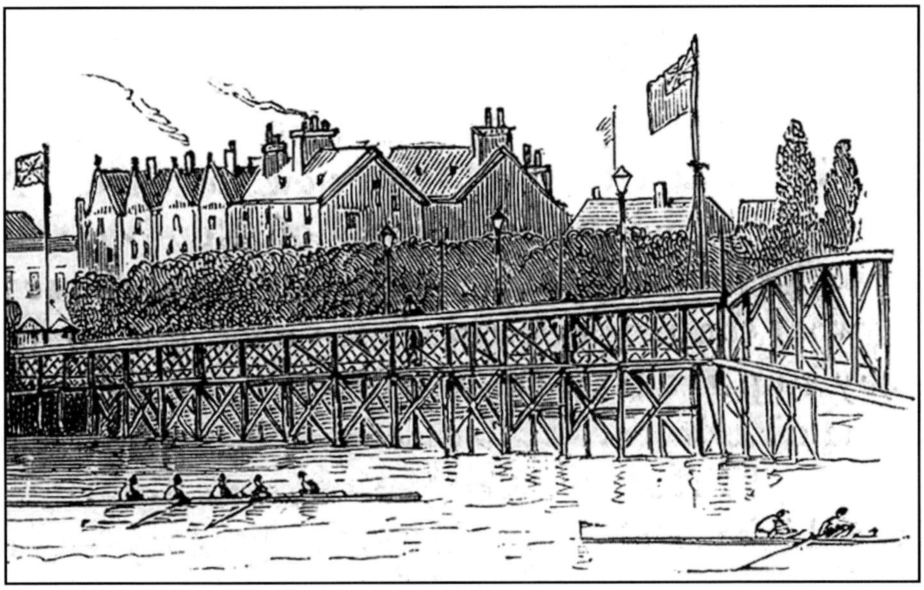

Left: ***New Ferry*** *Pier is seen from the River Mersey, with houses beyond the iron pier structure. The pier was 856 ft. long and opened to the public in 1865, operated by the Mersey River Steam Boat Company the ferry plied to and from Liverpool. Rowing was also a popular pastime as can be seen here*

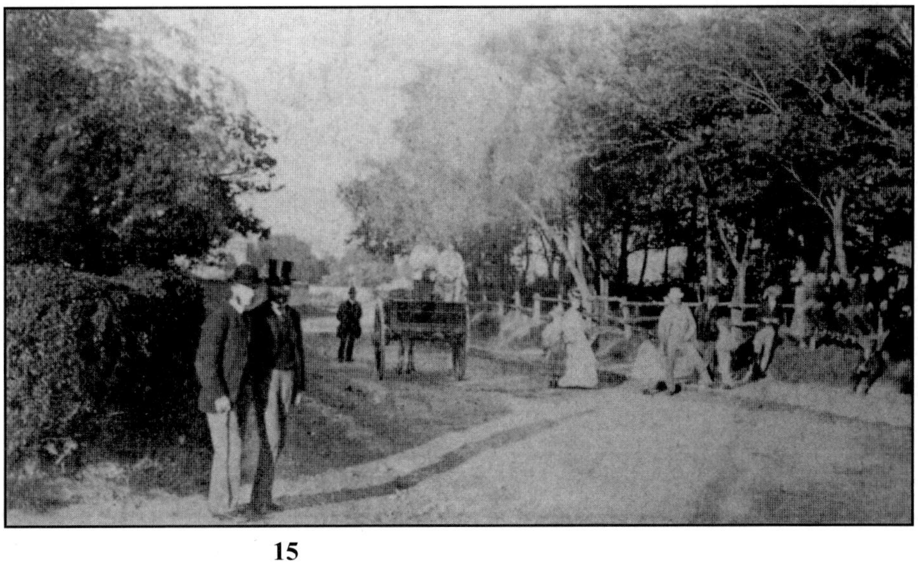

Right: *All the people seen in this photograph taken in Kings Lane Dacre Hill* ***Rock Ferry****, are looking at the camera including boys sitting on the fence to the right. The two men on the left must have been well-to-do as one has a bowler hat and the other a top hat*

1876

– The *Argyle Theatre,* Argyle Street **Birkenhead** changed its name to The *Princes of Wales Theatre* [see also 1891]

– The Holt Technical School was built at **Tranmere** - this was **Birkenhead's** first technical school but was not initially used for the original purpose as Tranmere was absorbed into Birkenhead in 1877. It was later used as a branch of the Laird School of Art

– Stamford Spence Schultz first played for **Birkenhead** Park Cricket Club. He was an excellent batsman who was born in Birkenhead, educated at Uppingham and then Cambridge University. In 1878 he became the first Birkenhead Park player to play for England on the 1878/9 tour of Australia[BPCC]

– **Birkenhead** Park Rugby Football Club took a prominent role in forming the Cheshire County Rugby Union[SOUV]

Jan **Oxton** Cricket Club prepared their new ground of six acres that they rented from the Earl of Shrewsbury (previously farmed by Mr Houghton who was paid £30 for disturbance) for an annual rent of £3. 3 shillings per acre - besides cricket and tennis, a ground was laid for croquet with a bowling green coming a year later, together with a cricket pavilion[SOUV]

May 15 A new landing stage for goods traffic constructed by Messrs Brassey between Morpeth Dock and low water basin in **Birkenhead**

June 1 St Catherine's Church, **Higher Tranmere**, consecrated after undergoing considerable alterations and extensions

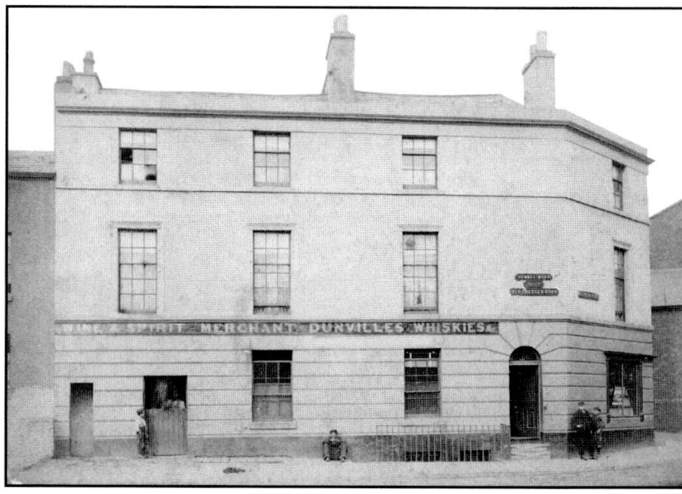

Above: *The* Farmers Arms *is pictured in Tunnel Road late Old Chester Road at the junction of Waterloo Place* ***Birkenhead***

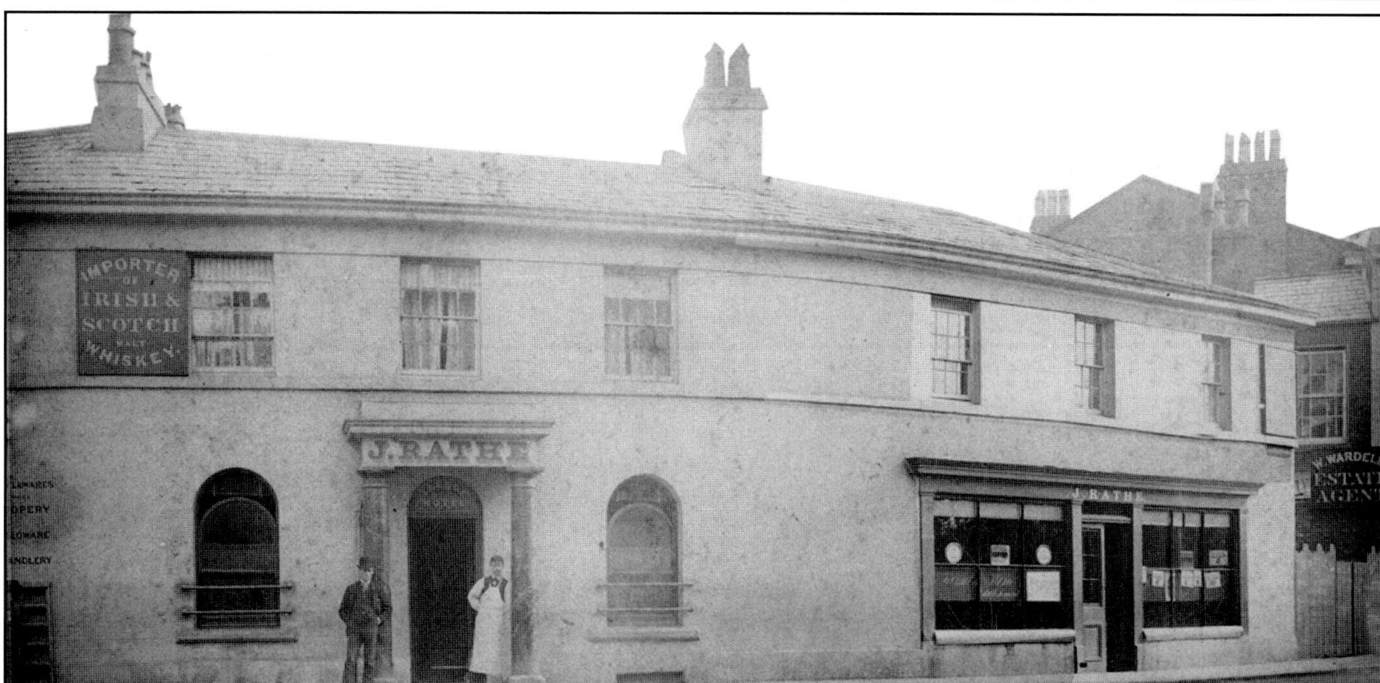

Above: *The* Talbot Hotel *is pictured in* ***Oxton*** *- the address then was No.2 Talbot Buildings, Claughton Firs. J Rathe was the licensee who was described as 'a Wholesale Wine & Spirit Merchant and Ale & Porter Bottler'. The* Talbot *dates back to at least 1850 when the victualler was a Thomas Lodge. The building was demolished in 1969 [now the site of the car park] and the replacement pub opened. On the extreme left were the signs for the Earthenware Dealer Margaret Thompson and on the right at No.1 Rose Mount was W Wardell, Estate Agent.*

1877

– The Townships of **Birkenhead, Claughton, Oxton, Tranmere** and part of **Higher Bebington** incorporated by Royal Charter - population 77,260[SOUV]

– **Tranmere** Conservative Working Men's Club was erected on a site in Old Chester Road presented by Major Orred. The building comprised a large billiards room, library, reading room and a turret with clock. There was a bowling green attached

– Nixon's, Provision Merchants, opened their first shop in **Birkenhead**[SOUV]

Jan 31 Death of Sir William Jackson, one of the Town's 'leading lights' who had lived at *The Manor House*, **Claughton**, which he had had built - he was buried at Flaybrick Cemetery[ROB]

Mar 28 Wirral Tramway which ran from Woodside Ferry, **Birkenhead**, to **New Ferry** - was opened to the public

April Brassey Street Mission - new premises opened in **Birkenhead** at a cost of £1,500[SOUV]

May 5 First edition of the ***Birkenhead** News* - price one penny - published & printed by Willmer Brothers in opposition to the *Birkenhead Advertiser* which had been founded in 1853[FB]

Oct 28 St Ann's Catholic Church opened in **Rock Ferry**

Oct 31 Statue of the late John Laird was unveiled in Hamilton Square, **Birkenhead**, facing the proposed Town Hall, which was not built for another 10 years (see also 1925)[SOUV]

Nov 14 First Municipal Election in **Birkenhead**

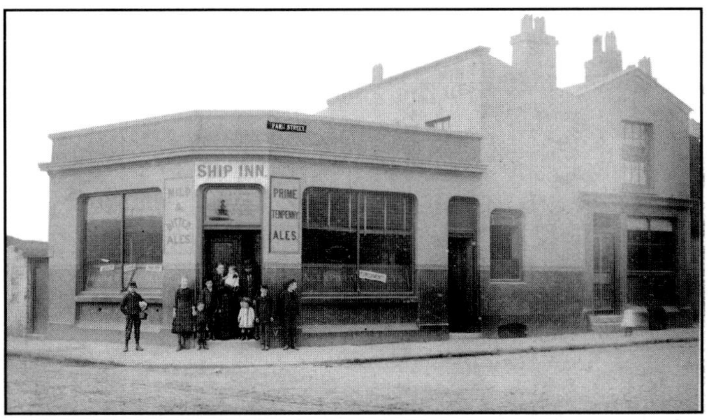

Above: *The* Ship Inn *is pictured in Park Street* ***Birkenhead*** *when the victualler was E Brown who is probably posing with his family in front of his pub*

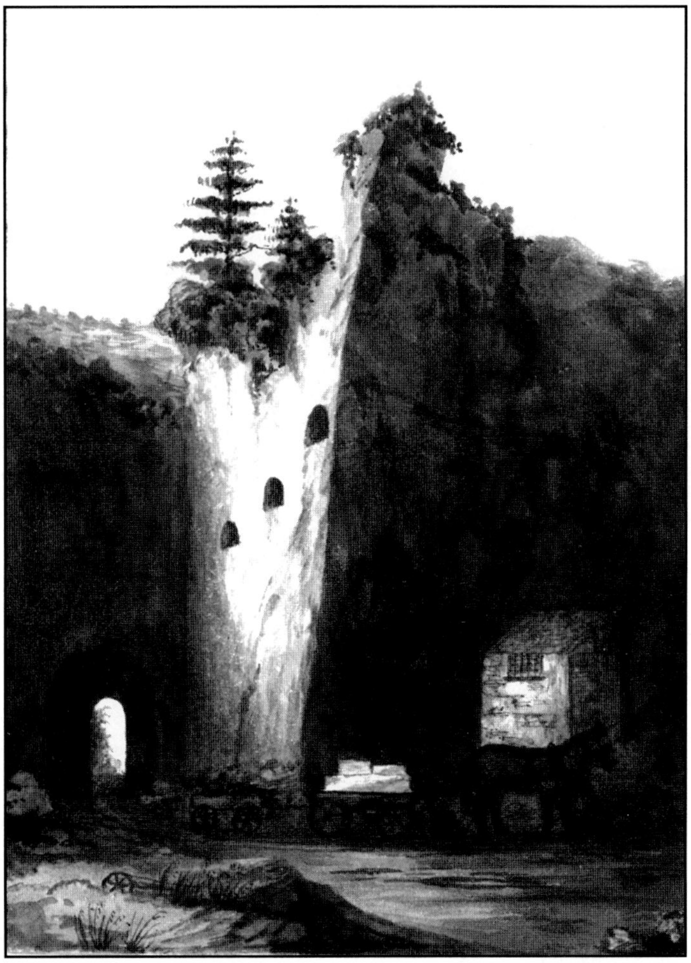

Above: *The Eastern approach to Mount Road tunnel in* ***Storeton*** *Quarry is seen in this watercolour, which is dated June 1877. The horse-drawn wagons are loaded with stone before descending the Storeton Tramway to the quay at Bromborough and then for distribution by sea. The tramway was opened 15 August 1838 - the event being celebrated with flags decorating the buildings along the route and wagons supplied to convey parties to view the completed tramway. There were many visitors - some travelling some distance with the formal meal for 50 invited guests being held in a local [large] house and the less formal dinner for the 200 workmen engaged on the tramway and quarry works was held in the Mount Road Tunnel pictured. Prior to the tramway opening, the stone was carried by horse-drawn wagon the 2.5 miles to Bromborough Dock on poor roads, made worse by these wagons, with each load taking up to three weeks! Where the old way would take about 20 days, the tramway would take that many minutes. Although the tramway closed in 1905, the quarrying continued for about 20 years the stone being transported by lorry. The existence of the tramway caused Mr Lever great annoyance and inconvenience as it went through their works with the rails standing several inches above the ground. However, this was resolved when the quarry and tramway were sold at auction 28-29 September 1911, being part of the late Sir Thomas Brocklebank's Estate, with Mr Lever buying the entire quarry and tramway land*[TST]

1878

– **Birkenhead** St Mary's Cricket Club formed in Birkenhead Park - it was originally affiliated to St Mary's Parish Church

– A Fire and Ambulance Station was established at **Tranmere** equipped with one fire engine, one escape appliance and one Ambulance. This station closed down in 1895 when the new Fire Station was opened at Whetstone Lane **Birkenhead** [see 1895][SOUV]

– **Birkenhead** received a "Grant of Arms"

Mar 29 Beerhouse - 37 Church Road Higher **Tranmere** (incl. Nos. 35 & 39) sold @ auction £2,470[LCP]

Apr 1 Monks Ferry Station closed to be replaced the same day by Woodside Station **to passengers**[RSoW]

May 3 **Tranmere** Conservative Club opened

Sept 17 Grand Eisteddfod held in **Birkenhead Park** for four days

1879

– Reginald Wood joined **Birkenhead** Park. He was their second cricketer to play for England when they toured Australia in 1886/7 [see also 1876][BPCC]

– The Dock Board's Lairages opened at **Birkenhead**

– The new floating roadway and landing stage opened at Woodside **Birkenhead**[MMB]

Oct 12 The **Birkenhead** Tramways Company purchased the Docks Route[BET]

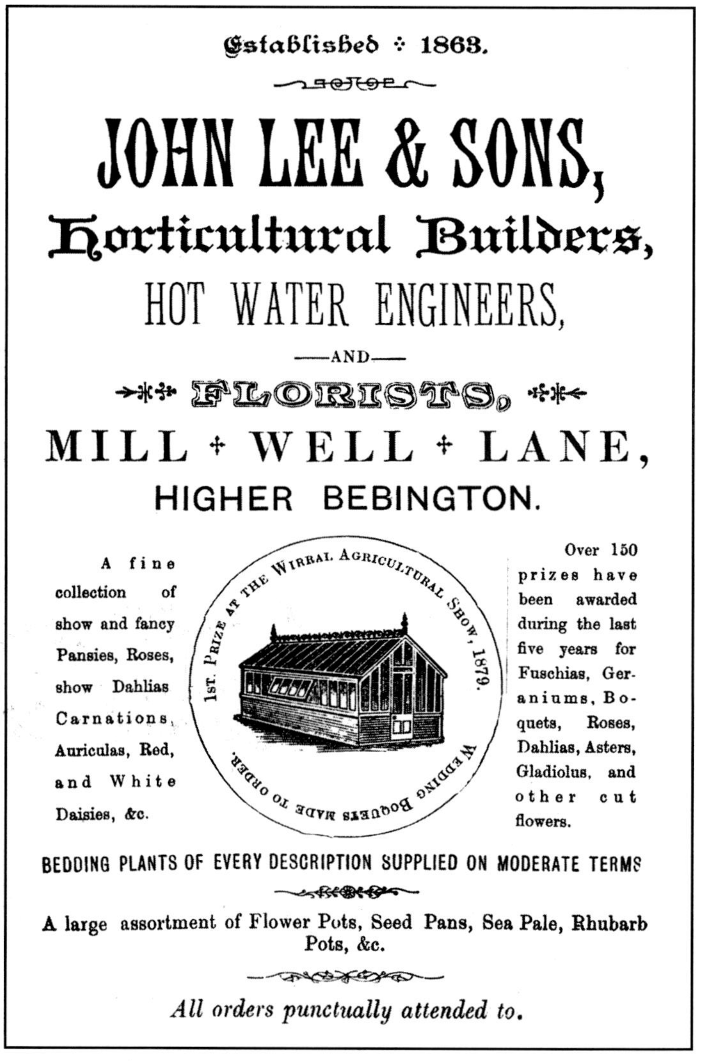

Above: *John Lee & Sons were established in 1863 and traded as Horticultural Builders and Hot Water Engineers from their premises in Millwell Lane, this was later shortened to Mill Lane*

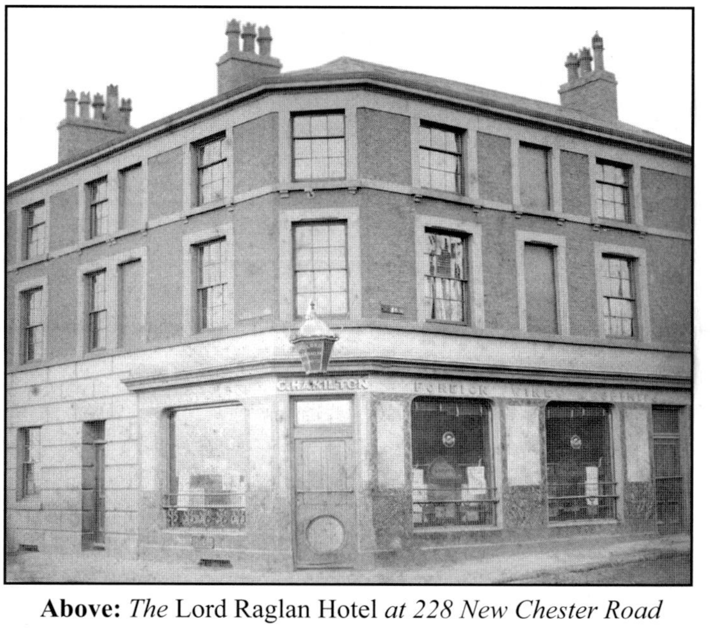

Above: *The* Lord Raglan Hotel *at 228 New Chester Road* ***Tranmere*** *is seen with Union Street on the right, when Charles Hamilton was the publican. The advert above the windows say 'Porter - Foreign Wines and Spirits' The pub which was later owned by Birkenhead Brewery, is still trading today [see 1909]*

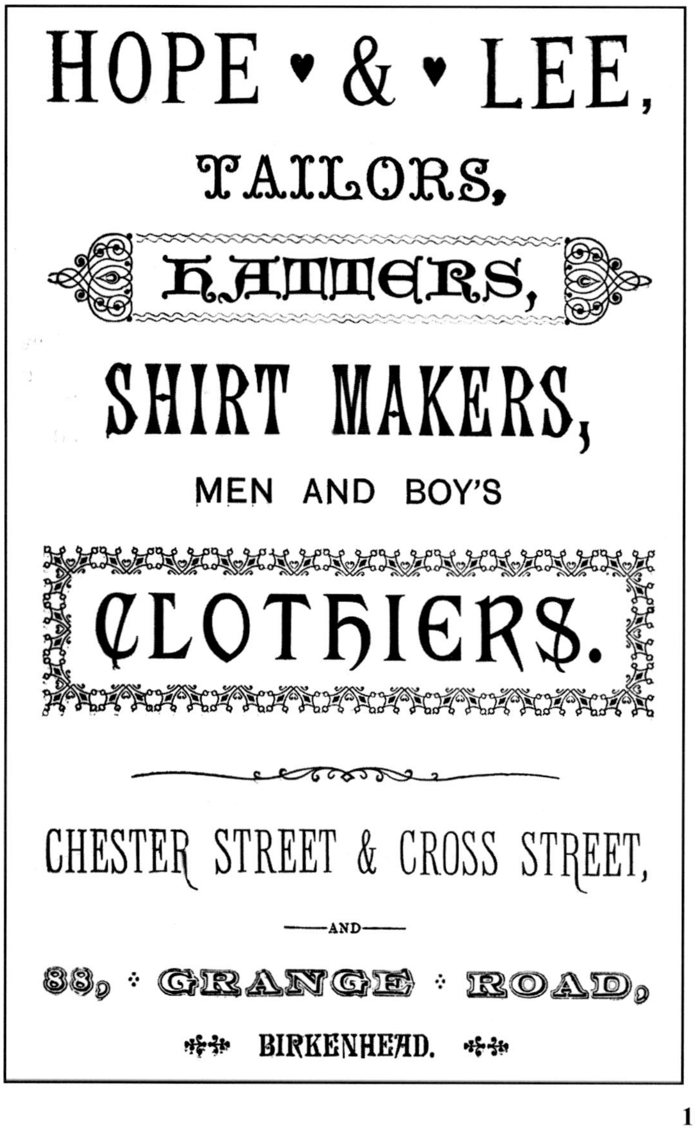

Left: *John Lee opened his first tailor's shop in* ***Birkenhead*** *in 1864 - later joining with a Mr Hope to become Hope & Lee - trading in Grange Road for many decades*

1880

– Mr JJ Martin and his brother Ralph opened a bakery at 45 Borough Road **Birkenhead** [in 1889 JJ Martin joined forces with CH Hubbard and traded as Hubbard & Martin]

June 17 Beerhouse & 3 houses 1-4 Prices Lane (Claughton Firs) **Oxton** sold @ auction £680[LCP]

June 30 An auction of the freehold estate of the late Miss C King included:- *Royal Oak* (+ 4 cottages) Village Road **Hr Bebington** sold £1,200[LCP] [see also 1958]; four cottages Village Road (next plot to the Royal Oak) sold £610; Quarry the west side of Storeton Lane [later called Storeton Road] with land - total 9,300 square yards not sold - reserve £280 per acre. In total there were 19 lots with 60 acres of land up for auction

1881

Mar 15 *Harp Inn* Chapel Street, **Birkenhead** (including house & shop) sold @ auction £1,125[LCP]

July 1 Corner stone of the Wirral Children's Hospital, Woodchurch Road, **Birkenhead**, was laid [see 1921]

Aug 26 *Victoria Vaults* 93-97 Oxton Road **Birkenhead** + 2 shops sold @ auction £1,100[LCP]

Oct 8 Tranmere Rovers played their first known game against Anfield at home on what is now Mersey Park **Rock Ferry** - they won 3-1

Oct 18 St Luke's Church consecrated on St Luke's Day in Lower **Tranmere** - total cost £6,000[SOUV]

Oct 29 The Mayors of **Birkenhead** and **Liverpool** respectively set in motion the engines either side of the Mersey for constructing the new Railway Tunnel

JONES & Co.,

IRONFOUNDERS;

ENGINEERS,

MILLWRIGHTS, WHITESMITHS, &C.,

CONWAY FOUNDRY,

232, CONWAY STREET,

BIRKENHEAD.

By order of the Trustees of the late Miss C. KING.

HIGHER BEBINGTON,

NEAR BIRKENHEAD.

PLAN & PARTICULARS

OF VALUABLE

FREEHOLD BUILDING LAND,

A PUBLIC-HOUSE,

FORMERLY CALLED "THE ROYAL OAK;"

FARM HOUSE AND OUTBUILDINGS,

SEVERAL COTTAGES,

AND

FREESTONE QUARRIES,

AT HIGHER BEBINGTON.

TO BE SOLD BY AUCTION,

BY

MESSRS. BAILEY & NEEP,

AT THE

LAW ASSOCIATION ROOMS,

14, COOK STREET, LIVERPOOL,

ON

WEDNESDAY, the 30th day of June, 1880,

At Half-past ONE for TWO o'clock in the Afternoon, precisely.

Above: *This was the cover for the auction catalogue for the Estate of the late Miss C King which included the* Royal Oak *in Village Road, Higher* ***Bebington*** *and the quarry on the west side of Storeton lane*

Below: *The gunpowder is being placed in the One O'Clock Gun by an official in a top hat at Morpeth Pier* ***Birkenhead*** *ready for firing electrically from Bidston observatory. High fencing was later erected between the gun and River Mersey [see 1867]*

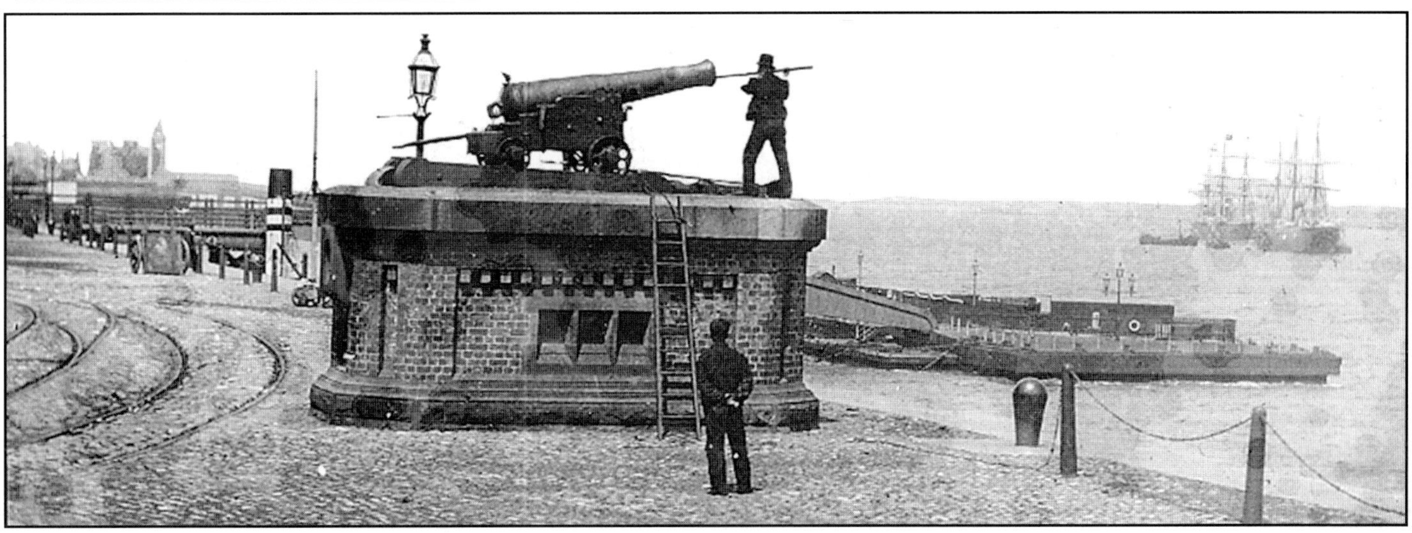

1882

– Argyle Street Baths opened in Argyle Street South **Birkenhead**

Feb 2 HRH Duke of Edinburgh visited the training ship *Indefatigable* moored off New Ferry

Mar 1 Mrs Francis Grant of **Rock Ferry** placed £100,000 in the hands of Trustees, the interest to be paid for the relief of the deserving poor, irrespective of class or creed

May 2 **Higher Tranmere** High School For Girls was inaugurated, being located in two houses knocked into one in Clifton Park [see 1888][SOUV]

May 24 *Sun Inn* 205-209, Bridge Street (corner Park Street) **Birkenhead** + house & warehouse sold @ auction £3,280[LCP]

June 3 **Birkenhead** Park (Rugby) Football Club Athletic Sports were held at the Wirral Agricultural Show

IRVING, LITTLE & CO.,
193, ∴ 195, ∴ & ∴ 197, ∴ CLEVELAND ∴ STREET,
AND
183, CHESTER STREET, BIRKENHEAD.
Paint, Oil, Colour, Varnish & Glass Merchants,
GENERAL SHIP CHANDLERS, IRONMONGERS, SAIL MAKERS, YACHT OUTFITTERS, &C.

Agents for Tuck & Co's Patent Elastic Steam Packing and India Rubber Goods. Lieuvain's Patent Lubricators, and Jesty's Patent Anti-Fouling Compositions.

Dealers in Waste, Tallow, Hemp, and Flax Packing, Patent Lubricating Packing, and Engine Stores of all kinds; Hemp, Manilla, Coir, and Wire Rope; Canvas, Twine, Pitch, Tar, Junk, and Oakum; Roofing, Sheathing, Boiler, and other Felts; Locomotive Antifriction, and Colliery Grease, Soft Soap, Glue, Black Oil, Torch Oil and Wick; Locomotive Coal, Salt, Ballast, and Fire Shovels; Nails, Brushes, Gunpowder, &c.

YACHT ∴ STORES ∴ OF ∴ EVERY ∴ DESCRIPTION.

F. KIRKHAM,
DEALER IN
PROVISIONS, POULTRY,
FRUIT,
FRESH BUTTER,
—AND—
NEW LAID EGGS,
VEGETABLES, &c.
6, YORK PLACE,
BALL'S ROAD,
BIRKENHEAD.

J. H. HURLEY,
Hair Dresser and Tobacconist,
5, MARKET STREET,
(ONE DOOR FROM CHESTER STREET),
BIRKENHEAD.
Genuine + Hamburg + Ground + Razors always + on + hand.

Below: *The* Refreshment Rooms *[known as Donavan's after John Donavan, the victualler from the 1870s to at least 1903], where men could partake of billiards and a beer with the ladies having high tea whilst waiting for the ferry boat to* **Liverpool***. Situated in Bedford Road* **Rock Ferry***, the ferry was only 50 yards to the right of the photographer*

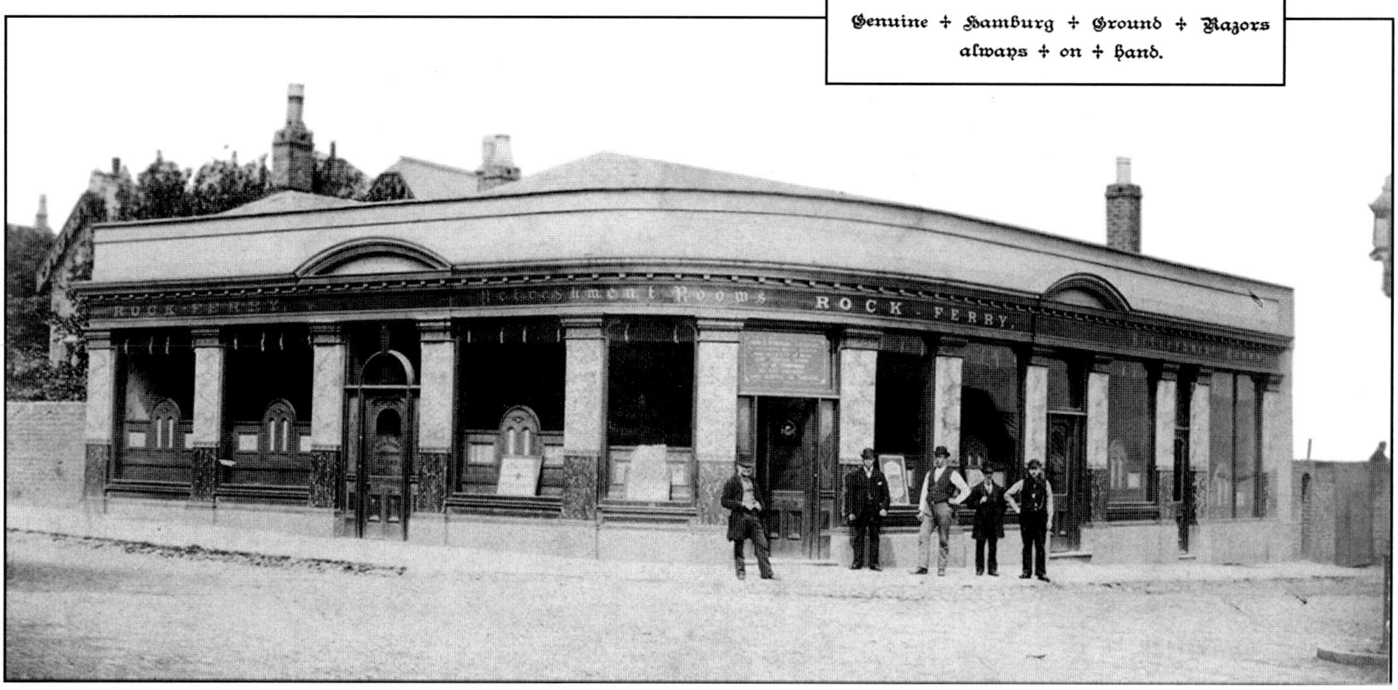

1883

– The Young Women's Christian Association opened a small hostel at 67 Argyle Street **Birkenhead**[SOUV]

June 21 Wirral Children's Hospital, Woodchurch Road, **Birkenhead**, was opened by the Duke of Westminster[SOUV]

July **Oxton** Cricket Club opened their extended pavilion plus new front - which cost a total of £300 - with a match Cricketers verses Quoiters[SOUV]

Sept 29 Claughton Higher Grade School opened in Borough Road **Birkenhead** when the school room under Christ Church, Woodchurch Road was full to overflowing [see also March 1941][SOUV]

Oct 10 Foundation stone laid for the Town Hall, Hamilton Square **Birkenhead**, by the Mayor TS Deakin Esq

Oct 11 The Premier, William Gladstone, inspected the Mersey Tunnel works

Oct 18 *Royal Oak* 44, Westbourne Road **Birkenhead** (incl. No. 11) sold @ auction £750[LCP]

1884

– The Liverpool Victoria Rowing Club was formed - they used facilities at the Great Float **Birkenhead** with their headquarters at the *Egerton Hotel* Canning Street Birkenhead [see article this page]

Jan 17 A partyof gentlemen (the first on record) walked through the Mersey Railway tunnel from **Liverpool** to **Birkenhead**

Jan 17 Reformatory ship *Clarence*, lying in the Mersey off **New Ferry**, burnt to the water's edge[see this page]

May 24 *St Luke's School, attached to the Church in Old Chester Road Lr* ***Tranmere*** *opened*

July The Wednesday edition of the ***Birkenhead*** *News* was first published[FB]

Oct 16 The Premier, William Gladstone, cut the first sod of the Wirral Railway in the show ground of the Wirral and **Birkenhead** Agricultural Society

Nov 20 The YMCA Photographic Group was formed at a meeting held at Berry's Grand Restaurant, **Birkenhead**, the club being affiliated to the YMCA and later became the Birkenhead Photographic Association [see 1937]

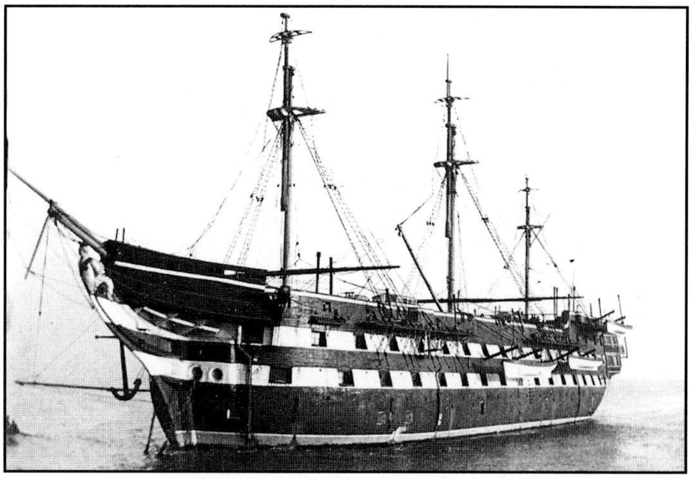

Above: *Reformatory ship* Clarence *lying in the River Mersey off* ***New Ferry*** *was burnt to the water's edge 17 January 1884*

The Liverpool Victoria Rowing Club was formed in 1884 - initially they used the facilities at the Great Float **Birkenhead** which was a natural inlet. Their headquarters were at the *Egerton Hotel* Canning Street Birkenhead. The members would change and run through the streets down to the dockside where they hired boats from a boatman. There was not much serious rowing in the early days and the Great Float was used by scores of people who would hire boats and picnic on the banks of the pool. They decided to have their own boathouse and boats so in 1892 they raised sufficient capital to built a small boathouse on the Wallasey Pool near the Halfpenny Bridge and bought their own boats from a club in Chester. They moved their headquarters temporarily to the *Pool Inn* until they built a new clubroom behind the boathouse

Below: *The invited guests look on from elevated seating at the laying of the foundation stone of* ***Birkenhead's*** *Town Hall which was performed by the Mayor Mr TS Deacon on 10 October 1883. The site chosen was the south-east side of Hamilton Square. The building, which cost £60,000 to build, took three years to erect and was officially opened in 1887. The Town Hall has twice been damaged by fire [see 1901 and 1935]*

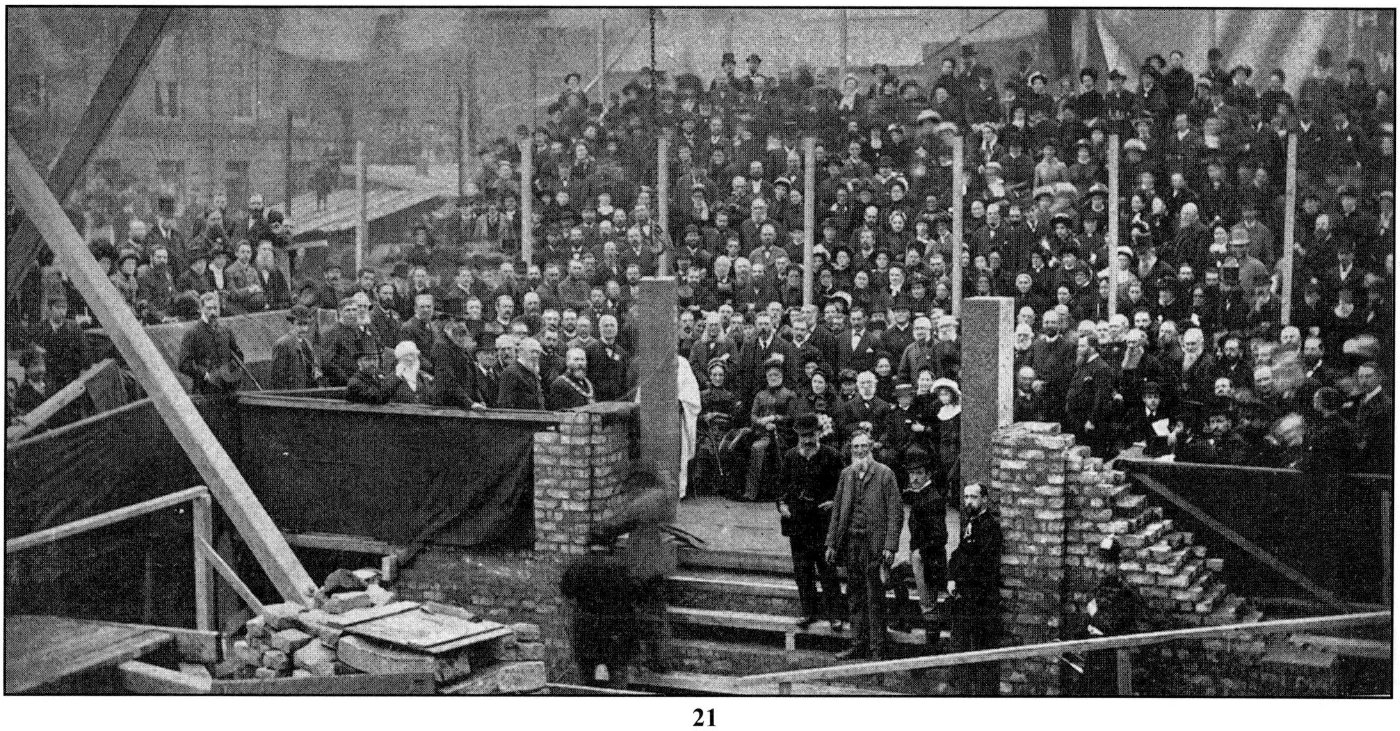

1885

– Christ Church, Kings Lane, Higher **Bebington** had an adjoining tower with shingled spire added, containing one bell [see sketch]

– **Prenton** Bowling Club was formed[SOUV]

Feb 12 The Mayors of **Liverpool** and **Birkenhead** met in the centre of the Mersey Railway tunnel and joined hands. They lunched afterwards at the Adelphi Hotel with shareholders

June A cast iron bandstand was installed in Lower **Birkenhead** Park - cost £150 [see 1929][TPG]

July 15 Mersey Park, **Tranmere**, comprising 21 acres opened by the Mayor of Birkenhead, Robert Paterson

Nov Inaugural meeting of the Wirral District Football Association held at the *Royal Castle Hotel*, Chester Street **Birkenhead** attended by:- Birkenhead Argyle; Birkenhead Rovers; **Bromborough Pool**; The Claughton; The Highfield, **New Ferry**; **Seacombe** St Paul's;The Tranmere; **Tranmere** Rovers and **Wallasey Village** [see also 1886][WDFA]

1886

– **Birkenhead** Sessions Court opened in the newly-built Town Hall

– Mersey Railway opened between Liverpool [James Street] and Green Lane **Tranmere**[RSoW]

– First final of the Wirral District Football Association Challenge Cup won by **Bromborough Pool** who defeated The **Claughton** 3-1[WDFA]

– **Prenton** Tennis Club formed using two grass courts

\- sharing Prenton Bowling Club's Pavilion until their own was opened in 1892[SOUV]

– **Birkenhead** Park Rugby Football Club moved to their present ground in Upper Park[SOUV]

Mar 18 *Haymarket Arms*, 73 Grange Road, **Birkenhead** sold at auction £550[LCP]

Oct 24 Church of Christ **Birkenhead** held their first meeting in *Claughton Music Hall*

Nov 27 The turret clock in the new **Birkenhead** Town Hall set in motion [see also 1901]

JAMES LLOYD,

TAILOR & DRAPER,

105, CHESTER STREET,

BIRKENHEAD.

All Coats cut by Reeves's American System.

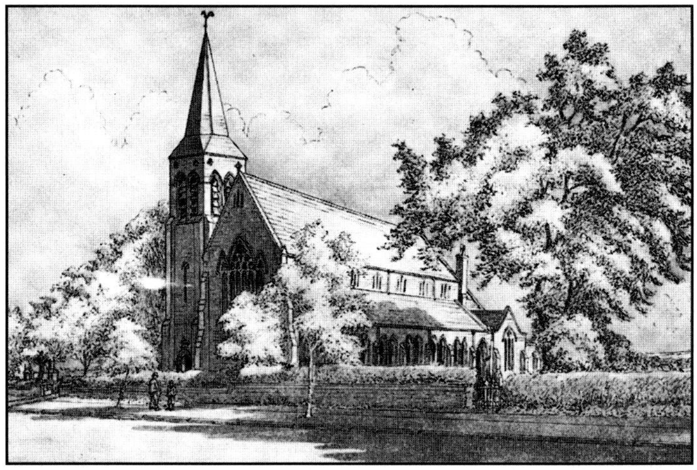

Above: *Christ Church, Higher* **Bebington,** *was consecrated in 1859 but a tower and spire on the original plans were not built due to the cost. However, the widow of Vincent Ashfield King, paid for this to be added to the Church in his memory - the tower and spire were consecrated in 1885*

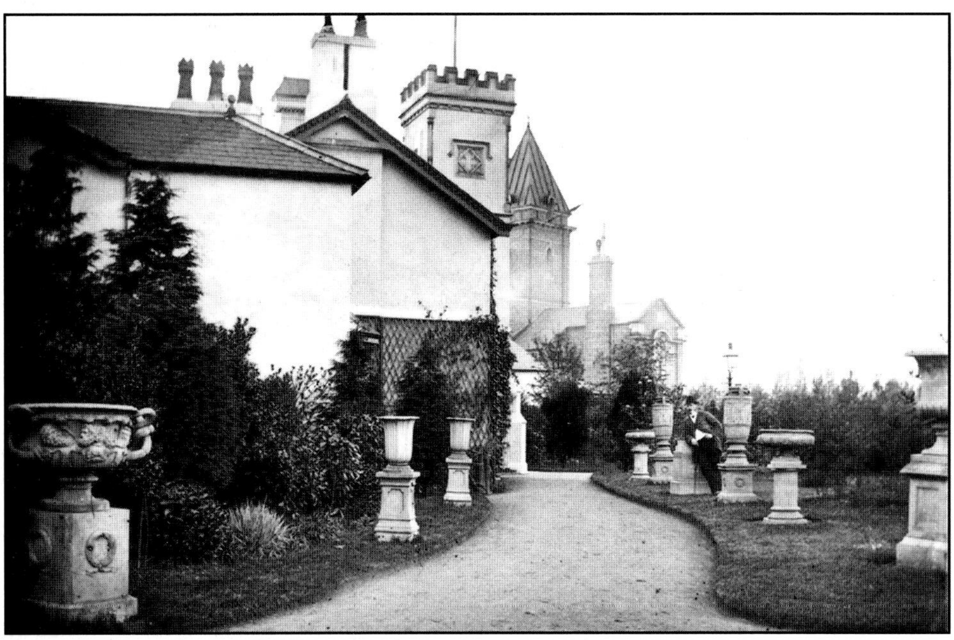

Above: *The garden of* Mayer Hall Lower **Bebington** [see 1870]

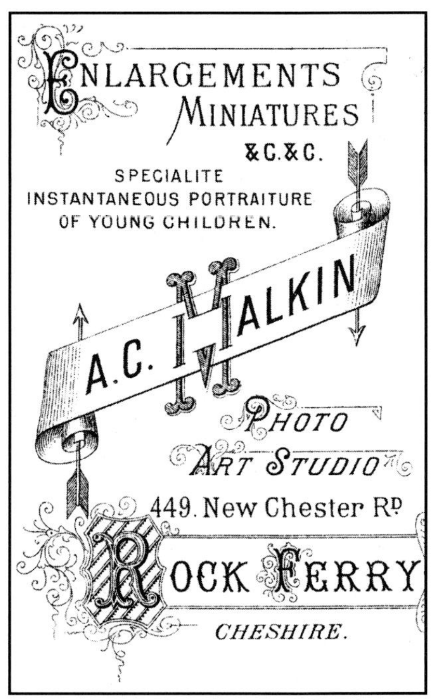

Above: *The reverse side of a portrait advertising AC Malkin's photography business at 449 New Chester Road* **Rock Ferry**

1887

– Greenbank Church in Greasby Road **Upton** was demolished

– **Birkenhead** public abbatoir opened at **Tranmere**

– Rugby International Ireland v Wales held at **Birkenhead** Park's ground[SOUV]

Feb 10 Some 5,000 people saw **Birkenhead**'s first Mayor, John Laird, open the new Birkenhead Town Hall [see photo][souv]

May 20 **New Ferry** Landing Stage carried away during a heavy gale

July 26 Henry Martin was convicted of murdering Henry Burrows in the cellar of the **Birkenhead** Brewery Company and sentenced to 20 years penal servitude[MMB]

Oct 9 First services of the Congregational Church **Prenton** held in the temporary premises of the Prenton Bowling Club Pavilion[SOUV]

Nov 1 Traffic on the Mersey was suspended due to heavy gales - **Tranmere** Stage was damaged

A. ELLIS
Manufacturer of Bassinettes, Landaulettes, Mail Carts, Invalids' Carriages, &c.
161 & 163 GRANGE ROAD, BIRKENHEAD
Bassinettes, Perambulators, Invalids' Carriages, Lent on Hire.
REPAIRS OF EVERY DESCRIPTION PROMPTLY ATTENDED TO.

P. J. FEEHAN,
Stevedore, Contractor,
AND
SHIP'S BALLAST DEALER.
YARD:—CLEVELAND ST. & TAYLOR ST.
Macadam, Paving Stones, &c., Gravel for Garden Walks, Rockery from the Red Sea.
RESIDENCE—329, CLEVELAND STREET, BIRKENHEAD.

E. LEWIS,
Billposter & Deliverer,
(LESSEE OF PRIVATE STATIONS),
2, GRANGE STREET,
BIRKENHEAD.
TOWN & COUNTRY ORDERS PROMPTLY ATTENDED TO.

Below: *There were over 5,000 peaple watching the first Mayor of* ***Birkenhead****, John Laird and invited guests present at the opening of the Birkenhead Town Hall 10 February 1887. This was early days of photography with the shadowy figure of a man who had moved, looking up at the dignitaries in front of the soldiers who did not move*

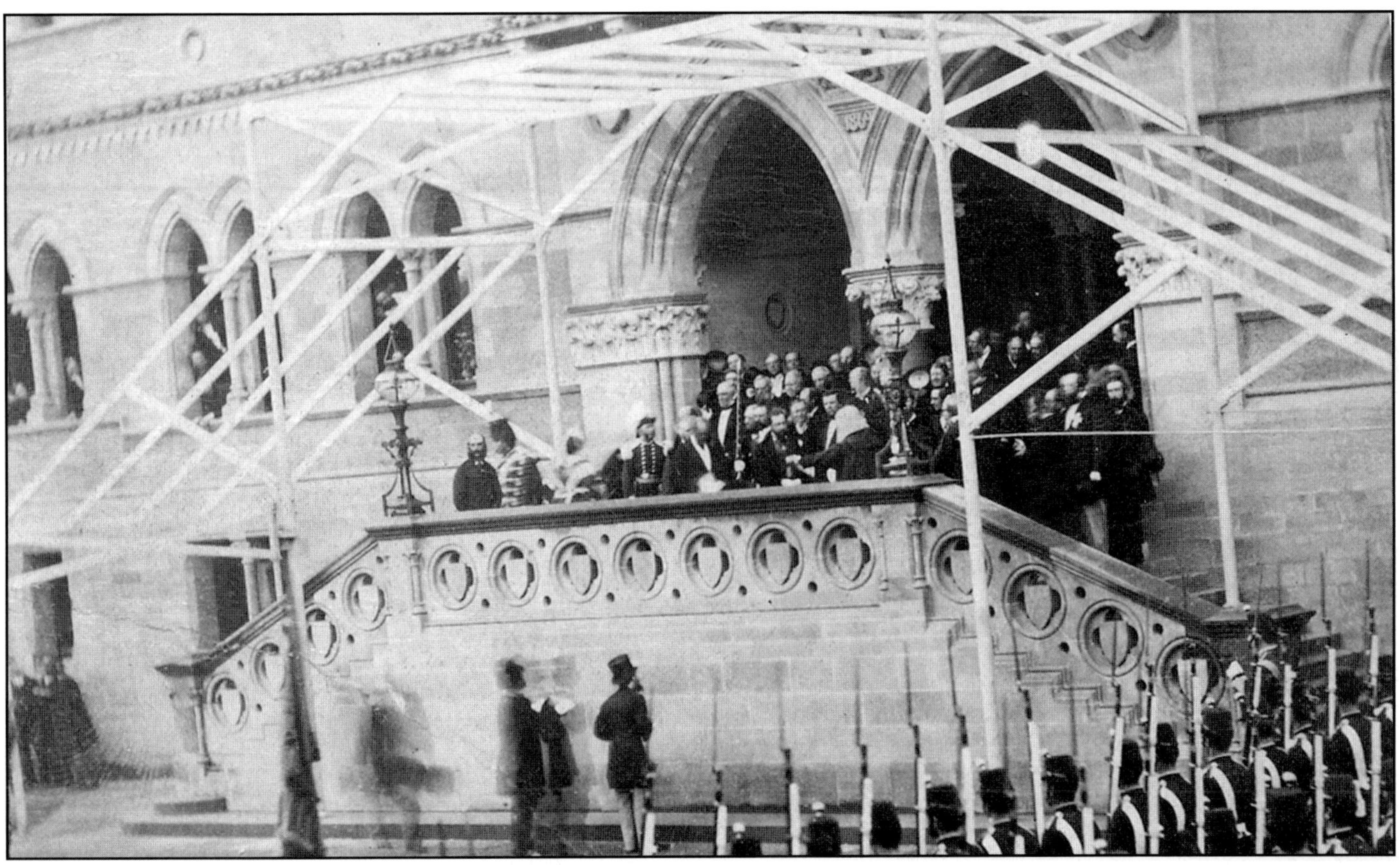

1888

– Brassey Street Mission **Birkenhead** opened a new gymnasium - total cost £657[SOUV]

– The **Birkenhead** Salt Co founded[SOUV]

– **Higher Tranmere** High School for Girls moved from Clifton Park to a larger house in Devonshire Park which had a large assembly hall (built in 1890) and also a large basement

– Wirral Joint Hospital Board formed to provide accommodation for the treatment of infectious diseases. An Isolation Hospital was developed adjoining the Workhouse at **Clatterbridge**

– Land in Lower **Birkenhead** Park which had not been sold, was used as a recreation ground with skittle alley, bowling alley and quoiting ground established[TPG]

Jan 2 Mersey Railway extension opened linking **Wallasey, Hoylake** and **West Kirby** with **Liverpool** via **Birkenhead**

May 8 *Cleveland Hotel* 1, Cleveland Street **Birkenhead** sold @ auction£2,790[LCP]

May 15 *Railway Hotel* ph. Bedford Road, **Rock Ferry** sold @ auction £4,350[LCP]

Aug 11 Foundation stone laid of St Matthew's Church, Park Road East **Birkenhead** by the Mayor Francis Thornely

Sept 4 *Mersey Hotel* ph. 25, Lord Street **Birkenhead** sold @ auction £2,450[LCP]

Sept 4 *Elephant & Castle*, 56 Park Street, **Birkenhead** sold @ auction £3,175[LCP]

Oct 30 *Farmers Arms* 12, Waterloo Place **Birkenhead** sold @ auction [licence withdrawn][LCP]

Nov 20 *Great Eastern* steamship sold by auction over five days and realised £58,000 - to be broken up [see catalogue cover this page]

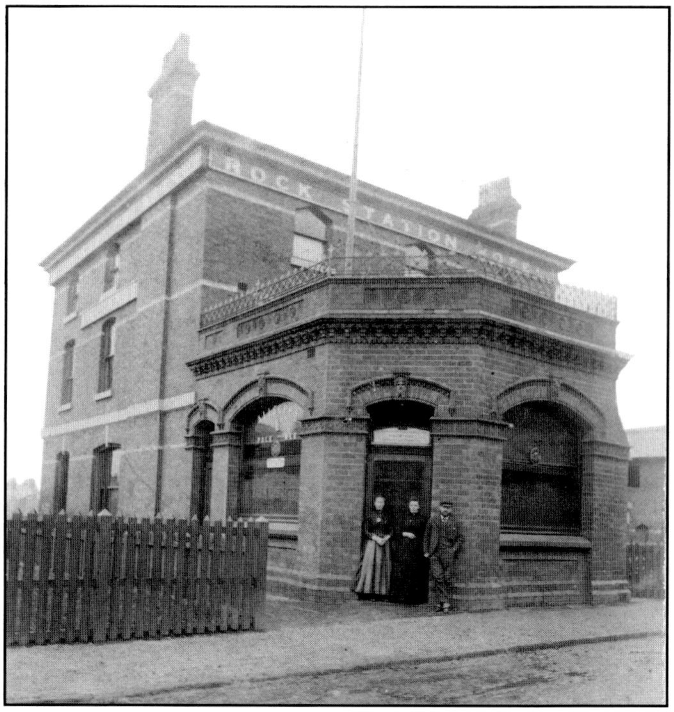

Above: *The* Rock Station Hotel *is seen at 1 Highfield Road (off Bedford Road)* ***Rock Ferry****. Originally the Rock Ferry Station was on the south side of Bedford Road but was moved to the other side in 1891 [see also 1959]*

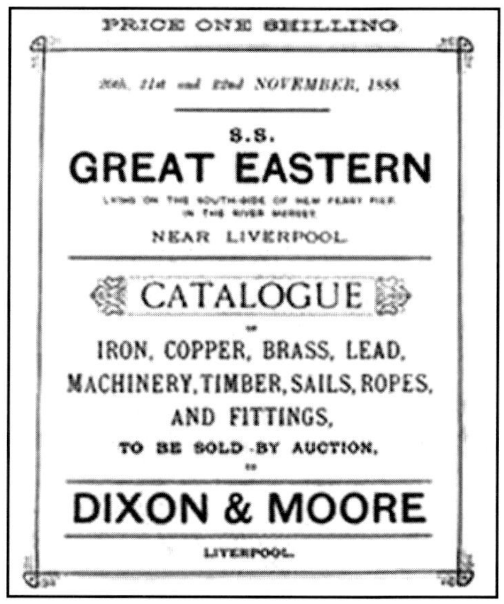

PRICE ONE SHILLING

20th, 21st and 22nd NOVEMBER, 1888

S.S.

GREAT EASTERN

LYING ON THE SOUTH-SIDE OF NEW FERRY PIER IN THE RIVER MERSEY

NEAR LIVERPOOL

CATALOGUE

OF

IRON, COPPER, BRASS, LEAD, MACHINERY, TIMBER, SAILS, ROPES, AND FITTINGS,

TO BE SOLD BY AUCTION,

BY

DIXON & MOORE

LIVERPOOL.

Above: *This was the catalogue cover for the auction of the contents of the* Great Eastern *before she was broken up [see 1890]*

Below: *The* Wellington Hotel *at 10 Bebington Village Lower* ***Bebington*** *dates back to the days when this was on the the main coaching route from* ***Birkenhead*** *to* ***Chester*** *- this being a suitable stopping place for refreshments for both horses and passengers. The vehicle pictured outside was a horse-drawn delivery cart. Note the window to the left of the entrance has been blocked in to save Widow Tax but was opened up when the hotel was refurbished. The victualler at this time was Thomas E Langley*

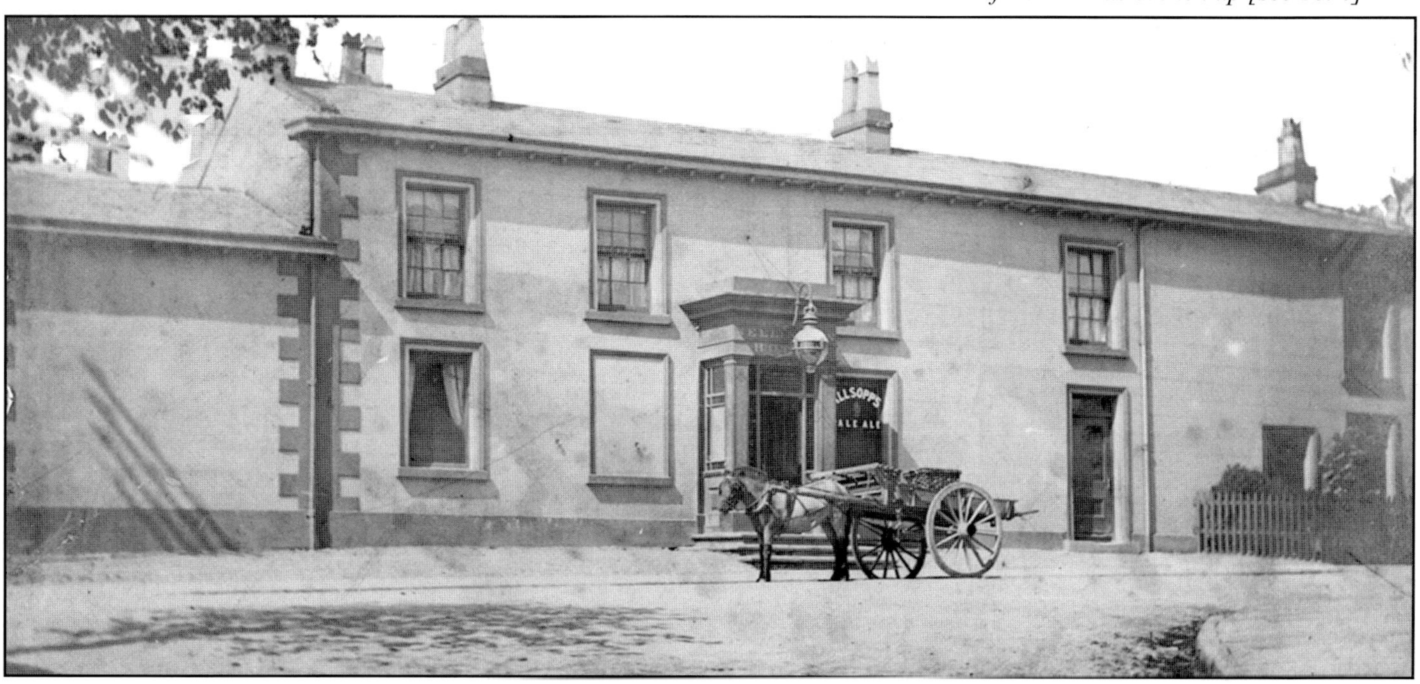

1889

– The **Birkenhead** Tramways Company, were in financial difficulties. In order to prevent the tramways closing, the Corporation purchased the rails and granted a lease to a new company called the Birkenhead United Tramways, Omnibus and Carriage Company Ltd[SOUV]

– **Oxton** Hockey Club formed[SOUV]

– JJ Martin joined forces with CH Hubbard and traded as Hubbard & Martin - their first branch was 12 Market Street South **Birkenhead**

Jan 12 **Birkenhead** Institute was opened by the Duke of Westminster with Mr WS Connacher being appointed as Headmaster from 184 applications with five members of staff for the 42 pupils - it had taken almost five years from its concept in 1883. Fees started at £1.10.0 per terms for boys under 12 to £3.0.0 per term for boys over 12 years old [see photo & rules this page][SOUV]

Aug 27 *Red Lion* (bh), Tunnel Road, **Birkenhead** + 2 cottages sold @ auction £1,050[LCP]

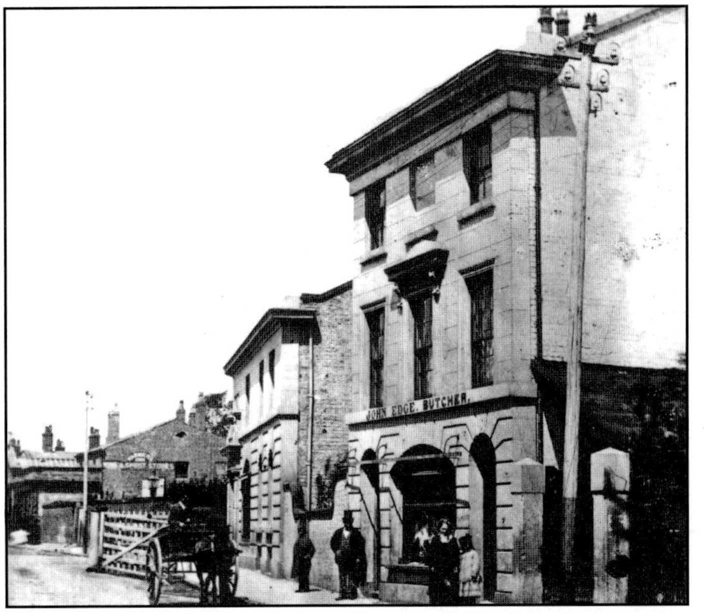

Above: *The toll bar gate can be seen behind the horse and carriage in New Chester Road. It had operated here until 1872*

Right: *This photograph of the boys and staff of* ***Birkenhead*** *Institute was taken in the first term that the school was founded in 1889.*

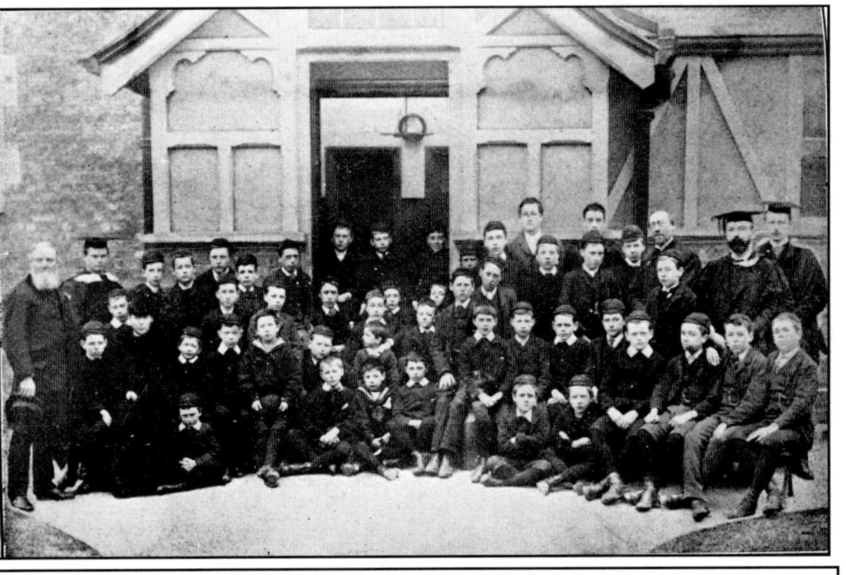

Below: *The* Halfway House *can be seen in Woodchurch Road* **Prenton** *looking towards* ***Woodchurch****. This was a wayside inn so called because it was halfway between Woodside* ***Birkenhead*** *and the village of Woodchurch. The sign for Storeton Road, which is off to the left, is seen on the corner of the inn between the 's's' of Yates's and 'es' of Ales. A new, much bigger, pub was later built to replace this inn [see 1931]*

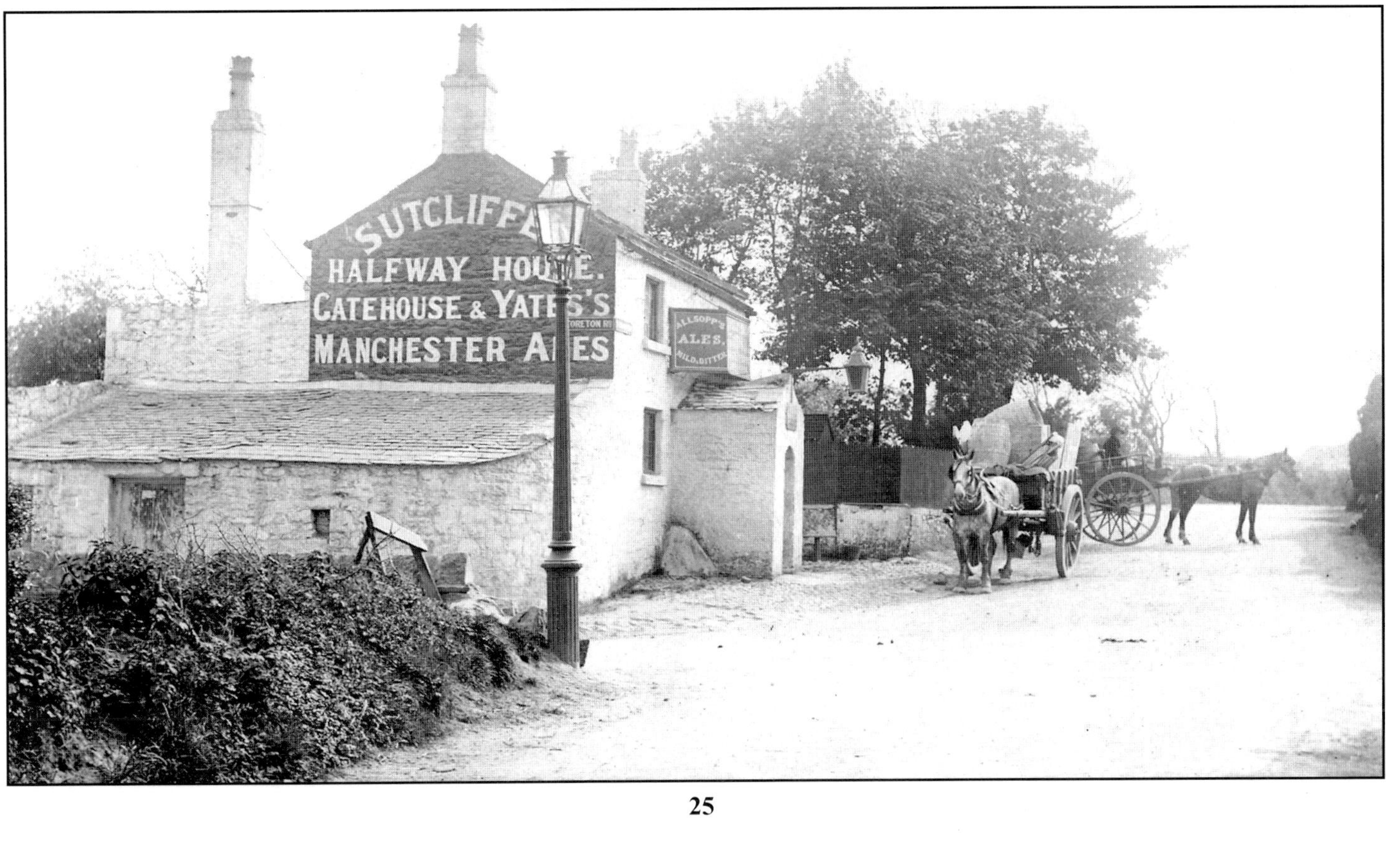

1890

– St Margaret's Convent, Mersey Road South, **Rock Ferry**, opened as a rescue home. A public laundry was opened to give the girls an occupation and as a means to support them. The laundry closed down in 1947 and the building was later turned into a Guest Home for retired ladies[DOS]

– Alfred Harding's removals business established in **Birkenhead**

– The *Great Eastern*, Brunel's ship, was broken up at **New Ferry** - it took 18 months to complete the job [see photo this page]

– Freehold Methodist Chapel built in Old Chester Road **Birkenhead**[OPB]

Feb 17 Beerhouse 28, Chapel Street **Birkenhead** sold @ auction £725[LCP]

Apr 18 The Congregational Church **Prenton** opened their first Chapel - which was later to become the Hall[SOUV]

May 15 Foundation stone laid for St Winifred Welsh Church, Westbourne Road **Birkenhead** [see sketch][SOUV]

Jul 2 *Blue Bell* (bh) Park Street, **Birkenhead** sold @ auction £1,040[LCP]

Nov 29 YMCA moved from 42 Conway Street to new premises in Grange Lane [later Grange Road] **Birkenhead**

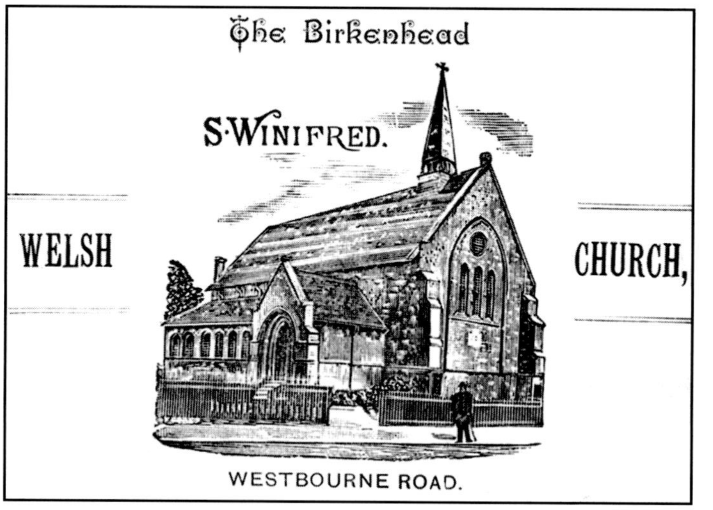

Above: *This is a sketch of St Winifred Church, Westbourne Road* ***Birkenhead*** *- foundation stone was laid 15 May 1890*

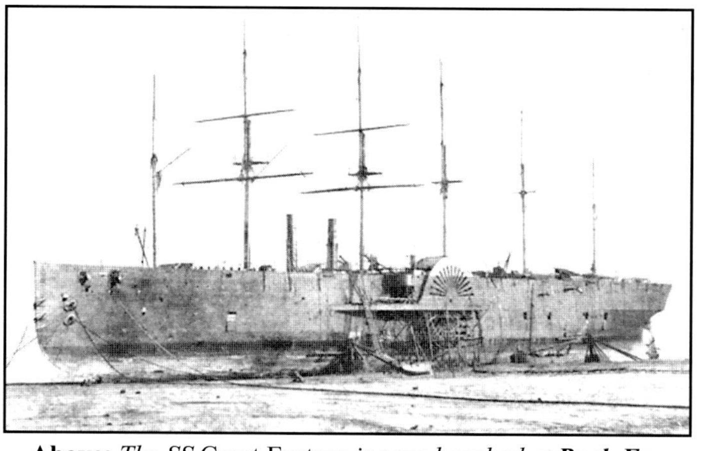

Above: *The SS* Great Eastern *is seen beached at* ***Rock Ferry*** *ready for breaking up which took 18 months - starting in 1889 and completed in 1890. She was an iron sailing steam ship designed by Isambard Kingdom Brunel and when launched in 1858 was the largest ship ever built. She had the capacity to carry 4,000 passengers around the world without refuelling with only the SS* Oceanic II *surpassing her in length in 1899 and the SS* Celtic II *in tonnage, launched 1901. At the time the ship was being broken up a local newspaper reported that when the workers broke into a compartment in the inner shell on the port side, they found a skeleton. When the* Great Eastern *was being constructed, it was discovered that two of the riveters, a worker and his apprentice, had disappeared. It was later believed that they had been sealed on the inside by accident. An hotel in* ***New Ferry*** *was named after the ship [see 1898]*

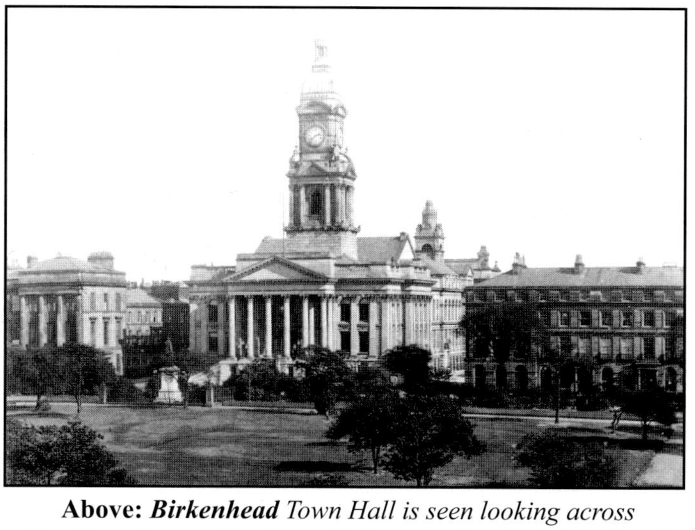

Above: ***Birkenhead*** *Town Hall is seen looking across Hamilton Square Gardens which are enclosed all round with railings as these gardens were privately owned until the council bought them in 1903 and opened them to the public. This shows the original spire which was destroyed by fire 10 July 1901 causing £15,000 worth of damage. The spire was replaced with a dome*

1891

– William Bernard established in Grange Road **Birkenhead**

– **New Ferry** Methodist Church opened[LBRB]

– Society of Friends Church built in Slatey Road **Birkenhead**[OPB]

– *Bidston Court*, a house in **Noctorum** built at a cost of £150,000 for Robert Hudson, soap manufacturer. [Moved to Royden Park in **Frankby** 1929 -31 and renamed *Hillbark*]

– **Birkenhead**'s *Argyle Theatre*'s name restored and Dennis Clarke became sole manager[SOUV]

– Boy's Brigade started at Brassey Street Mission **Birkenhead**[SOUV]

– **Birkenhead** & District Co-op founded

– *Thornton Manor*, **Thornton Hough** purchased by Wm Lever

Mar 5 *Shrewsbury Arms* + 2 cottages, Claughton Firs, **Oxton** sold @ uction £4,250[LCP]

Mar 14 St Winifred's Welsh Church opened Westbourne Road **Birkenhead** [see 1890][OCB]

May 7 St Saviour's Church, **Oxton**, consecrated

Apr 15 *Birkenhead Arms* (ph) 12, Market Street **Birkenhead** + shop, house & warehouse sold @ auction £5,750[LCP]

Jun 15 Green Lane, **Birkenhead** to **Rock Ferry** extension opened on Mersey Railway

June 30 Beer house, 23 Hope Street **Birkenhead** sold @ auction £2,150[LCP]

Sep 29 St Mark's Church, Devonshire Road, **Claughton** opened

Oct 21 *Manor Arms* (ph) 180/2 Chester Street, **Birkenhead** sold @ auction £1,605[LCP]

Nov 29 Church of Christ Alvanley Place **Birkenhead** opened [see 1917][SOUV]

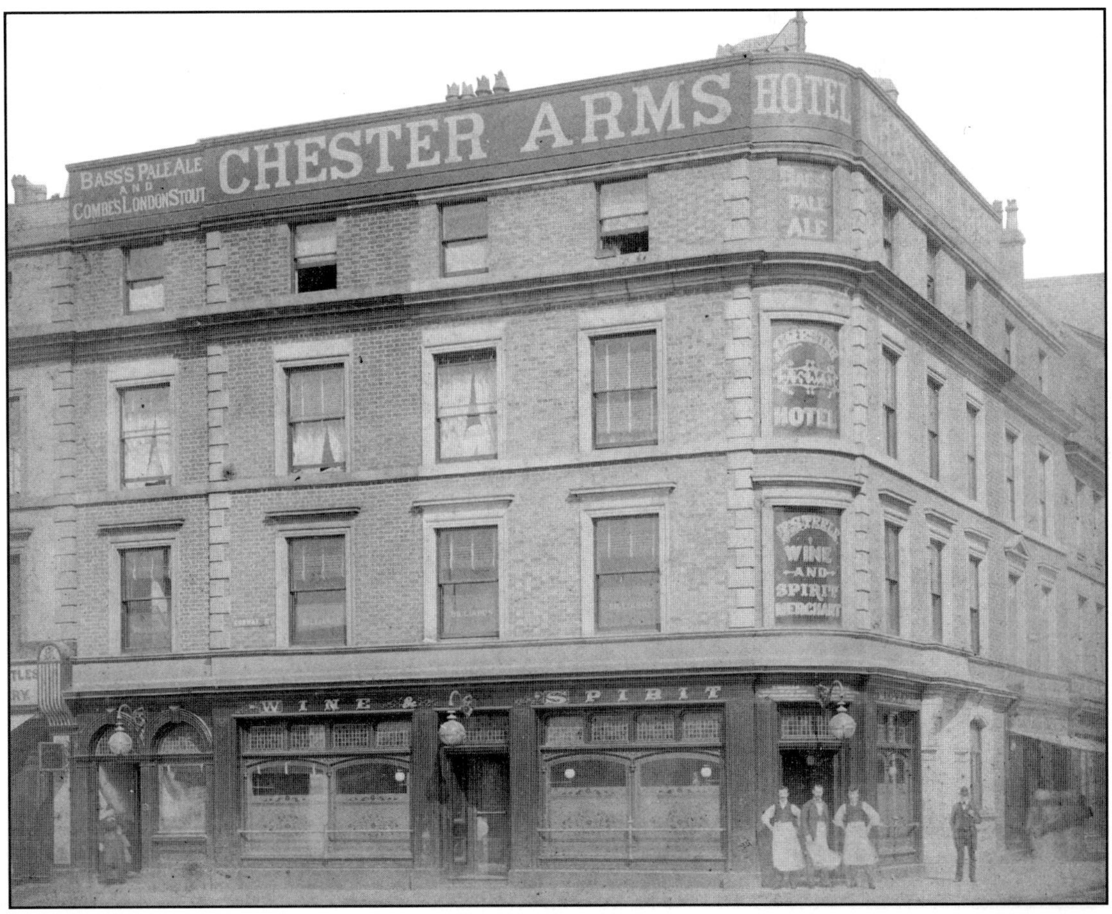

Right: *The* Chester Arms Hotel, *which dates back to at least 1850 when William Beggs was the victualler, is pictured in Conway Street at the corner of Hamilton Street - Thomas Steel the publican is the middle of the three men in the doorway. It must have been a thriving pub because many public houses of the Victorian era have one or more window blocked in to avoid paying the Window Tax. The pub was taken over by* ***Birkenhead*** *Brewery, surviving until 1971 when it was demolished and St Mark's House office block erected on the site*

1892

– Basketball introduced into **Birkenhead** YMCA. Game originated in America in 1891

– PS *Snowdon* built for the Snowdon Passenger Steamship Company by Laird Brothers **Birkenhead** [see photo]

Jan 9 Charles Thompson Mission's new premises opened in Hemingford Street, **Birkenhead** [still there today][YWPH]

Jan 26 Shrewsbury Lawn tennis Club founded in Shrewsbury Road **Oxton** - later to become Birkenhead Lawn Tennis Club [see 1960][BLTC]

May 20 Tower of St Saviour's Church **Oxton** dedicated [see photo]

Jul 18 First county cricket match at **Birkenhead** Park - Cheshire v Derbyshire[WBD]

Aug 10 *Theatre Hotel* 41 Henry Street, **Birkenhead** withdrawn at auction @ £1,040 reserve £2,000[LCP]

Sep 26 Birkenhead Pavilion & Roller Skating Rink opened in Park Road East, **Birkenhead**[BW]

Oct **Birkenhead** Park Rugby Club new pavilion built[BW]

Nov 5 Battleship *Royal Oak* launched at Laird shipyard, **Birkenhead** - she was the largest vessel to be built at that time on the Mersey[MOI]

AMIES & SONS
FAMILY
Boot & Shoe Manufacturers
235 GRANGE ROAD, & 30 MARKET STREET
BIRKENHEAD.
LARGEST AND BEST SELECTED STOCK IN TOWN.
Repairs Executed with Despatch.

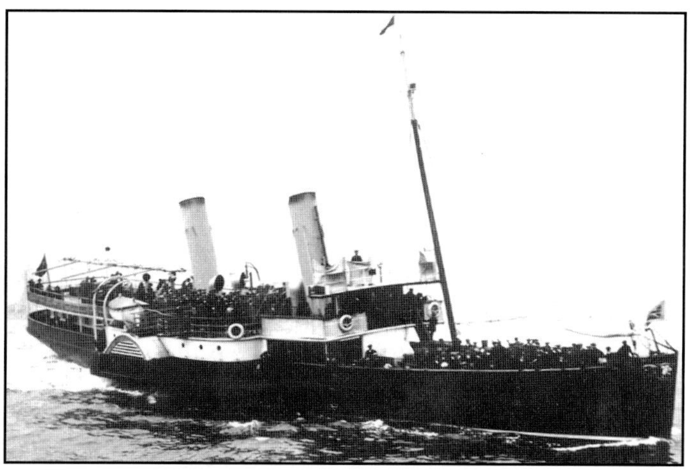

Above: *The two funnelled Paddle Steamer* Snowdon *was built by Laird Bros Birkenhead in 1892 for the Snowdon Passenger Steamship Company. She had a speed of 14 knots and a certificate for 462 passengers. She served as a minesweeper from Dover to Harwich during the First World War, resuming her North Wales passenger service in 1919 and was broken up in 1931*

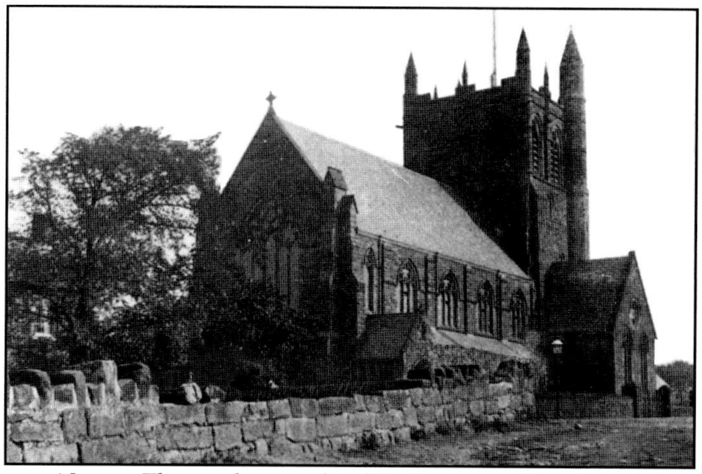

Above: *The newly-completed St Saviour's Church at the junction of Bidston Road and Gerald Road straight ahead, was taken from Townfield Lane. Originally* **Oxton** *was part of the Parish of Woodchurch but in 1851 the first Church was built here and Oxton became a separate Parish. However, due to an increase in population, the Church was not big enough so a new one was built on additional land donated by the Earl of Shrewsbury, finally being consecrated 7 May 1891 and the Tower dedicated 20 May 1892. There are stunning views from the tower looking west towards North Wales and east towards Liverpool. The Church was badly damaged during the Second World War when a land mine fell on the Carnarvon Castle Hotel nearby [see 1941 and 1948]*

BIRKENHEAD ROYAL PAVILION,
ELITE SKATING RINK,
PARK ENTRANCE.
MONDAY, 31st October, and during the Week.
TWO EXHIBITIONS DAILY.
Engagement at Enormous Expense of
Chevalier T. H. CROWTHER,
The Plus Ultra of SKATERS, BICYCLISTS & SWORDSMEN,
King of all Skaters. King of the Wheel.
Patronized by H.R.H. the Prince of Wales and Royal Family
The Refined Performances of this World Renowned Artiste are astounding feats of graceful skill and daring in the use of
Skates, Unicycle, Bicycle and Sword.
Every Afternoon 4-30 and Evening 8-30.
NOTE—See this most Wonderful Artiste previous to his departure to the Chicago Exhibition. POSITIVELY FOR ONE WEEK ONLY
ADMISSION - - - - 6d.

Above: Chevalier T.H. Crowther was the star attraction at the ***Birkenhead*** *Royal Pavilion*, Elite Skating Rink, opposite the main entrance to Birkenhead Park, for the week commencing 31 October 1892. Although a foreign sounding gentleman he came from Bradford and gave an interview at his rooms at the *Queens Hotel* to the *Birkenhead Wasp*. He was known as the King of Skaters who had travelled in every country except Australia. One of his most daring feats was to ride on his bicycle across Niagara Falls of America on a plank of wood nine inches wide in front of 10.000 people

1893

- William Lever replaced old, unhealthy cottages with new at **Thornton Hough**
- The Wirral Amateur Cup (football) introduced for the 1892/3 season with **West Kirby** FC the first winners - the same season saw the introduction of the first League in the district called The Wirral & District Association Football League [see also 1906][WDFA]
- Temporary Laird Street Council School opened in **Birkenhead**[WBD]

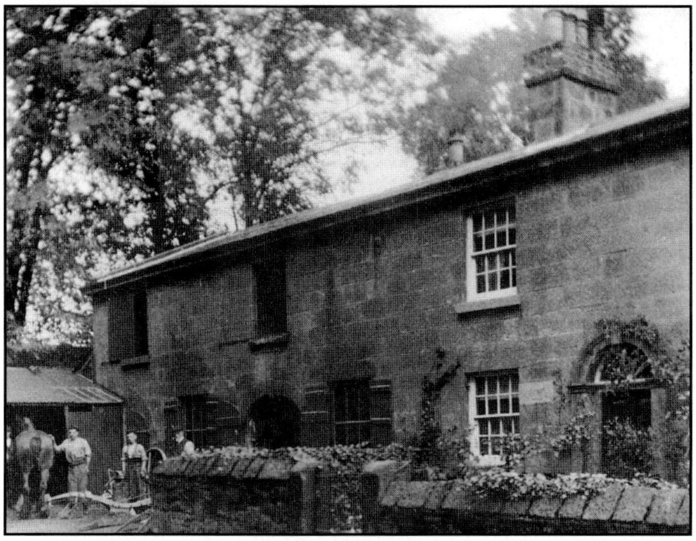

Above: *The Smithy at **Woodchurch** which faced onto the main road from Woodchurch to Upton*

ROBB BROTHERS

Compete with Liverpool Establishments.

—LADIES' DEPARTMENTS.—

MILLINERY.	UNDERCLOTHING.
Mantles	*Baby Linen*
Hosiery	*Corsets*
Gloves	*Ribbons*
Trimmings	*Laces*
Knitting Wools	*Flowers*
Umbrellas	*Jewellery*

GENTS' DEPARTMENTS.

Shirts	*Scarfs*
Hosiery	*Braces*
Collars	*Handkerchiefs*
Gloves	*Umbrellas*

11, 13 & 15, CROSS STREET

AND

234 & 236, GRANGE ROAD, BIRKENHEAD.

MRS. FERGUSON

152 GRANGE ROAD

English and French Confectionery.

SUPERIOR CREAM ICES. & GENUINE HOME-MADE TOFFEES.

PARTIES SUPPLIED WITH ICES.

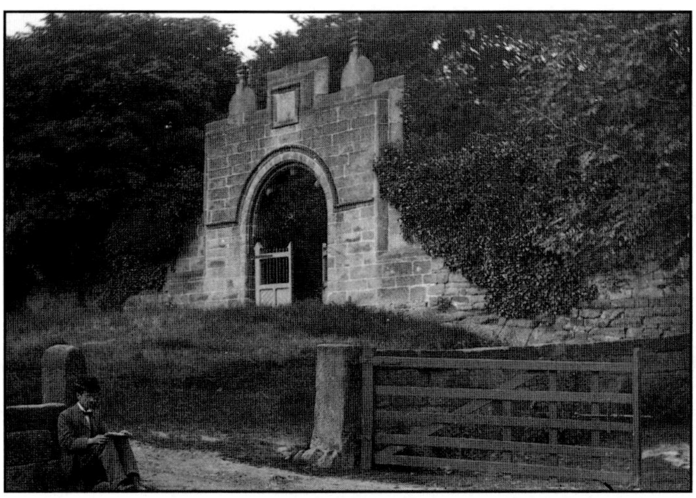

Above: *The entrance to **Bidston** Hall is seen above the gate post. The original building probably dates back to the 16th Century when it was used by the Stanley family as a hunting lodge. It was rebuilt by William the 6th Earl of Derby who died in 1642. Charles the 8th Earl was the last member of the Stanley family to reside here in 1653. The property was sold to Robert Vyner c1680. The Hall remained in the Vyner family until 1966 when it was purchased by Mr & Mrs Faulkner by which time it was in a serious state of disrepair. They had restored most of the building to its original splendour by 1969 when they sold it*

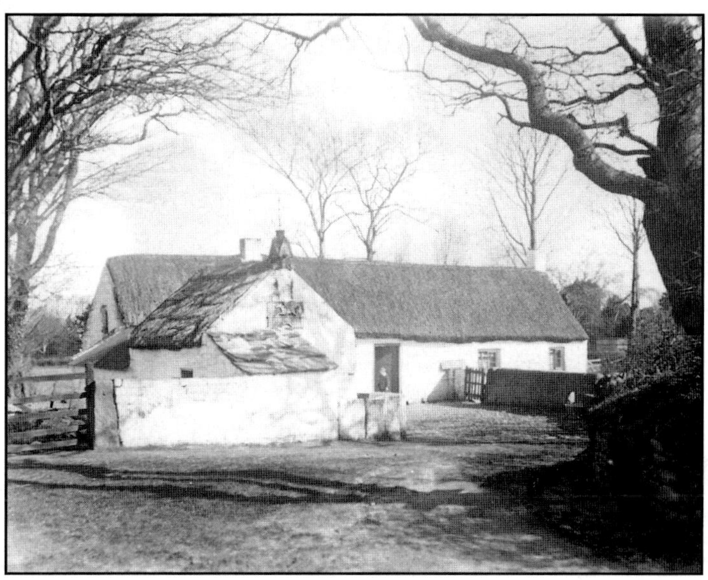

Right: Tam O'Shanter's Cottage *at **Bidston** was so named in 1837 by Richard Lea, a stone mason who lived here and carved a scene from Robert Burns' poem "Tam O'Shanter". This can be seen on the side of the cottage above the sloping roof*

1894

– Willmer Brothers moved to bigger premises, acquiring land in **Birkenhead** bounded by Chester, Duncan, Albion and Brandon Streets - for their printing works[FB]

– Della Robbia Pottery opened its works at 2 Price Street **Birkenhead** under the managership of Harold Rathbone[DRPB]

– Birkenhead YWCA moved from Argyle Street to larger premises at 42 The Woodlands **Birkenhead**[SOUV]

– **Bidston** Windmill, which had fallen into decay, was restored at the expense of RS Hudson of *Bidston Court* [see 1898] - to coincide with the opening of Bidston Hill to the public[WPPB]

– Branch Library opened in Price Street **Birkenhead** and also Grove Road **Rock Ferry**

Jan 6 International rugby union match England v Wales held at **Birkenhead** Park[SOUV]

Feb Wirral Ladies Golf Club instituted in **Bidston**[WLGC]

Feb 19 *Derby Arms* (ph) + workshops etc, Nelson Road **Rock Ferry** sold @ auction £4,600[LCP]

Mar 8 Serious fire on board American line SS *Paris* lying in **Birkenhead** Graving Dock

Apr 27 First portion of **Bidston** Hill acquired by **Birkenhead** Corporation

May 15 The temporary Church of St Stephen, an iron and timber building which became the Church Hall in 1897, was opened in Prenton Lane **Prenton**[SOUV]

May 25 Queen Victoria opened the Manchester Ship Canal

Jun 14 Stone Quarry, Holt Hill, **Tranmere** sold @ auction £305[LCP]

Aug 3 Grand opening of Lipton's Provision Market at 168 Grange Road **Birkenhead**[MB]

Oct 13 Explosion aboard the T & J Harrison steamer *Explorer* in Alfred Dock **Birkenhead**, due to coal gas - killed four men

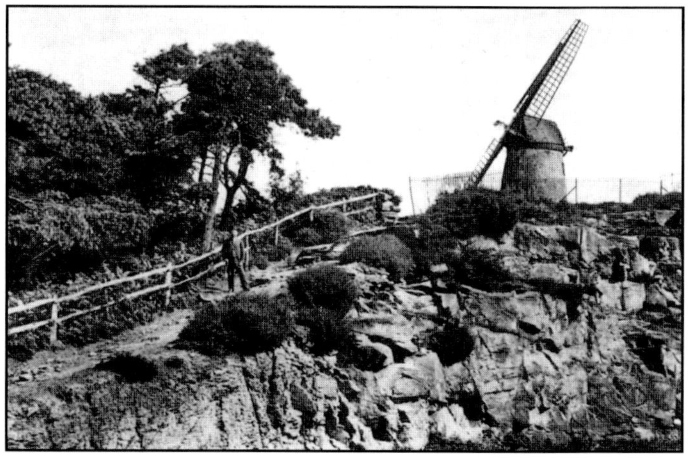

Above: *Bidston* *Windmill photographed for an 1894 publication shows it in a state of disrepair with one arm missing - the mill was repaired at the expense of RS Hudson of* Bidston Court

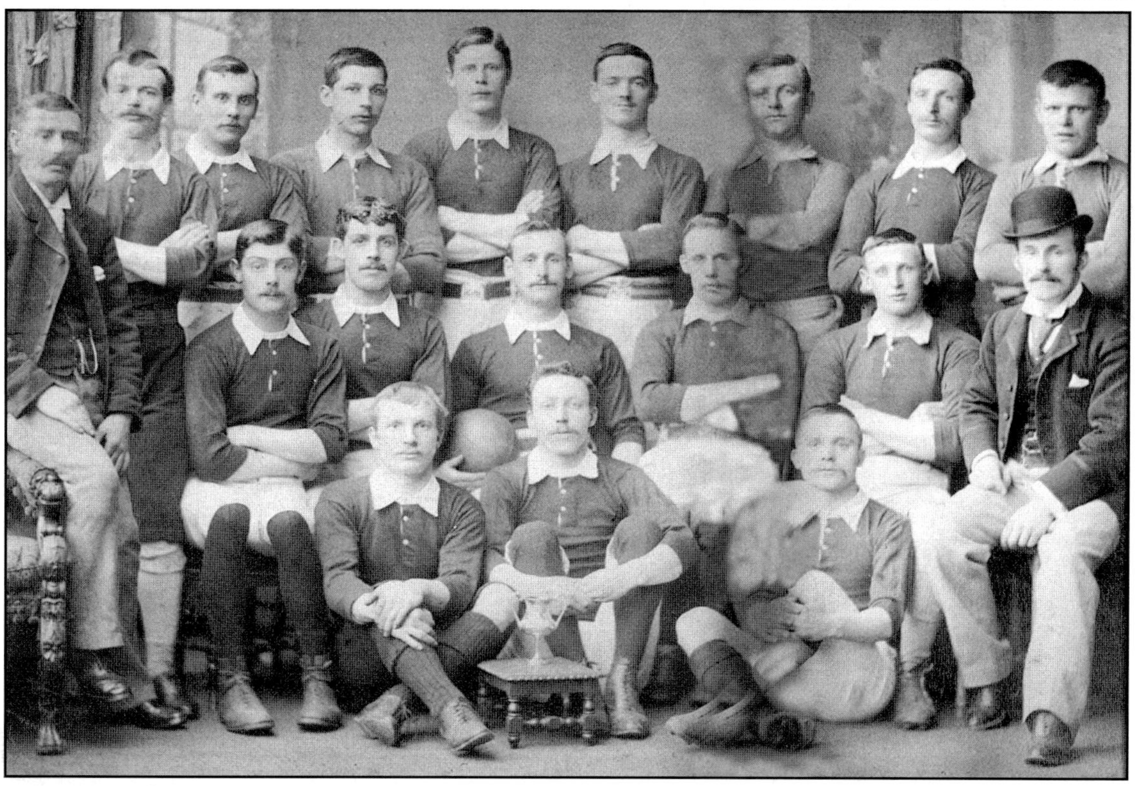

Above: *Birkenhead* *Wanderers 'A' team winners of the Liverpool & District Rugby League Cup 1894-5: W Monaghan J Edwards E Dixon J Glover j Grey J Lightfoot W Carter C Holmes F Glover D Atkinson A Goat (Captain) R Hesketh F Cooper J Love (Hon Secretary) A Herbert C Keegan G Webb [see article right of photo]*

Left: Birkenhead Wanderers were initially a Rugby Union club founded in the early 1880s. - their headquarters were in the Queen's Hotel opposite the Park Entrance. They later switched from Union to League playing in the Lancashire Second Competition of the professional Northern Union to allow their players to be paid. Although they won the Liverpool and District Rugby League Cup in 1894-5 they did not have much other success. They shared Tranmere Rovers' ground from 1903, then located in Temple Road**.** However, the club ceased playing in 1904

1895

– **Birkenhead** Fire Station opened in Whetstone Lane [see 1958]

– Tramway lines purchased by **Birkenhead** Corporation from Wirral Tramway Co following financial difficulties, then granted them a lease to operate the tramways [the Corporation thus became owners of all the tramlines in the Borough][SOUV]

– **Wallasey** Co-operative Society amalgamated with **Birkenhead** Co-operative Society

– South End Destructor opened in **Birkenhead**

– Woodland Junior Mixed & Infants School opened in Borough Road **Birkenhead**[OPB]

– The **Birkenhead** Savings Bank, which opened in 1839 with premises at 46 Hamilton Square, finally closed[souv]

Feb River Mersey froze in parts and ice floes floated down the river [see photos]

Feb 3 Fire at Congregational Church, **Liscard**

Mar 10 **Birkenhead** Infectious Diseases Hospital opened in Tollemache Road

May 1 Bebington Station became **Bebington** & **New Ferry** Station[RSoW]

June 1 Branch railway line from **Bidston** to **Seacombe** & **Egremont** opened with intermediate station at **Liscard** and **Poulton**

Nov 18 *Graving Dock Hotel* (ph) **Birkenhead** sold @ auction £8,550[LCP]

BIRKENHEAD WEDDING RING DEPOT.

FRANCIS UNTHANK,
Watchmaker & Jeweller
96 OXTON ROAD,

Begs to inform the inhabitants of this town that he has just added to his Stock a large selection of GUINEA GOLD WEDDING RINGS of the Latest Fashions; he also wishes to inform his patrons that he has made a Genuine Reduction in Price, and guarantees to defy any house to sell at a lower price. All Rings sold by Weight, being of the highest quality and best make. ALL SIZES, SHAPES, AND FASHIONS.

N.B.—Each Purchaser will be presented with Half-Dozen serviceable Teaspoons, with his name stamped on.

Watches Cleaned 2/6. **Clocks Cleaned from 2/-.**

M. HARKER
Confectioner,
AND
FANCY BREAD BAKER,
35 GRANGE ROAD WEST,
BIRKENHEAD.

Tea Parties and Balls catered for on the shortest notice.

RICH BRIDES' CAKES
MADE TO ORDER.

Y.W.C.A. Hostels
42 & 44 The Woodlands, BIRKENHEAD.

TERMS (per week.)	
Single Rooms	8/- to 10/-
Cubicles	6/6 to 8/-
MEALS.	
Breakfast	8d.
Dinner (residents)	1/-
" (non-residents)	1/3
Tea (residents)	9d.
" (non-residents)	1/-
Supper	7d.
EXTRAS.	
Tea	1d. per cup
Cocoa, Milk, etc.	2d. "

"By love serve one another."

1. It is earnestly desired that each resident in these Hostels should help to foster a spirit of Christian fellowship and partake in all the advantages of the Hostels and Club.
2. Family Prayers at 9-20 p.m. daily.
3. Each resident is requested to make her own bed and leave her room tidy.
4. One meal, at least, should be taken in the Hostel each day, and no food is allowed to be taken into the cubicles.
5. No washing to be left in the cubicles. Residents are requested not to use the kitchens for any purpose except for airing their linen.
6. No petrol or cleaning spirit should be taken into the bedrooms.
7. The Hostels are closed at 10-30 each night, Saturday at 11 o'clock, and lights turned out one half hour later. Quiet should be observed after these hours.
8 Tenancy to be terminated by a week's written notice on either side. The Committee reserves the right to terminate any tenancy should occasion demand.
9. All communications regarding the Hostels to be made to the Superintendent.

Above: *This advert giving the prices and terms for the* ***Birkenhead*** *YWCA shows they have moved into their new premises at 42-44 The Woodlands from Argyle Street*

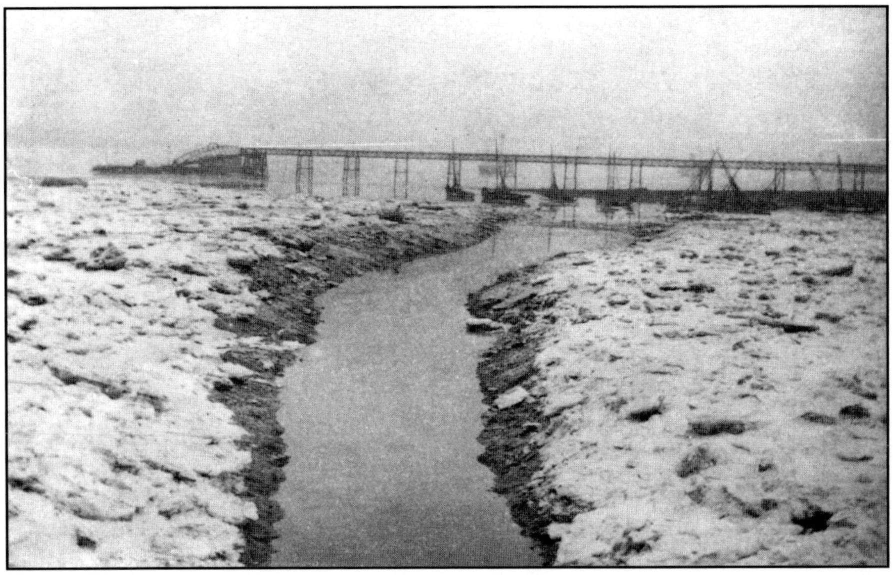

In February 1895 Arctic weather conditions caused large ice-floes to come down from the upper reaches of the River Mersey bringing small icebergs. At low tide the river had the appearance of a vast ice field. In Birkenhead and Wirral hundreds of houses were completely frozen up and water carts were sent round town, also warm clothing and free food were supplied to the needy. These conditions remained for a few weeks before the thaw set in.

Above: *The cleared channel leads to New ferry Pier*

Right: *A scene in Laird Brothers' yard where the ice was particularly thick*

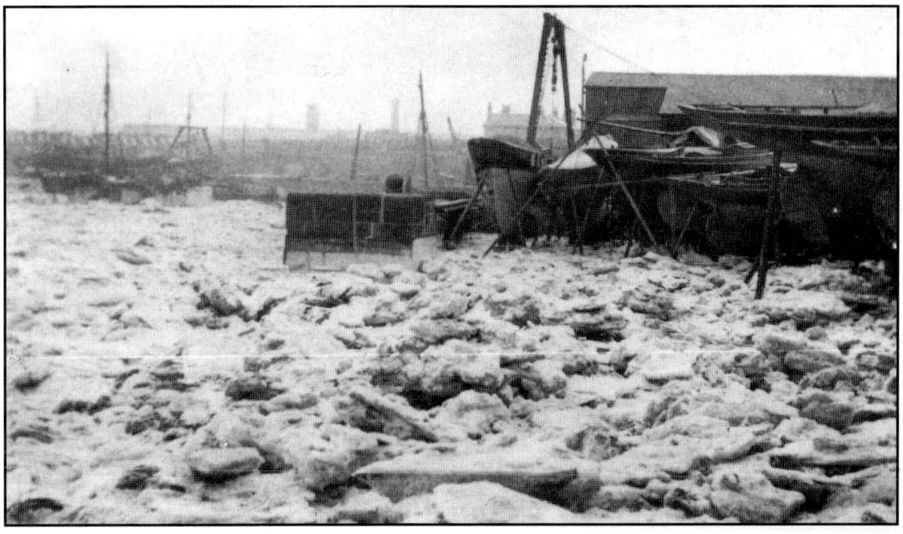

1896

– Cathcart Street Council School **Birkenhead** opened

– Harry Lauder first appeared at the *Argyle Theatre*, **Birkenhead**

– St Winifred's Welsh Church, Westboume Road, **Birkenhead**, consecrated[OPB]

– **Birkenhead** Council commenced to supply electricity

– Egerton Street **Birkenhead** Improvement Scheme sanctioned

– **Rock Ferry** FC founded - used a ground in Bedford Park

Mar 16 **Bidston** to **Wrexham** railway line opened for goods with intermediate stations at **Neston, Storeton** [later Storeton for **Barnston]** and **Upton** - opened May 18 for passengers

May 18 **Bidston** to Harwarden railway line opened to passengers. Intermediate stations at: **Neston, Storeton** and **Upton**

Sept **Birkenhead** Corporation commence to supply electricity

Nov 9 *Argyle Theatre*, Argyle Street **Birkenhead** showed films - reputed to be the first time moving pictures were shown outside London[RP]

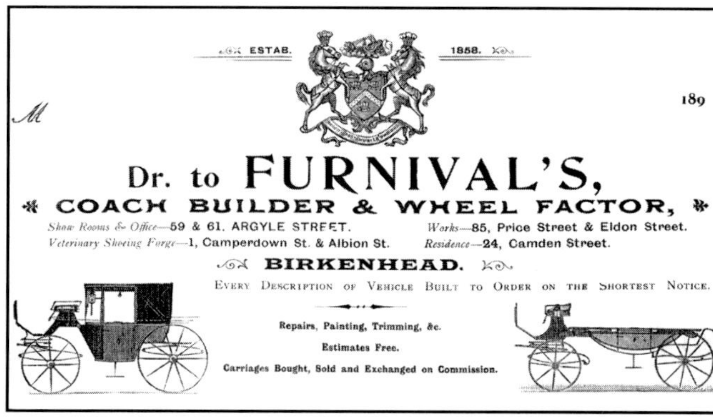

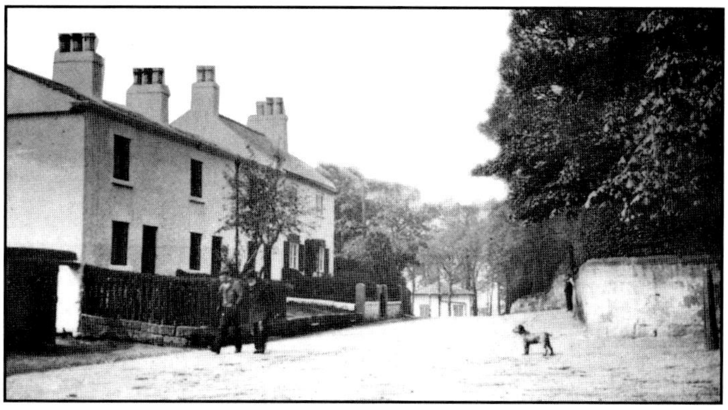

Above: *The two men on the left are walking into* ***Upton*** *Village from* ***Greasby****. The Toll Bar can be seen in the distance [see 1901] and behind the wall on the right was Upton Hall Convent. The cottages were demolished in the 1960s and the road layout altered*

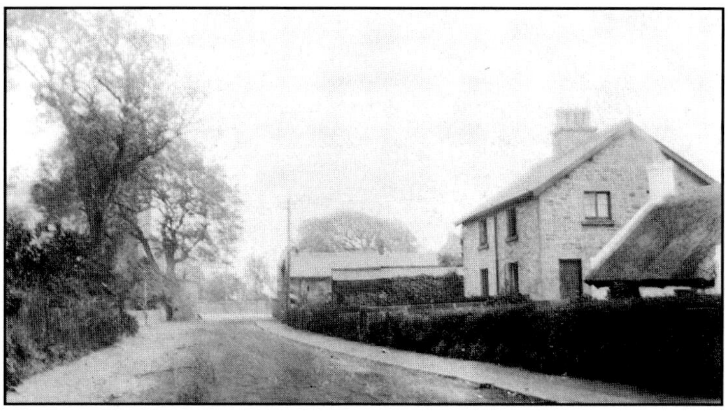

Left: *Looking up School Lane* ***Bidston*** *with St Oswald's Church behind the tree on the left at the junction of Boundary Road which is seen in the distance. The building on the right of the junction was* Stone Farm *formerly the* Ring O' Bells *[see 1864]*

MRS. JAMES

Servants' Registry Appointment Rooms

36 GRANGE ROAD WEST,

BIRKENHEAD.

Superior Servants waiting to be engaged.

WINDOW BLINDS

Manufactured by Patent and Special Machinery and painted in every variety of Colourings.

ALSO

SPRING ROLLER BLINDS

In all the Newest Materials.

FLORENTINE BLINDS.
GAUZE WIRE BLINDS.
INSIDE VENETIAN BLINDS.
SPANISH BLINDS.
DWARF BLINDS.

R. J. REED

237a GRANGE ROAD,

BIRKENHEAD,

Manufactory—ELIZABETH STREET.

Right: *The tramcar seen on the left at* ***Birkenhead*** *Woodside, which is pulled by one horse, is on the single track for the Docks route. Beyond the horse and carriages were the other two tracks also used by the horse trams until the electric trams replaced them in 1901. The Ferry Terminal building is straight ahead and Woodside Station is out of the picture to the right*

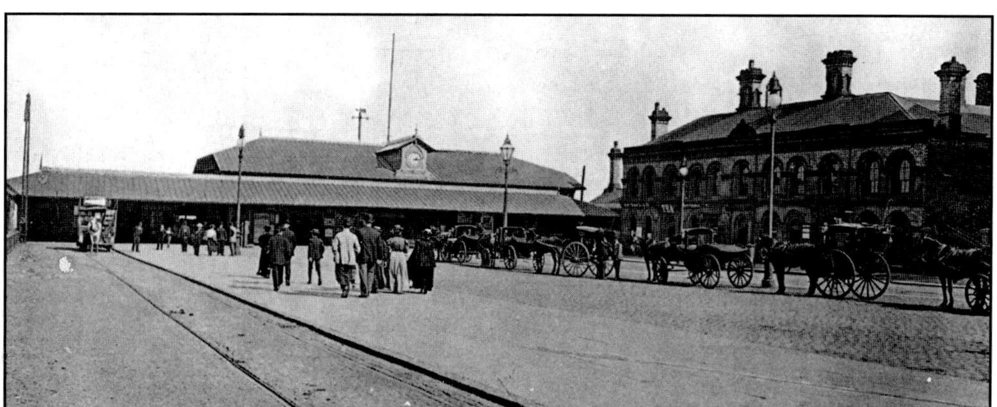

1897

– Holy Trinity C of E School opened in Eldon Street **Birkenhead**[WBD]

– Extension of the Infectious Diseases Hospital in Tolemache Road **Birkenhead** opened

– Council purchased **Rock Ferry** & **New Ferry** cross river services

– Victoria Hall, **Hr Bebington**, was erected in Village Road at a cost of £1,850 to commemorate Queen Victoria's Diamond Jubilee

May 26 Mr James Lever died. He was father of the founders of Lever Bros, **Port Sunlight**

June 19 Queen Victoria's Jubilee was celebrated in **Birkenhead** by a grand procession through the town to the Park where 12,000 children took part in a Sunday School fete which was marred by heavy rain

June 22 Queen Victoria's Jubilee Day was celebrated at **Birkenhead** in the evening with displays of electric lights and fireworks from many steamers in the Mersey

July 1 Over 62 acres of land on **Bidston** Hill acquired for public use at a cost of £18,550 with Birkenhead Corporation paying £8,500 and public subscription for the rest

Nov 1 St Stephen's Church Prenton Lane **Prenton** opened - cost £10,000 [see drawing below and also 1946][SOUV]

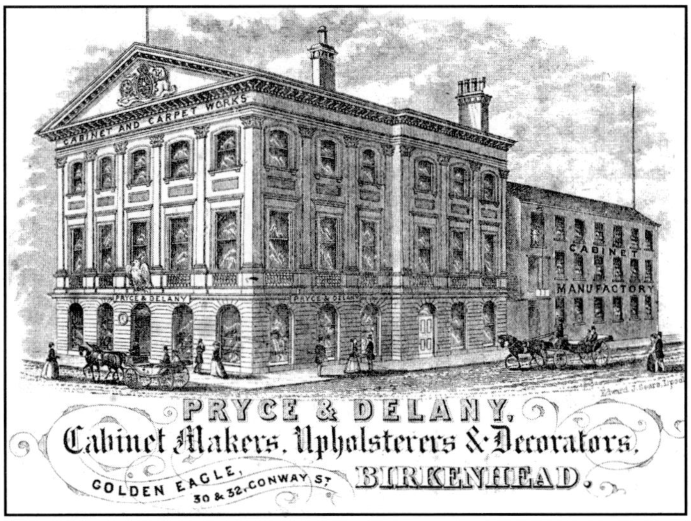

Above: *This was an advertising card showing the cabinet, carpet works and showroom of Pryce & Delany who were advertised as Cabinet Makers, Upholsterers & Decorators at 30 & 32 Conway Street [Bank Street on the right]* ***Birkenhead****. The premises later became the premises of the Mersey Motor Company and in 1917 opened as the* Birkenhead Empire Picture Hall *[the building remained as a cinema until 1991]*

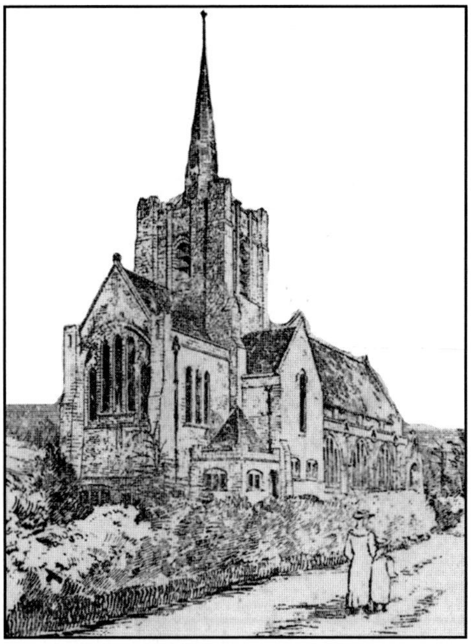

Above: *This sketch of St Stephen's Church Prenton Lane* ***Prenton*** *which opened 1 November 1897 and cost £10,000 - shows the spire which was in the original design but never built due to lack of funds*

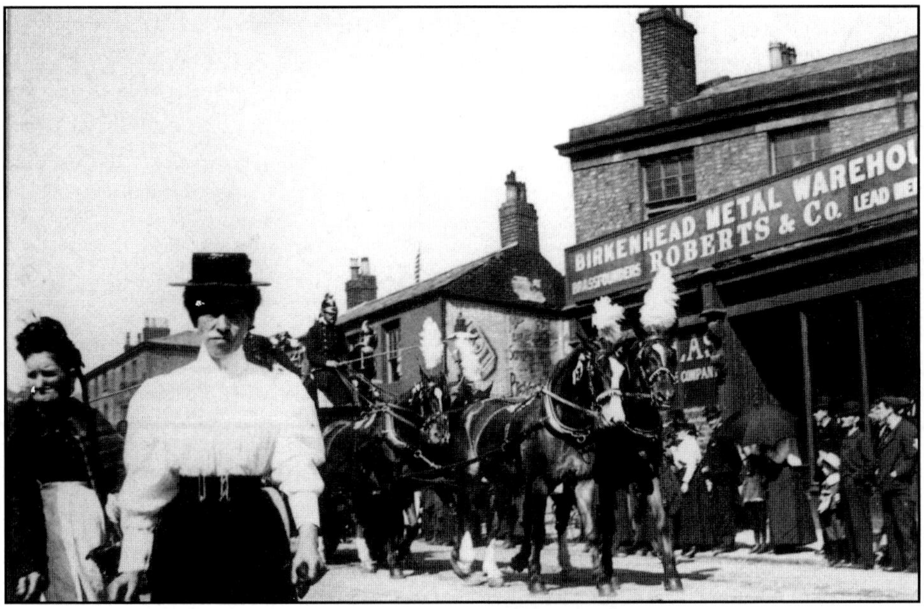

Above: *To the right of the two ladies pictured in Argyle Street* ***Birkenhead*** *is the horse-drawn Birkenhead Fire Brigade taking part in a parade and passing in front of the Birkenhead Metal Warehouse, belonging to Roberts & Co which was opposite the* Argyle Theatre

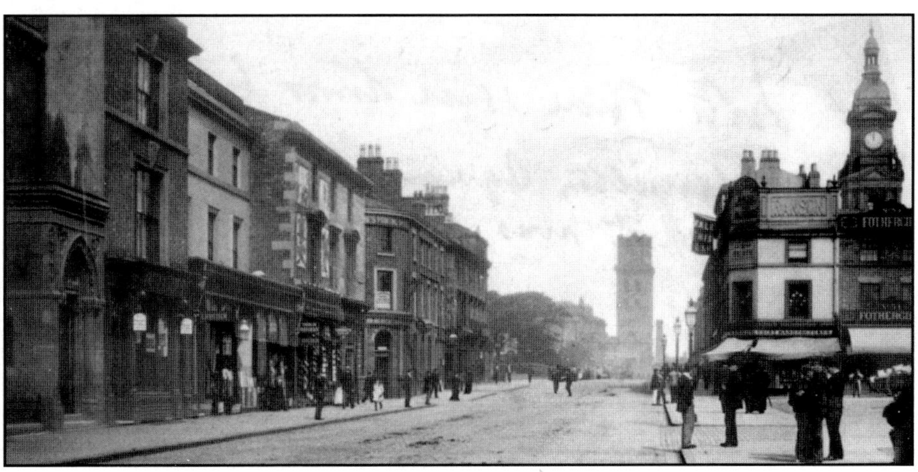

Right: *This view in Hamilton Street was taken when there were no crowds - so the* ***Birkenhead*** *Market to the right must have been closed. Note the original tower to Birkenhead Town Hall, top right, which was burnt down in 1901*

1898

- – The *Theatre Royal* in Argyle Street **Birkenhead** was acquired by MR WW Kelly
- – **Birkenhead** Cycling Club formed[SOUV]
- – Ford water pumping station opened near **Upton** station
- Jan 6 St Michael's and All Angels Church Carlton Road was consecrated - being the daughter church to Christ Church **Birkenhead** [see also November 1958][SOUV]
- Jan 21 Princess Louise and Marquis of Lorne visit **Birkenhead**[WBD]
- Mar 28 Beerhouse - 37, Church Road (+ No 35) Hr **Tranmere** sold @ auction £80[LCP]
- April 1 **Birkenhead** Municipal Borough formed into one civil parish, amalgamating with it the former townships of **Claughton, Oxton, Rock Ferry, Bebington** and **Tranmere**
- July 19 Bidston Court Estate, Vyner Road **Bidston**, was put up for auction by RW Hudson, the soap manufacturer
- Aug *Atlantic Hotel* (ph), 255 Price Street, **Birkenhead** + lock-up shop sold @ auction £12,500[LCP]
- Sept 25 The mission of St Joseph's RC Church North Road **Birkenhead** opened[DoS]
- Oct 21 Marble bust of John Laird unveiled in **Birkenhead** [see also 1877]
- Dec 14 *The Great Eastern Picnic Hotel*, New Ferry Road, **New Ferry** sold @ auction £8,400 - bought by Birkenhead Brewery [see photo][LCP]

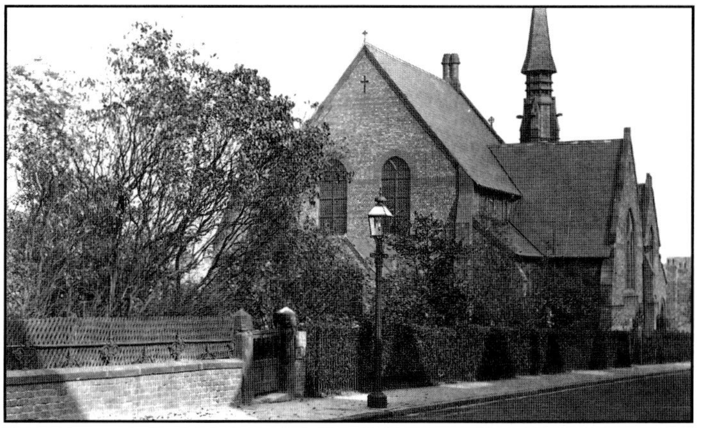

Above: *St Michael's and All Angels Church, Carlton Road* ***Claughton-cum-Grange*** *which seated 850 was consecrated. she was the daughter church to Christ Church Birkenhead*

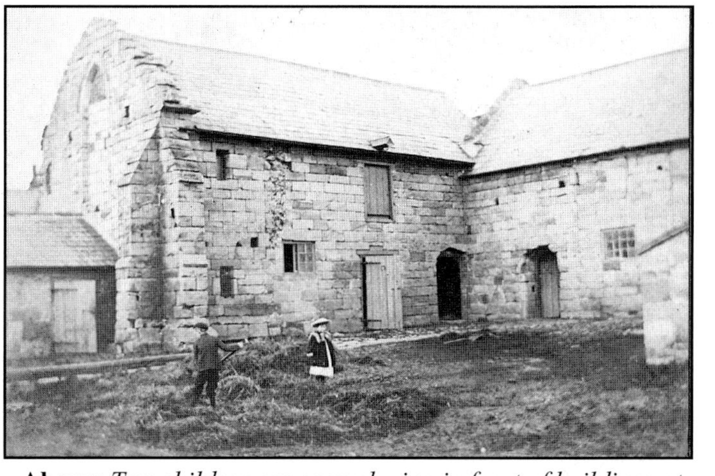

Above: *Two children are seen playing in front of buildings at* ***Storeton*** *Hall Farm. The Hall, which was built by Sir William de Stanley, dates back to c1360 and remained in the Stanley family until 1848. The remains of the east gable end of the Great Hall, seen on the left, have been incorporated into the farm buildings*

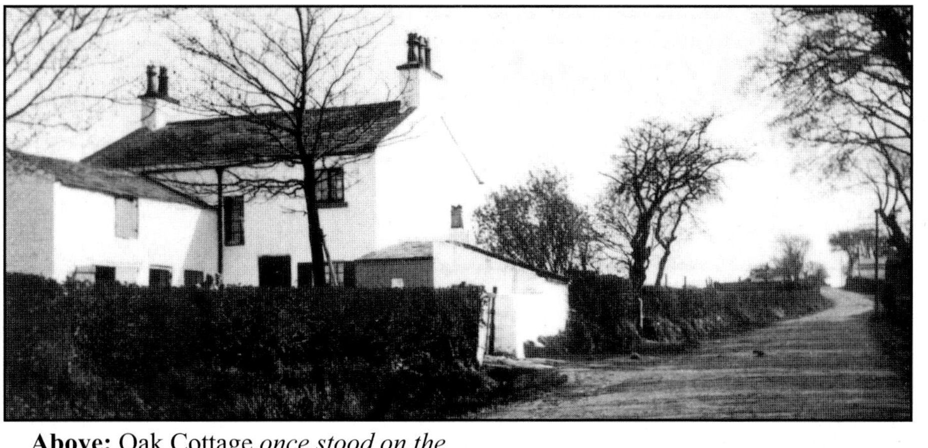

Above: Oak Cottage *once stood on the road from* ***Upton*** *Village to Arrowe Park [the garage opposite the police station now stands on or near the site]*

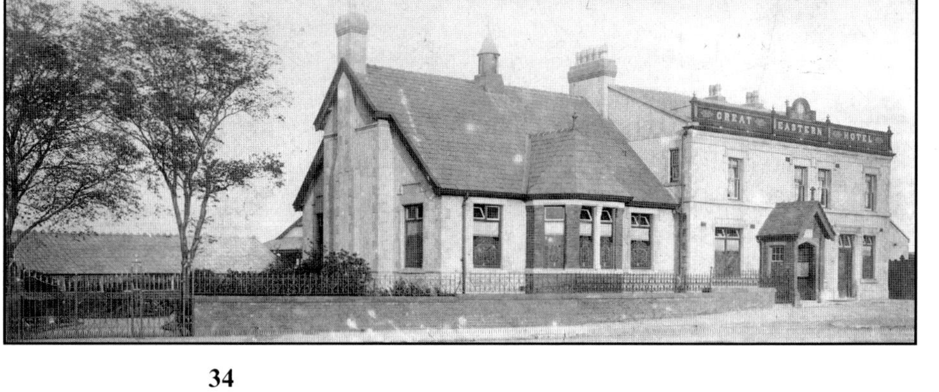

Right: *The Great Eastern Picnic Hotel, New Ferry Road,* ***New Ferry*** *was bought at auction 14 December 1898 by Birkenhead Brewery for £8,400. The hotel was named after the great Brunel ship of that name, which was dismantled for scrap on* ***Rock Ferry*** *shore with some of the items being bought for the hotel*

1899

- – Willmer Brothers, publishers of the the ***Birkenhead*** *News*, inaugurated the Wallasey News
- – Well Lane Council School **Rock Ferry** opened[WBD]
- Mar 11 Launch of the HMS *Glory* at **Birkenhead**
- May 17 An electric tramway scheme adopted in **Birkenhead**
- June 30 Triangular ferry service commenced linking **Liverpool, Rock Ferry** and **New Ferry**
- July 16 Holy Name of Jesus RC Church opened [consecrated in 1921] in Beresford Road **Oxton** - built on land belonging to the house *Overdale* which had been acquired by Bishop Carroll shortly before his death [see 1931 Birkenhead School][DoS]
- July 19 Duke of York distributed prizes won by HMS *Conway* cadets
- July 26 The Catholic reform ship *Clarence*, lying in the Sloyne off **New Ferry**, was burnt to the water's edge - 235 Officers and boys were rescued
- Oct The Arudy Estate, Bebington Road, **Hr Tranmere**, comprising The Towers and Rockleigh House sold @ auction for £11,350[LCP] - bought by the Birkenhead Corporation
- Dec 7 HMS *Glory*, built at **Birkenhead**, left to be placed in commission

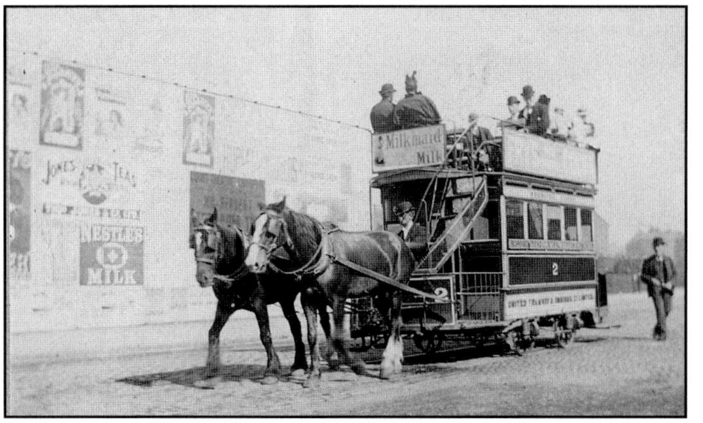

Above: *The **Birkenhead** United Tramway & Omnibus Company car No.2 is seen passing the advertising hoardings in Borough Road by Central Station - the lower destination board indicated "Borough Road, Central Station & Prenton". This double-deck car was one of 10 purchased in 1890 and is pulled by two horses, although originally only one horse was used. These cars operated until the electric trams replaced them in 1901*[TBW]

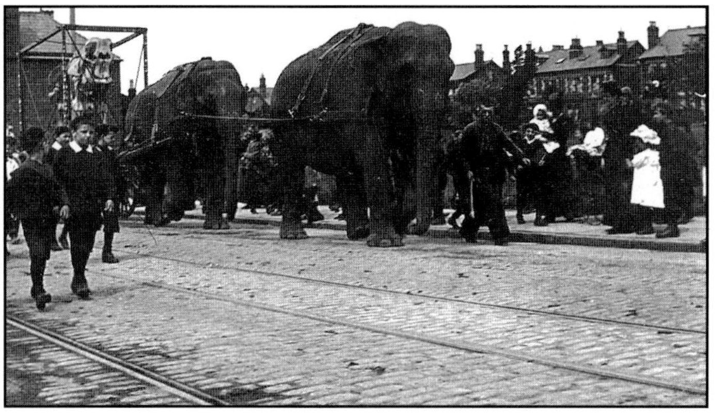

Above: *Lord George Sanger's circus is in town! This view of the elephants leading the circus parade was taken in Borough Road - this was the only way they could get the large animals to the venue from the railway station - which was their mode of transport then.*
This was also good publicity as the streets would be lined with excited children who would tell their friends who would want their parents to take them to the circus

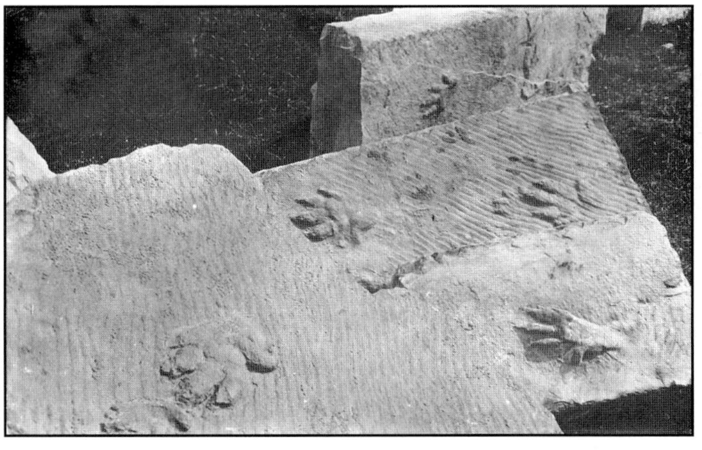

Above: *A section of the cheirotherium dinasaur footprint, which was found in Storeton Quarries, was built into the wall in the porch of Christ Church Higher **Bebington** opposite the main door*[SOUV]

Right: *The horse and cart on the left is standing in front of the Unitarian Chapel in Grange Road West **Birkenhead** which was erected in 1851 at a cost of £1,600. It was sold off in 1900 and replaced with an ornate curved building with several shops including the Liverpool Savings Bank which opened in 1903. The Church was resited in Bessborough Road, also opening in 1903. Looking across Charing Cross - The Grange Hotel, which was owned by the Birkenhead Brewery with T Lloyd the then licensee, was on the corner of Atherton Street to the left and Grange Road straight ahead. It was demolished in the mid 1980s and replaced with a McDonald's fast food restaurant. A policeman can be seen standing under the big lamp post*

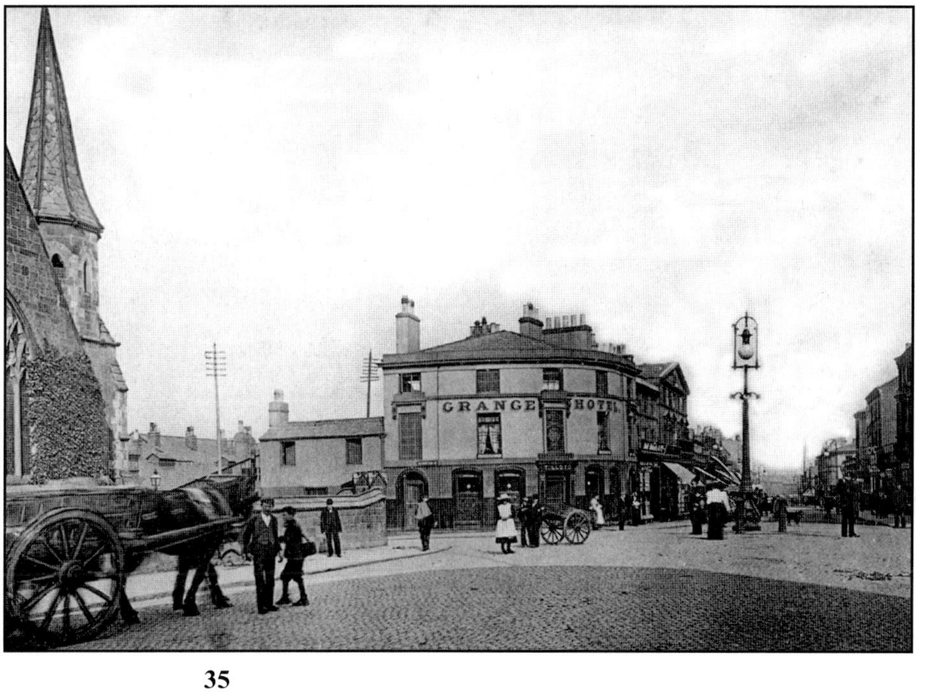

1900

– Livingstone Street Baths **Birkenhead**, opened with two swimming baths, slipper and shower baths[WBD]

– Birkenhead Corporation extended electric supply to **Bidston** and **Noctorum**

– St Paul's Presbyterian Church North Road **Tranmere** built [see photo next page][OPB]

– Hubbard & Martin opened a purpose-built Electric Bakery in Pilgrim Street **Birkenhead** to supply their branches

Feb *York Hotel* and *Park View Hotel* both in Price Street and *Charing Cross Hotel* Grange Road West **Birkenhead** sold together for £37,000[LCP]

Feb 15 St Elizabeth's Convent Park Road North, **Birkenhead**, opened[DoS]

Mar 10 In his will, Thomas Ismay of **Thurstaston** left the **Birkenhead** Children's Infirmary £1,000 and £2,000 to the training ship the *Indefatigable*

May 7 Mafeking relieved - great rejoicings

May 11 **Upton** Presbyterian Church of England - new church officially opened[OPB]

June 28 A collision occurred off **Rock Ferry** between the SS *Orpheus* which sank with the loss of six of the crew and SS *Vigsnaes*

July 10 Property sold in **Upton** Village at auction including: shop + weighing machine £66; 3 shops incl. Post Office £1,030 and workshop & clubroom £525[LCP]

Aug St Joseph RC Church North Road **Birkenhead**, opened[DoS]

Aug 3 The Wirral and Birkenhead Agricultural Show at **Bidston** wrecked by gales[WBD]

Sept 9 George Fell, caretaker at Conway Street Post Office, **Birkenhead** was found murdered - case remains unsolved[MMB]

Dec 11 A fire at Laird Brothers shipyard **Birkenhead** - the pattern shop was destroyed - total damage £20,000

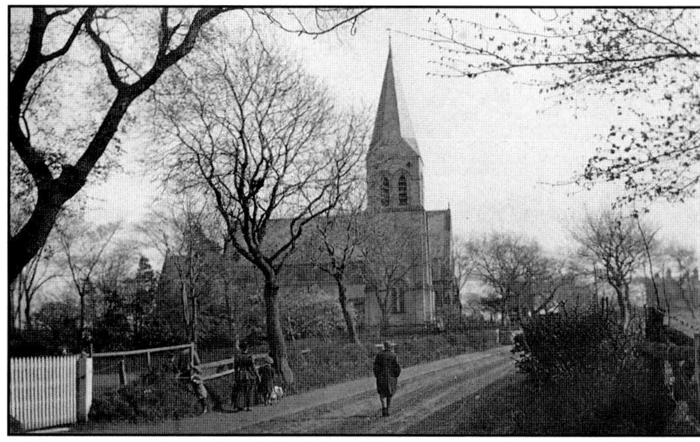

Above: *Christ Church Higher **Bebington** is seen when Kings Road was a country lane. The Church was consecrated 24 December 1859 on land given by Colonel King, who also supplied Storeton stone to build it with - the tower being erected in 1885, the same year that a copy of the prints from the Cheirotherium, found in Storeton Quarry in 1835 were displayed in the Church porch [see 1885]*

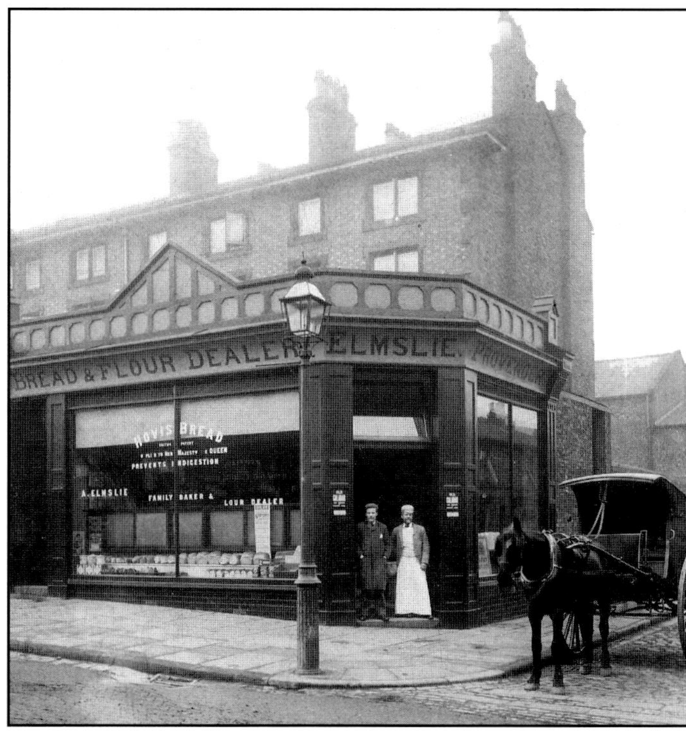

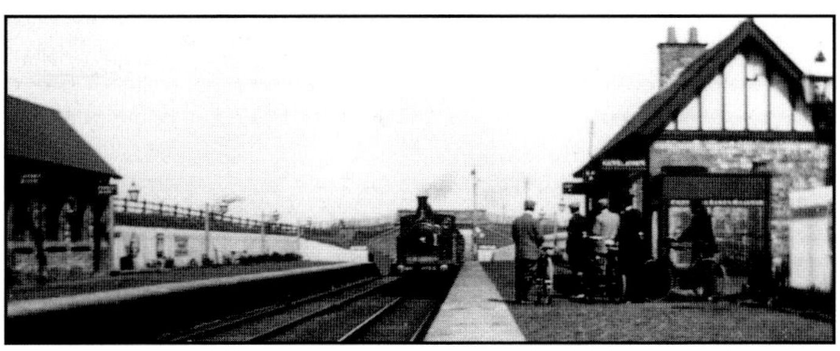

Above: ***Storeton** Station is seen at the turn of the last century. The group of cyclists are waiting for the train arriving from the Upton direction. This station opened on the North Wales and Liverpool Railway in 1896 which ran from **Bidston** to **Wrexham***

Above Right: *Alexander Elmslie is seen standing in the doorway of his shop at 122 Oxton Road on the corner of Derby Street **Birkenhead** his horse and cart advertising that he was a Bread and Flour dealer is seen on the right. This shop was later owned by Alex Green who ran a Cycle shop here for many years [see photo on right]*

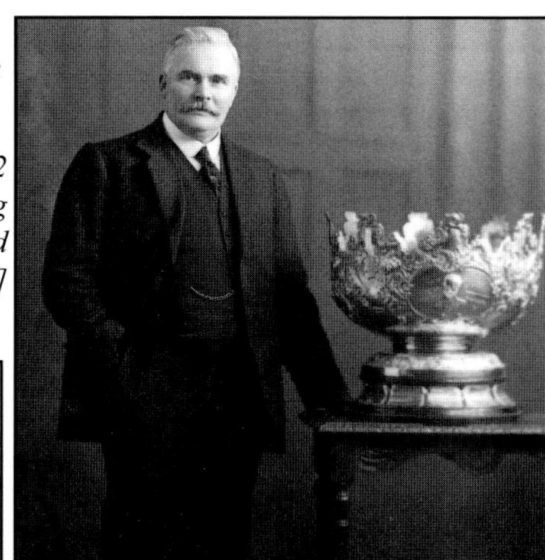

Above: *In 1900 Alexander Elmslie won a prize for his Hovis bread and is seen here standing proudly with his silver trophy.*

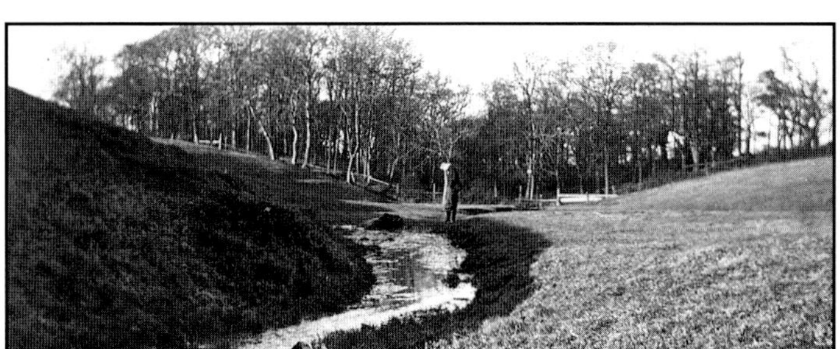

Right: *This rural scene with the girl watching the meandering brook, was of **Prenton** Dell when the land belonged to Prenton Hall Farm [see 1954]*

1901

– Hurst's Bakery founded in Claughton Road **Birkenhead** [still in business today]

– Mount Road Water Pumping Station opened in **Tranmere**

– **Raby** Village School closed - children accommodated at **Thornton Hough**[YW8]

Jan Bidston Avenue Junior School **Claughton** opened

Jan 14 **Birkenhead** North End Cycling Club founded at a meeting at the *Pacific Hotel*[SOUV]

Jan 22 Country mourns the death of Queen Victoria

Feb 2 Funeral of Queen Victoria

Feb 4 **New Ferry** to Brandon Street **Birkenhead** electric tram service commenced - extended to Woodside 6 June[BET]

Mar 11 Woodchurch Road Primary School **Birkenhead** opened in a temporary iron building constructed in the school yard with 14 children - by December of this year there were 229 pupils and 12 staff [see also December 1904][WRPS]

May 17 United Reformed Church opened in Old Chester Road **Tranmere** - built at a cost of £3,081[SOUV]

May 17 **Tranmere** Congregational Church opened in Old Chester Road[OPB]

May 18 First match at **Upton** Cricket Club - founded by Mr WSS Hannay, a wealthy cotton broker who lived in Upton [see 1906][PROG]

July 10 **Birkenhead** Town Hall damaged by fire with damage assessed at £15,000[WBD]

Aug 1 New Victoria Park at **Tranmere**, comprising an area of 29 acres formerly opened by the Mayor of **Birkenhead**, Thomas Cook[SOUV]

Aug 14 New electric tramway service opened from Woodside **Birkenhead** to Bebington Road Higher **Tranmere**; Laird Street and also the Claughton Road Route[BET]

Aug 31 HMS *Exmouth* launched Laird's shipyard **Birkenhead**

Sept 27 The last Birkenhead horse tram ran along Borough Road when the Borough Road depot and stables closed and the new **Prenton** electric tram service commenced[BET]

Oct New Women's Ward of 22 beds opened at the **Birkenhead** Borough Hospital Park Road North[SOUV]

Dec 24 Line of Docks tram route opened in **Birkenhead**[BT]

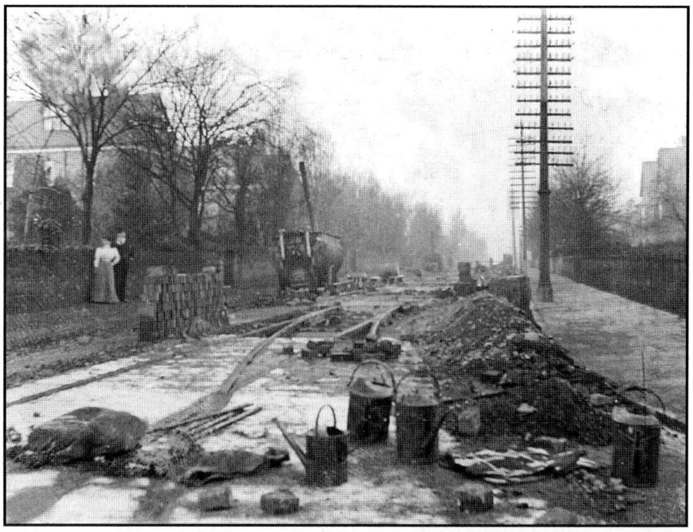

Above: *This photograph was taken in Shrewsbury Road* **Oxton**, *where the road curves to the right and Gerald Road is off to the left, on 24 November 1901. The work on laying the tram lines for the Circle Route has closed the whole road and not a workman is in sight. The Oxton & Claughton Circle Route opened 2 March 1902*

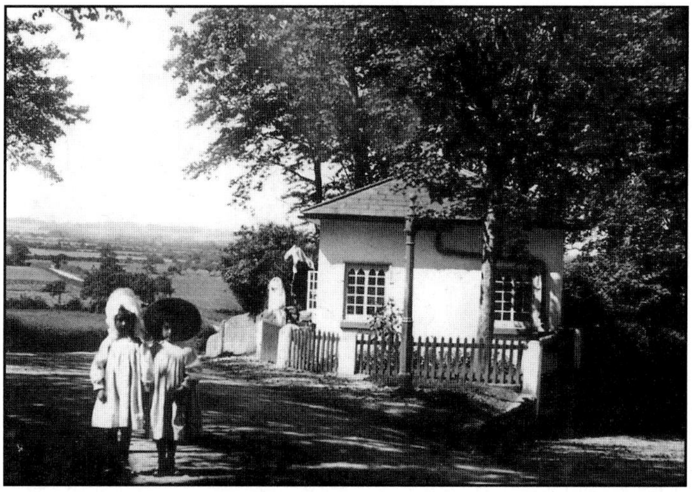

Above: Toll Bar Cottage **Upton** *sometimes known as* All Hill Cottage *is seen at the junction of Saughall Massie Road to the right and Greasby Road to the left - the original stone holding the gate can be seen to the right of the girls. This delightful, historical cottage was demolished in the 1960s when the road junction was altered*

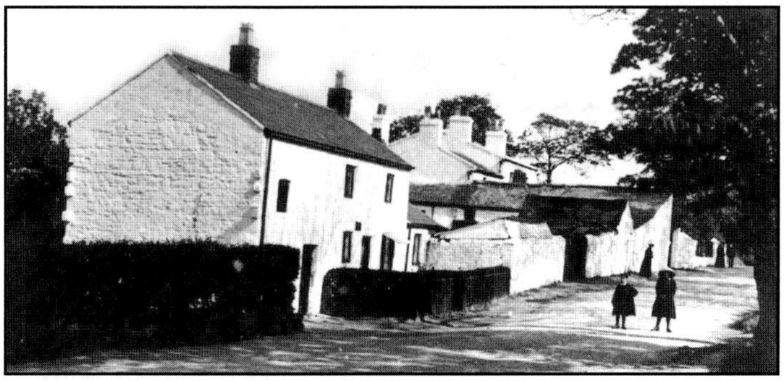

Above: *The two children are standing in Boundary Road* ***Bidston*** *outside Rose Cottage which was lived in by George Knight who was a gardener in the 1890s. His wife later served refreshments to passers-by. All the buildings seen here were demolished when the road was widened and the site is now part of the land in front of the houses in Worcester Road. Vyner Road North is now either side of the photographer [see also 1939]*

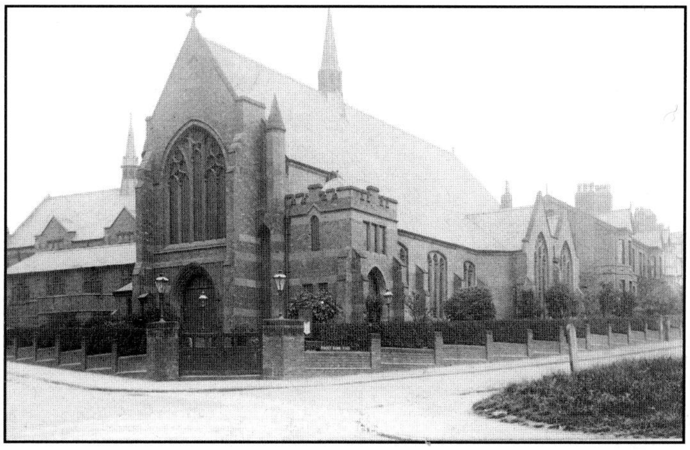

Above: *St Paul's Presbyterian Church of England, which was opened in 1900 with 570 sittings, is seen in North Road* ***Birkenhead*** *with Rocky Bank Road to the right*

1902

– **Birkenhead** Corporation Act passed authorising the corporation to acquire Hamilton Square Gardens

– Slatey Road Branch Police Station opened in **Birkenhead**[WBD]

– Price Street Branch Police Station opened in **Birkenhead**[WBD]

– North & South Wales Bank, later to become Midland Bank, opened at Charing Cross, **Birkenhead**

Jan 11 New Headquarters of the 1st Volunteer Battalion, The Cheshire Regiment, opened in Grange Road West **Birkenhead** - a Ball was held in the new building with the elite of the district present [see also 1914][4BTCR]

Mar 2 **Oxton & Claughton** Circle tram route opened[BET]

Jun 1 **Boer War - Peace declared**

Jun 18 Reception for the Service Sections of the 1st Volunteer Battalion, The Cheshire Regiment, on their return from the Boer War, was held in their new building in Grange Road West **Birkenhead** [see also 1914][BTCR]

Aug 9 Coronation of Edward VII - oak trees were planted to commemorate the occasion in **Birkenhead** Park, Mersey Park and Victoria Park **Tranmere**[TPG]

Sept 10 Diamond Jubilee of the Wirral & Birkenhead Agricultural Society at the new permanent show ground at **Bebington**[YW8]

Sept 23 *Brown Cow Vaults*, Bromborough Road **Bebington** purchased by Birkenhead Brewery £3,475[LCP]

Oct 16 Many **Birkenhead** charitable institutions benefited under the will of Mr George Rae

Nov Mersey Docks and Harbour Board were contemplating abandoning **Bidston** Observatory and disposing of the assets

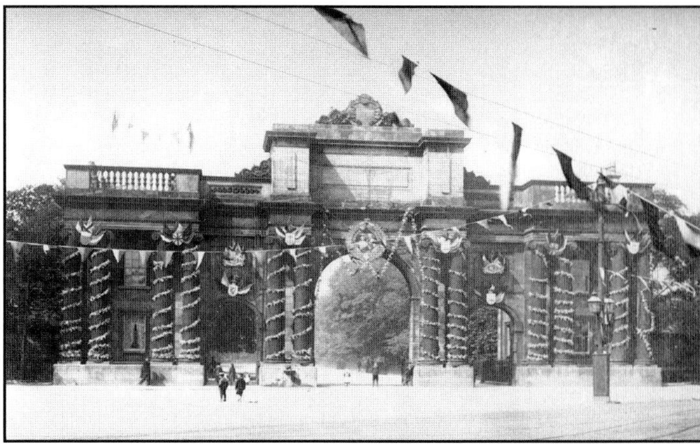

Above: *The main entrance to **Birkenhead** Park is decorated to celebrate King Edward VII's Coronation Day on 9 August 1902 - in a similar way to how the Town Hall was decorated [see photo below]*

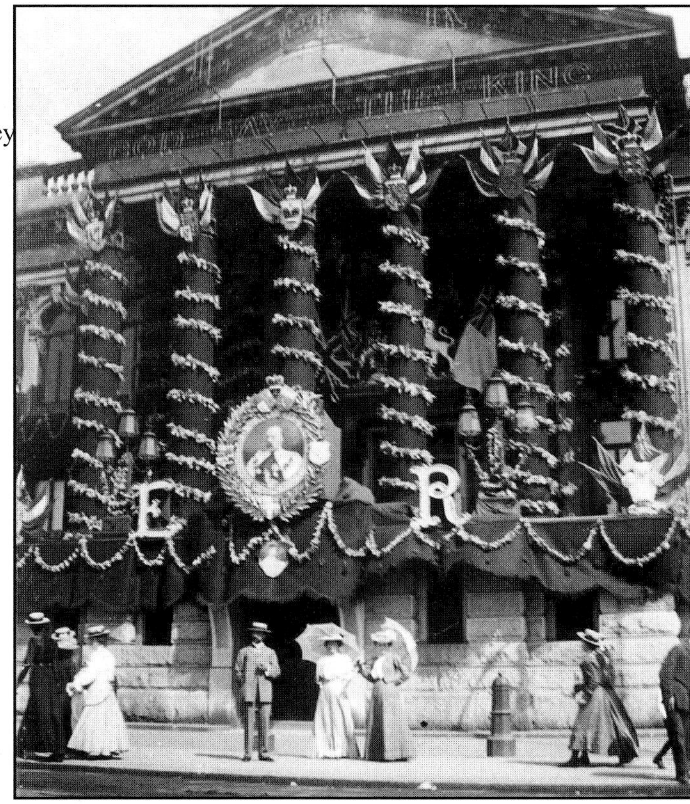

Above: ***Birkenhead** Town Hall is decorated to celebrate King Edward VII's Coronation Day on 9 August 1902 - a large picture of him is displayed above the entrance and "God Save The King" is seen at the top of the building [see also above]*

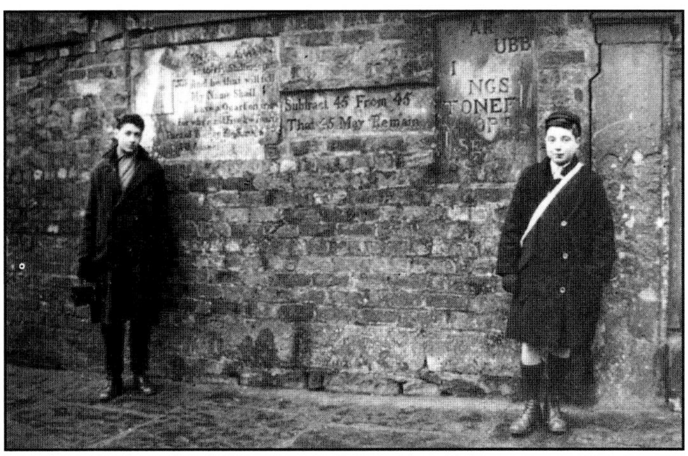

Above: *The 'puzzle stones', seen here on the wall of a house in Lower **Bebington**, were the work of the eccentric stone mason Thomas Francis [see 1869 and 1903]*

Below: *Woodside Tram Terminus, Ferry building ahead and Woodside Station on the right are all bedecked with flags and bunting to celebrate the Royal occasion*

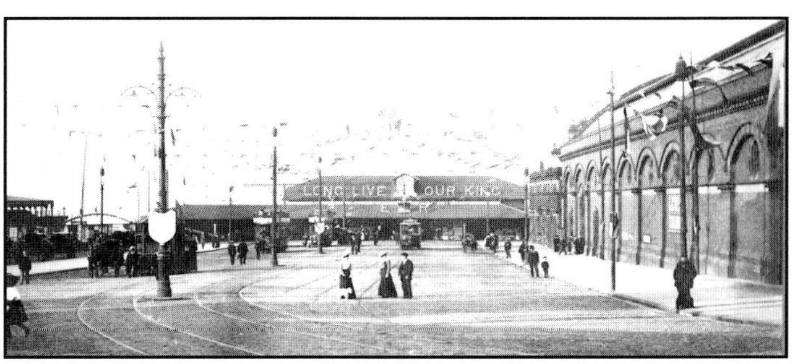

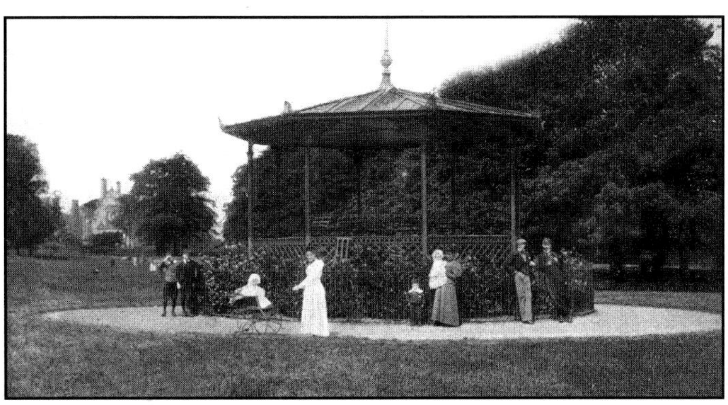

Left: *The bandstand pictured in **Birkenhead** Park was replaced in 1929 and then re-sited in Mersey Park [see 1950]*

1903

– Hamilton Square Gardens acquired by **Birkenhead** Corporation[SOUV]

– Conway Street School opened in **Birkenhead**[OPB]

– **Birkenhead** Corporation extend electricity supply to **Prenton** and **Upton**

– Special Council School opened in Claughton Road **Birkenhead**[WBD]

– WW Kelly, an American, took over the *Theatre Royal* in Argyle Street **Birkenhead**

– Tutteys Stores opened in Oxton Road, **Birkenhead** operating here until 1937 when Rostances took over

– **Birkenhead** shipbuilding firm Laird Brothers amalgamated with the Sheffield-based steel manufacturer Cammell to form Cammell Laird & Co Ltd[OPD]

Feb 13 Charles Thompson, founder of the mission in **Birkenhead**, died

Mar 19 Birkenhead Unitarian Church, Bessborough Road, **Birkenhead**, opened

May 3 First electric train ran through the Mersey Tunnel from **Liverpool** to **Birkenhead**[RSoW]

May 27 Memorial window in St Mary's Parish Church **Birkenhead** unveiled by the Archbishop of Sydney

Jun 12 New wing of Wirral & **Birkenhead** Children's Hospital opened by Thomas Royden - Cost £3,500[SOUV]

July A branch of the Liverpool Savings Bank opened in new premises at Charing Cross **Birkenhead**

July 23 HM cruiser *Topaze* launched at Cammell Laird **Birkenhead**

July 25 HM Torpedo boat destroyer *Blackwater* launched at Cammell Laird Shipyard **Birkenhead**

Sept 26 Nurses home opened to the rear of the Borough Hospital, Park Road North **Birkenhead**[SOUV]

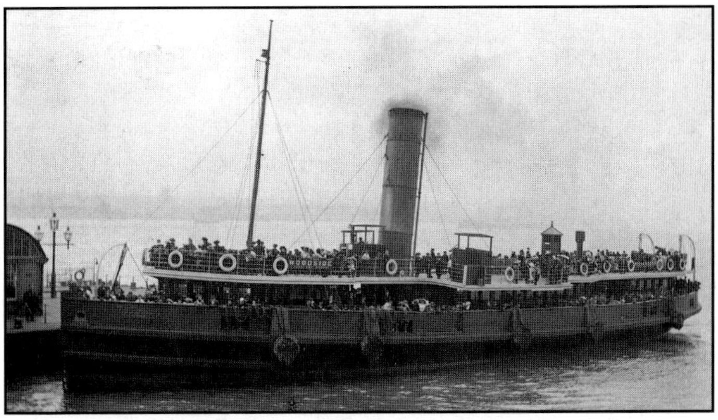

Above: *This photograph of the ferry boat* Woodside *was taken at Woodside* ***Birkenhead*** *by Arthur Maycock of Parkgate on 30 July 1903. The* Woodside *was built for Birkenhead Corporation*

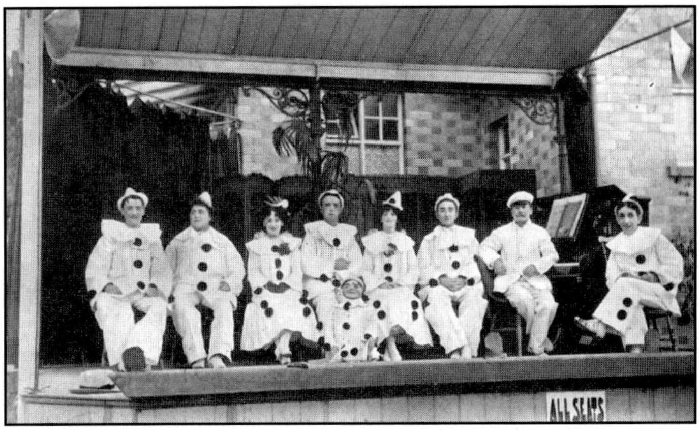

Above: *Prince's Pierrots on the stage at the Olympian Gardens,* ***Rock Ferry****, which was sited at the rear of the* Royal Rock Hotel *- they closed in 1925*

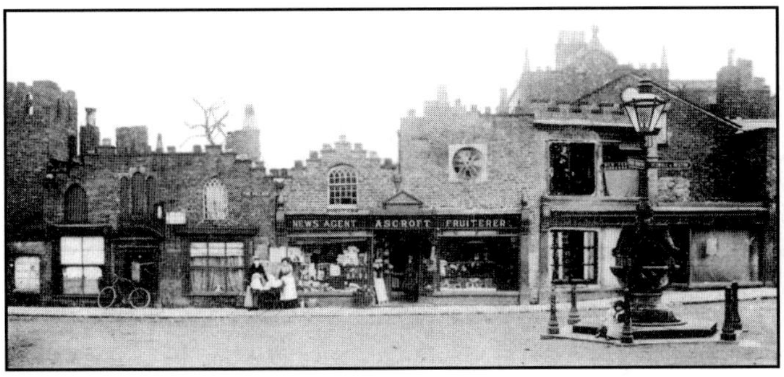

Above: *The drinking fountain is seen from Heath Road Lower* ***Bebington*** *in the middle of The Village. It had been donated to Bebington by Charles Hill in 1863 but due to road widening was moved into Mayer Park in 1905. It was moved back in 1996 and now stands in the middle of a roundabout in almost the same position as seen here. The castellated buildings ahead were built by Thomas Francis, an eccentric [see 1869 and 1902]*

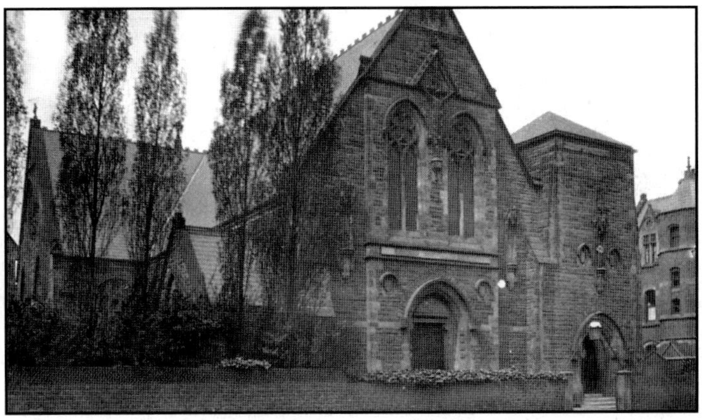

Above: *St Anne's Roman Catholic Church, pictured here in Highfield Road,* ***Rock Ferry*** *was opened in 1877 replacing the original Church, which opened 1864*

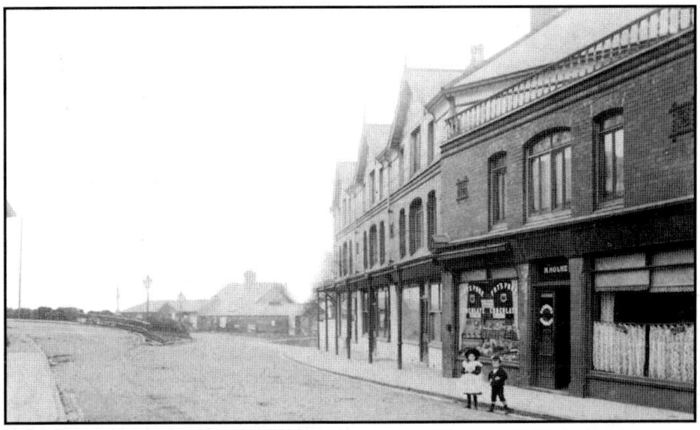

Right: *The two children on the right looking at the photographer are standing in front of the row of shops in New Ferry Road which led down to the* ***New Ferry*** *Pier. These shops did good business until the ferry closed down in 1922 and were later converted into flats*

1904

– Major sewer road works carried out in Grange Vale, **Birkenhead**

Feb 24 St Barnabas' Church Russell Road **Rock Ferry -** consecrated - built at a cost of almost £5,000 [see photo][SOUV]

Mar 6 St John The Evangelist, Bebington Road **New Ferry** the chapel opened on the upper floor of the building together with club rooms - the school rooms on the ground floor opened 5 September 1904 - total cost £4,607[DoS]

April St Joseph's School opened in **Birkenhead**[DoS]

April 23 **Birkenhead** Co-op opened its new bakery

July 16 HMS *Pathfinder* launched at **Birkenhead**

July 19 Royal Yacht *Victoria & Albert* which was moored off **Rock Ferry**, sailed from Mersey after King Edward VII had laid the foundation stone for the **Liverpool** Anglican Cathedral

Sept 5 Woodchurch Road Primary School, **Birkenhead**, transferred to new building [see photo][WRPS]

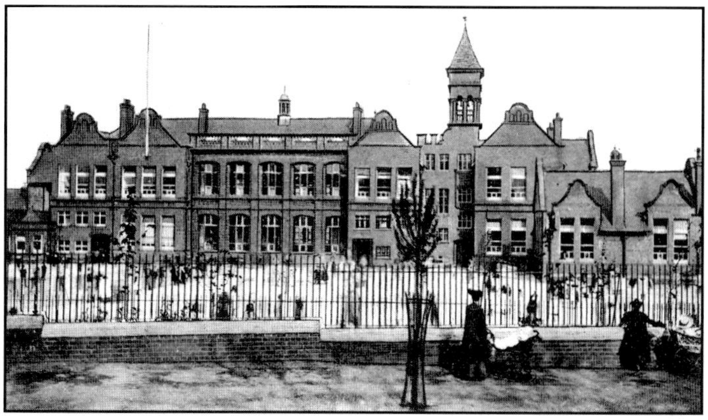

Above: *This postcard was sent in 1904, the year Woodchurch Road* ***Birkenhead*** *Primary School opened, having transferred from their previous premises at 77 Woodchurch Road, which had originally been the Hermitage British School*

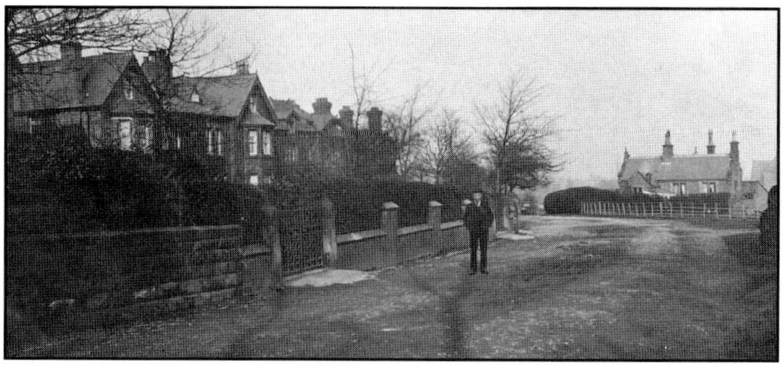

Above: *The boy is standing in Egerton Park* ***Rock Ferry.*** *This was an enclosed residential park with a similar design to Rock Park - houses around the outside of an oval road, those in the middle forming an island and access either end which was guarded by a toll house [see 1908]*

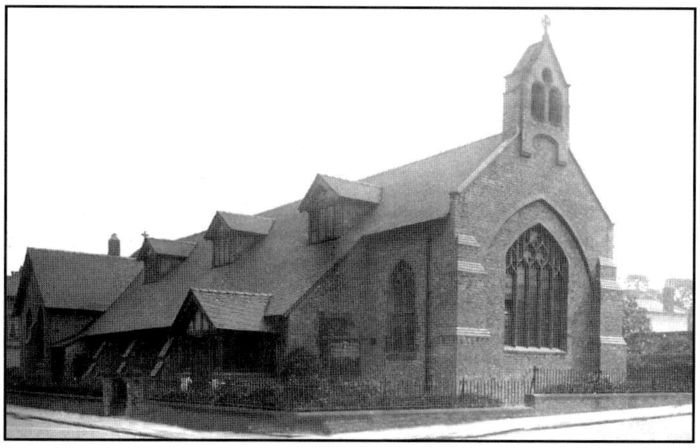

Above: *St Barnabas' Church Russell Road, on the corner of Ebenezer Street,* ***Rock Ferry*** *was consecrated 24 February 1904 - it was built at a cost of almost £5,000*

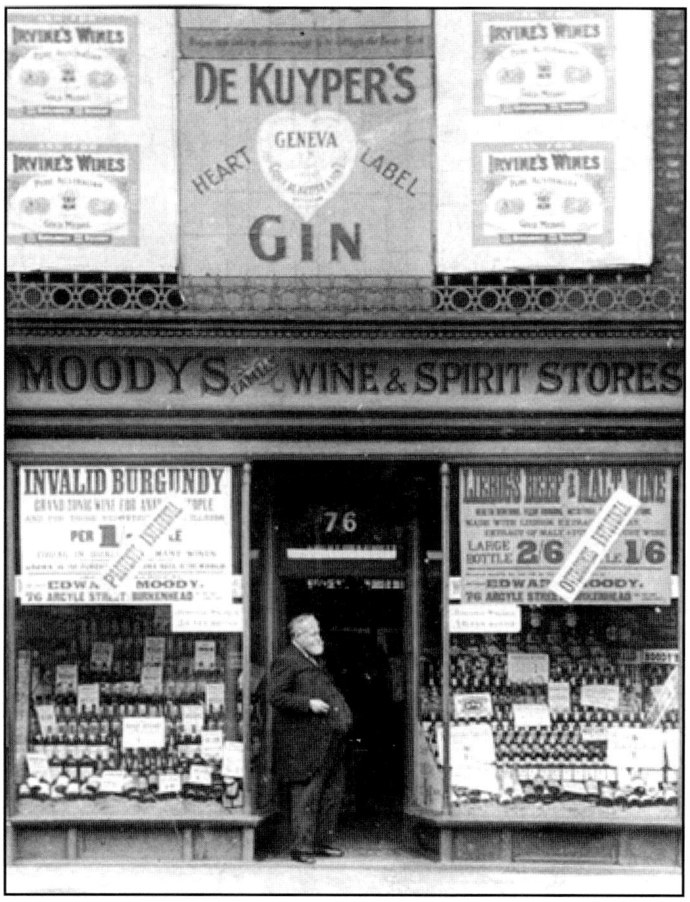

Above: Edward Moody first opened a wine and spirit shop in Great Charlotte Street Liverpool *c.1*901. He moved to 76 Argyle Street Birkenhead in 1904, and established "Moody's Wines" living above the shop with his wife Millie. His sons, Edward Percy and Arthur, worked their passage to Canada in 1902 to try their luck with lumberjacking and laying the railroad. When Edward died in 1908, Edward Percy came back to Birkenhead and took over the management of the shop with his mother. During the First World War he met a French sailor in Gibraltar and they became firm friends. After the War, Percy bought a motor bike and sidecar. He was able to use his friendship with Louis to further his French language skills and with his wife Ann visited contacts in vineyards in different parts of France and Spain, buying wine to be delivered to Argyle Street. By the 1950s, Percy had built up Moody's Wines with 8 branches: 18 Church Road Lower Bebington; 65 Church Road, Higher Tranmere; 149 Laird Street, Birkenhead; 116 Bedford Road Rock Ferry; 44 New Chester Road New Ferry; 457 Borough Road Birkenhead; 67 Woodchurch Lane Prenton and 63 Station Road Ellesmere Port. He registered brands for the Port and Sherry that were blended and bottled in the shop: Little Brown Jug, El Capitan, Old Doubloon, Tesoro, Brillante and O Pharol. When his son Arthur returned after the war in 1946, he worked for his father, until the shops were sold to Bents Brewery by 1960, then worked as a representative for importers of fine French wines, until he retired. Arthur's son Tony currently owns a vineyard in Australia

1905

– **Birkenhead** Corporation stables and depot opened in Cleveland Street

– Birkenhead High School moved to new premises in Devonshire Place, **Oxton** from Village Road

– Higher Elementary and Secondary Schools opened in **Birkenhead**[WBD]

– Woodlands Council School opened in **Birkenhead**[WBD]

– Mersey Park Council School opened in **Hr Tranmere**

– Fountain in the centre of **Bebington** Village moved into Mayer Park [see 1903]

– **Birkenhead** Corporation authorised by Local Government Board Provisional Orders Confirmation (No.4) Act 1904 to borrow for Gas Works purposes, with sanction of Local Government Board

– Laird Street Infants School; opened in **Birkenhead**[WBD]

– Laird Street Presbyterian Church opened in **Birkenhead**[OPB]

– New smithy at **Thornton Hough** opened Major sewer road works still being carried out in Grange Vale **Birkenhead**

– **Storeton** Tramway closed [see 1877]

Feb 18 **Prenton** Golf Club formed

Feb 20 Ceremony of affiliation of St Aidan's Theology College **Oxton** to Liverpool University at **Birkenhead** Town Hall

May 29 Famous escapologist Houdini appeared at the *Argyle Theatre* **Birkenhead**[YWPH]

Oct 26 The Queen Eleanor Cross was unveiled in Hamilton Square Gardens **Birkenhead** in memory of Queen Victoria

Dec 11 Mersey Railway Company started a new Motor Bus Service between **Oxton** and Central Station, **Birkenhead** - ceased 17 March 1906 due to legal action by Birkenhead Corporation[TBB]

Dec 26 County Hockey match held at **Oxton** between Cheshire and Lancashire[SOUV]

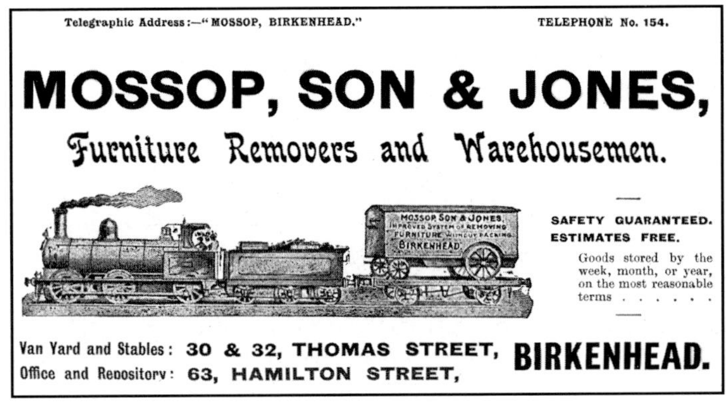

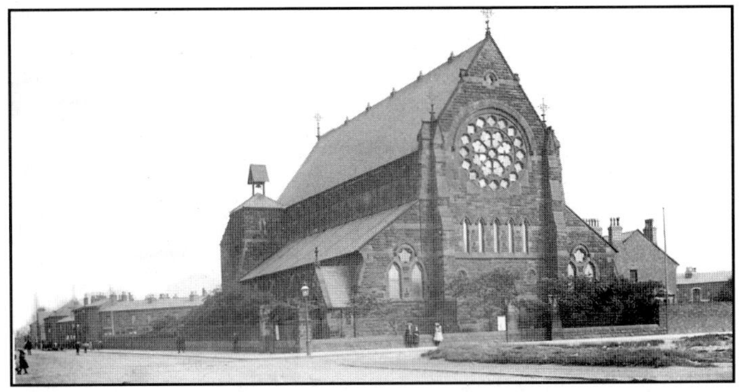

Above: *Roman Catholic Church of Our Lady is seen in Price Street* ***Birkenhead****. Erected in 1867, it cost £8,000 to build and had 800 seats*

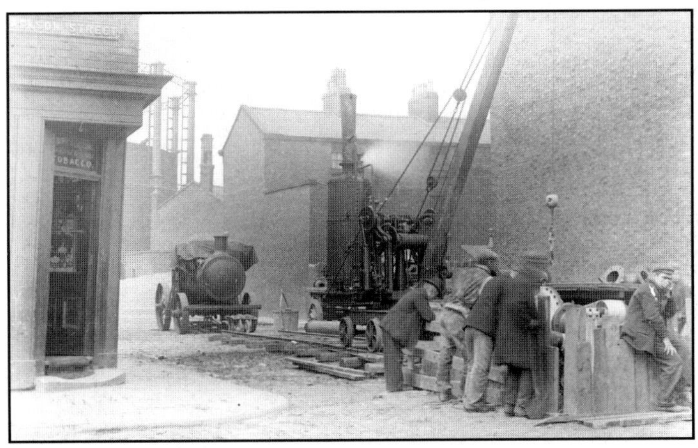

Above: *Putting down a pumping station on the corner of Jackson Street* ***Birkenhead*** *in connection with the Grange Vale Sewer Scheme*

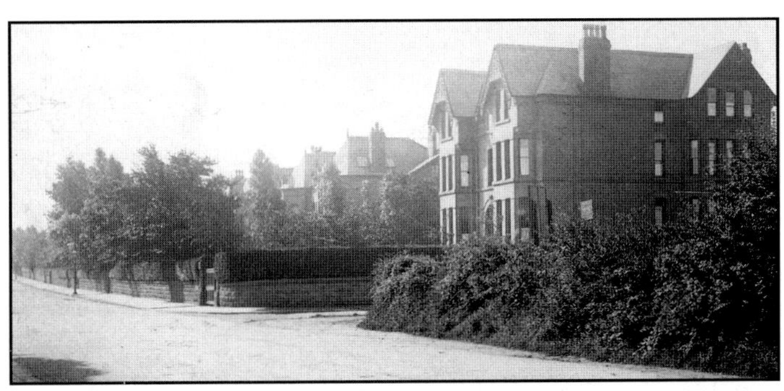

Above: *The first three buildings on the right in Bidston Road* ***Oxton****, beyond the corner of Howbeck Road, belonged to Kensington House School for Ladies. This private school took boarders - but due to falling numbers closed in 1934 - flats now occupy the first building on the right*

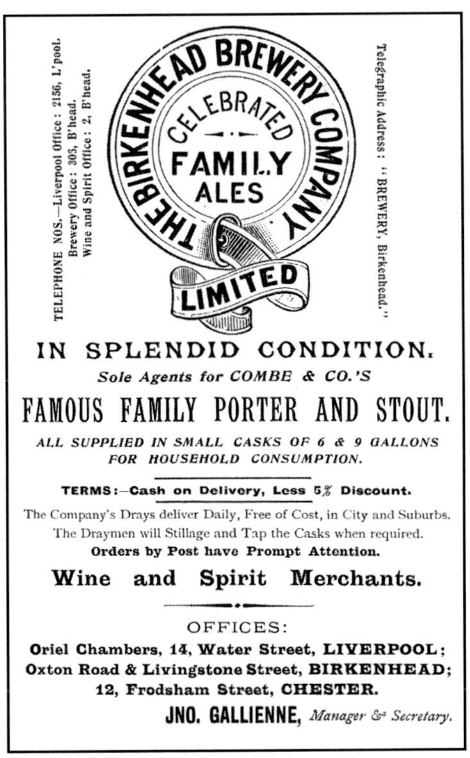

Left: *The* ***Birkenhead*** *Brewery was founded when two family breweries merged in 1865 - the Cook family had a brewery in Oxton Road and the Aspinall family had one in Cleveland Street. They became the main controller of public houses in and around Birkenhead and Wirral. By the time they were taken over in 1964, they had 200 licensed premises and employed over 1,200 people*

1905` continued

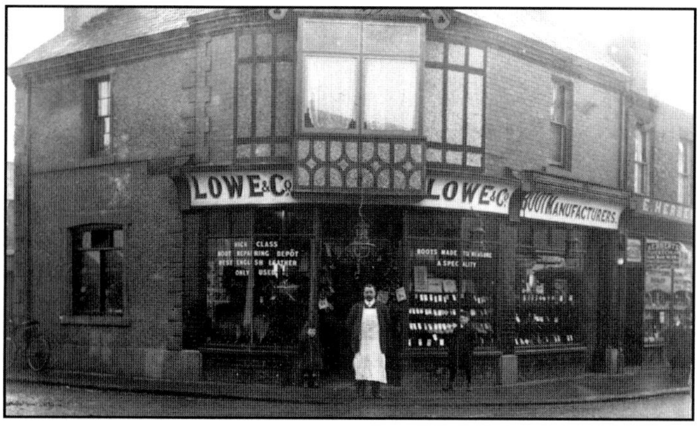

Above: *Lowe & Co Boot Manufacturers 15 Bebington Road* ***New Ferry*** *- advertised as 'High Class Boot Repairing Dept.' 'Boots Made to Measure' - also had a branch at 31 The Village Lower* ***Bebington***

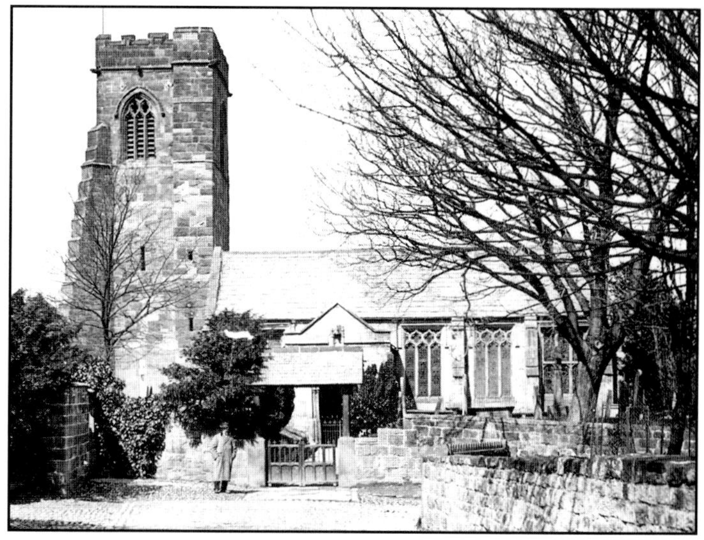

Above: *Parts of this Parish Church at* ***Woodchurch*** *date back to the 12th century with additions in the 14th, 16th and 20th centuries. The Parish of Woodchurch originally covered a larger area of Wirral including Oxton, Prenton, Noctorum and parts of Claughton. Until the large Woodchurch housing estate was built in the 1950s, this was a rural community*

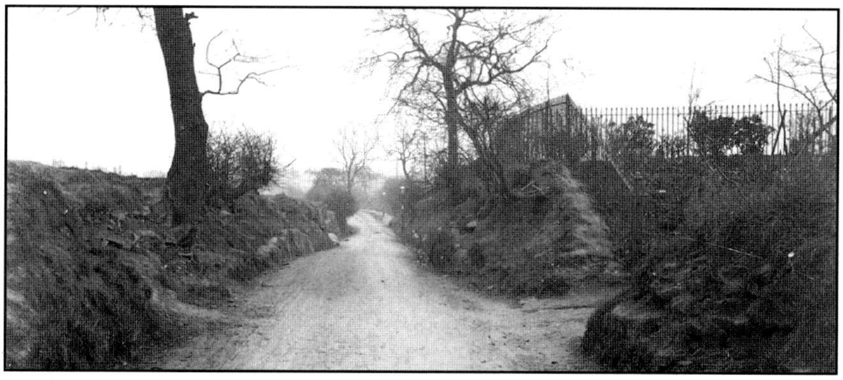

Left: *This view and the two below were all taken in Well Lane* ***Tranmere*** *in 1905, prior to road improvements being implemented. This was probably looking up Well Lane towards Church Road with the view below in the distance*

Right: *Continuing up Well Lane* ***Tranmere*** *from the picture above, behind the three children can be seen the terrace of houses known as Apple Grove. On the left behind the shrubs at the bend of the road were the cottages below*

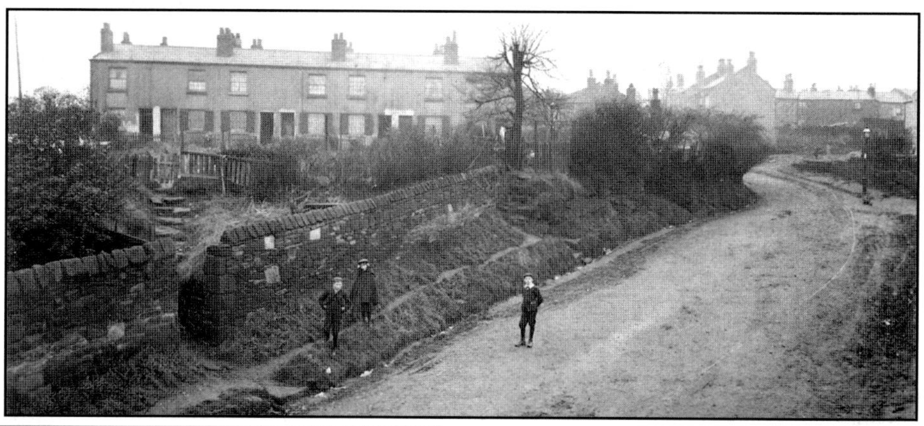

Below: *These two cottages - No.105 on the left and 107 on the right in Well Lane* ***Tranmere*** *are hidden behind the shrubs on the bend in the road seen in the picture on the right. They had both been demolished by 1915 and the road widened*

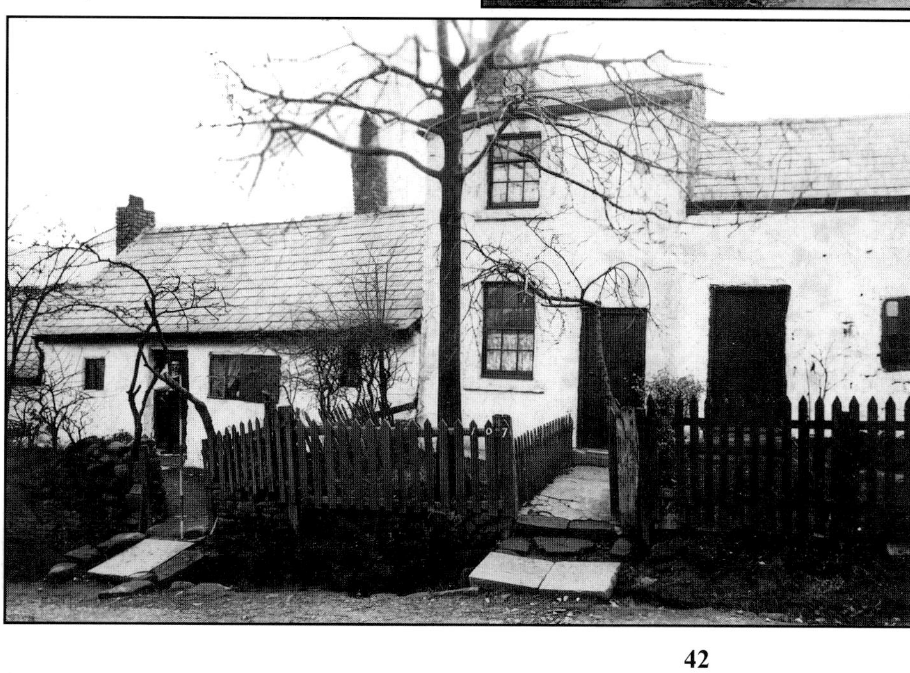

1906

– Girls' secondary school opened in Conway Street - transferred to new building in Park Road South **Birkenhead** in 1928

– Woodchurch Road Welsh Methodist Church opened in **Birkenhead**[OPB]

– Park Road and Cleveland Street temporary schools opened in **Birkenhead**[WPD]

– GPO opened in Argyle Street, **Birkenhead**

– Sir WH Lever, Bart., elected MP for Wirral

– The Wirral & District Association Football League changed its name to TheWest Cheshire League[WDFA]

– **Thornton Hough** Congregational Church opened

– **Upton** Village saddler, Mr Fred Salisbury, sold his shop with weighing machine in front, in Upton Village, to Mr Shone who sold and repaired bicycles and then became the first retailer of petrol in the village - the family retained the business for many decades

– **Upton** Cricket Club erected a large wooden pavilion which survived 71 years before being replaced in 1972 [see also 1901 & 1929][SOUV]

Jan 13 Launch at Cammell Laird's shipyard **Birkenhead** of the triple screw steamer *St George* built for service between Fishguard and Rosslare

Apr 6 **Prenton** Golf Club's new course officially opened

Apr 11 Foundation stone laid for St George's Congregational Church at **Thornton Hough**[YW8]

Apr 12 Japanese battleship *Katori* arrived in **Birkenhead** [see below]

Dec 5 Following the closure of the Della Robbia Pottery, **Birkenhead** there was a three day auction of vases, pottery etc at their Liverpool shop

Dec 5 Highfield Bowling Club founded at **Rock Ferry**

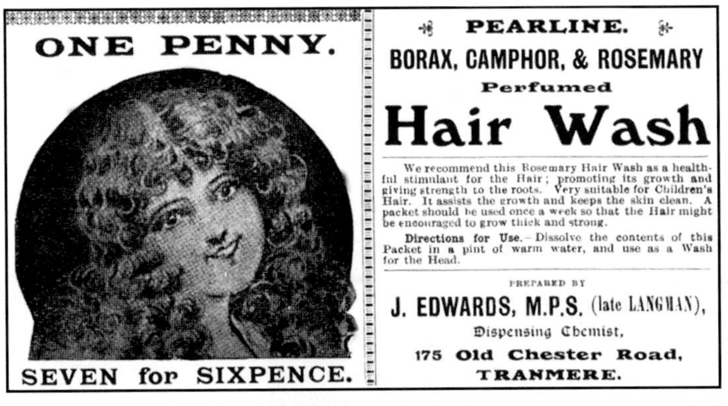

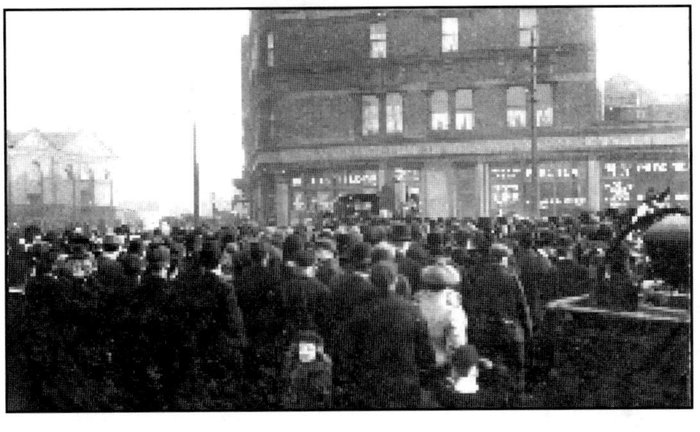

Above: *Sir William H Lever addressing a crowd in the Haymarket* ***Birkenhead*** *- he became Liberal MP for the Wirral Division of Cheshire 24 January 1906*

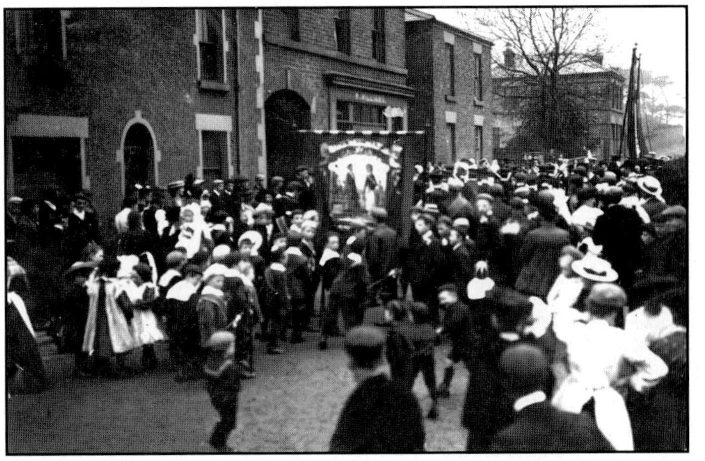

Above: *The Shepherd's Club walking up Village Road Higher* ***Bebington*** *with Mount Road in the distance*

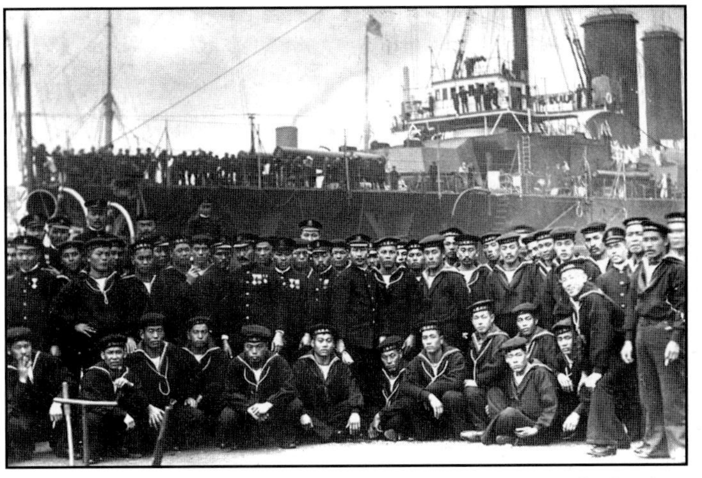

Above: *The Japanese battleship* Katori *is seen in the background, behind her crew who are posing for a photograph during their visit to* ***Birkenhead*** *12 April 1906*

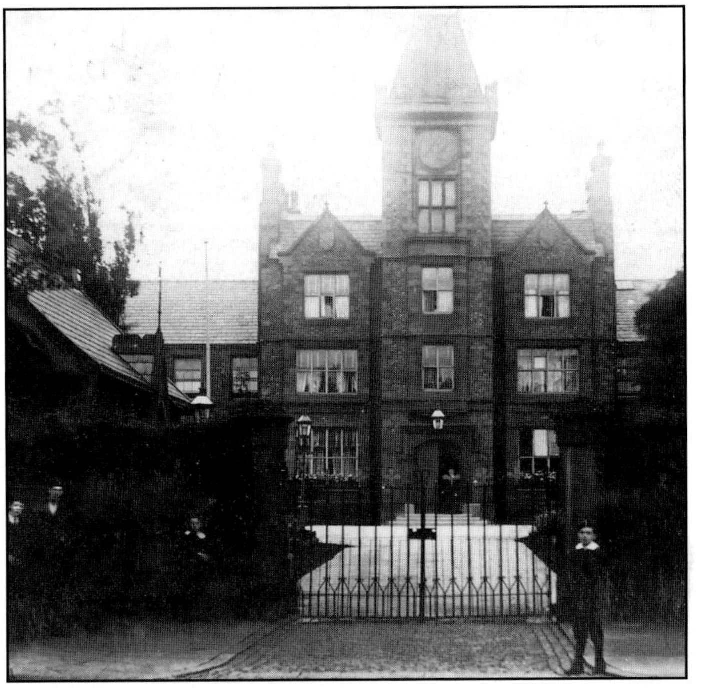

Above: *The caption for this picture postcard dated 5 October 1906 states 'Workhouse Entrance* ***Tranmere****'. Originally built as the Tranmere Workhouse in 1862/3, it was taken over by the Council in 1929 and became an infirmary known as St Catherine's Hospital*

1907

– **Bidston** Hill dedicated as an open space[OPB]

– Mersey Park Junior Mixed and Infants School opened in Higher **Tranmere**[OPB]

– The Corporation of **Birkenhead** obtained an Act of Parliament empowering it to impound the waters of the Rivers Alwen and Breinig in Denbighshire and create the Alwen Dam to supply water to **Birkenhead**[IAWSB]

May 4 Highfield Bowling Club opened in Highfield Road, **Rock Ferry**

May 16 *Plough Vaults* corner of Bebington Road and Woodhead Street **New Ferry** sold at auction - bought by Birkenhead Brewery for £400 [see photo][LCP]

May 29 St George's Congregational Church dedicated at **Thornton Hough**

July 16 New liner *Lusitania* arrived in the Mersey

Sept 7 Cunard liner *Lusitania* leaves the Mersey for New York on her maiden voyage

Dec 7 HMTBD *Swift* launched from Cammell Laird **Birkenhead**

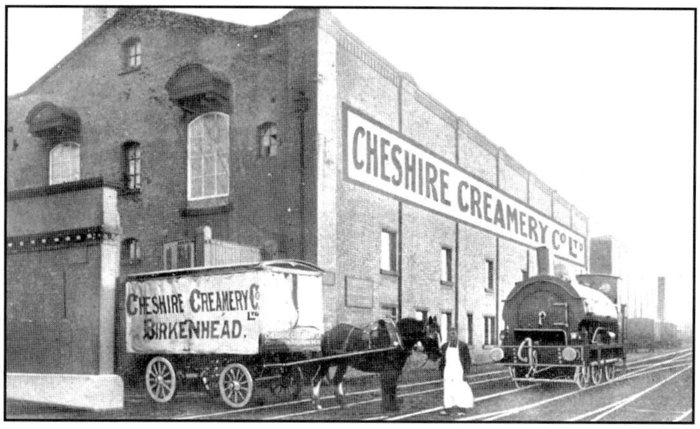

Above: *This advertising postcard for the Cheshire Creamery & Co Ltd Vittoria Wharf* ***Birkenhead****, which stated it as being the "best placed factory in the kingdom", was posted in 1907. A train has been superimposed into the picture to add credibility to their sweeping statement. However, they must have delivered throughout the country as this postcard was confirmation of an order from a customer in Catford London*

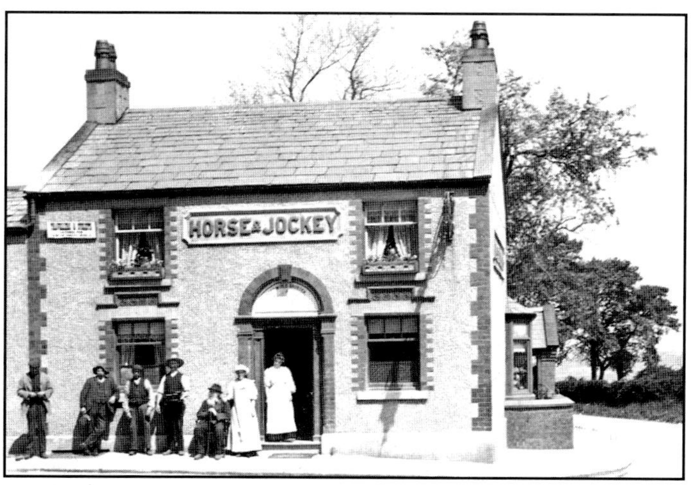

Above: *The* Horse & Jockey Inn *is pictured in* ***Woodchurch*** *c1907 when the new victualler, Septimus Broster, took over. He ran the pub until he died in 1936, a year before it was demolished then replaced by the* **Arrowe** Park Hotel *[see 1937]*

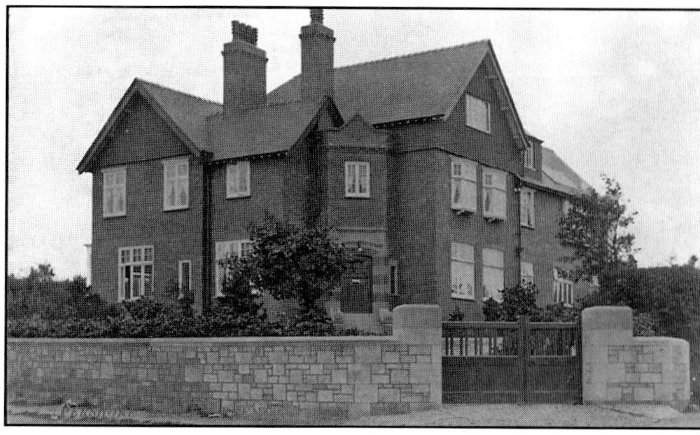

Above: *This newly-built house stood on the corner of Prenton Lane and Prospect Road in* ***Prenton - it later became Pershore House School***

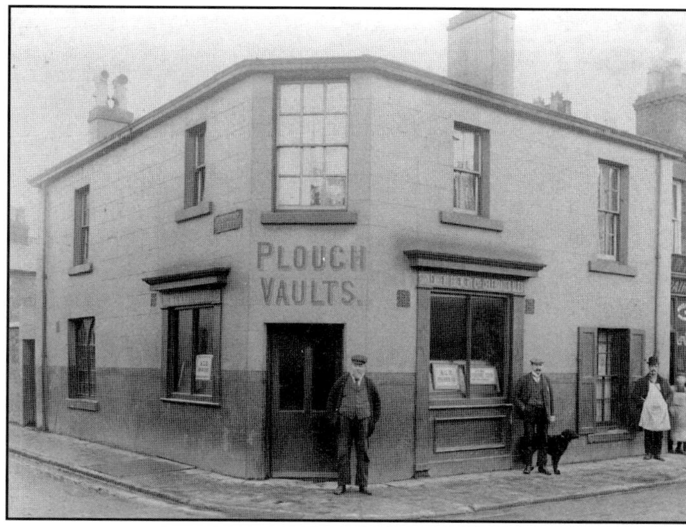

Above: *The* Plough Vaults *is seen on the corner of Bebington Road and Woodhead Street* ***New Ferry****. It was bought by Birkenhead Brewery at auction 16 May 1907 for £400*

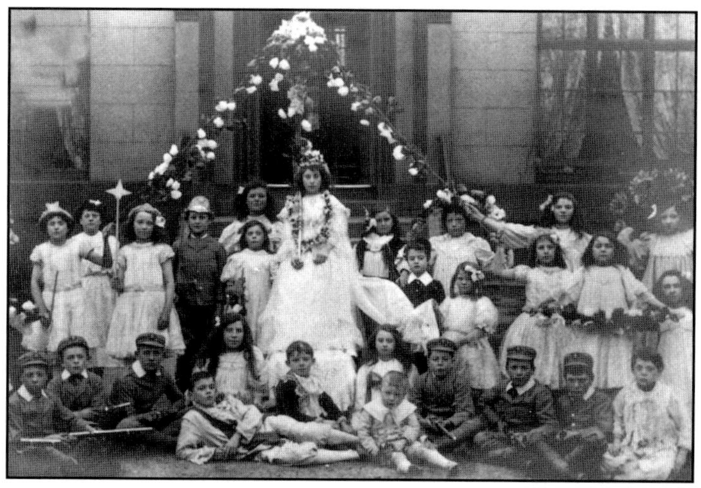

Above: *The crowning of this Rose Queen, who is with her attendants and other children from the Charles Thompson Mission, took place on 24 May 1907 at the Mission in Hemingford Street* ***Birkenhead*** *[see 1892]*

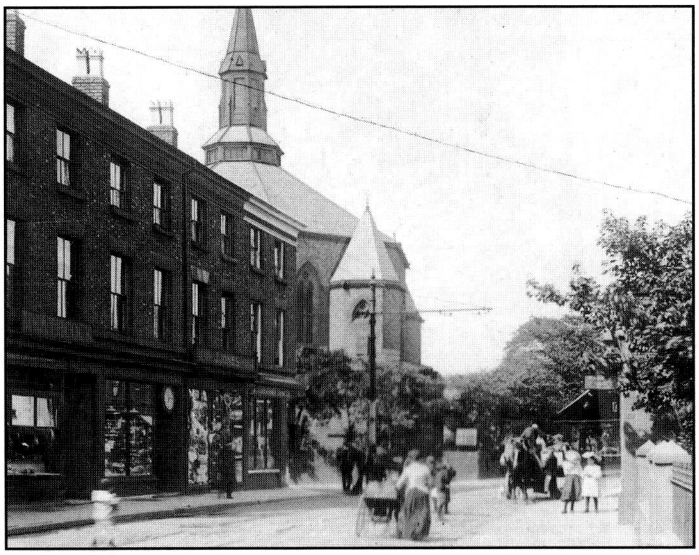

Above: *The imposing church building behind the shops in Church Road Higher **Tranmere** was the Wesley Church, otherwise known as the 'Pepperbox'. Tranmere's first Methodist Chapel was erected in Queen Street c1840 and in 1860 it was decided to build a new Chapel. The first service was held on 21 August 1862. During the First World War the men's activities were suspended but the ladies of the church opened a canteen in the lecture hall for the Bantam Battalion who were training in Birkenhead. Due to damage caused to the spire by a bomb on 21 December 1940, it was decided in 1946 to remove the spire*

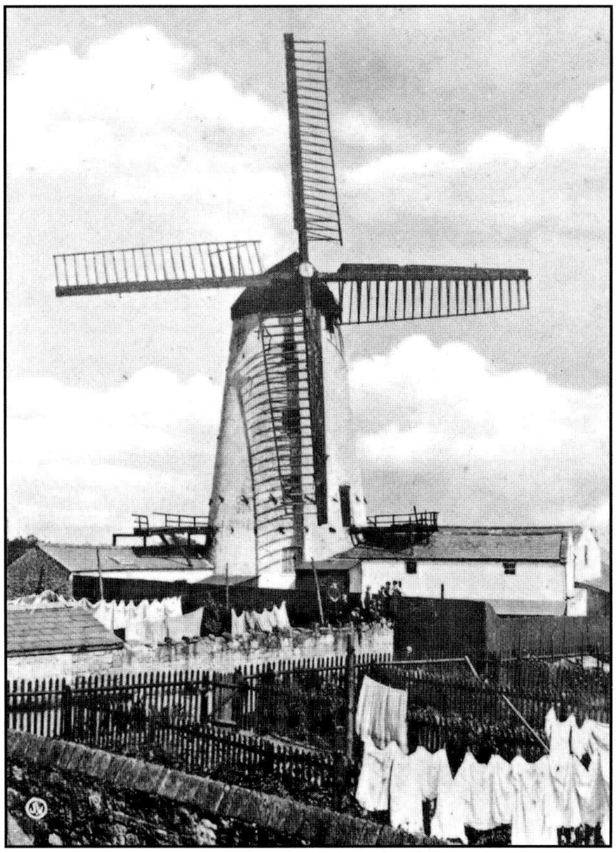

Above: *Higher **Bebington** tower mill is seen in School Lane, diagonally opposite the old school. This mill dates back to the early 19th century and operated until the beginning of the 20th century. The sails were taken down during the First World War. It was used for storing machinery and during the Second World War used as a look-out post. In 1963 it was listed as "a building of special architectural and historic interest" - but despite this, was demolished c1971*
[see also 1936]

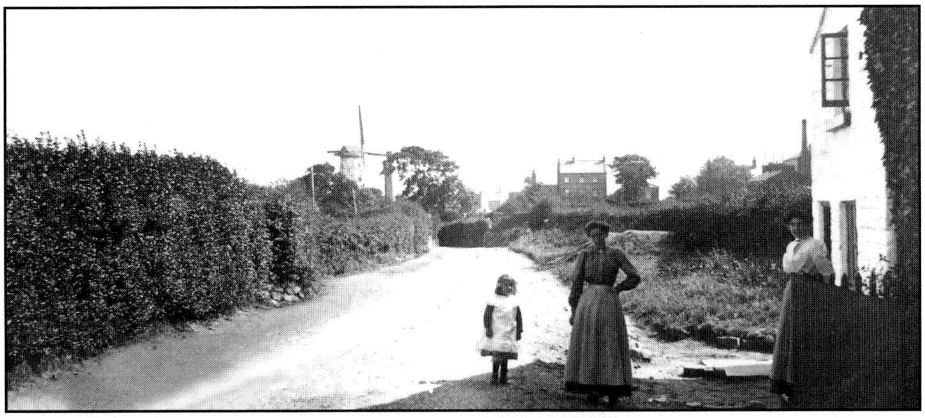

Above: *The Higher **Bebington** Mill seen in the distance on the left is the one pictured above*

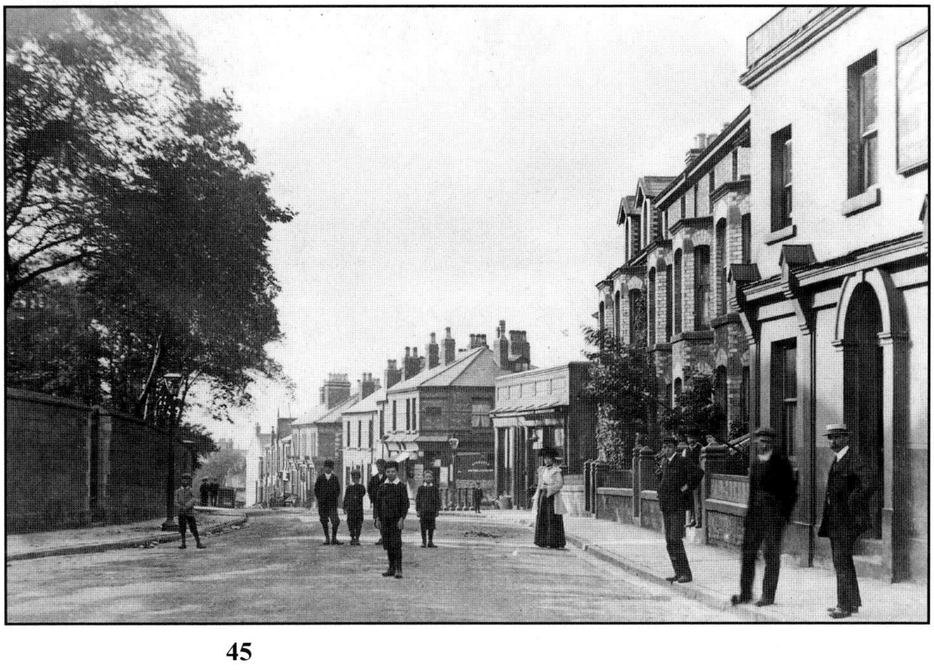

Right: *This postcard dated 1907 shows a group of people posing for the photographer, who is standing in the middle of Whetstone Lane, Higher **Tranmere**. Behind the high wall on the left was Holt Hill Convent which was originally a private residence with commanding views across the River Mersey. In 1856 it was purchased by the Faithful Companions of Jesus and opened as a girls' boarding school*

1908

– Lee Tapestry moved their business from their factory in Warrington to new premises in the North End of **Birkenhead**[TTM]

– **Prenton** Road West Congregational Church built[OPB]

– Extension to **Bidston** Hill recreation ground[WBD]

Jan 24 Boy Scout movement inaugurated at **Birkenhead** YMCA in Grange Road Birkenhead by Baden Powell [see 1929]

Feb 28 **Prenton** Golf Club's new club house opened [see photo]

Apr 25 **Tranmere** Rovers became Combination champions

June 29 New Post Office opened in Argyle Street **Birkenhead**[WBD]

Sept 5 Women's Suffrage demonstration at St George's Hall **Liverpool** which included the **Birkenhead** and Wirral Branch

Sept 7 ***Birkenhead*** *Hippodrome* in Grange Road opened it was part of the theatre syndicate known as the De Freece Circuit. The first manager, Mr Walter De Freece, was the husband of the famous Vesta Tilley, who was the main attraction at the opening

Oct 22 North Branch Carnegie Library **Birkenhead** opened by Alderman JT Thompson

Oct 27 Launch from the **Tranmere** Bay Developments Company's works, of the largest dredger in the world

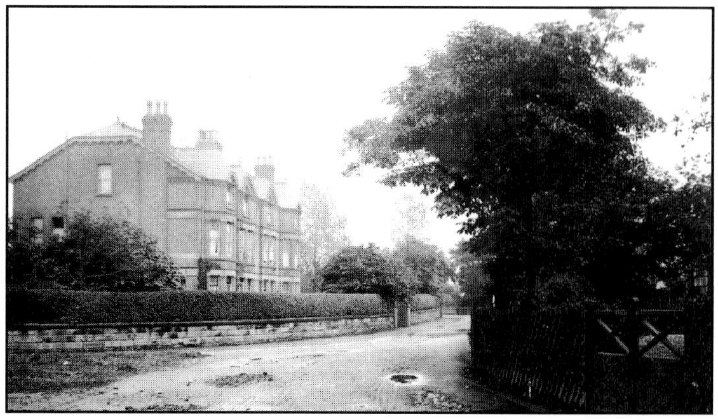

Above: *This postcard of Egerton Park, the Bebington Road entrance,* ***Rock Ferry*** *was posted in 1908 exactly 100 years after the park was first laid out. It was designed on similar lines to Rock Park - enclosed with an oval road and houses around the outside and also in the middle. Gate posts were placed at the entrance either end, fronting on to Bebington Road (seen here) and Old Chester Road*

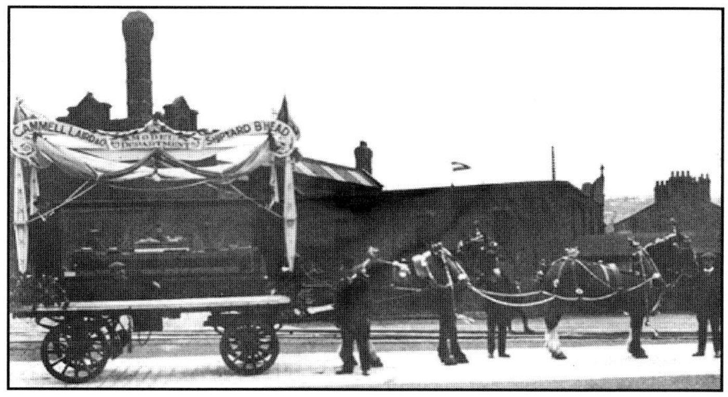

Right: *Cammell Laird Model Department are transporting one of their models to an exhibition on a horse-drawn wagon*

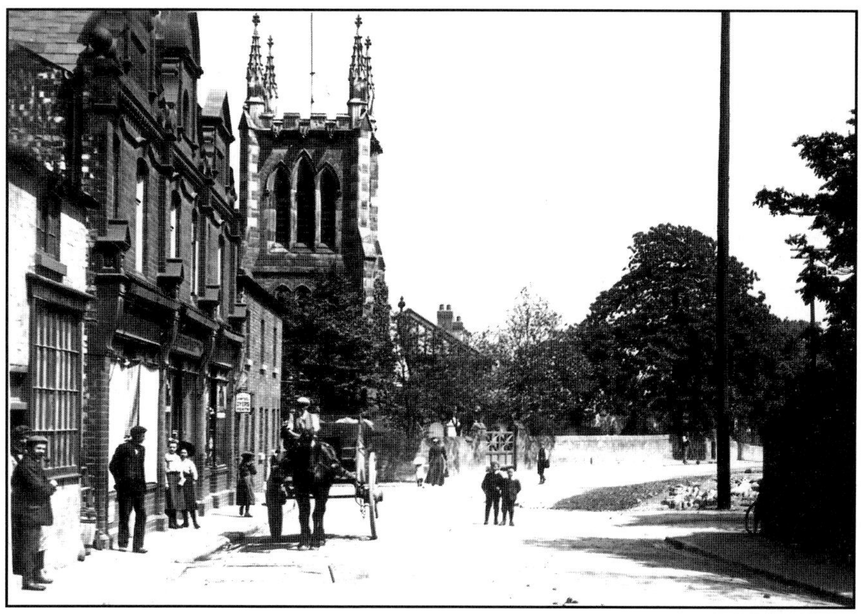

Right: *The horse and cart is standing outside the shops in* ***Upton*** *Village with St Mary's Church behind. The shop on the extreme left was bought in 1908 br Mr Shone who ran a cycle shop and later on also had petrol pumps [see 1917]*

Below: ***Prenton*** *Golf Club's new club house can be seen on the right, which was opened 26 February 1908. The club was formed 18 February 1905. Originally they shared a ground on what is now part of Waterpark Road, with cricket, rugby and hockey clubs. They purchased a 43 acre site in the summer of 1905 together with some fields which now form part of their present course. The new course was officially opened 6 April 1906. Prenton Waterworks can be seen on the left horizon - the houses to the left of it in Reservoir Road are:-* Norway Lodge, Ashley *and* Alfreton

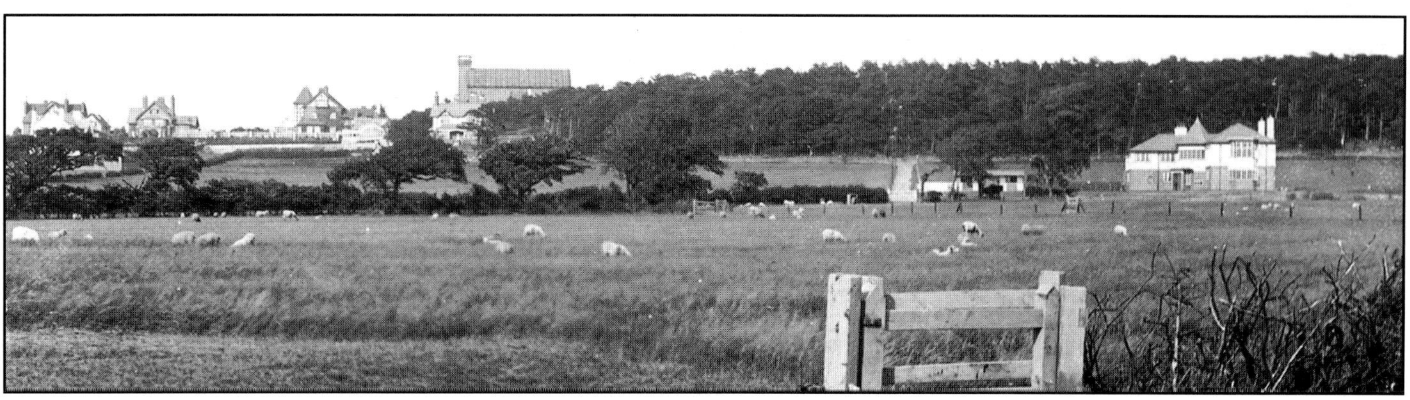

1909

– St Matthew's C of E Church Park Road East was built in **Birkenhead**[WBD]

– Hemingford Street Council School opened in **Birkenhead**[souv]

– 4th Battalion Cheshire Regiment spent summer camp at Abergaveny

– St Stephen's Church, **Prenton**, completed [see photo][OPB]

Mar 6 **Birkenhead** Dock disaster - 14 workmen killed [see photo opposite][YWPH]

Jun 15 New covered extension to **Birkenhead** Market opened[YW2]

Oct 19 New **Birkenhead** Central Library opened in Market Street South [see photo]

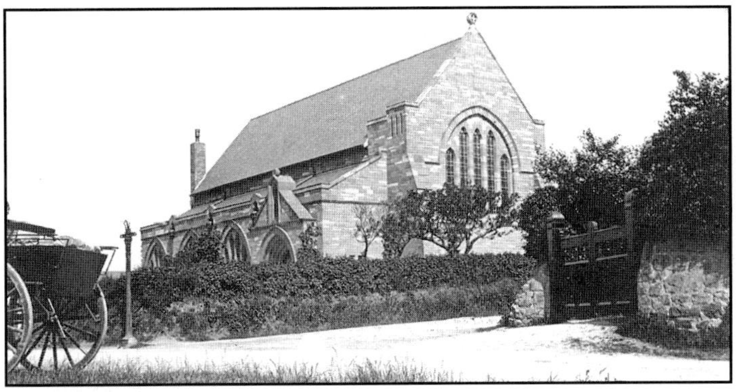

Above: *St Stephen's Church Prenton Lane* ***Prenton*** *opened 1 November 1897 - cost £10,000 - completed 1909 [see 1897]*

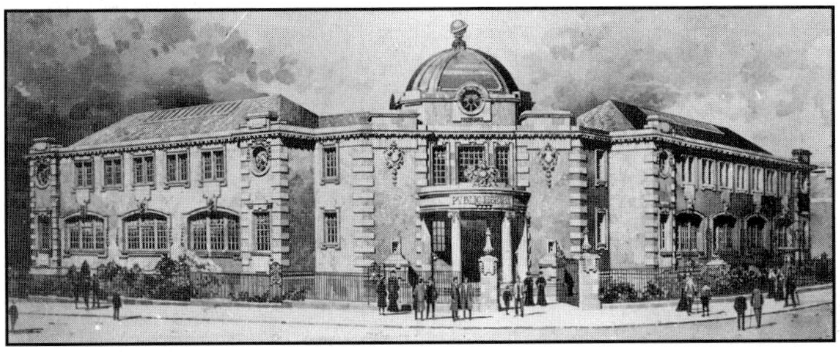

Above: *Architect's drawing of the new* ***Birkenhead*** *Central Library which opened in Market Street South 19 October 1909*

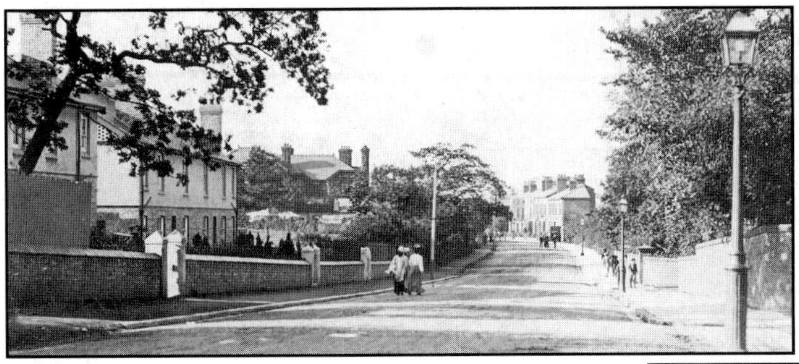

Above: *This was the view in Old Chester Road, Dacre Hill,* ***Rock Ferry*** *taken by the postcard publisher George Davies in 1908 and posted in 1909*

Right: *This 1909 postcard taken in New Chester Road* ***Tranmere*** *shows children posing for the photographer outside M Byrne's Cyclist's Rest & Tobacconist shop on the corner of Clare Street. The* Lord Raglan Hotel *is pictured on the right on the corner of* Union Street

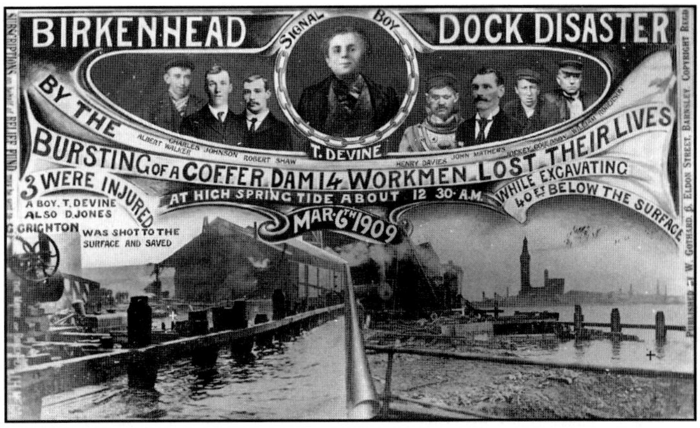

Above: *This was a postcard was sold to raise funds following the* ***Birkenhead*** *Dock disaster on 6 March 1909 - when a coffer dam burst due to a high spring tide and strong winds. A total of 14 workmen lost their lives, with 3 injured*[YWPH]

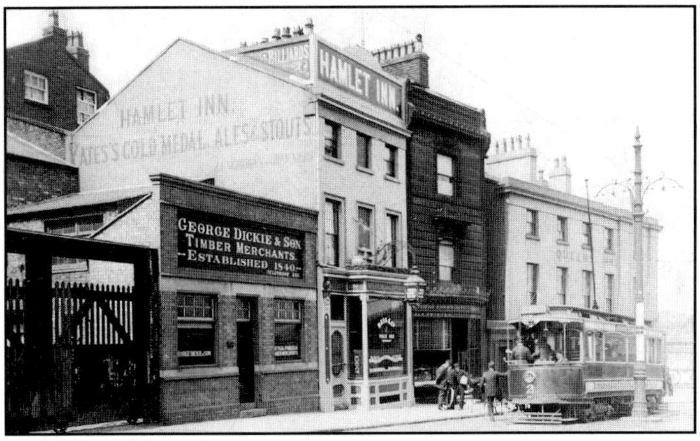

Above: *The single-deck* ***Birkenhead*** *tramcar No.2 is in Chester Street in front of the* Queen's Inn, *then William Brewitt, dining room keeper,* Hamlet Inn *& G Dickie timber merchant*

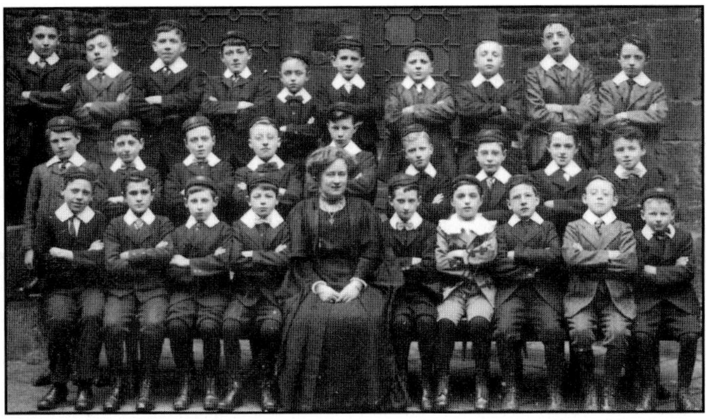

Above: *This* ***Birkenhead*** *Institute school photograph was taken in 1909 [Geoffrey Nicholson 2nd left middle row]*

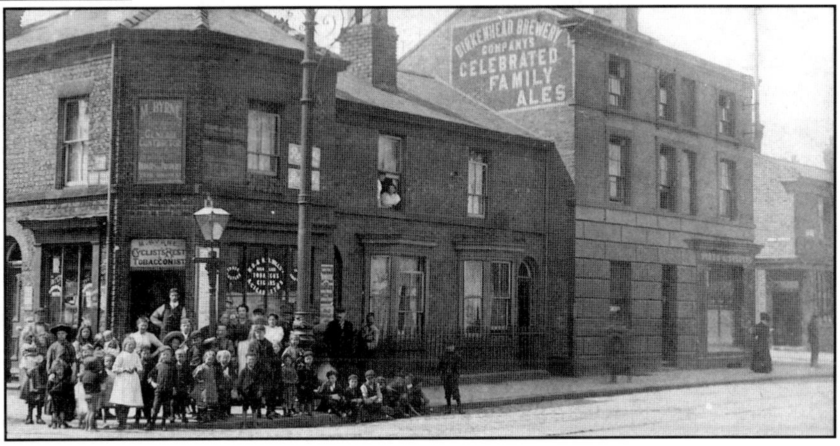

1910

–	Laird street Baptist Church opened in **Birkenhead**[OPB]
–	**Birkenhead** & District Co-op central offices opened in Catherine Street
–	All Saints' Church, Shrewsbury Road **Oxton** was consecrated as the Parish Church - which was formed out of **Oxton** and **Bidston** Parishes and St Bede's (a Chapel of Ease to Bidston) was handed over to All saint's and became the Parish Hall[PROG]
Jan 1	**Birkenhead** Brewery first introduced milk stout[BB]
Apr 10	Chief Scout Robert Baden-Powell unveiled the tablet in the YMCA Grange Road **Birkenhead**: "In this Hall the Boy Scout Movement was publicly inaugurated by Lieutenant General Sir Robert SS Baden-Powell, KCB, on January 24th 1908. This Tablet was unveiled by the Chief Scout Sir Robert SS Baden Powell on April 10th 1910"
May 6	**King Edward VII died**
Dec 30	Brassey Street Mission **Birkenhead** new buildings opened - cost £4,050 which had been paid before the extension scheme opened[SOUV]

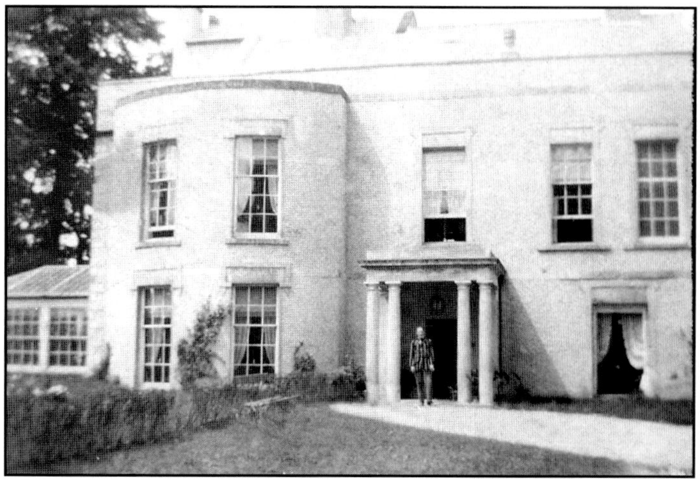

Above: *This small-sized postcard of* Bebington Hall *was posted in 1910 and had an embossed address stamp for 'The Old Rectory Lower Bebington Cheshire'. This building stood at the junction of The Village and Heath Road in Lower* ***Bebington.*** *Built in the 1830s for private occupation, it was later used by St Andrew's Church, as seen here, and eventually demolished with the Town Hall erected on the site in 1956. The Bebington Central Library and Health Centre opened later in 1971*

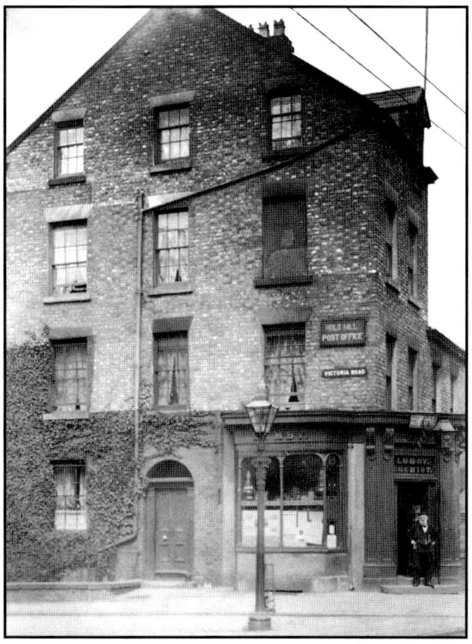

Above: *This postcard dated 1910 shows Hr* ***Tranmere*** *Post Office, which was also Lumby, Chemist, at 12 Church Road, Holt Hill at the junction with Victoria Road. The Post Office later moved across the road*

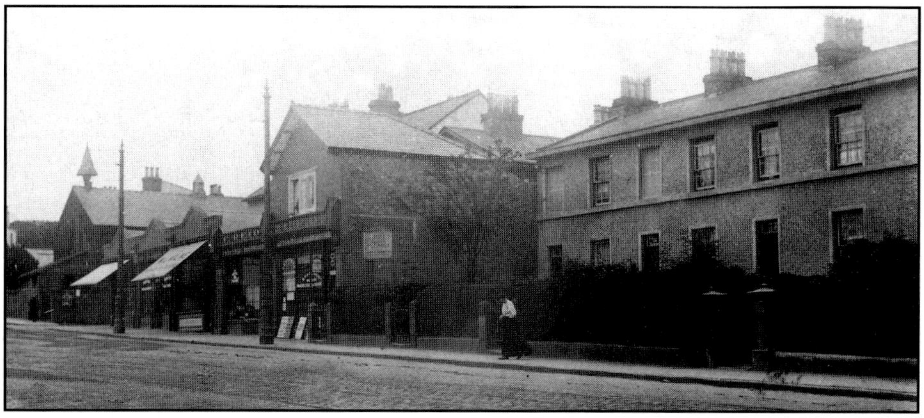

Above: *The shop behind the nearest street pole was TR Bedford who was a Stationers & Newsagents at No.20 Upton Road* ***Claughton****, who also ran the Post Office. The terrace of houses set back from the shops, with two of the windows being blocked off to save window tax, had a row of shops built in their front gardens and extended to the pavement including G Jones, Plumber, whose sign can be seen this side of the Post Office*

Right: *The* Horse & Jockey *Hotel, a Yates's Manchester Ales pub, is seen in Upton Road,* ***Upton*** *Village, with Rake Lane off to the left. Rake Lane was then the main road to* ***Woodchurch*** *before the by-pass was opened in 1938. The new* Horse & Jockey *was opened there in the 1960s and the old pub seen here was demolished and a supermarket built on the site*

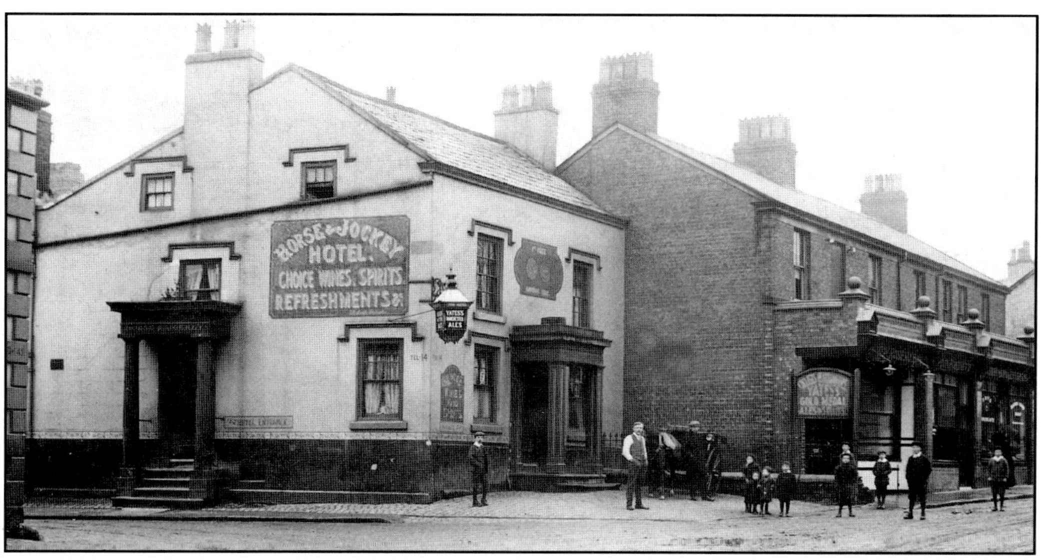

1911

- – Brassey Street School in **Birkenhead** and **Rock Ferry** Council School opened[souv]
- – Foundation stone laid for Alwen Reservoir in North Wales, which was to supply water to **Birkenhead**
- – Building commenced on the King Edward VII Memorial Clock, erected in Argyle Street **Birkenhead**[BPH]
- – Whetstone Lane Fire Station extended in **Birkenhead**[WBD]
- Jan Baden Powell Girl Guides - 1st **Birkenhead** West formed[TW]
- Jan Parish of All Saints & St Bedes **Birkenhead** formed
- June 22 Coronation of King George V - public bonfires at **Birkenhead** Park and Mersey Park, **Tranmere** [see photo]
- Sept 28 Auction of the estate of the late Sir Thomas Brocklebank, one of the pioneer ship-owners, at **Bebington, Storeton** and **Tranmere** - including the Storeton Railway and quarries [see photo]
- Nov 4 *Electric Picture House* opened in New Chester Road **Rock Ferry**[SSW1]
- Nov 11 **Birkenhead** Masonic Hall opened in Oliver Street[WON]

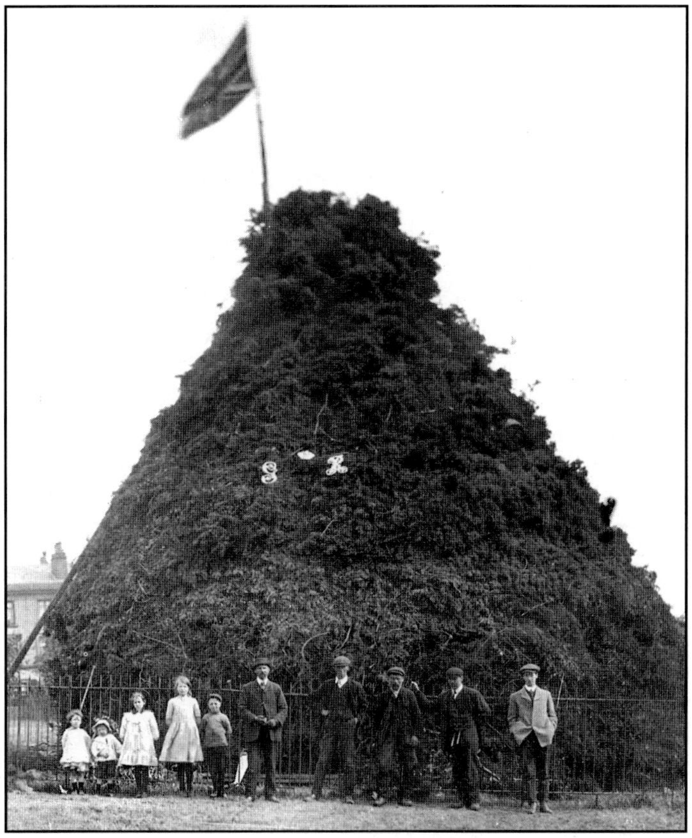

Above: *A group of children are posing in front of the Coronation Bonfire with some of the adults who built it in Mersey Park to celebrate the Coronation of George V which was held on 22 June 1911. There was also a firework display following the lighting of the bonfire [see below]*
Below: *The bonfire seen above is well alight in Mersey Park* ***Tranmere***

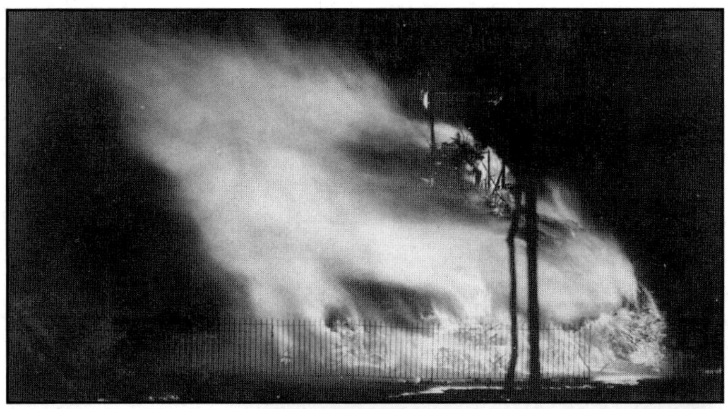

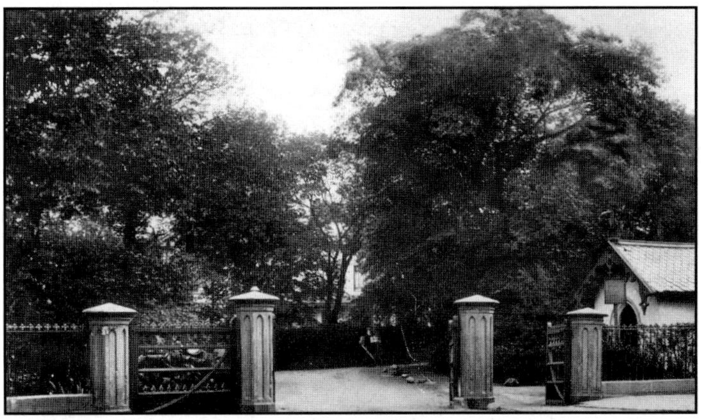

Above: *These were the entrance gates to Rock Park* ***Rock Ferry.*** *Designed in 1837 the imposing houses were completed by 1850. The Toll Cottage on the right collected from visitors*

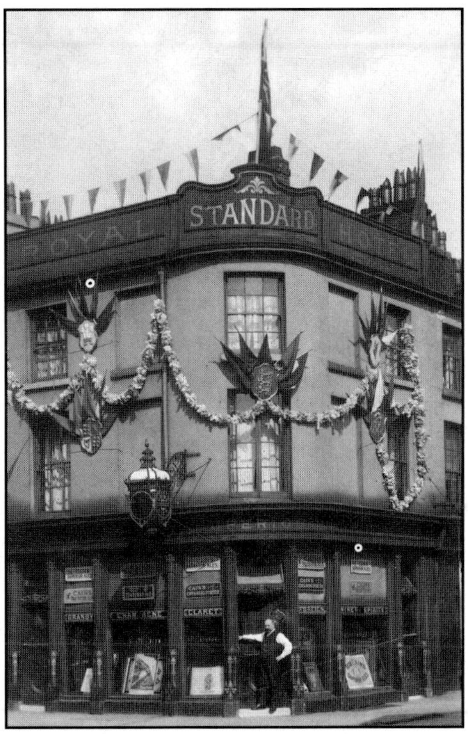

Left: *The landlord of the* Royal Standard Hotel, *338 New Chester Road* ***Tranmere,*** *is standing proudly outside his Caine's Brewery pub, which is decorated for the Coronation of King George V*

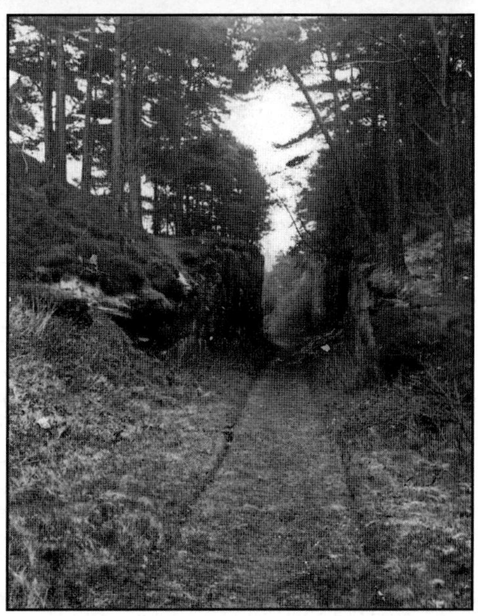

Right: *This view of* ***Storeton*** *Quarries was taken 18 March 1911. It shows where the rail track ran from the Great Cutting, which was the main entrance to the North Quarry, after the rails were removed following the closure of the railway in 1905 - although stone was removed from the quarry by lorry for the subsequent 20 years*[ST]

1912

Mar 4 **Birkenhead** Museum and Art Gallery opened in the old library building in Hamilton Street[WBD]

Mar 9 Tranmere Rovers new ground in Borough Road, **Prenton** was opened with a match against Lancaster Town - Tranmere won 8-0[TR1881]

Mar 30 The Arno recreation ground opened - six acre site in **Oxton** [see photo][WBD]

Apr 3 **Birkenhead** Chamber of Commerce formerly inaugurated[WBD]

Apr 15 The ill-fated Cunard liner *Titanic* sank on her maiden voyage

Aug 14 Largest floating dock in the world launched at Cammell Laird **Birkenhead**[MOI]

Aug 22 Foundation Stone for the New Chapel **Rock Ferry**
laid by Sir WH Lever [see photo]

Oct 24 King Edward VII memorial clock unveiled in Argyle Street **Birkenhead** [later moved to its present site - see 1929][BPH]

Nov 12 St Peter's [Church] Hall Morecroft Road **Rock Ferry** opened - specially designed as a Parish Hall - it cost £5,468 (debt paid off in 1921)

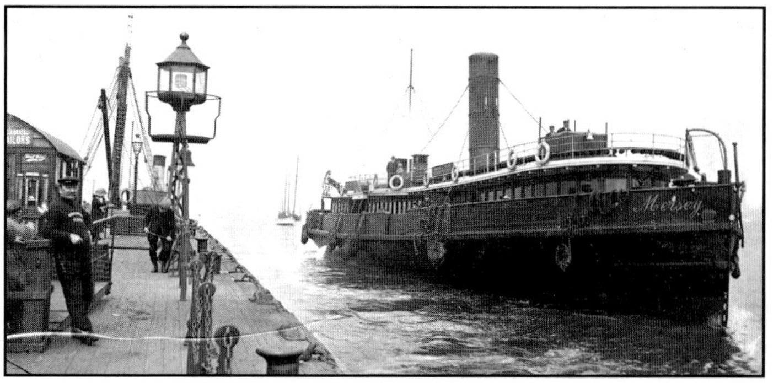

Above: *The ferry boat* Mersey, *with not many passengers aboard, is seen off the* ***Rock Ferry*** *landing stage*

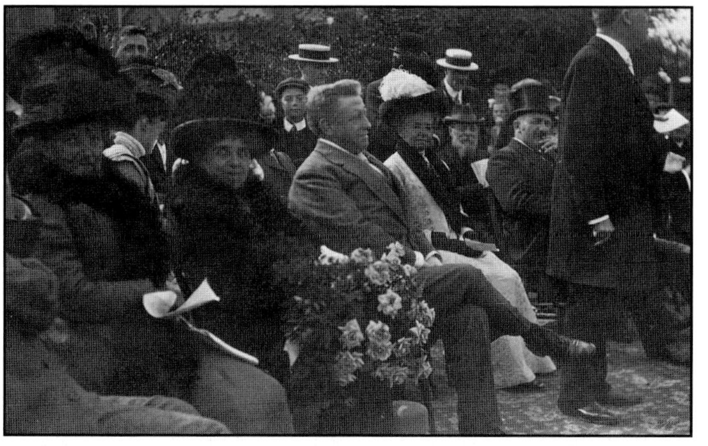

Above: *This photograph shows Sir William and Lady Lever at the ceremony for the laying of the foundation stone for the new chapel at* ***New Ferry***

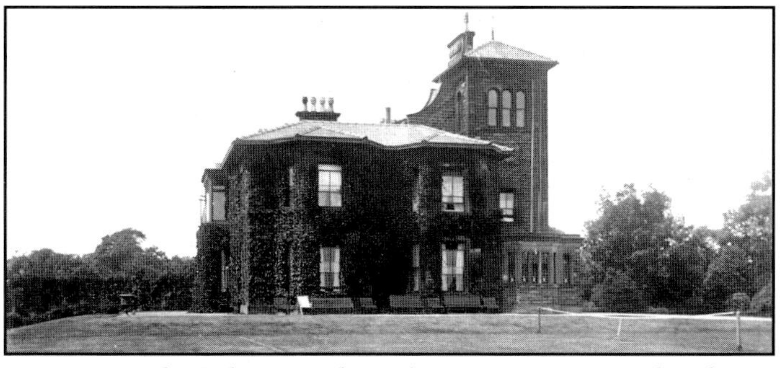

Above: *The Salacres, a large house in* ***Upton*** *was lived in about this time by David Richards, a ship owner and prominent Presbyterian - it was converted into flats in the 1930s*[SUAH]

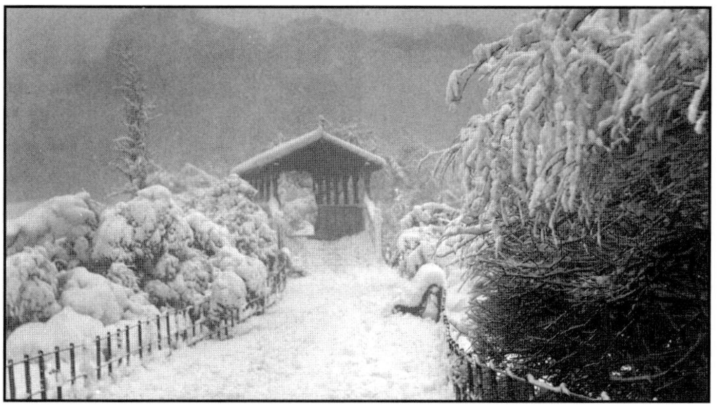

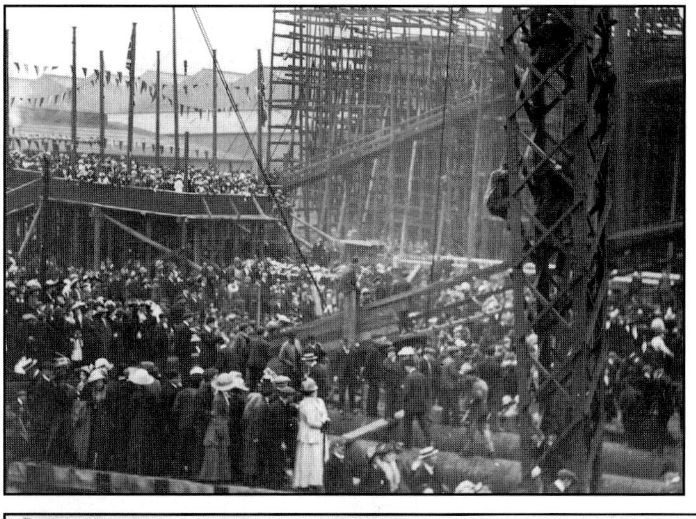

Left: *The vast crowds are watching the launch of HMAS* Melbourne *at Cammell Laird* ***Birkenhead*** *30 May 1912. Built for the Australian Navy, she survived the First World War and was broken up in 1929*

Above: *This snow scene was taken of the Swiss Bridge in* ***Birkenhead*** *Park*

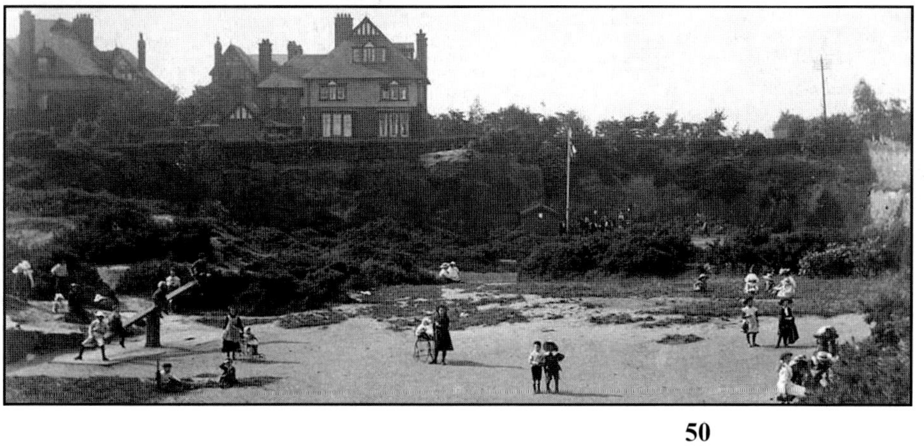

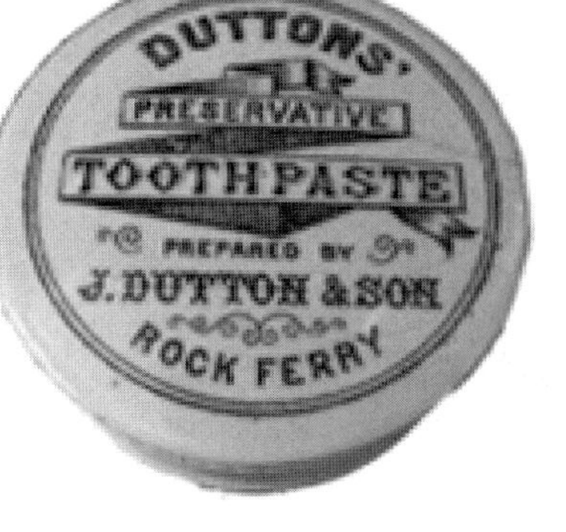

Left: *The six acre Arno Recreation Ground. which was converted from a quarry, opened in* ***Oxton*** *30 March 1912*

1913

– **Bidston** Lighthouse last used [see 1872][WPPB]

– Higher **Bebington** School in School Lane closed, replaced by Higher Bebington Junior School in Mill Road

– Launch of HMS *Audacious* (Super Dreadnought) at Cammell Laird **Birkenhead**[MOI]

June **New Ferry** tradesmen's Walk [see two photos]

July The new wing of **Birkenhead** Institute Whetstone Lane opened - the two-storey building accommodated Junior School and in the basement were the kitchens and dining room as well as storage rooms for old desks etc[SOUV]

July 13 Foundation stone laid for St Edmund's Orphanage, Heath Road **Bebington** [see photo 1914][DoS]

Nov 13 Foundation stone laid for the Masonic Hall in Oliver Street [back of Grange Road] **Birkenhead**

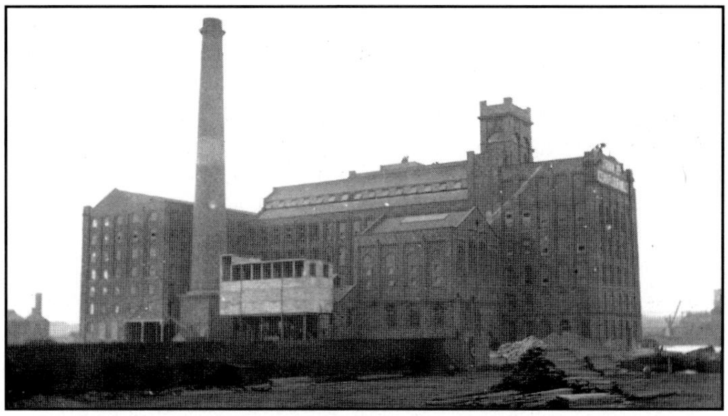

***Above:** The Ocean Flour Mills of Joseph Rank, are pictured at **Birkenhead** - which is where the new method of bulk flour transportation by container was first developed. The mill closed in September 1988 as it was no longer cost efficient*

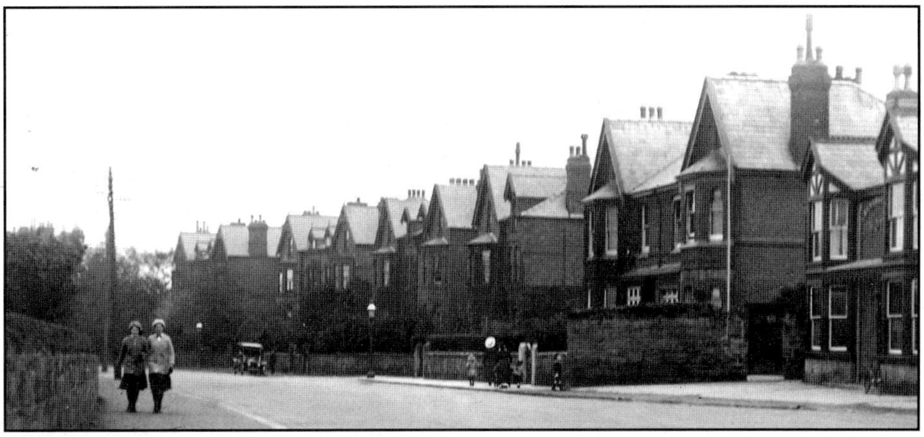

Left: *The building on the extreme right was the* Carnarvon Castle Hotel *in Bidston Road, **Oxton** which dated back to at least 1850, when John Knowles was the victualler. Seen here before the First World War - it was the Second World War that changed the buildings pictured here. The pub was reduced to rubble and also the large semi-detached next door in March 1941 when it was hit by a land mine. To the right of the lamp post is Silverdale Road and the house seen the other side lost part of its roof during the bombing and was repaired with the new roof being lower [see 1941 & 1956]*

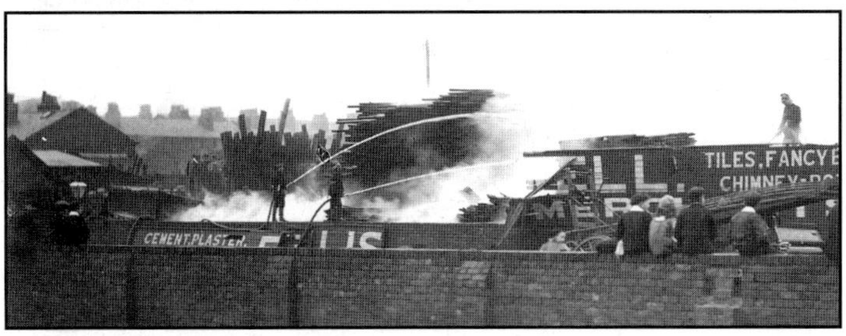

Above: *The children sitting on the wall have a front-seat view of the serious fire at the timber yard of Ellis & Powell at 320 New Chester Road **Rock Ferry** [see 1914]*

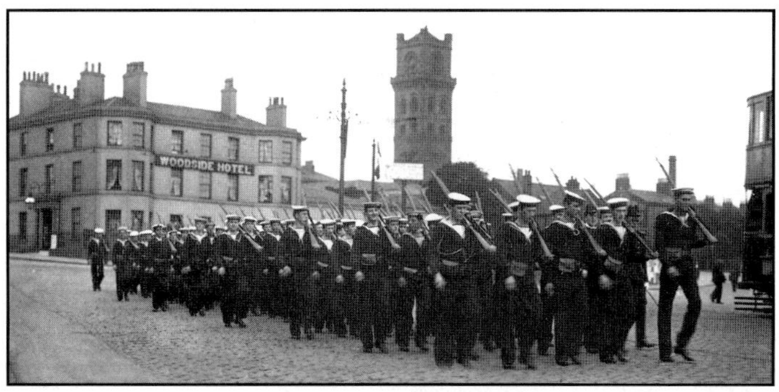

Above: *This group of **Birkenhead** Naval Volunteers are marching towards the ferry at Woodside to catch the boat across to **Liverpool** where they were going on special duty during the visit of King George V. The* Woodside Hotel *can be seen in the background*

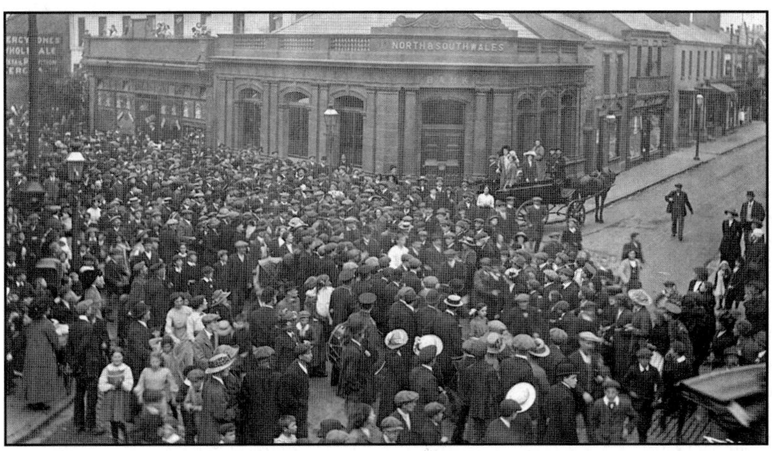

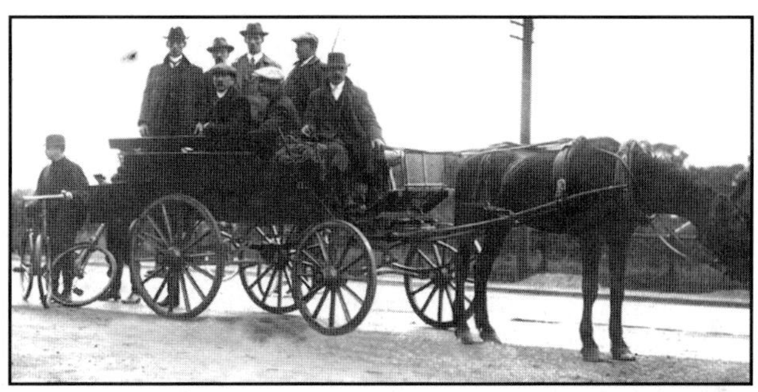

Above: *The crowd is gathered at **New Ferry** for the annual Tradesmen's Walk - this took place in June, starting and ending at the Toll Bar Corner pictured. The course was 16.25 miles long, **Whitby** being the turning back point. The winner in white is seen in the middle of the throng of people in front of Parr's Bank at the junction of Bebington Road and New Chester Road.*

Above right: *The officials of the Tradesmen's Walk are pictured in the horse and carriage where they would get a moving grandstand view of the walkers*

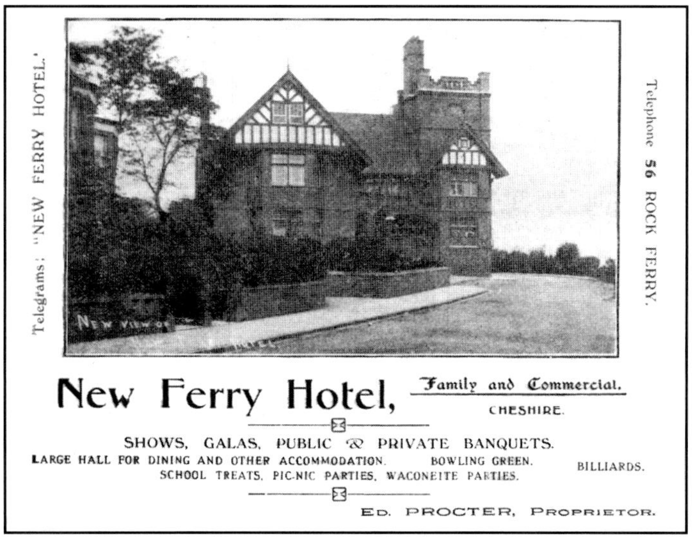

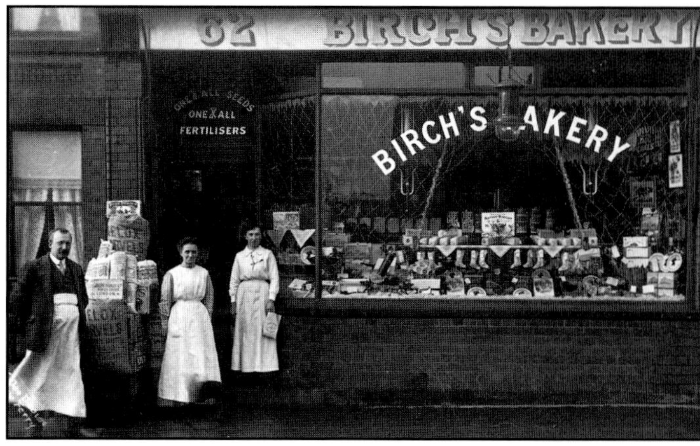

Above: *Birch's Bakery shop is pictured at 62 Bebington Road* ***New Ferry*** *- not only did they sell bread etc, but also pet food, fertilizers, seeds etc*

Right: *St James' Church in Laird Street* ***Birkenhead*** *which was completed in 1858 occupied an island site where one side was Laird Street and the other side Hoylake Road. It was built to serve the workers' flats known as Dock Cottages - part of which can be seen on the right [also see 1938]*

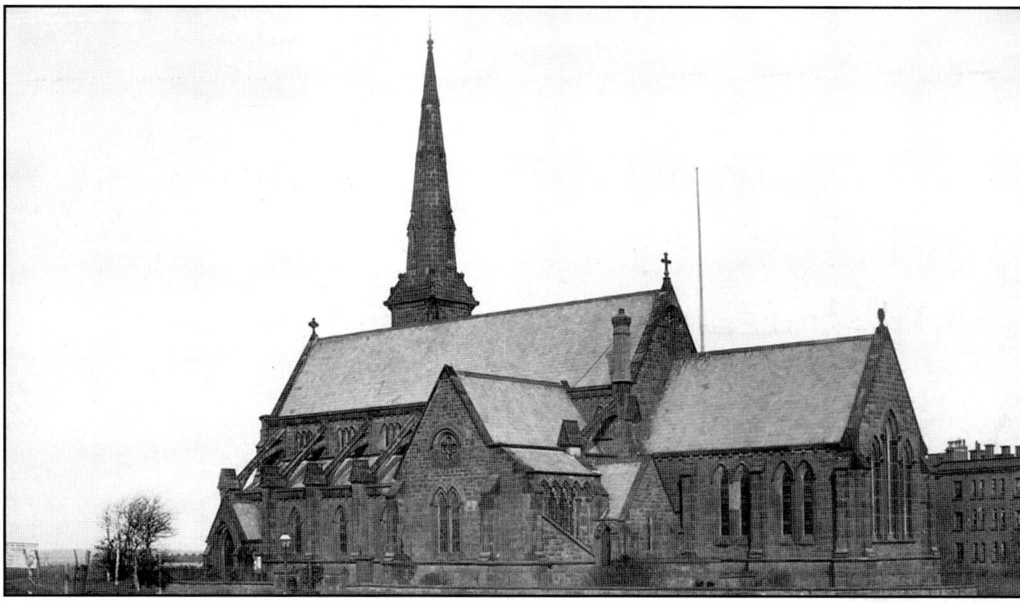

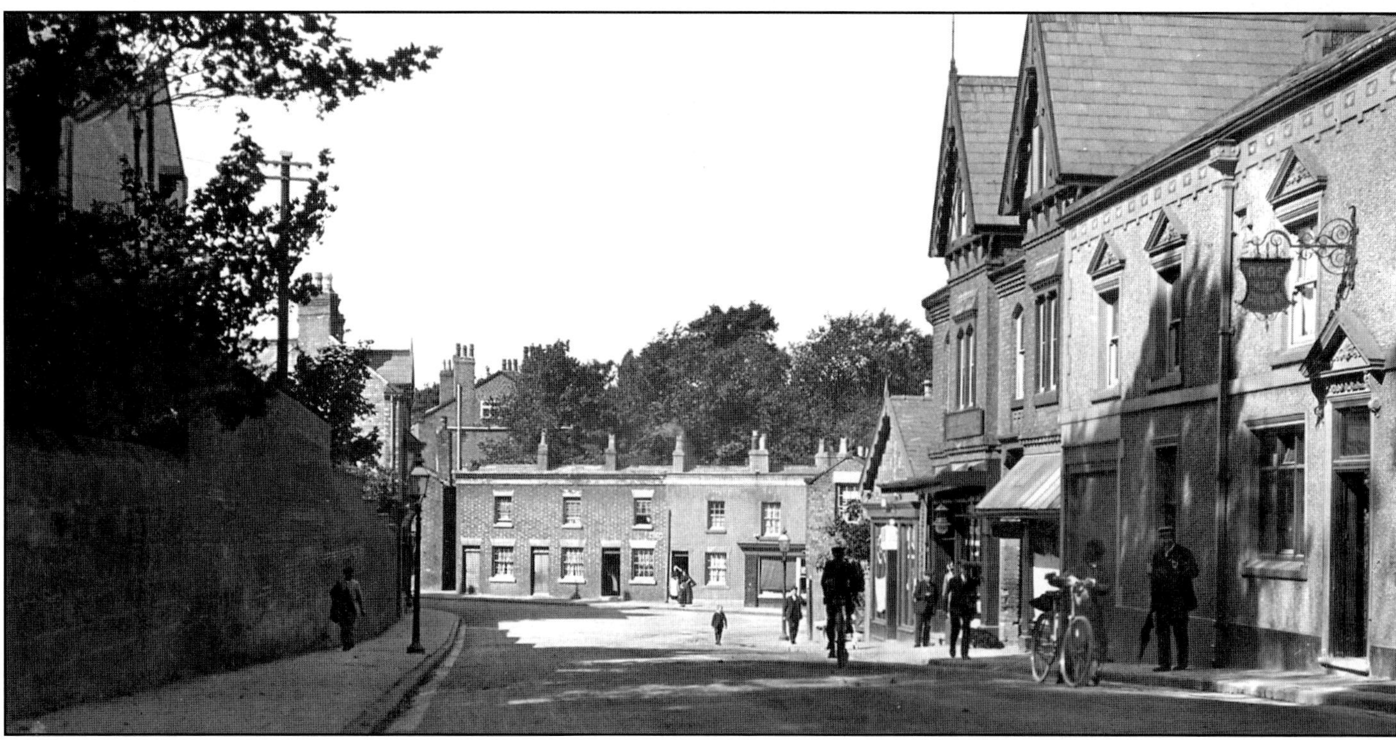

Above: *Looking down Church Road Lower* ***Bebington*** *just before the First World War, with Heath Road to the left of the houses ahead - the fountain which was in the middle of the road in front of the houses, was removed to Mayer Park - The* Rose & Crown *pub on the right is the only building pictured that is still standing today. The Town Hall and Civic Centre are now on the left*

1914

– St Edmund's Orphanage opened in Heath Road **Bebington** [see photo][DoS]

– Temple Road School opened in **Birkenhead**[souv]

– The Tranmere Territorial Company - the 4th Battalion of the Cheshire Regiment marched through the night from Birkenhead to Rhyl and arrived in good condition for breakfast[4BTCR]

Mar 25 King George V & Queen Mary visited the Wirral Borough - their itinerary included:-
Tour around Cammell Laird shipyard, **Birkenhead**
Opened the public park on **Bidston** Hill
Laid the foundation stones for **Wallasey** Town Hall and Lady Lever Art Gallery, **Port Sunlight**

June 2 "Home Comforts Exhibition" held for 10 days at the Claughton Rink **Birkenhead** (see advert next page)[PROG]

July 31 **Birkenhead** Corporation obtained parliamentary powers to run motor omnibuses within the Borough and to **Moreton, Upton, Woodchurch** and **Bromborough**[SOUV]

Aug 4 Outbreak of the First World War

Aug 8 First wounded Belgians were received at **Birkenhead** Borough Hospital

Aug 19 ***Birkenhead** News* Prince of Wales War Relief Fund inaugurated[VS]

Aug 23 Local Women Suffrage Societies abandon propaganda work and offer to help towards the war effort[VS]

Aug 25 St Catherine's Hospital **Tranmere** became a Military Hospital[VS]

Sept 5 Major Strong addressed a recruiting meeting in the Haymarket **Birkenhead**[VS]

Sept 12 ***Birkenhead** News* started its Patriot's Gallery in its newspaper - by the end of the war over 6,000 portraits had appeared[VS]

Oct 2 Over 50 Belgian Refugees arrived at *The Towers*, Victoria Park **Tranmere** [see photo - also 1957][VS]

Nov 4 Red Cross Society opened at 19 Palm Grove **Oxton** as a convalescent home or temporary hospital[VS]

Nov 18 Alfred Bigland started the Bantam's Battalion in **Birkenhead** - previously men under 5'6" high were refused entry into the army but were now admitted[VS]

Dec 3 **Rock Ferry** Council School buildings given to the 2nd Battalion Bantams[VS]

Dec 9 The 4th Cheshires leave **Birkenhead**[VS]

Dec 25 Over 100 wounded soldiers arrive at Woodside Station **Birkenhead**[VS]

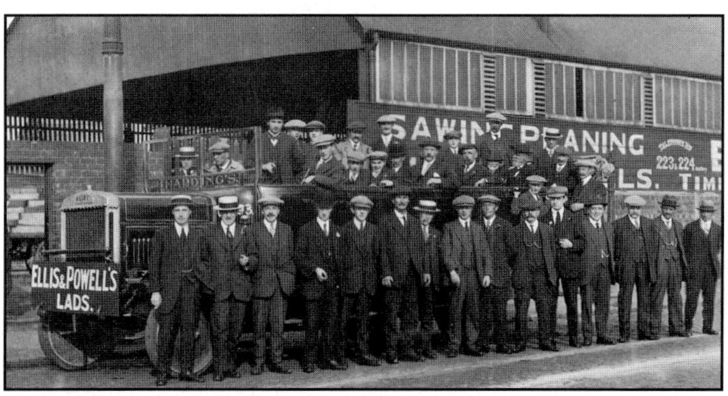

Above: *This Harding's charabanc is pictured outside Ellis & Powell's Timber Yard at 320 New Chester Road* ***Rock Ferry****, with the sign at the front of the vehicle which says: "Ellis & Powell's Lads" - they were probably volunteers being taken to sign up for war*

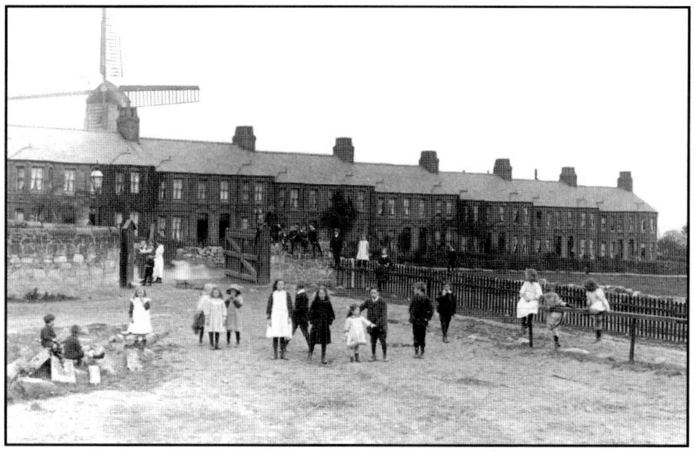

Above: *The children are posing for the photographer in front of houses in Mill Terrace Higher* ***Bebington*** *- the Mill looms in the background [see 1924]*

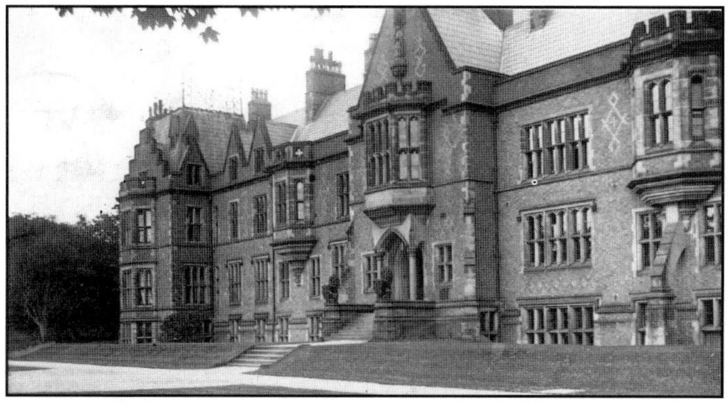

Above: *The front entrance to St Aidan's Theological College is seen in Shrewsbury Road* ***Oxton.*** *Founded in 1846, this building was erected in 1855 at a cost of £40,00, in five acres of land - it was demolished in 1969 and houses built on the site*

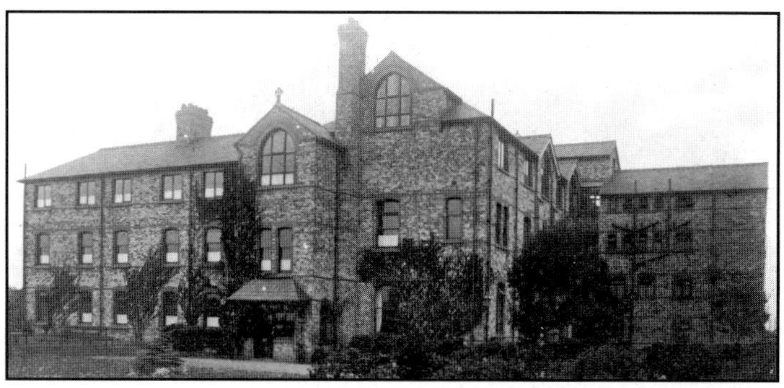

Above: *St Edmund's Orphanage and School, which cost £8,000 to build, was opened in Heath Road* ***Bebington*** *and was surrounded by large playing fields and well laid out gardens. It was run by the Sisters of Charity and accommodated 120 boys*

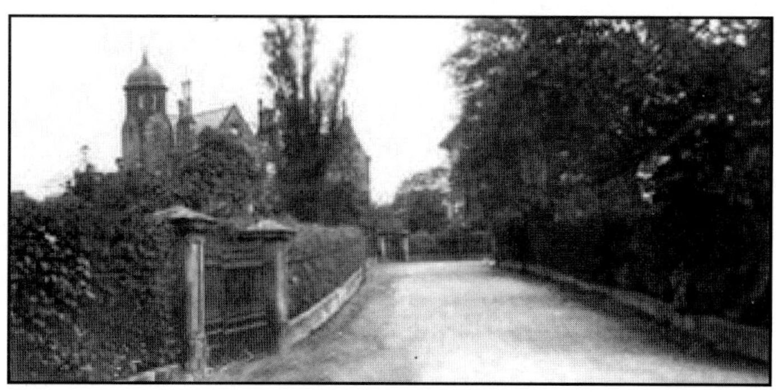

Above: *This is a view in Rock Park,* ***Rock Ferry*** *which was laid out in 1837. It originally only had one entrance which was controlled from a Toll-cottage [see 1911]*

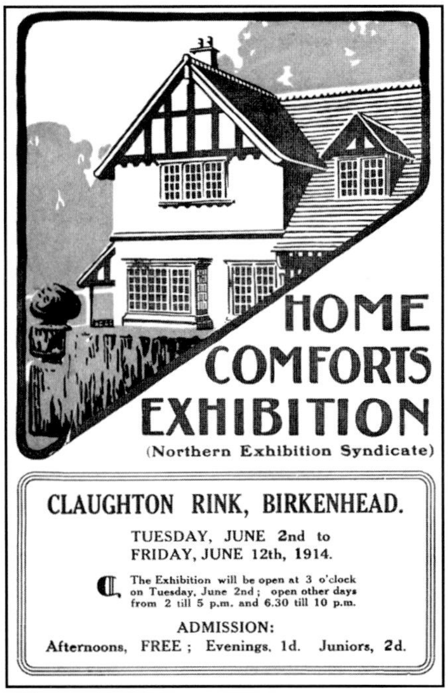

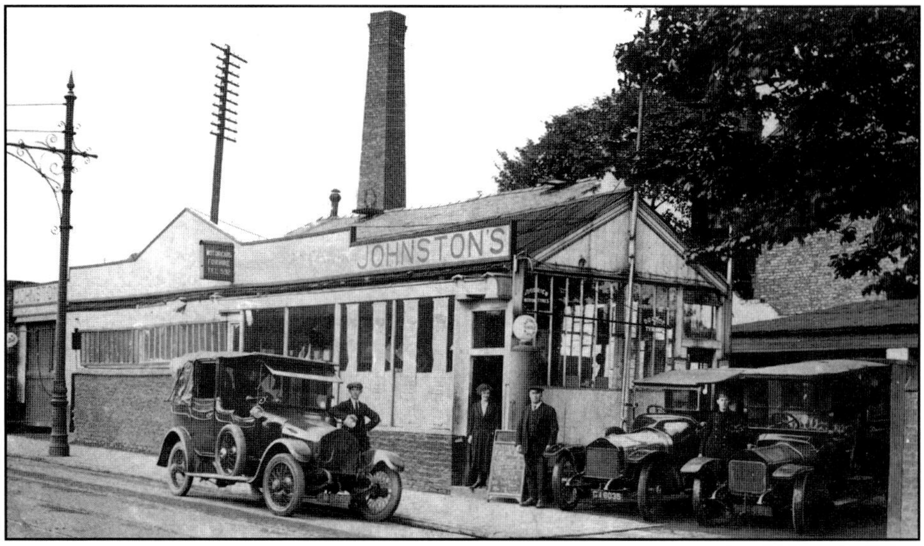

Above: *Two Johnston Brothers, John and Edward set up business as taxi cab proprietors in Borough Road,* ***Birkenhead*** *at the junction with Kingsland Road and are seen here with their taxis. They also operated a bus service to* ***Heswall*** *using a Daimler 20 seater and 32 seater Leyland char-a-banc. They sold the Heswall bus service to Hardings on 1 October 1924 who sold it to Crosville in October 1925*

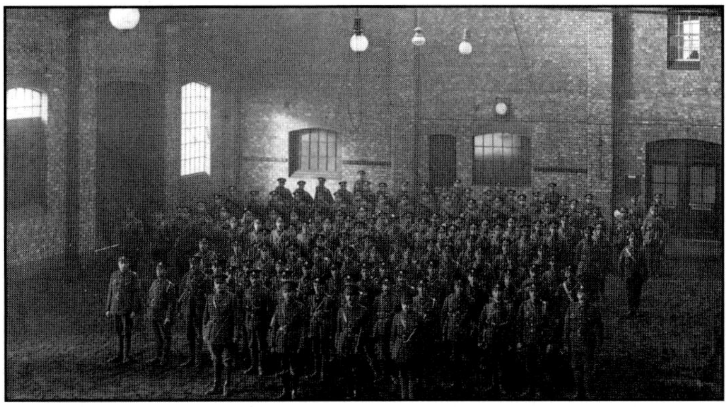

Above: *This was a postcard sent from a soldier who had been stationed at this Drill Hall in Grange Road West* ***Birkenhead*** *which was the headquarters of the 1st Volunteer Battalion, The Cheshire Regiment. The building, which opened 11 January 1902, is still standing today and used as a sports centre*

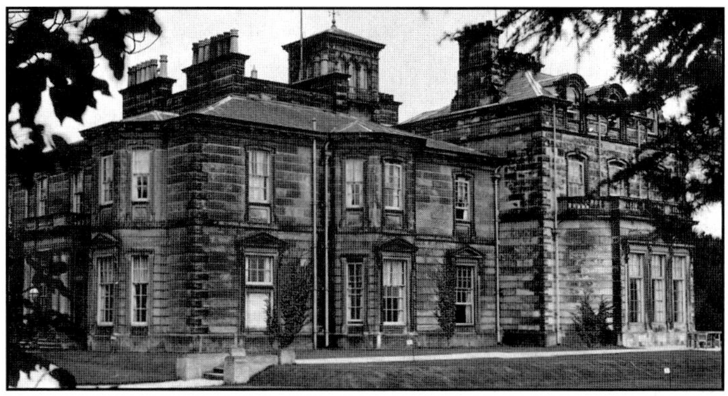

Above: Upton Manor *(then known as* Harefield House*) was built c1857 for the ship owner William Inman. The Belvidere tower, pictured between the chimneys, was built before 1875 as a viewing tower so he could see his ships in the River Mersey. William Inman purchased the Lordship of the Manor of Upton in 1865 and the mansion was then known as* Upton Manor. *The Manor was extended by the then new owner, Mr Stern. From 1951 to 1984 it became the junior department of Upton Hall Convent*

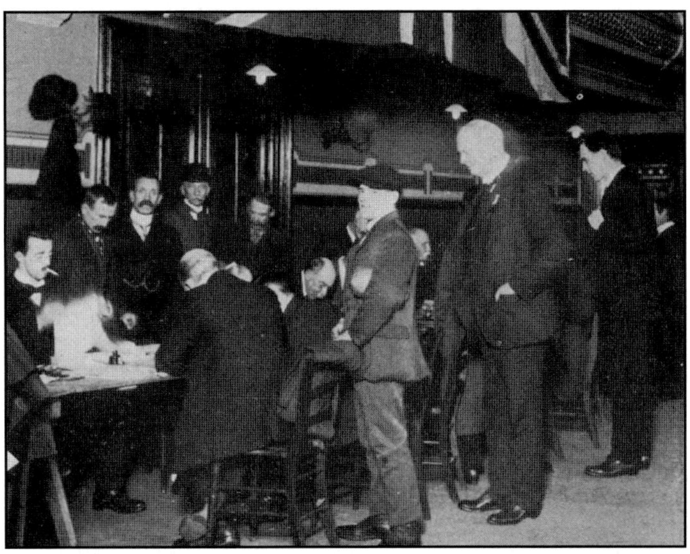

Above: *Mr Alfred Bigland is the taller man looking on as some new recruits are signing on for the Bantams at* ***Birkenhead*** *Town Hall. It was he who persuaded Lord Kitchener to allow smaller men under the regulation height to sign on in November 1914 - Birkenhead recruited the first Bantams Battalions. They were overwhelmed with the response from all parts of the country*

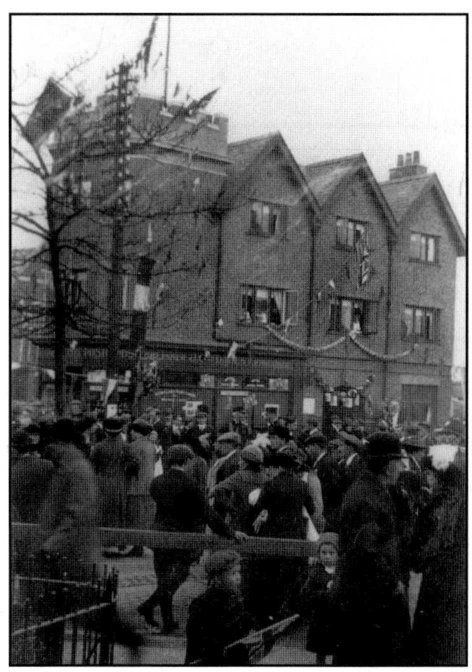

Right: *The crowds are gathered on the 25 March 1914 for the visit to* ***Birkenhead*** *and* ***Port Sunlight*** *of King George V and Queen Mary. The shop in the background, which is bedecked with flags at 125 New Chester Road* ***New Ferry,*** *belonged to J George Davies, who was the official photographer to Lever Brothers.*

1915

– **Birkenhead** YWCA opened a new boarding house at 44 The Woodlands, next to their premises at No. 42[SOUV]

Feb 22 Harry Lauder appeals for recruits at the *Argyle Theatre* **Birkenhead**[VS]

Feb 26 Wounded soldiers given an open invitation to the Argyle Theatre **Birkenhead**[VS]

Mar 12 Gas workers strike in **Birkenhead** [see next page][VS]

Mar 21 Lord Kitchener inspects **Birkenhead** Bantams at St George's Hall **Liverpool**[VS]

Mar 31 Hemingford Street Schools **Birkenhead** to be given to the Army Council for wounded soldiers[VS]

May 7 *Lusitania* torpedoed off Ireland - many of the crew were from Merseyside

May 10 '*Lusitania* riots' in **Birkenhead** [see photo below][MMMB]

May 24 The Great Belgian National Band performed at the *Hippodrome Theatre* Grange Road **Birkenhead** to raise funds for the War effort

July 16 Girl Guides entertainment held at St Saviour's Church Parish Hall **Oxton** to provide funds for water carts in France[VS]

July 22 **Birkenhead** High School for Girls, raised funds for the Victoria League Club for Soldiers[VS]

Sept 13 First six lady tram conductors started duty in **Birkenhead**[TBW]

Oct 26 ***Birkenhead** News* Edith Cavell Fund started[VS]

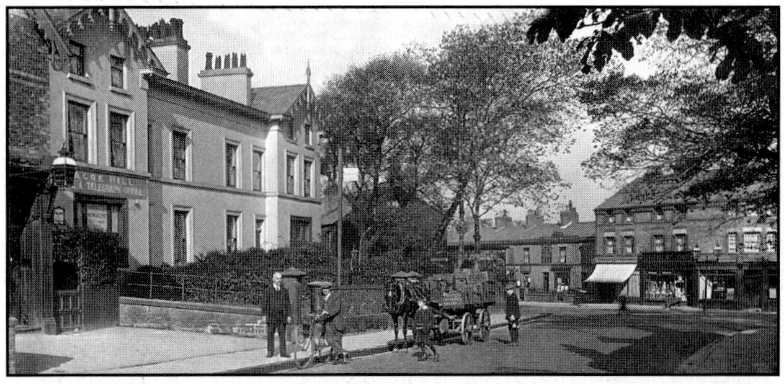

Above: *To the left of Wrightson's horse and cart delivering their mineral water, is the Dacre Hill Post Office and Telegraph Office* ***Rock Ferry*** *. It was situated in Old Chester Road which bends to the left with Rock Lane West to the right*

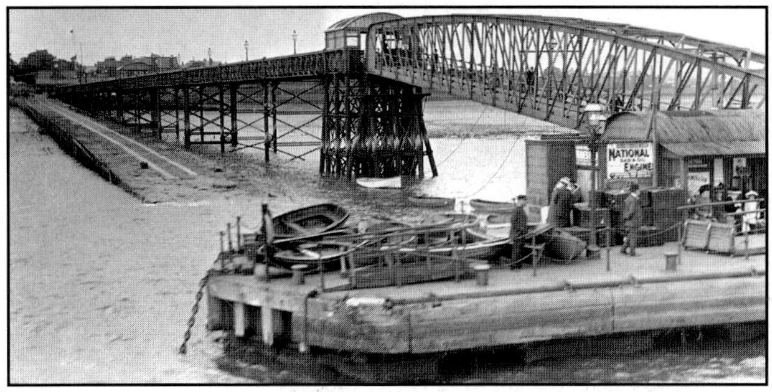

Above: *The floating landing stage is seen at* ***Rock Ferry*** *with passengers waiting on the right and others walking down the bridge connecting the pier and stage. The slipway seen on the left dates back to 1820 when it was built by Thomas Morecroft to enable passengers to board the ferries. Due to falling numbers of passengers, the service closed in 1939*

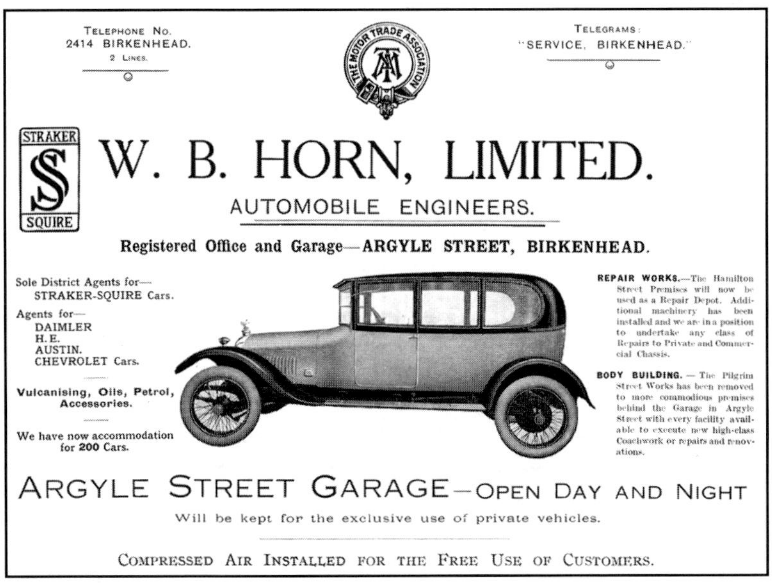

Below: *This was the scene after the building in Old Chester Road had been attacked by anti-German rioters following the sinking of the* Lusitania *7 May 1915. Many of the ship's crew were from Merseyside and the day after the sinking rioting broke out in* ***Liverpool*** *targeted against German and Austrian businesses. Fearing that the trouble would spread to* ***Birkenhead*** *pubs were closed on Monday which is when the rioting started - it lasted a day in which time 24 shops or houses were attacked - several people were charged with rioting*

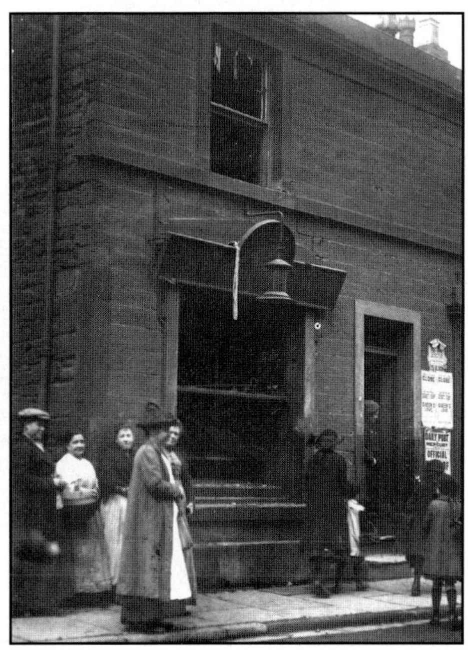

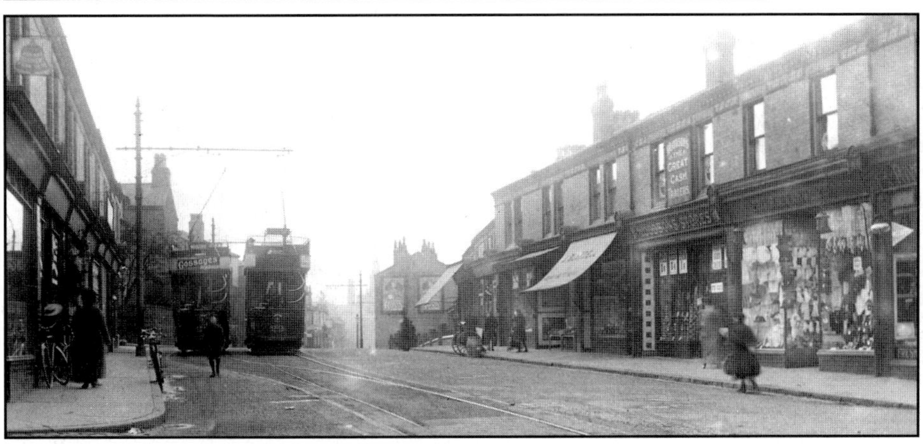

Above: *Tramcar No. 29 on the right, is passing another tram in Church Road Higher* ***Tranmere.*** *The shop on the right with the sign above saying "Woodsons The Great Cash Traders" belonged to Woodson's the Grocers at 221 Church Road*

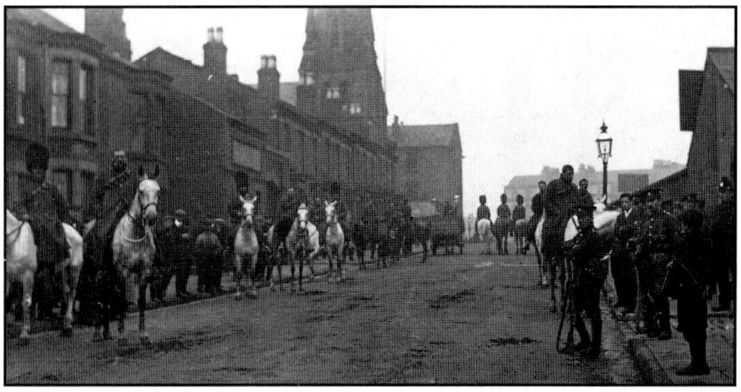

Above: *The Scots Greys are on escort duty following a strike of workers at the* ***Birkenhead*** *Gas Works. They were guarding the workers who were not on strike*

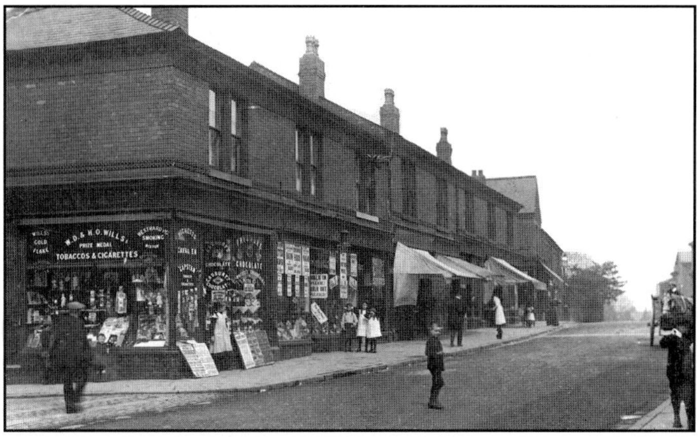

Above: *This 1915 postcard view of Derby Road* ***Higher Tranmere*** *shows Davis's Newsagents and Tobaccanist at No.50 on the corner of Maybank Road and beyond at Nos.46 & 48 is Constantine's Grocers shop - whose slogan was: "Walk in please - Walk out pleased". The newspaper boards feature the Gallipoli Campaign*

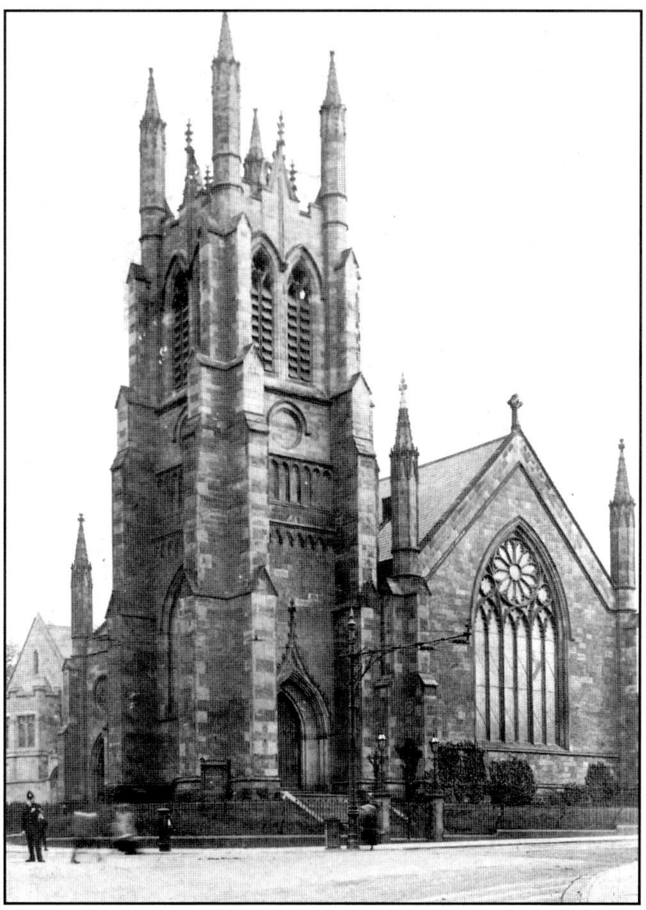

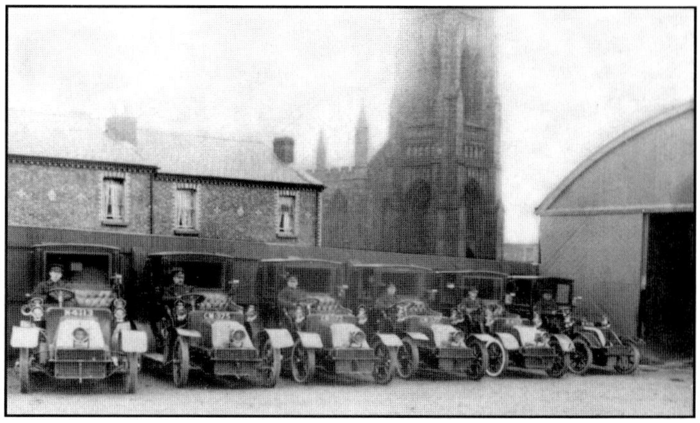

Above: *These Provincial Motor Cab Company cars were lined up at their garage on the corner of Duke Street and Beckwith Street - opposite Park Station. St Anne's Church is seen behind*

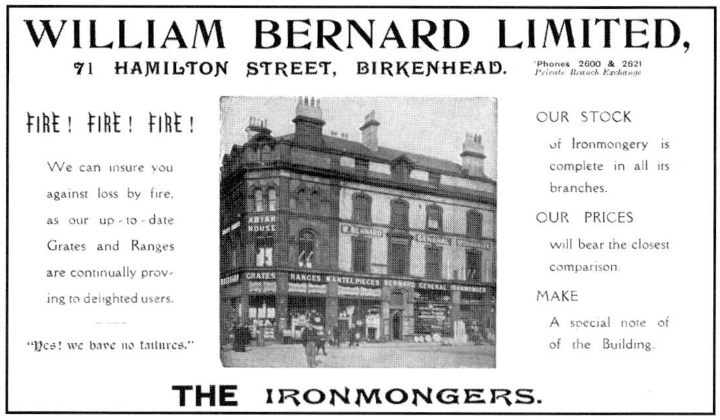

Above: *An advert for William Bernard, Ironmongers Hamilton Street* ***Birkenhead*** *[see also 1940]*

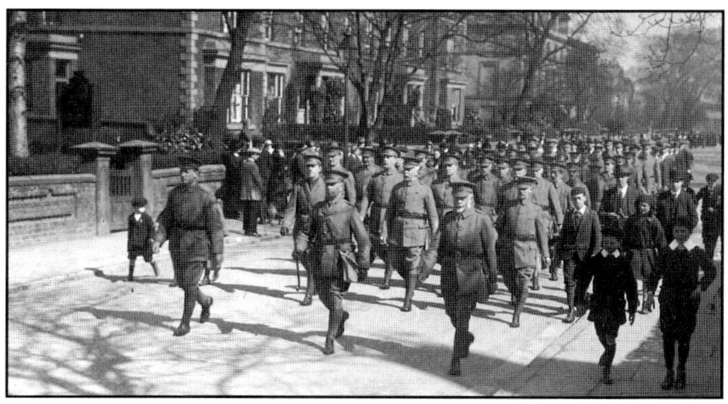

Above: *The* ***Rock Ferry*** *section of the Volunteer Defence Corps on their first march April 1915*

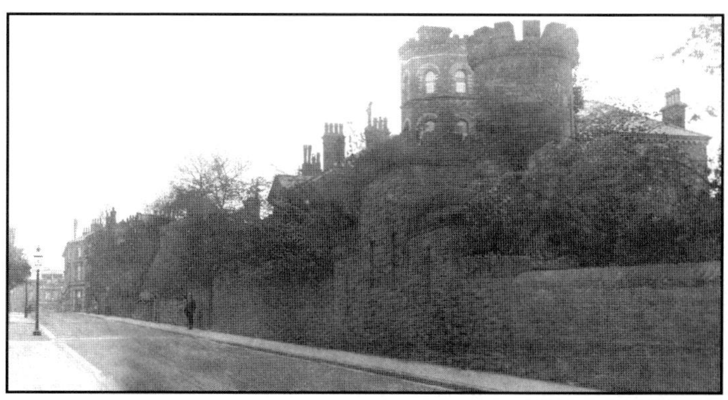

Above: *Mrs Alice Braithwaite's Claughton College and Music Academy for young girls is pictured on the right at* Normanston *14 Christchurch Road* ***Claughton****. Originally built in 1866. It was converted into flats and remains so to the present day*

Left: *The Congregational Church at the junction of Woodchurch Road and Balls Road* ***Birkenhead*** *was erected in 1858 [see 1922]*

1916

– **Storeton** Village School closed

– **Birkenhead** Borough Hospital extensions completed - number of beds doubled from 72 to 156[SOUV]

Jan 1 A great gale caused a building to collapse at the **Bebington** Showground, killing Pte Tinsley and injuring 11 other soldiers [see photo of funeral]

Jan 1 YMCA hut opened in **Bidston** Village with a New Year's supper for 800 men[VS]

Jan 31 **Birkenhead** Tram collections started for War Funds[VS]

Feb 1 Abbotsford Red Cross Hospital opened at **Rock Ferry** [see photo][VS]

Feb 19 **Rock Ferry** Red Cross Hospital opened for public inspection - also Hospital Flag Day[VS]

March Bentley Bros. bought 7 & 9 Grange Road **Birkenhead for** £2,100[LCP]

Mar 6 **Birkenhead** National Eisteddfod postponed

May 16 **Birkenhead** Corporation employees including grave diggers, road and sanitary men return to work after two weeks strike - wages increased[VS]

Aug 9 Domestic Servants' Garden Party for the wounded at **Oxton** Cricket Club[VS]

Oct 31 Presentation of the Rowland Jackson Ambulance in **Birkenhead** - funds raised by public subscription [see photo of Red Cross ambulance][VS]

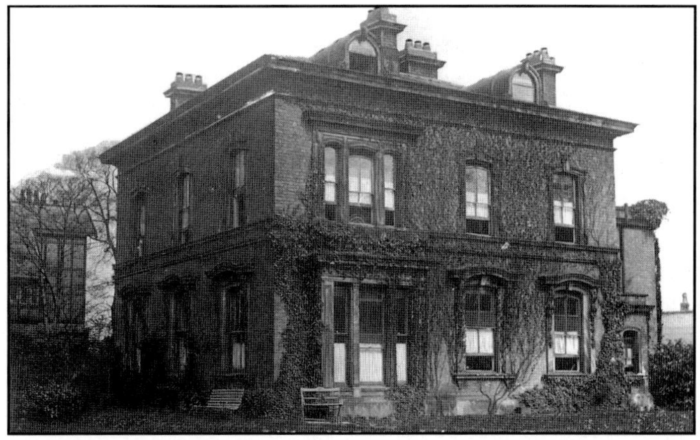

Above: Abbotsford, *the home of Mr C May Massie at 591 New Chester Road* ***Rock Ferry,*** *was loaned to the Red Cross to be used as a Military Hospital. It was opened 1 February 1916 and received its first patients 10 May. By the time it closed down 10 May 1919, it had treated 409 in-patients and 20 out-patients*

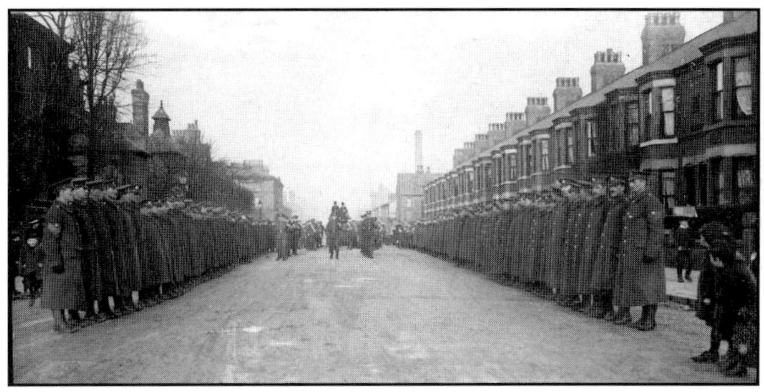

Above: *The guard of honour in Livingstone Street* ***Birkenhead*** *was for the funeral of Private Tinsley who was killed in the* ***Bebington*** *Showground disaster 1 January 1916. Bantam's Battalions were billeted at the showground [now known as the Oval Sports Ground] when a fierce gale caused the building to collapse with many injuries but only one fatality*

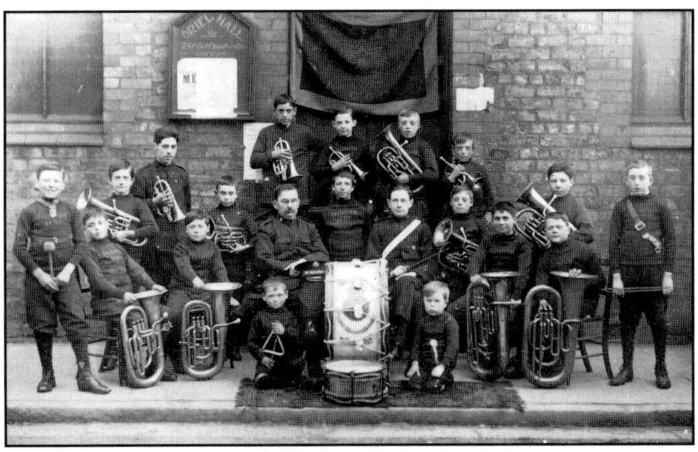

Above: *The Salvation Army Rock Ferry Junior Band is pictured outside Oriel Hall at 240 Old Chester Road,* ***Rock Ferry***

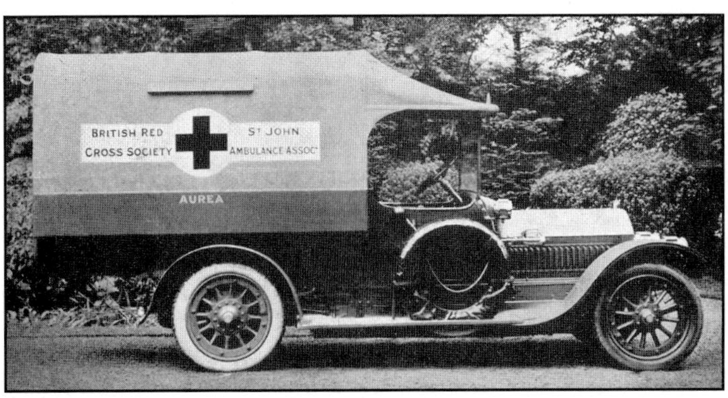

Above: *This was one of a fleet of ambulances purchased by the Red Cross with contributions from the general public as well as individual donations. Thousands of wounded men were transported by special hospital trains from the south coast to Woodside Station* ***Birkenhead*** *and from there conveyed to military hospitals across Wirral by these ambulances*[VS]

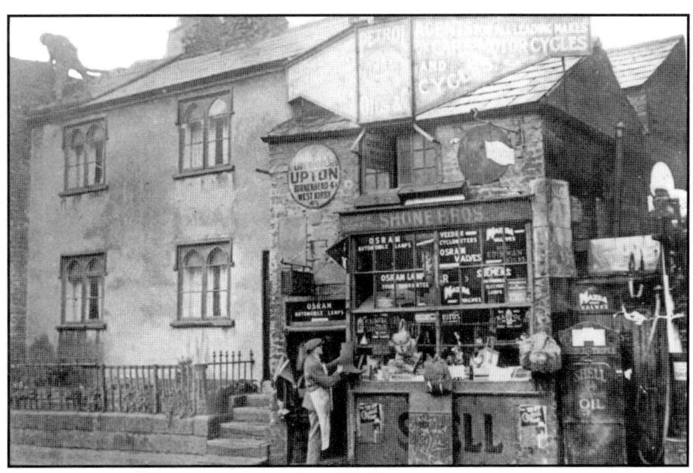

Above: *Shone Brothers' cycle shop with petrol pumps seen in* ***Upton*** *Village. The advertising board at roof level tells that they were agents for all leading makes of cars, motor cycles and cycles. They bought the shop in 1908 and continued into the 1970s. Above the entrance is a round sign giving distances from Upton - Liverpool 5.5 miles; Birkenhead 4.5 miles and West Kirby 4.25 miles*

1917

– The tennis court at the Presbyterian Church of England in **Upton** was used to produce vegetables for the war effort[SOUV]

– German Prisoner of War Camp established at **Bidston**[WPPB]

Jan 3 **Birkenhead** Chief Constable authorised to employ paid women police[VS]

Mar 10 ***Birkenhead*** *News* price increased from 1d to 1.5d[VS]

Apr 16 War time Economy Food lectures at **Birkenhead** YMCA[VS]

May 14 King George V and Queen Mary visit Cammell Laird, **Birkenhead**, during a two day war-time visit to Merseyside[VS]

June 16 **Birkenhead** Tramway employees' pay increased[VS]

July 12 Meeting at **Birkenhead** Town Hall to discuss the collection of waste paper[VS]

Aug 9 Domestic servants entertain wounded soldiers at Birkenhead School **Oxton**[VS]

Aug 23 German prisoners of war start work on River Birket scheme at **Bidston**[VS]

Sept 5 Royal National Eisteddfod held in **Birkenhead** Park. A pavilion was erected to accommodate 10,000 people - the event was marked by a Logan stone in the park - the Prime Minister, David Lloyd George, visited the event and was given the Freedom of the Borough[VS]

Sept 6 Prime Minister, Lloyd George's official visit to Wirral commenced[VS]

Oct 17 Grand Concert held at Hemingford Military Hospital **Birkenhead**[VS]

Oct 22 Fire at Vernon's warehouse **Birkenhead** Docks[VS]

Nov 23 Bridge Drive at St Saviour's Parish Hall **Oxton** in aid of the Bantams' Battalion[VS]

Dec 5 Miss AA Laird was the first woman Councillor in **Birkenhead**[VS]

Dec 29 Copies of the ***Birkenhead*** *News* sent to local troops on active service [see below][VS]

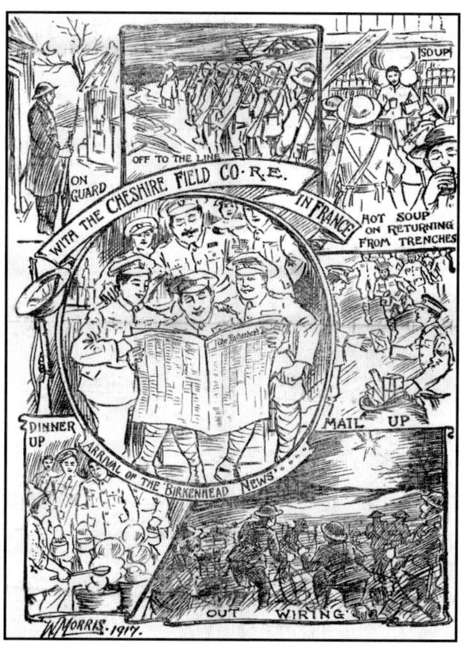

Right: *A cartoon by W Morris of life on the Western Front - several small sketches of soldiers' duties and in the central sketch "With the Cheshire Field Co RE in France – arrival of the* **Birkenhead** News

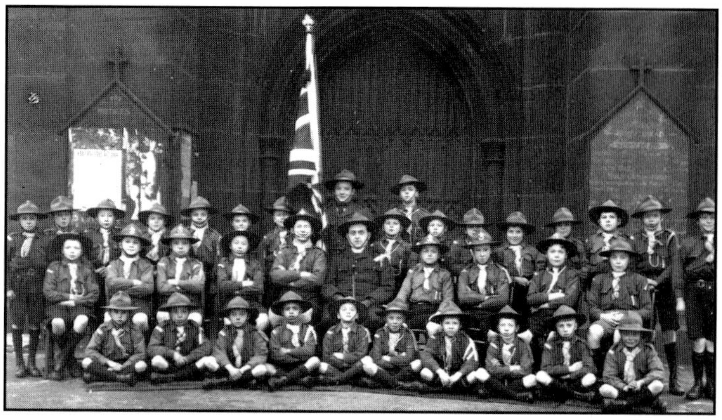

Above: *This Scout group was connected to St Anne's Church of England Beckwith Street* ***Birkenhead***

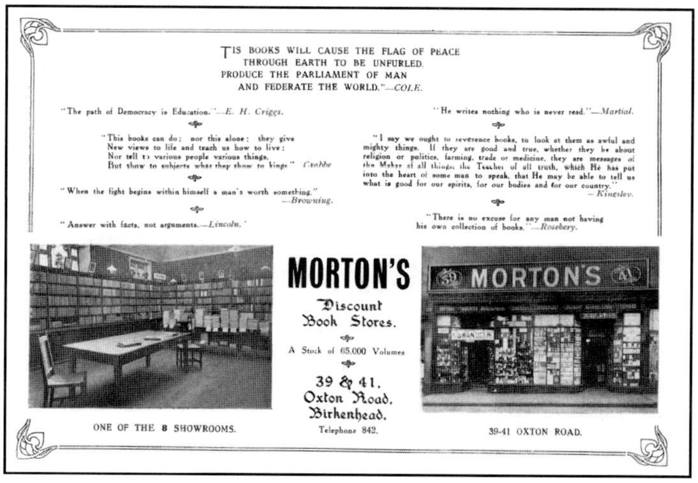

Above: *This was an advert for Morton's Discount Book Stores at 39-41 Oxton Road* ***Birkenhead***

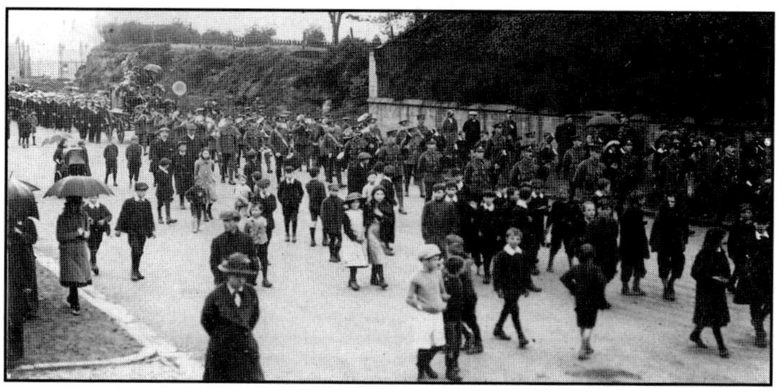

Above: *The army band are leading the funeral cortege for Mr Haldon who was a fireman on board the HMS* King Orry *- a contingent of the Royal Navy follow behind - some were probably members of the crew of the* King Orry

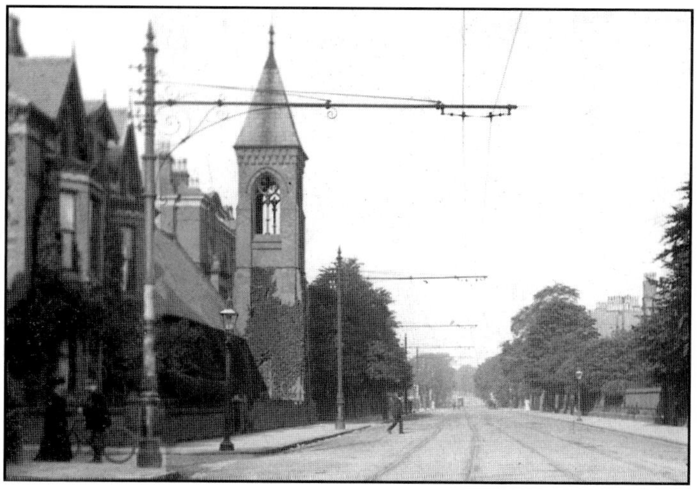

Right: *Looking down Park Road South* ***Birkenhead*** *the road to the left of the tram line pole was Alvanley Place, the church beyond on the corner of Merton Place was the Catholic Apostolic Church - this was purchased by the Church of Christ, opening 12 May 1951*

1918

Jan 12 Exhibition held at Allanson's store, Grange Road **Birkenhead** of articles made at the British Red Cross depot, Balls Road **Birkenhead**[VS]

Jan 26 Mr Isaacson held a Concert Party at Arrowe Hall Military Hospital **Woodchurch**[VS]

Jan 30 Whist Drive held at St Peter's Hall **Rock Ferry** for the Bantams' comfort fund

Feb 14 Letter from Lord Derby regretting the necessity for the breaking up or amalgamating of the Wirral Bantams[VS]

Mar 21 Meat ration cards introduced in **Birkenhead**[VS]

Apr 13 May*or* and Mayoress of Birkenhead entertain wounded in **Tranmere** Military Hospital[VS]

May 18 Mrs Edith Jones, a tram conductress died when she was crushed between two trams at Woodside **Birkenhead** *[see photo]*

June 4 Lieut. W Ashcroft bequeathed £500 for War Memorial at Birkenhead School **Oxton**[VS]

June 7 Sale of soldiers' needlework at **Tranmere** Military Hospital[VS]

July 1 National coal rationing order came into force[VS]

July 13 French Red Cross Day - case of 1906 Clicquot Champagne auctioned by the Mayor of **Birkenhead** for £155 in aid of funds[VS]

Jul y25 Carmelite Convent set up in Grosvenor Place **Oxton**[DoS]

Sept 14 Baseball match at **Bebington** between American and Canadian soldiers[VS]

Oct 17 **Birkenhead**'s War Savings over one million pounds[VS]

Nov 4 The death occurred of Lieut Wilfrid T Owen MC, old boy of **Birkenhead** Institute, recognised as one of the greatest of the English War poets - he died one week before the Armistice at the age of 25[SOUV]

Nov 11 Armistice Day - 'The war to end all wars' had come to its victorious finish and 'never again' was the hope - there were jubilant scenes in Hamilton Square **Birkenhead**[VS]

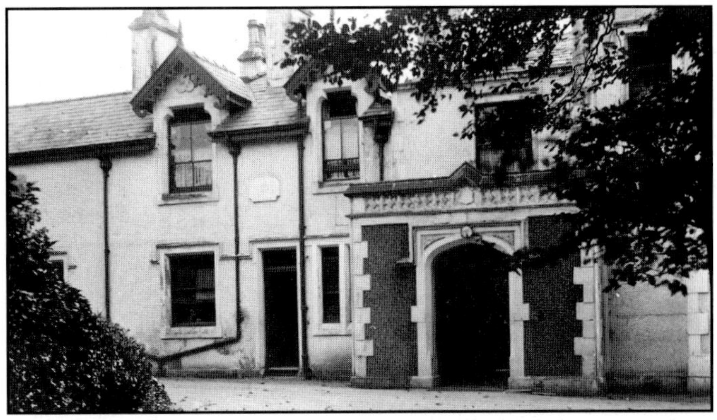

Above: *This was the main entrance to* Greenbank *which was a large house in* **Upton**, *standing on an elevated position looking across to the Welsh Hills, owned by Thomas S Hannay, a cotton broker. Thomas Hannay and his wife were ardent workers for the Presbyterian Church and also the community. It was Mr Hannay who founded Upton Cricket Club in 1901 and also funded a hall which served the community. In 1936 evacuees from the Spanish Civil War were accommodated at* Greenbank. *During the Second World War it was used by the army in connection with the munitions camp in Arrowe Park Road. It was demolished after the war and part of the site is now occupied by the* Horse & Jockey *pub*

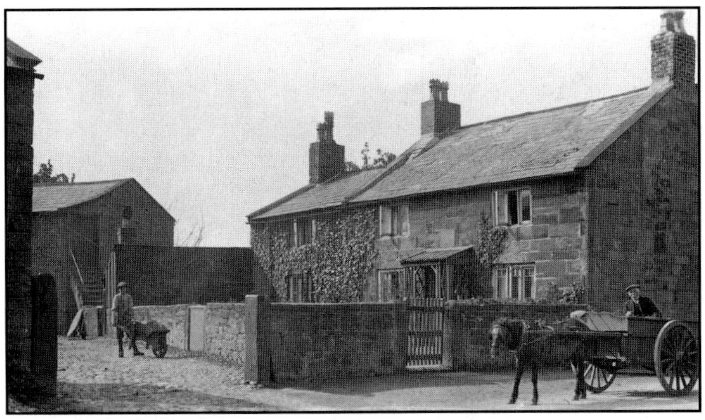

Above: *The man in the pony and trap is posing for the photographer outside Ford Farm, Ford Road,* **Upton**. *The area was known as Ford after the ford where the road crossed the River Fender, the Upton side of the station, prior to the old bridge being built. The farm house and buildings were demolished in the 1930s when the land was sold - a row of shops and houses were built on the land*

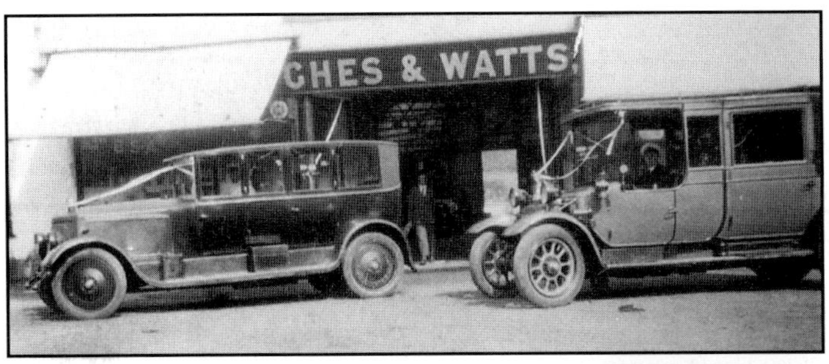

Above: *Vehicles outside Hughes & Watts Garage in Woodchurch Road* **Prenton**. *They operated from here until the late 1950s and were then taken over by Kirby's Motor Engineers. They sold out to Sainsbury's who opened their new store in 1982, building their car park on the site of the garage*

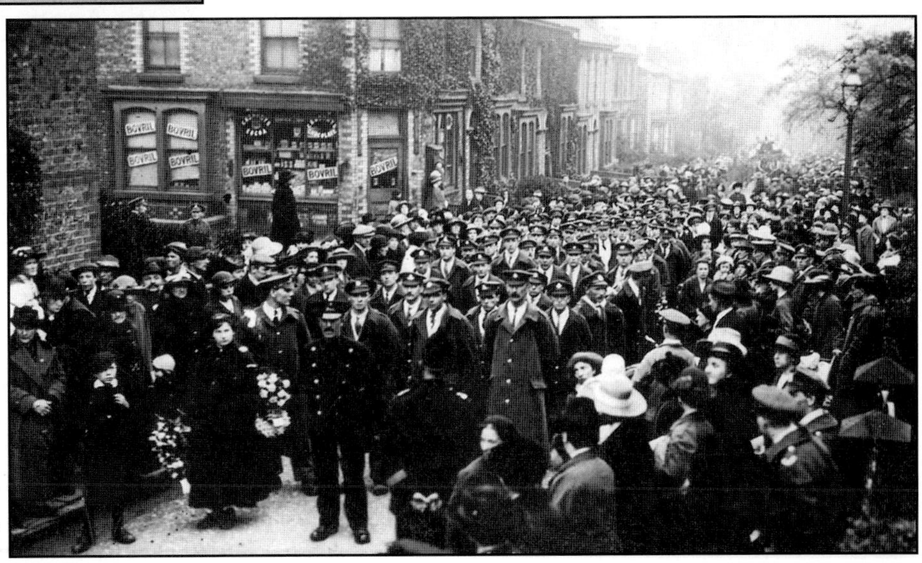

Right: *The funeral procession in Frodsham Street Hr* **Tranmere** *was for Mrs Edith Jones, a tram conductress who died when she was crushed between two trams at Woodside* **Birkenhead** *18 May 1918. Due to the war there was a shortage of tram conductors, so from 13 September 1915 conductresses were employed*

1919

– *Theatre Royal*, Argyle Street, **Birkenhead** sold to a cinema company

– **Prenton** War memorial dedicated [see photo]

– Demise of **Rock Ferry** Cricket Club resulted in two brothers HW & JP Hodgson joining **Birkenhead** Park - HW went on to score 11,723 runs and took 986 wickets for the Park club - he also played for Cheshire and the Minor Counties[BPCC]

Jan 15 The White Ensign from HMS *Birkenhead* placed in St Mary's Church **Birkenhead**

March **Rock Ferry** Auxiliary Military Hospital closed[VS]

May 3 Testimonial match for Ralph Holden at Tranmere Rovers [see photo]

July 12 First motor bus route commenced between **Rock Ferry** Pier and Park Station **Birkenhead** - extended to **Moreton** Cross 30 August [see photo][TBB]

July 19 Peace celebrations

July 26 The Chapter House at **Birkenhead** Priory was reopened as a Chapel at a dedication service[SOUV]

Aug 1 **Birkenhead** Police joined the national strike over pay and conditions. This was followed by looting and rioting then on the 2/3 August 500 troops arrived in the town. On 18 August peace was restored and the troops withdrawn. All sergeants and constables who had taken part in the strike were dismissed. New pay scales were introduced by the end of August[MQP]

Oct **Tranmere** admitted to the Central League when Leeds were expelled[TR1881]

Dec 21 Memorial window dedicated to members of the **Tranmere** Congregational Church who gave their lives in the First World War

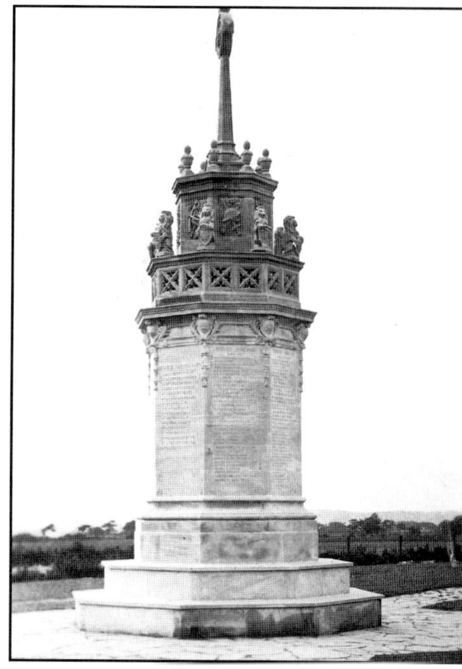

Right: *The* ***Prenton*** *War Memorial was erected on a piece of land in Prenton Lane at its junction with Osmaston Road in 1919 - in memory of the men of Prenton who gave their lives during the First World War [see also 1960]*

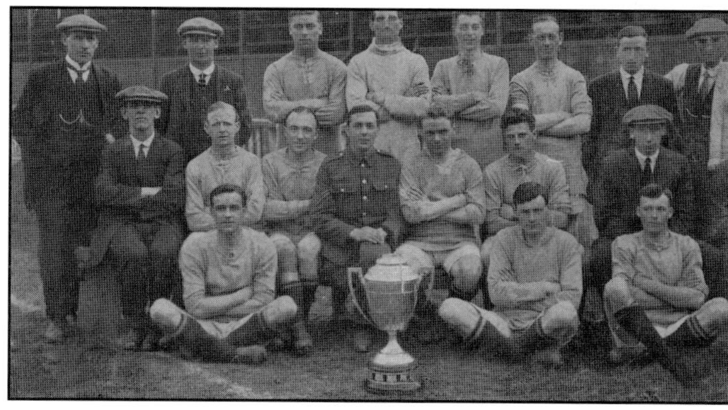

Above: *This was one of 500 postcards of the Tranmere Rovers team - who were winners of the Lancashire Combination Cup 1913-14 - sold at 2d each at a testimonial match for Ralph Holden, a former captain of* ***Tranmere*** *Rovers, who lost a leg in the Great War. The match against Liverpool was played at Prenton Park 3 May 1919. This event raised £450 for him, which included the gate money, raffles etc*

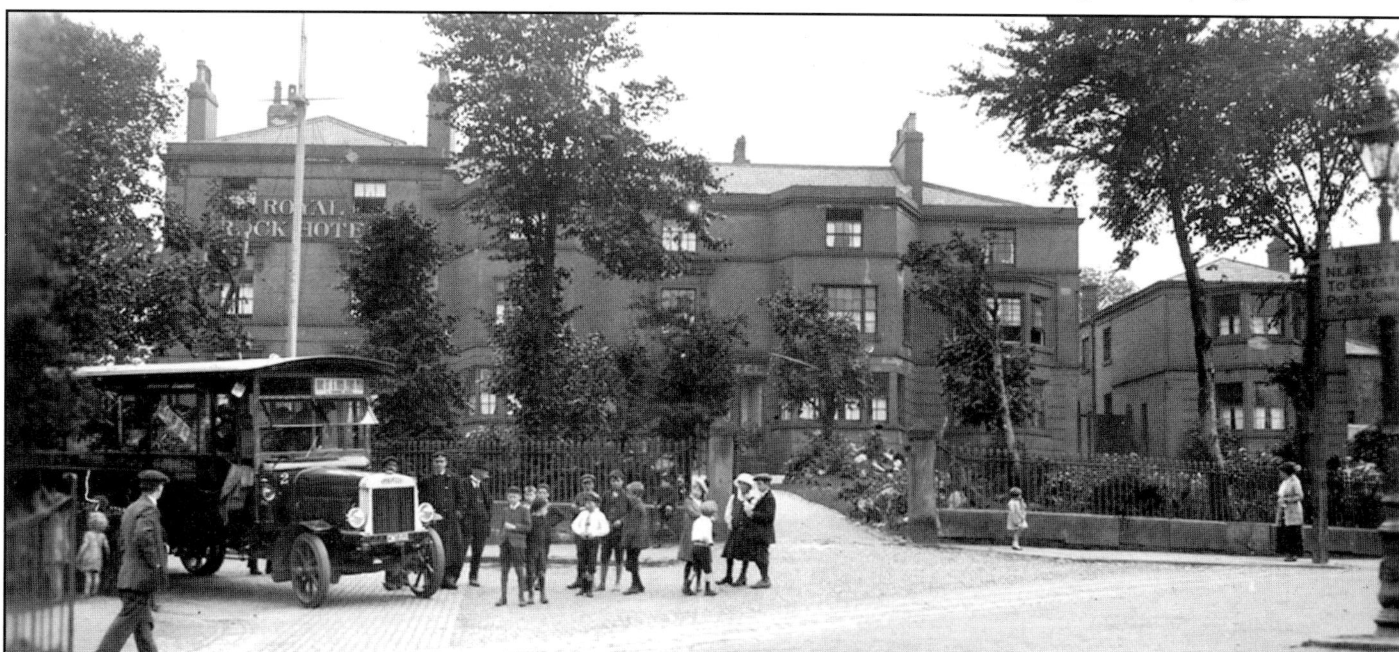

Above: *The young children are looking in awe at the motor bus parked outside the entrance to the* Royal Rock Hotel ***Rock Ferry****. Birkenhead Corporation started their bus service between Rock Ferry Pier and Park Station* ***Birkenhead*** *on 12 July 1919 using Leyland 32 seater 'O' type buses - No.2 is seen here. The* Royal Rock Hotel *was erected c1805 and in 1836 the hotel and pleasure Gardens were extended. The 'Royal' title was conferred by King George III who stayed here whilst visiting friends. The hotel was demolished in the 1960s when the Rock Ferry by-pass was built*[BB + RF]

1920

– Wirral Joint Hospital Board provided new wards for general and maternity patients and a new nurses' home
– *The Elms*, a large house with grounds in **Upton** Village, was bought by public subscription for £2,000 - a War Memorial was erected in the front of the building and the building opened as a sports and social centre called Victory Hall [see photo 1921]
– Application was made by three policewomen in the **Birkenhead** Police Force to be placed on the same pay scale as men. The Chief Constable stated that in his experience "they were only fit for the lighter parts of police work and that they are considerably below the value of policemen". Two of the policewomen resigned and the other one left the force in March 1921[MQP]
– The Chief Constable of **Birkenhead** reported that following the police strike the previous year "the force had improved in both contentment, efficiency and discipline"[MQP]
– **Bidston** War Memorial unveiled[WPPB]
– **Birkenhead** Park Rugby Football Club doubled the size of its stand[SOUV]
– War Memorial in the form of a bronze tablet was unveiled at the Wesley Church, Higher **Tranmere** for those members of the church who died in the Great War[SOUV]
– Great Disaster at Alfred Dock, **Birkenhead**
– The Wirral and District Association Cup was 'lost' for two years 1921 and 1922[WDFA] [see photo 1923]

Mar 25 **Thingwall** Hall gifted in Miss MC Twigge's will as a country home for sick children

Mar 31 **Bidston** Aerodrome opened - organised by the Great Northern Syndicate Ltd. The Golden Eagle Aviation Co Ltd used the GE1 - a war machine of the De Haviland type - modified and which had been adapted for passengers, also the DH6 which had been used during the First World War [see advert]

Mersey Window Cleaning Co.,
7. LOWWOOD GROVE,
WOODLANDS.
'Phone 1385.
Contractors for every description of Window Cleaning.

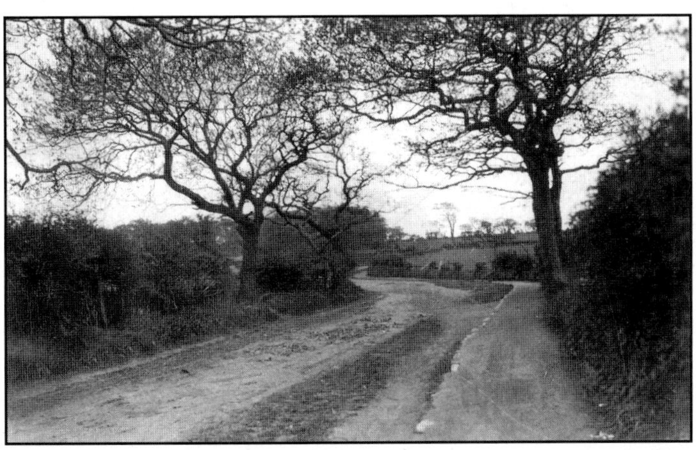

Above: *Kings Lane Higher **Bebington** was once surrounded by fields before the road widened and houses built either side in the 1930s. It is seen here with not a brick in sight! [see 1932]*

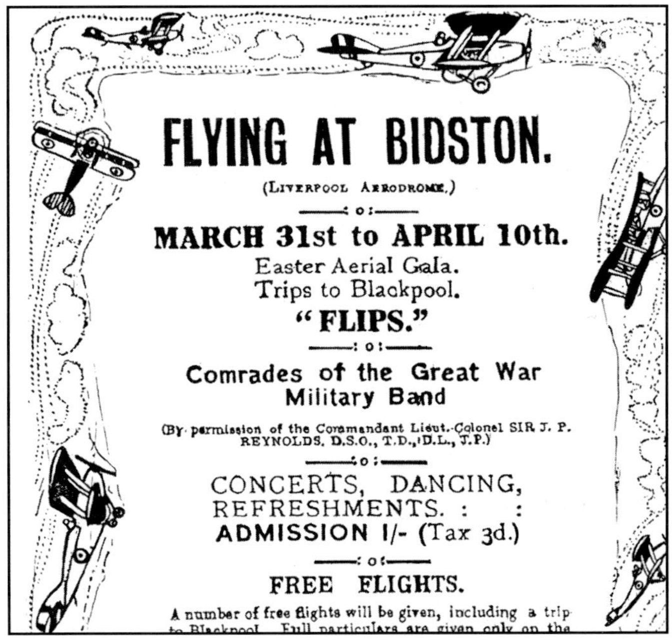

Above: ***Bidston** Aerodrome opened 31 March 1920 - organised by the Great Northern Syndicate Ltd. The Golden Eagle Aviation Co Ltd. They used a modified GE1 - a war machine of the De Haviland type - which had been adapted for passengers and the DH6 which had been used during the First World War. Bidston was advertised as '**Liverpool** Aerodrome'*

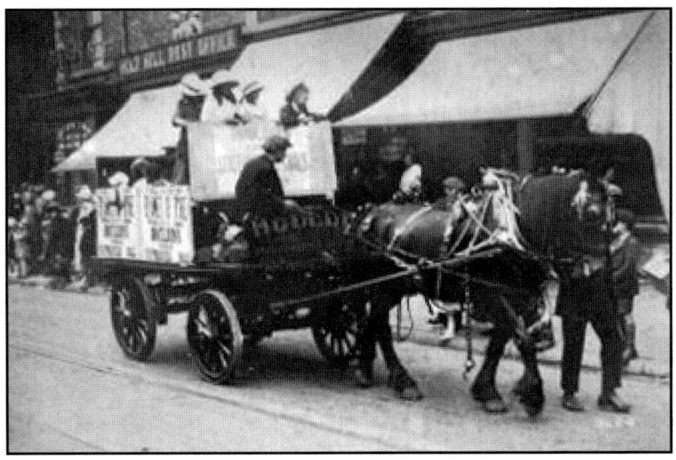

Above: *Houldin's decorated lorry is passing Holt Hill Post Office, Church Road Higher **Tranmere***

KNOWLES & JONES,
General Drapers & House Furnishers.

Departments: BLANKETS. SHEETS. QUILTS. PRINTS. MUSLINS. DRESS GOODS. COSTUMES. MANTLES. MILLINERY. FANCY GOODS.

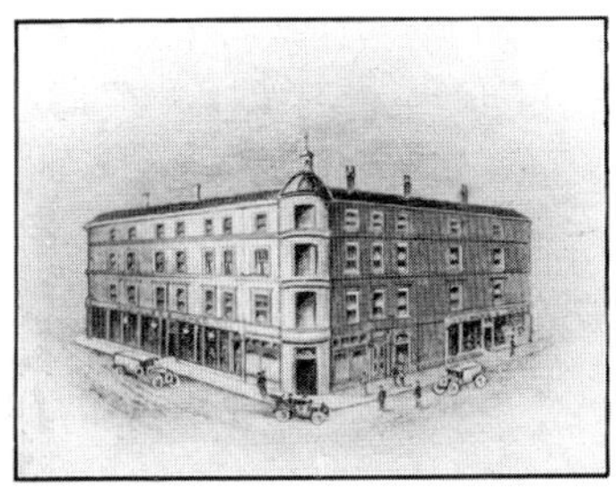

Departments: GLOVES. CORSETS. HOSIERY. CARPETS. OILCLOTHS. LINOLEUMS. BEDSTEADS. BEDDING. BLINDS. FURNITURE.

4, 6 & 8 Conway Street, and 96, Hamilton Street.
Telephone 342. BIRKENHEAD. Estimates Free.

Above: *The company of Knowles & Jones, general drapers and silk merchants, 4 - 8 Conway Street **Birkenhead,** dates back to the 1870s - they sold the business between the wars - George Sturla and Son later traded here*

1921

– Brass Tablet War Memorial placed in St Peter's Church **Rock Ferry** inscribed with the names of Church members who gave their lives in the First World War[SOUV]

– Holy Name RC Church, Beresford Road, **Oxton**, consecrated [see also 1899 & 1931][DoS]

Mar 19 Bus service commenced between Charing Cross, **Birkenhead**, and **Seacombe** Ferry[TBW]

July 20 **Upton** War Memorial unveiled outside the Victory Hall in memory of those killed in the First World War [see photo][SUAH]

Aug 15 Alwen Water Scheme completed and opened - supplying water to the **Birkenhead** area from North Wales - via the Cross Hill Reservoir at **Thingwall**

Aug 21 **Tranmere** Rovers played their first Football League game at home against Crewe Alaxandra in the Third Division North which they won 4-1[TR1921]

Sept 17 Disaster at Clover Clayton's Dry Dock, **Birkenhead** when five apprentices were killed whilst dismantling the ex-German Submarine *Deutschland*

Oct 21 **Birkenhead** YWCA opened its new Fearnley Hall - built at a cost of £2,034[SOUV]

Oct 24 Bus service commenced between Charing Cross, **Birkenhead** and **Liscard** Village[BB]

Nov 11 James Williams, a **Birkenhead** fireman, was injured when a maroon (gun) blew up at Hamilton Square for the Armistice Day Gun Salute in front of the Town Hall - he died five days later

Dec A Palm House was erected in **Birkenhead** Park [see photos][TPG]

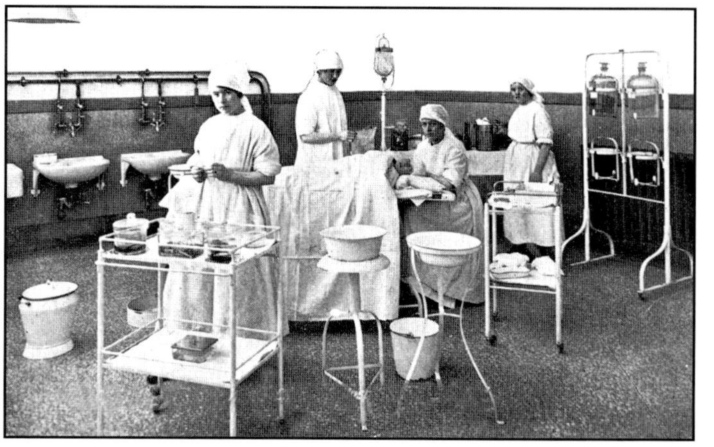

Above: *This postcard of the operating theatre, Wirral Children's Hospital, Woodchurch Road* ***Birkenhead****, was one of a series of postcards sold to raise funds for the hospital*

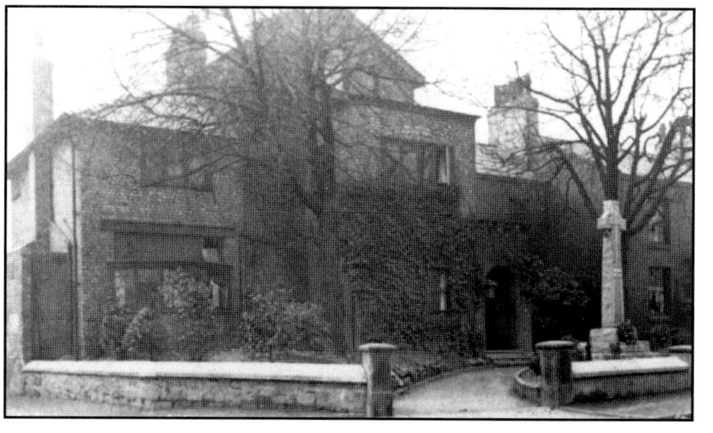

Above: *The Elms, a large house with grounds, on the corner of Upton Road and Salacre Lane* **Upton** *Village, was bought by public subscription for £2,000 in memory of those men of Upton who were killed in the First World War. The War Memorial on the right was erected in the front of the building and unveiled 22 July 1921. The building opened as a sports and social centre called 'Victory Hall'*

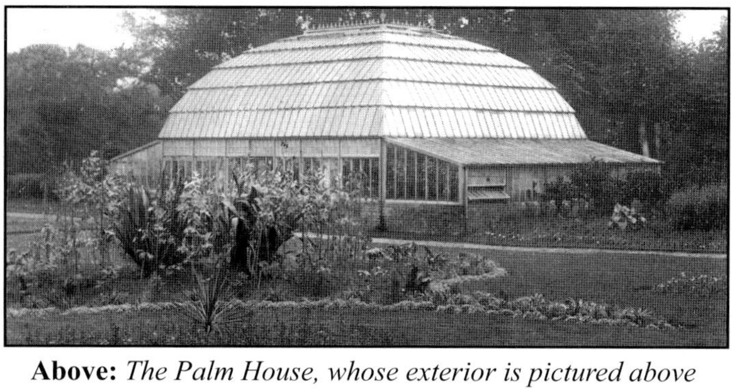

Above: *The Palm House, whose exterior is pictured above was erected in the Upper Park in* ***Birkenhead*** *Park, using the unemployment relief scheme, in 1921. It was demolished in 1947 with the site later being occupied by the conservatory which was built in the 1950s*

Below: *Interior of the Palm House with fine looking statues*[BP]

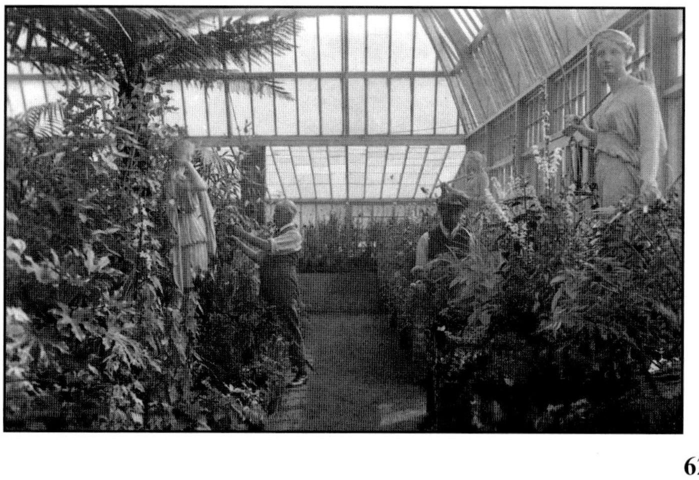

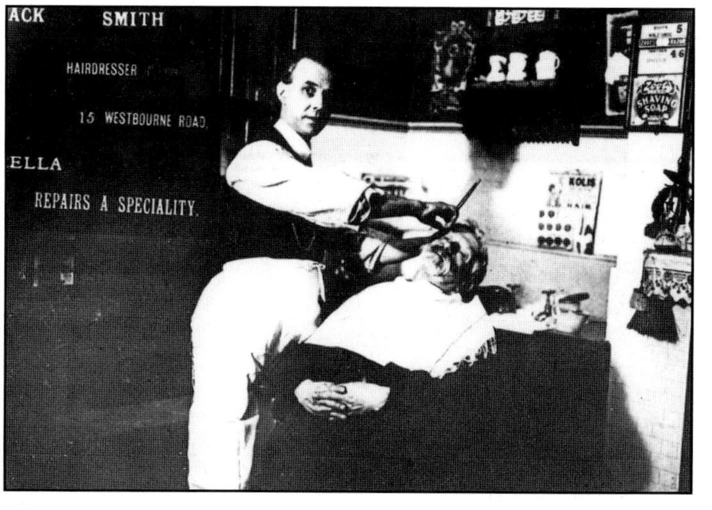

Above: *This photograph of a gentleman being shaved by a barber was shown twice nightly in the advertisments at the* Argyle Theatre *Argyle Street* ***Birkenhead****. As can be seen at the back it was for Jack Smith - Hairdresser - 15 Westbourne Road Birkenhead. The cost of a haircut then was 2/6d (12.5p)*

1922

– 1922 was a year of widespread unemployment with Government departments making economies. **Birkenhead** Police had to comply and reduce the strength of the force also a 2.5% reduction in pay[MQP]

– The **Birkenhead** YWCA Hostels at 42-44 The Woodlands for the first time had not been full owing to a lack of employment in the town[SOUV]

– Star Yachts (Model Boats) founded by Franz Denye in Birkenhead[YWPH]

Jan 31 **New Ferry** ferry service closed following demolition of the pier by a drifting steamer

Feb 5 **Oxton** Congregational Church gutted by fire [see photo]

Apr 15 **Upton** Racecourse opened on Moreton Road between Upton and **Moreton** [now the Upton spur road for the M53 Motorway - see Advert][OTT]

Dec 6 A fatal accident occurred at **Birkenhead** Park Station when the driver of a train arriving from **West Kirby** misread the signal in the misty dusk and collided with a departing train. This was the first (and only) fatal accident involving a passenger on the Wirral Railway[RSoW]

Dec 16 Lady Lever Art Gallery, **Port Sunlight**, opened

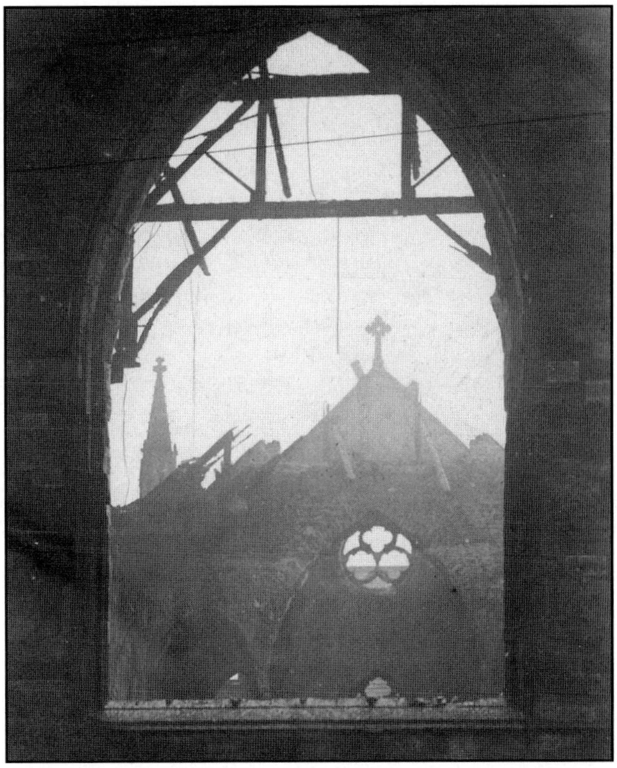

Above: *The ruins of Oxton Road Congregational Church* ***Birkenhead*** *can be seen after a fire gutted the Church 5 February 1922 only one month after re-opening following re-decoration and alteration. Built at the junction of Woodchurch Road and Balls Road it opened in 1858. The church re-opened September 1923*

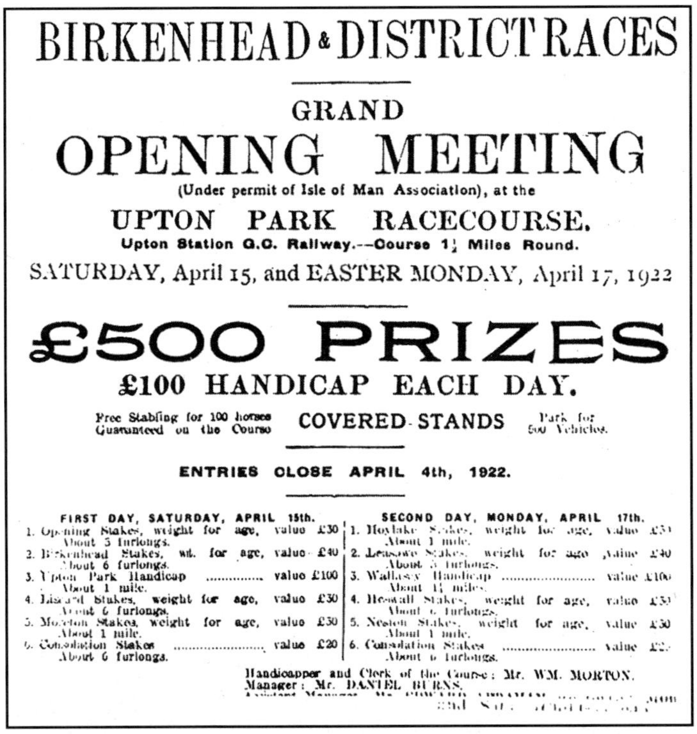

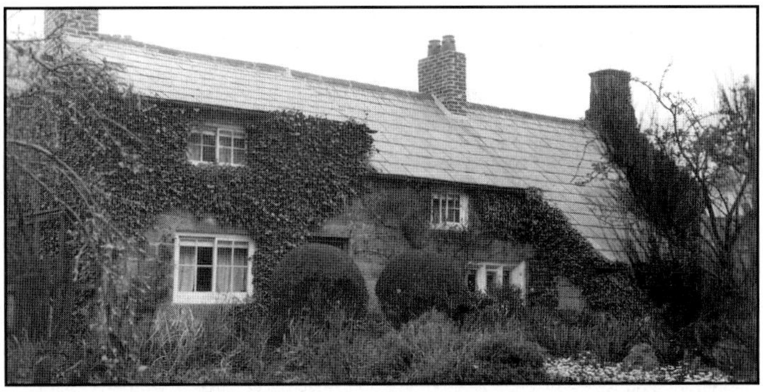

Above: *The original school, pictured here at* ***Bidston****, dated back to 1636. Living accommodation for the headmaster was added to the school house c1810. Due to an increase in demand, a new school was built in Bidston Village Road for £350, opening 13 August 1838. Following an air raid on 12/13 March 1941, the original schoolhouse was destroyed by incendiary bombs*

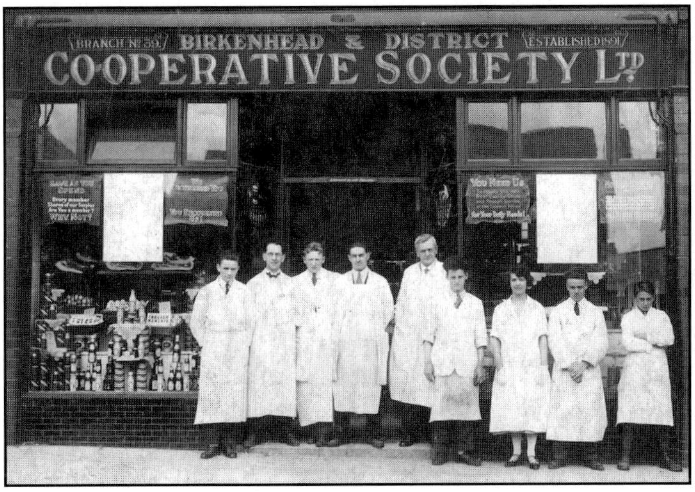

Above: *The staff of* ***Birkenhead*** *Co-op branch No.39 pose outside the shop probably for a company photograph*

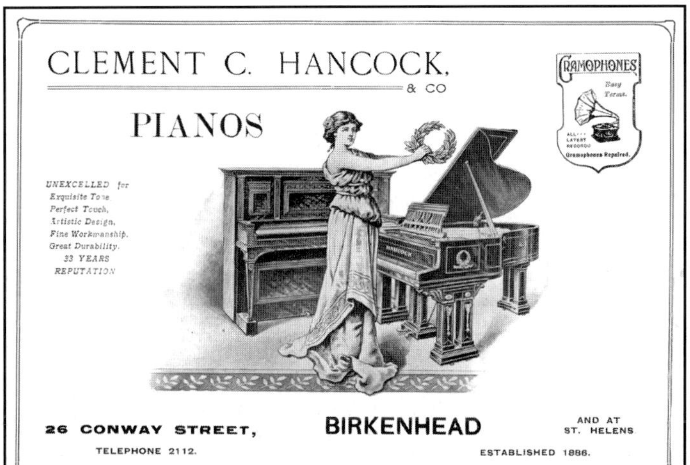

1923

Jan 1 Wirral Railway absorbed into the London, Midland and Scottish Railway[RSoW]

Apr 30 Captain AC Dawson appointed the new Chief Constable of **Birkenhead**[MQP]

Sept 27 **Oxton** Road Congregational Church, Birkenhead, reopened following restoration after fire [see 1922]

Oct **Birkenhead** Police purchased a four-speed motor cycle combination for £91. This was the founding of the 'modern' Traffic department[MQP]

Oct 14 War Memorial near St Andrew's Church Lower **Bebington** unveiled [see photo][SOUV]

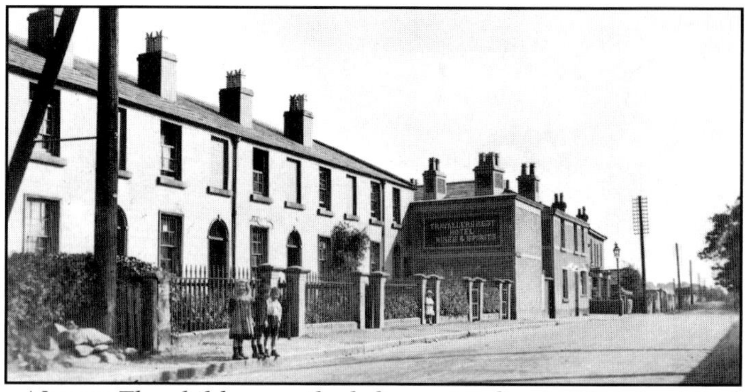

Above: *The children on the left are standing in Storeton Road near the* Travellers Rest Hotel *on the corner of Village Road Higher* ***Bebington*** *- note the size of the telegraph poles*

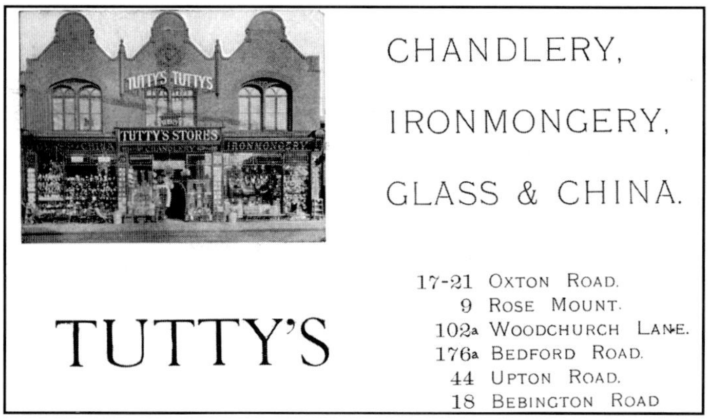

Above: *This was an advert for Tutty's Stores and shows their Oxton Road* ***Birkenhead*** *store which operated from 1904 to 1937 when they sold out to Rostances*

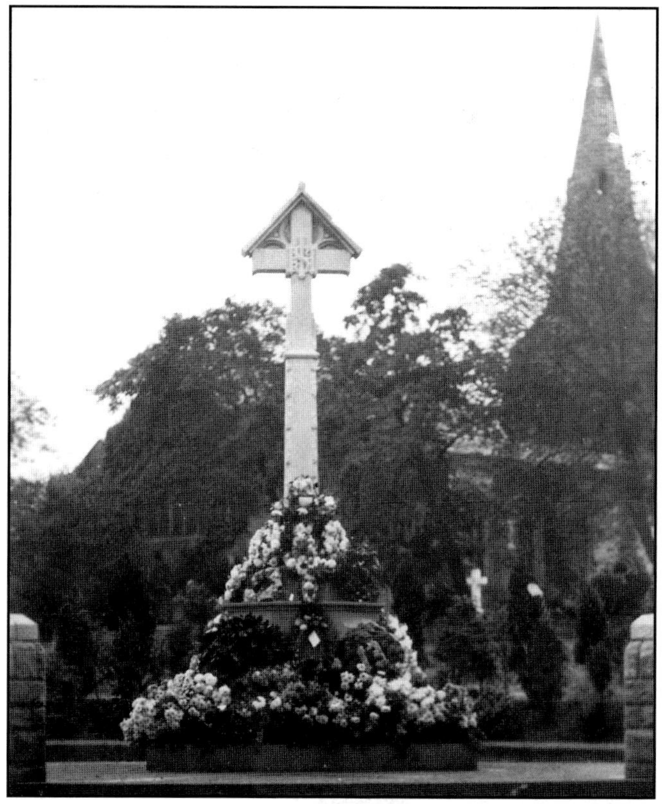

Above: ***Bebington*** *War Memorial, pictured in Church Road with St Andrew's Church in the background, was unveiled 14 October 1923 - the names of those connected with the church are inscribed on an oak Memorial Tablet in the Church*

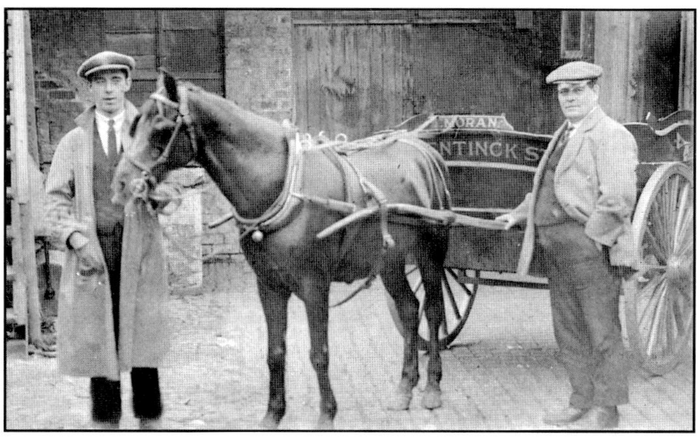

Two horses and carts used for delivering:- **Above:** *belonged to T Moran of 101 Bentinck Street* ***Birkenhead*** *- described in 1923 as a 'milk dealer'*
Below: *CA Birss 7 Greenway Road Hr* ***Tranmere*** *- dealer in fish, poultry and greengrocer*

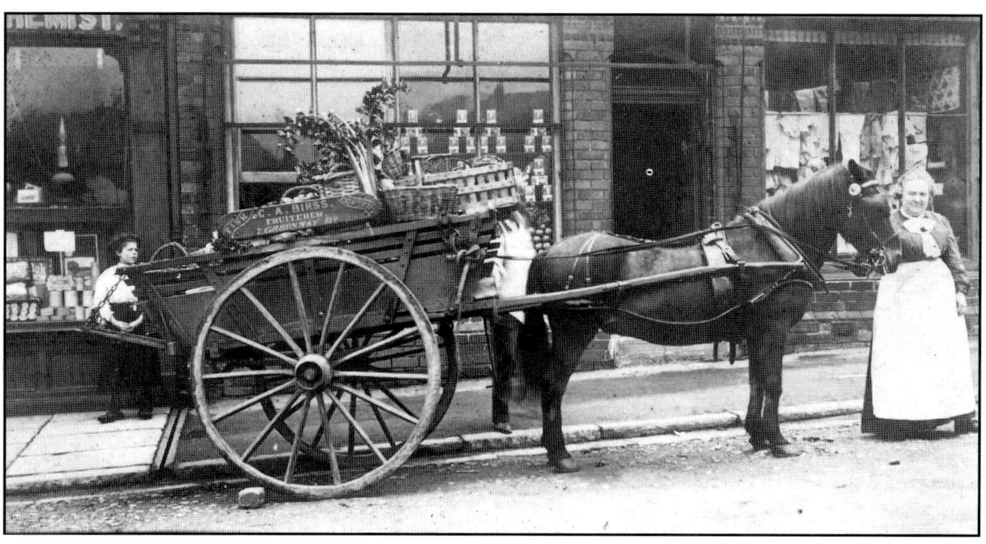

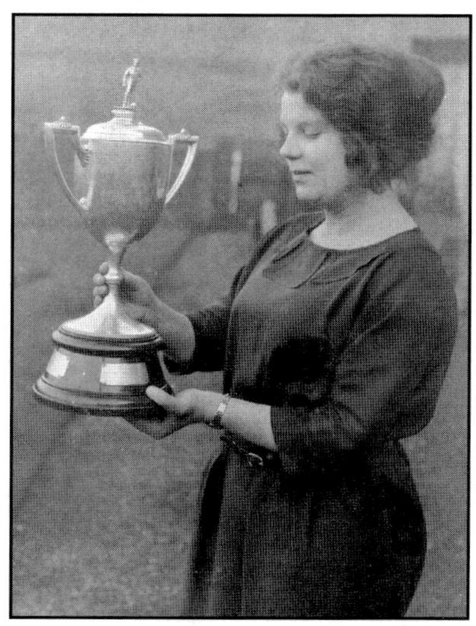

Above: *The Wirral Football Amateur Cup introduced in 1892 was lost for two years - the finder is pictured in 1923*

1924

– **Oxton** Cricket Club third team wicket was laid - with a tent being used until a new pavilion was built in 1927 - two new tennis courts were also laid then[SOUV]

Apr 9 Opening of Gorsey Lane, **Wallasey**, the new Highway Link between **Wallasey** & **Birkenhead** at a cost of £14,000

June 2 An attempt on Mount Everest resulted in the death of Mr Leigh Mallory and Mr AC [Sandy] Irvine [both of **Birkenhead**]. A report of 21st June said they were last seen within several hunderd feet of the summit - it may never be known whether they were the first to conquer Everest [see 1957]

Aug 24 Last Meeting at **Upton** racecourse - the land was later purchased by **Wallasey** Corporation - 111.5 acres for £30,335 17s 6d[OTT]

Sept 13 Dixie Dean made his debut for **Tranmere** Rovers, having been transferred from **Pensby** FC [see photo][TR1921]

Sept 28 New Church building of the Church of Christ, Grange Road West **Birkenhead** opened [see sketch][SOUV]

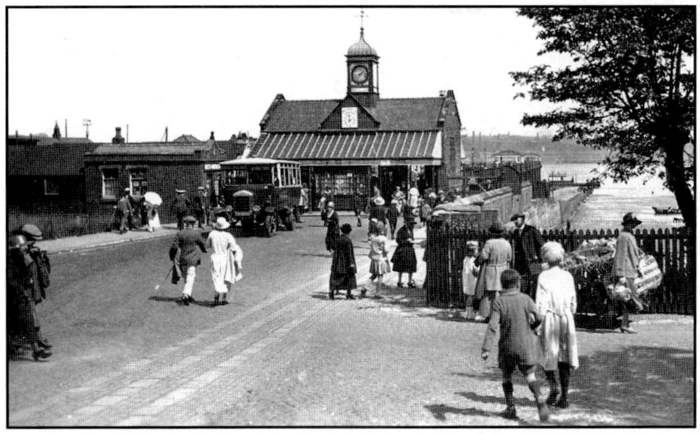

Above: *A busy scene at* ***Rock Ferry*** *Pier where the Birkenhead Corporation Straker Squire 'A' single-decker bus is waiting for passengers from the ferry boat to transport them to Moreton. The square white clock above the entrance to the ferry shows the time the next boat leaves for Liverpool. Although popular here, by 1939, due to lack of passengers, the ferry closed down [see 1939]*

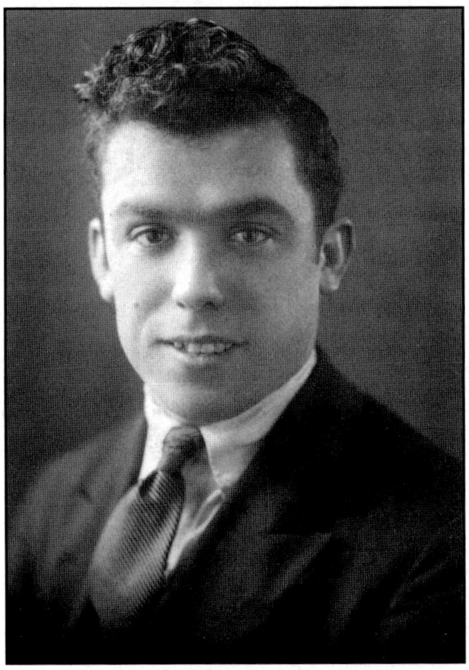

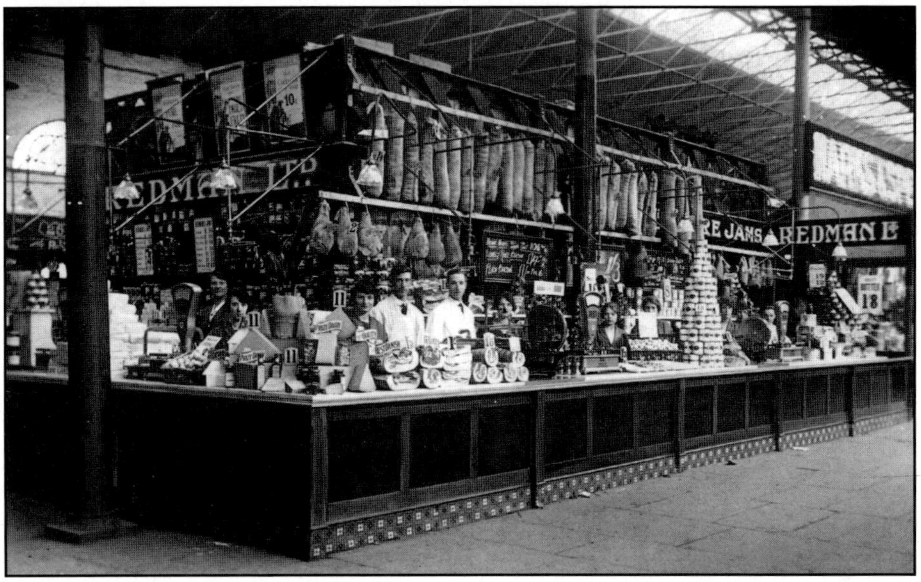

Left: *Dixie Dean, pictured above, was signed by Tranmere Rovers from Pensby AFC in 1924 and after 30 games and 27 goals he was transferred to Everton in 1925 for £3,000*[TR1921]

Above: *One of two Redman's grocery stalls in the old* ***Birkenhead*** *Market*

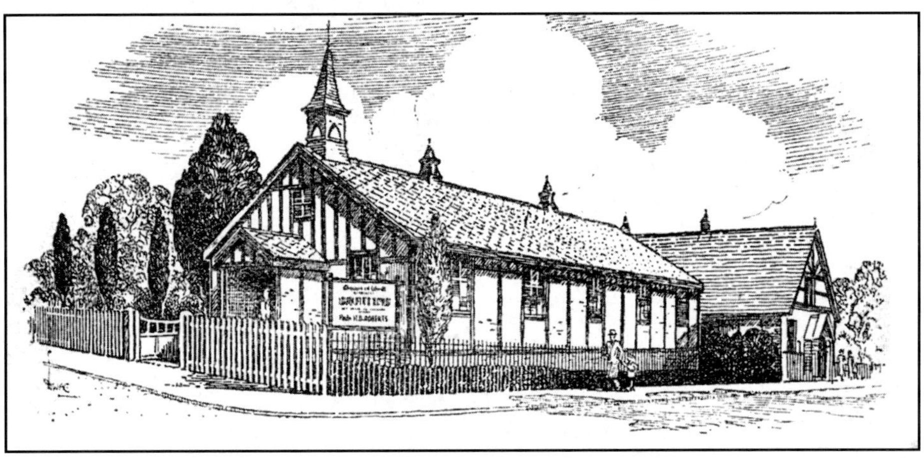

Above: *The Church of Christ in* ***Birkenhead*** *was founded in 1886 with being held services in the* Claughton Music Hall, *until their first Church was built in Alvanley Place in 1891. The new Church, pictured left, was opened in Grange Road West in 1924 and was used until 1951 when they bought the Catholic Apostolic Church in Park Road South [see 1951]*

OPEN-AIR

GYM. DISPLAYS

BY

Y.M.C.A. Gym. Members

IN BIRKENHEAD PARK

(Balaclava Ground)

On THURSDAY, 28th AUGUST, 1924,

At 7-30 p.m., ALSO IN

VICTORIA PARK (TRANMERE)

ON

MONDAY, 1st SEPTEMBER, 1924,

At 7-30 p.m.

The POST OFFICE MILITARY BAND will play at Birkenhead Park.

Y.M.C.A. GYM. PARTICULARS.

Gym. re-opens 20th September, 1924, at 7-45 p.m.

CLASSES and FEES:

	Y.M.	Gym.	Total
Seniors (under 21) -	7/6	7/6	15/-
,, (over 21) -	10/-	10/-	20/-
Juniors (Boys under 17)	5/-	2/6	7/6
Ladies - - - -		7/6 per quarter	
Junior Ladies - -		6/- ,,	
Girls - - - -		5/- ,,	
Boys - - - -		5/- ,,	

H. COURTENAY BICKLEY, *Hon. Sec.*
CHAS. LORD, B.A.P.T., M.I.H.
W. H. RALSTON, *Gen Sec.*

1925

– **Rock Ferry** & Park High [**Birkenhead**] schools for boys established[SOUV]

– SS *Upton* built by Cammell Laird **Birkenhead** for the **Rock Ferry** to **Liverpool** route. When the service closed in 1939 it was kept for the Woodside service as a back-up boat[WCS]

– Luggage boats *Oxton* & *Bidston* launched at Cammell Laird **Birkenhead** for the transportation of vehicular traffic across the Mersey. Following the opening of the Mersey Road Tunnel in 1934, trade on this route declined and the service closed July 1941. The boats were then fitted with cranes and used to unload aircraft , in mid-river during the war, brought over by boat from America

– The ***Birkenhead*** *News* introduced the 'Children's Corner' an idea of Miss Gladys Fitzpatrick who became 'Aunty Gladys' [see this page][FB]

Jan 10 Nellie Clarke, an 11 year old girl, was murdered in **Rock Ferry** - the murderer was never found[MMB]

Mar 14 Dixie Dean played his last game for **Tranmere** Rovers having scored 27 goals in 30 games - he was transferred to Everton FC for a record fee of £3,000[TR1921]

May 18 Referendum for Ratepayers on Mersey Tunnel Bill - in favour by majority of 4:1

July 5 Cenotaph in Hamilton Square, **Birkenhead**, unveiled in memory of the 1,293 men of Birkenhead who fell in the First World War [see photo][SOUV]

Nov 6 **Birkenhead** Institute's Pavilion was opened in the newly acquired seven acres of playing fields in Ingleborough Road and named the "Mount Road Memorial Ground" as a memorial to the old boys who died in the First World War[SOUV]

Dec 16 The first Mersey Road Tunnel shaft sunk at the ceremonial inauguration by HRH Princess Mary and Viscount Lascelles

Dec 17 Princess Mary launched the battleship HMS *Rodney* at Cammell Laird, **Birkenhead**[MOI]

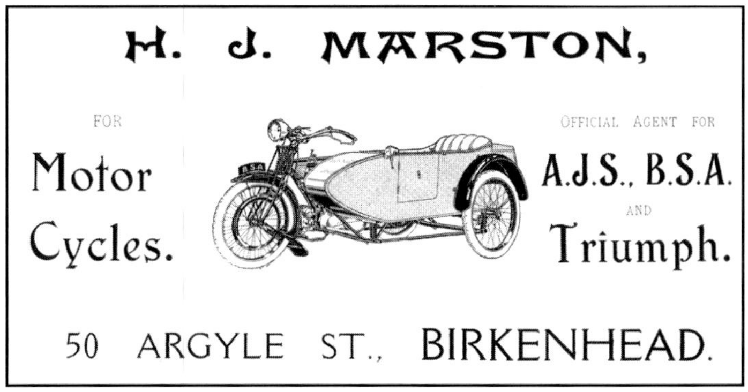

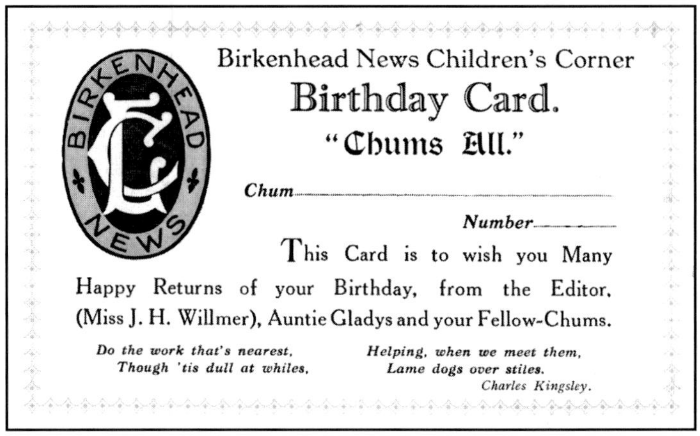

Above: *This was one of the birthday cards sent by 'Aunty Gladys to a 'chum'. The idea of a 'Children's Corner' for the* **Birkenhead** News *was that of Miss Gladys Fitzpatrick who became 'Aunty Gladys'*

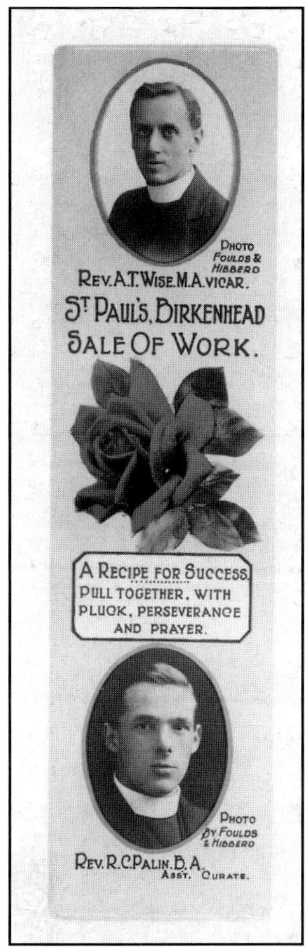

Above: *This bookmark was sold at St Paul's Church in Argyle Street* ***Birkenhead*** *in aid of their 'Sale of Work' and featured pictures of the then Vicar Rev AT Wise and the assistant Curate Rev RC Palin*

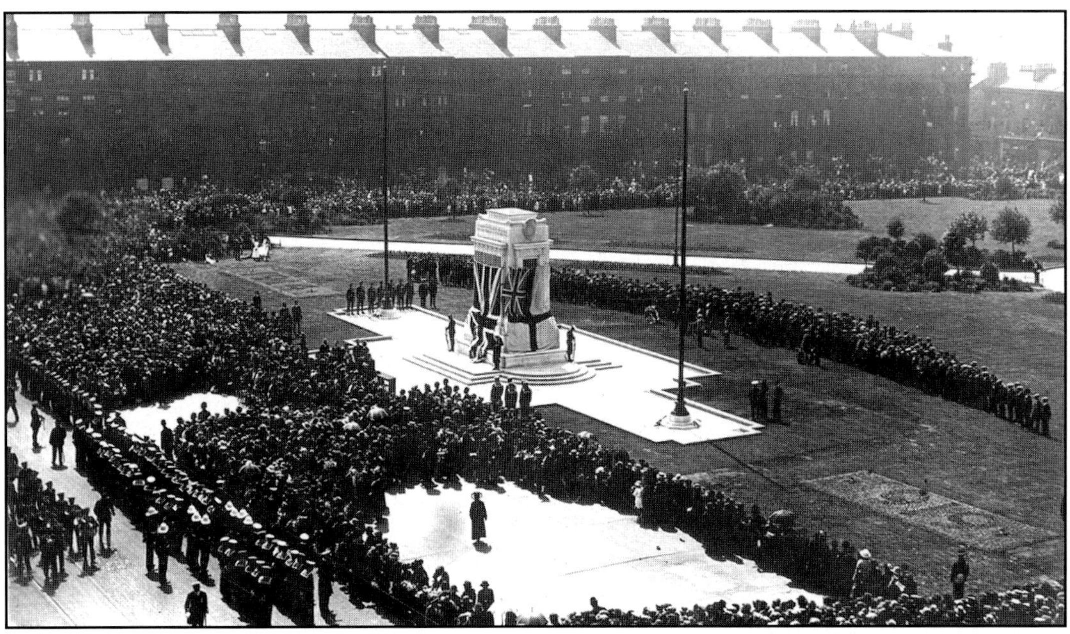

Above: *The vast crowds are seen around Hamilton Square,* ***Birkenhead****, at the unveiling of the Cenotaph in front of the Town Hall 5 July 1925. They reflected the feelings of the nation who were indebted to those who had given their lives in the Great War. The group behind the Cenotaph were those Birkenhead men who had taken part in the fighting - which had ended seven years previously*

1926

– **Birkenhead** Borough Hospital in Park Road North changed its name to Birkenhead General Hospital[RPW]

– **Birkenhead** Amateur Operatic Society gave their first performance "In the days of good Queen Bess"

– Additional water to supply **Wallasey** from Lake Alwen, North Wales agreed with **Birkenhead** Corporation

May 3 General Strike began - **Birkenhead** was more fortunate than others parts of the country during the General Strike where only two persons were before the court for disorder arising out of that crisis[MQP]

May 11 Police escort for **Birkenhead** Corporation buses on the **Rock Ferry** and **Prenton** routes, which were manned by volunteers - the windows were protected by wire netting[TBB]

Aug Lord Leverhulme sold 425 acres of **Arrowe** Park to Birkenhead Corporation [see photo 1927]

Aug 14 Last recorded meeting at **Bidston** Racecourse[OTT]

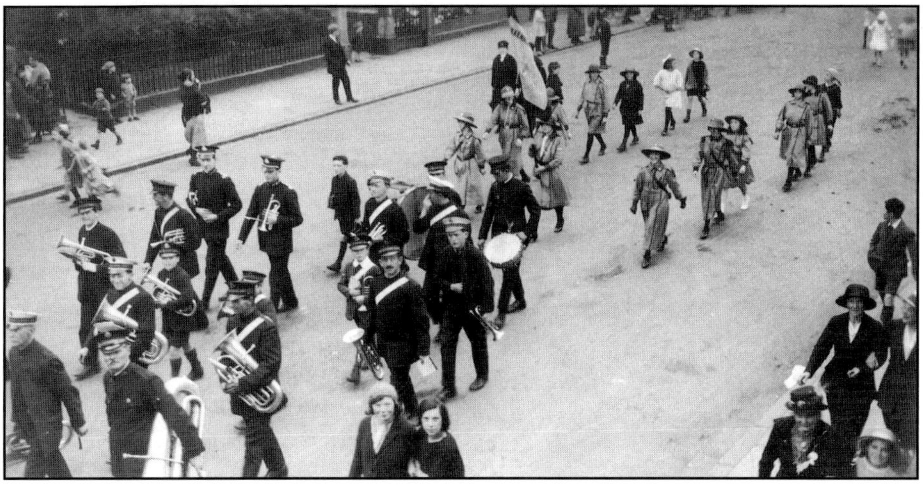

Left: *The Salvation Army Band are followed by a small group of Girl Guides, who were taking part in the Children's Day procession, walking down Cleveland Street* ***Birkenhead***

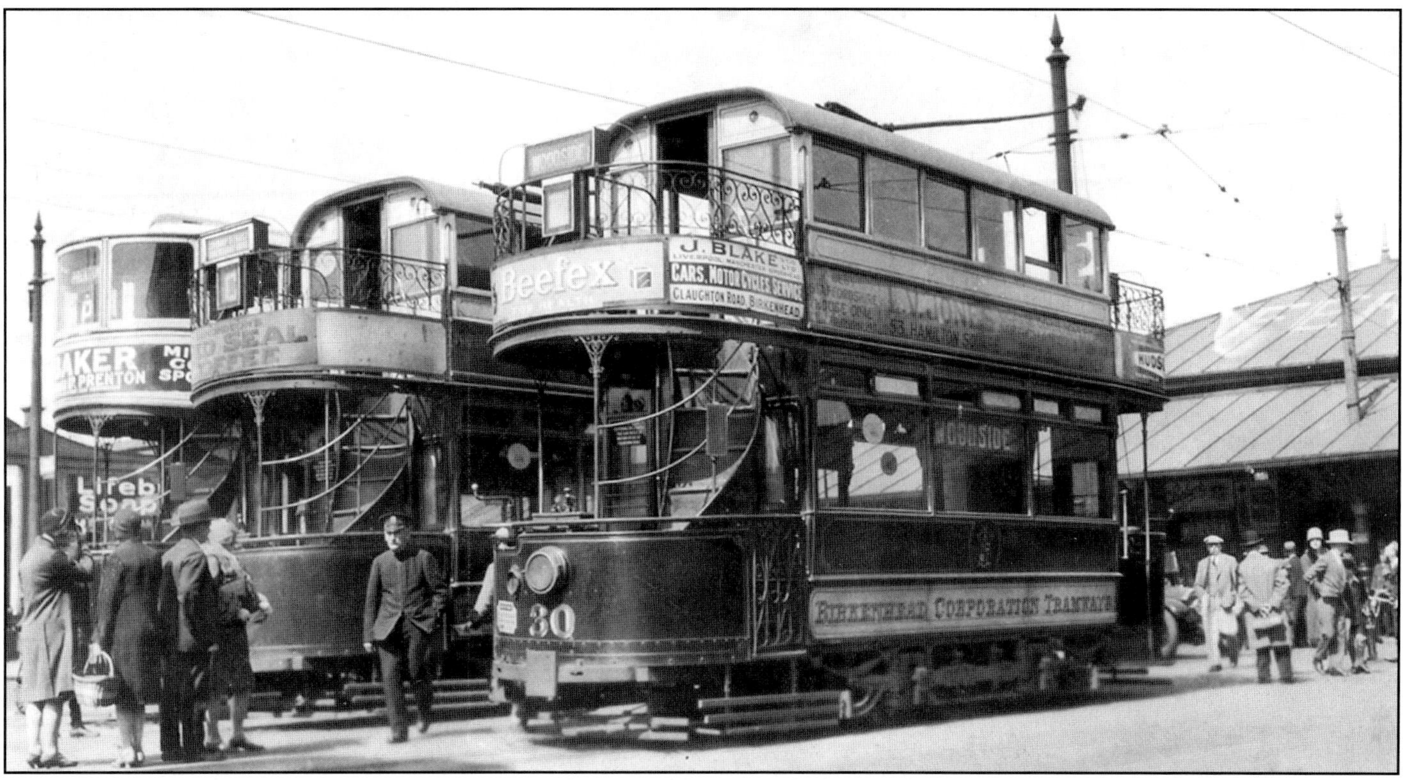

Above: *Three* ***Birkenhead*** *Corporation trams wait for passengers outside the Woodside Ferry Terminal entrance. The drab state of the trams was due to lack of funding as the end of the tram system was in sight - to be replaced by buses when the tramway closed in 1937*

1927

– Sir Ian Walker made a gift to Birkenhead Corporation of 15 acres of land on the western boundary of the Borough for a public park at **Prenton.** Its boundaries **were** Prenton Lane in the north, Golf Links Road to the east and Prenton Golf Club to the south.
During the Second World War the park was used as allotments for local residents to grow their own vegetables. The park was restored to its original state after the war in 1946

Jan 4 Blue Star line ship *Arondura* launched at Cammell Laird

Jan 21 Wirral Ladies Golf Club bought the land they had previously leased from the Earl of Shrewsbury in Bidston Road **Oxton** for £17,000[WLGC]

Feb 17 The new organ at Christ Church Hr **Bebington** was dedicated - followed by a Recital[SOUV]

May 23 Boys Brigade 6th Birkenhead Company formed at **Tranmere**

Jun 26 to 2 July - celebrations were held to mark **Birkenhead** Borough's 50th Anniversary 1877 to 1927[PROG]

Jun 27 Procession of Tramcars Ancient and Modern from the Laird Street Depot, **Birkenhead** led by a horse-drawn tramcar which was in use 50 years previously in 1877; a decorated and illuminated electric tramcar in service 25 years previously and a motor bus of the latest type - a band accompanied the procession on a different route for each of five days [see photo][PROG]

July 20 Birkenhead School **Oxton** held an Elizabethan Fayre to celebrate the Borough's 50th Anniversary - all the boys and masters dressed up in Elizabethan costume - the events included pageants, plays, stalls, maypole, music etc[BSPH]

Aug 13 HMS *Rodney*, build at Cammell Laird, left the Mersey for Portsmouth where it was commissioned into the Royal Navy

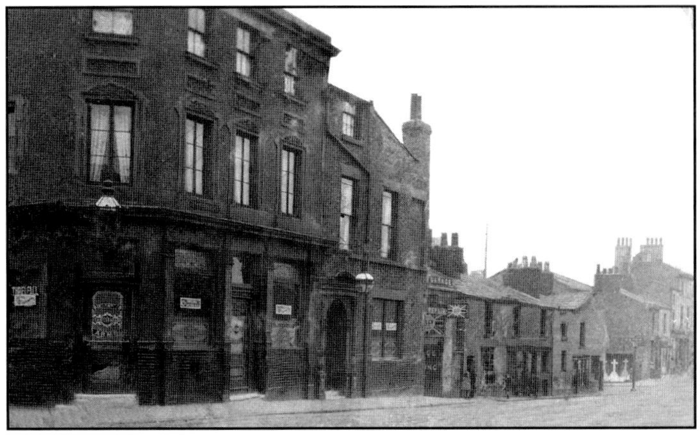

Above: *The* Birkenhead Arms *can be seen in Chester Street* ***Birkenhead*** *on the corner of Grange Street*

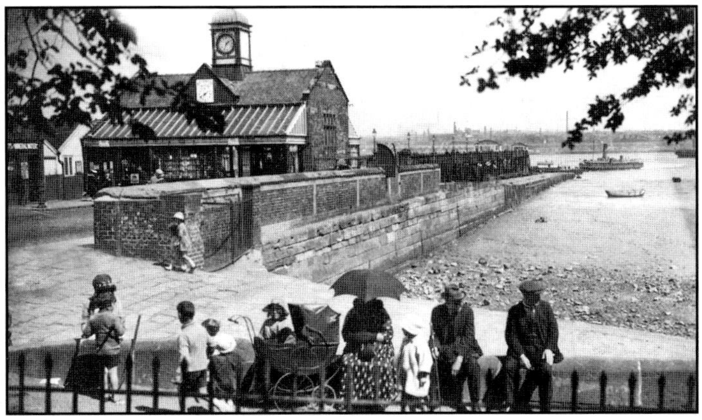

Above: ***Rock Ferry*** *ferry terminus building is on the left - the original slipway on the right dated back to 1820 when it was built by Thomas Morecroft to enable passengers to board ferries whether high or low tides. Due to falling passenger numbers (one likely reason was the opening of the Mersey Queensway Tunnel in 1934) the service closed in 1939 [see 1939]*

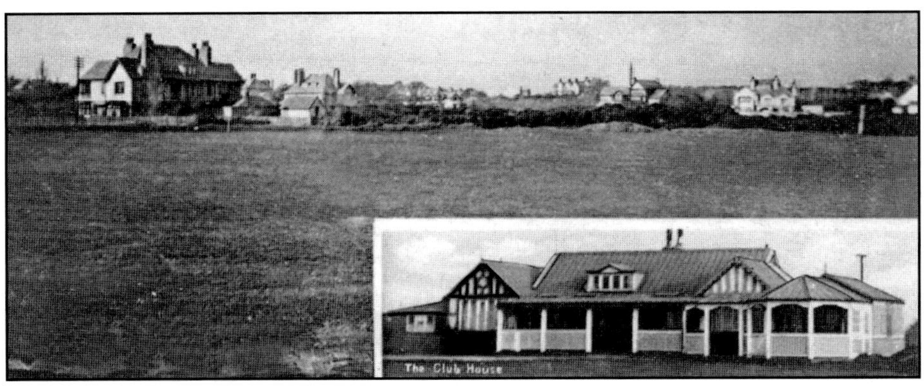

Right: *Part of the Wirral Ladies' Golf Club course in Bidston Road* ***Oxton*** *and the original clubhouse [as an inset] are seen on this postcard. The club was founded in 1894 but it was not until 1921 that they bought the land they had previously leased from the Earl of Shrewsbury for £17,000*

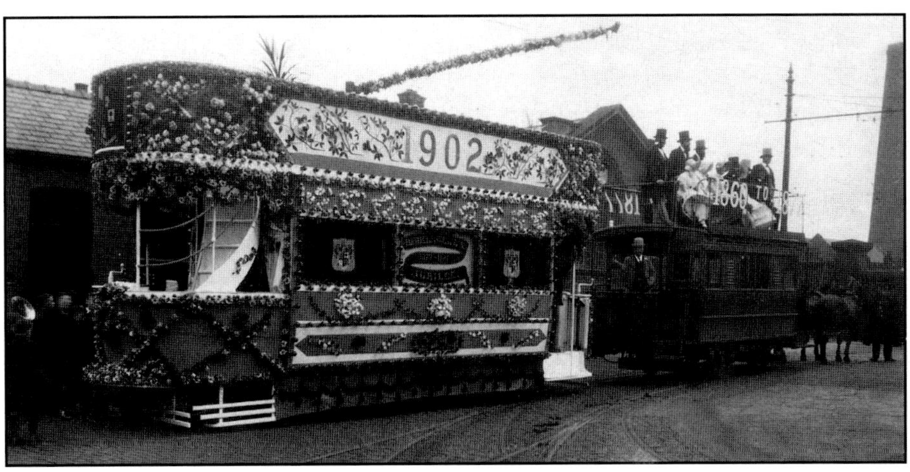

Left: *Two* ***Birkenhead*** *trams are pictured at the Laird Street depot. They both took part in the Procession of Tramcars Ancient and Modern from here led by the horse-drawn tramcar on the right, which was in use 50 years previously in 1877 - note the passengers on top in period costume. The decorated and illuminated electric tramcar on the left had been in service for 25 years. A motor bus of the latest type followed behind - then a band accompanied the procession on a different route for each of the five days. This was part of the celebrations for the Borough's 50th anniversary*

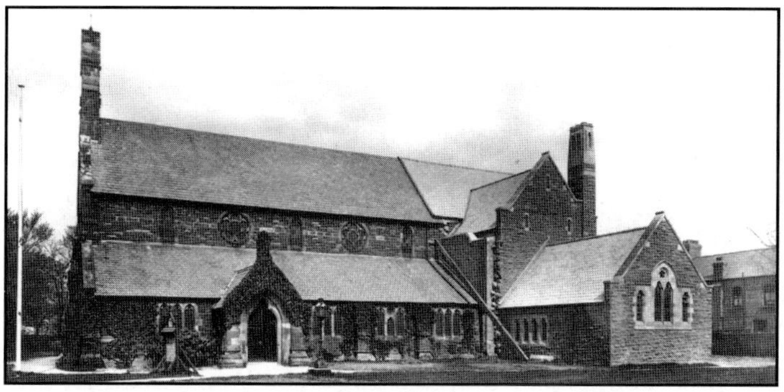

Above: *St Mark the Evangelist Church, pictured in New Chester Road* **New Ferry**, *was opened in 1867 at a cost of £3,500. It was built of red sandstone in the early English style and had seating for 600 people*

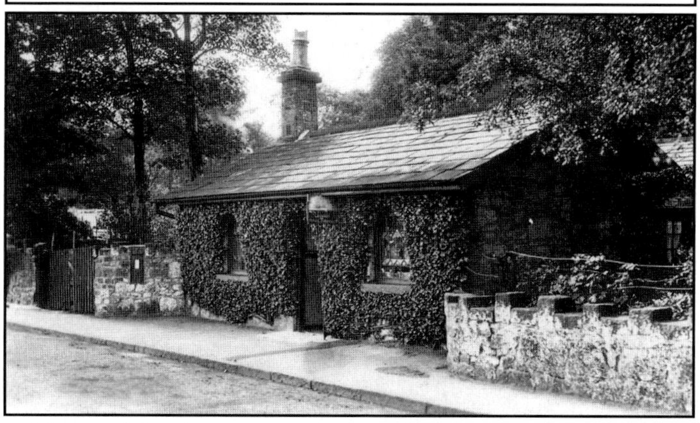

Above: *This tiny, ivy-covered cottage in Church Lane was used as the* ***Woodchurch*** *Post Office [see the post box set into the far wall]. It dated back to at least 1850 when William Peilin was the Sub Postmaster - the building was demolished in the late 1930s when the roads here were widened*

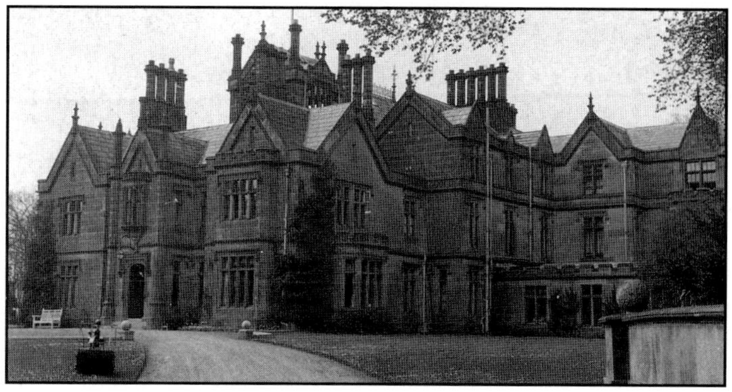

Above: ***Arrowe*** *Hall was a neo-Elizabethan building, built for John Ralph Shaw [changed his name from Nicholson to Shaw in order to inherit his great-uncle's estate] in 1835. It was enlarged in 1844, and extended several times since. During the First World War it was used as a military hospital. It was bought, together with 425 acres of parkland, from Lord Leverhulme by Birkenhead Corporation in August 1926. It was the ideal venue for the World Boy Scout Jamboree in 1929 [see 1929] and finally opened to the public in 1931. During the Second World War it was again used as a military hospital and American soldiers camped in the grounds for the build-up to 'D' Day*

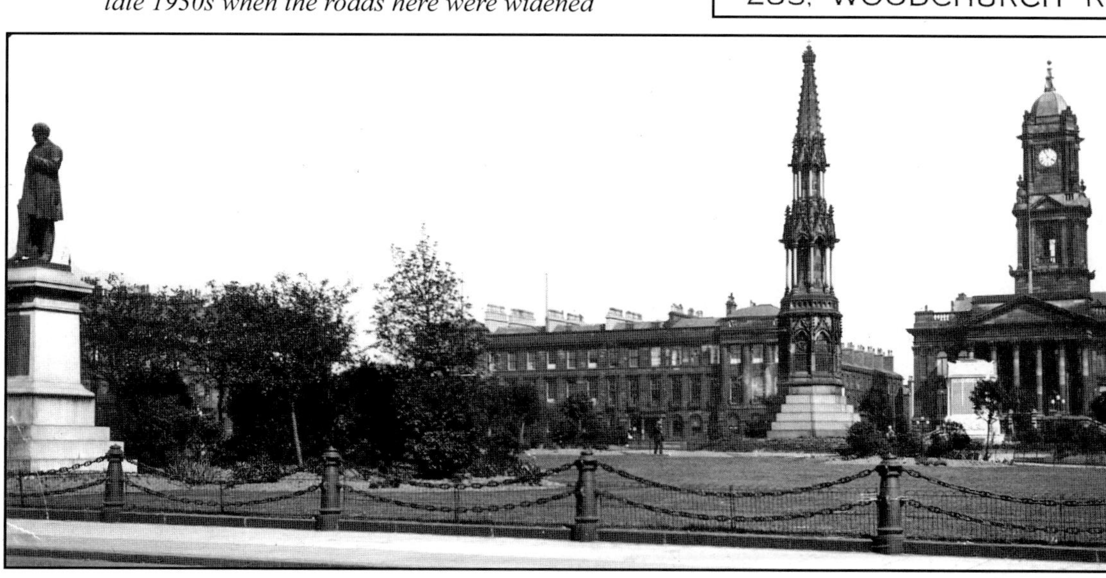

Left: *John Laird's Statue is seen on the left with his back to the* ***Birkenhead*** *Town Hall. Originally he was in front of and facing the Town Hall but was moved to make way for the Cenotaph [the white monument to the right - also see 1925]. There was a great debate at the time as it was thought that the founder of Birkenhead should not be moved*

1928

– **Birkenhead** Borough boundaries extended to include **Landican, Thingwall, Prenton** and part **Bidston**[SOUV]

– North-End sub Fire Station opened in Laird Street, **Birkenhead** [near St James' Church] - this was nearer to the docks and also eased the pressure on the Whetstone Lane Station[SOUV]

– **Oxton** Cricket Club purchased their ground in Townfield Lane from the Earl of Shrewsbury for £4,000[SOUV]

– **Birkenhead** Co-op purchased 168-170 Grange Road Birkenhead from Liptons for £7,500[LCP]

– Old Parkonians Rugby Football Club was formed [see 1950]

April 3 The road tunnels under the River Mersey from **Birkenhead** and **Liverpool** met in the middle and broke through

July 14 **Birkenhead** Corporation opened their **Prenton** bus route which terminated at Osmaston Road until it was extended to Prenton Dell Road October 1930[BB]

Sept 28 Park High School for Girls opened in Park Road South **Birkenhead**, having transferred from Conway Street[SOUV]

Oct 26 Two day "Flanders Bazaar" was held at the YMCA Hall Grange Road Birkenhead by the **Birkenhead** Branch & Women's Section of the British Legion[SOUV]

Dec Police Station opened in Well Lane **Tranmere** - twelve Police houseswere built next to the station up Well Lane[MQP]

Dec Due to the unemployment and shortage of funds **Birkenhead** YWCA decided to sell their annexe at 44 The Woodlands[SOUV]

Dec 1 Williamson Art Gallery opened in Slatey Road, **Birkenhead** [see photo next page]

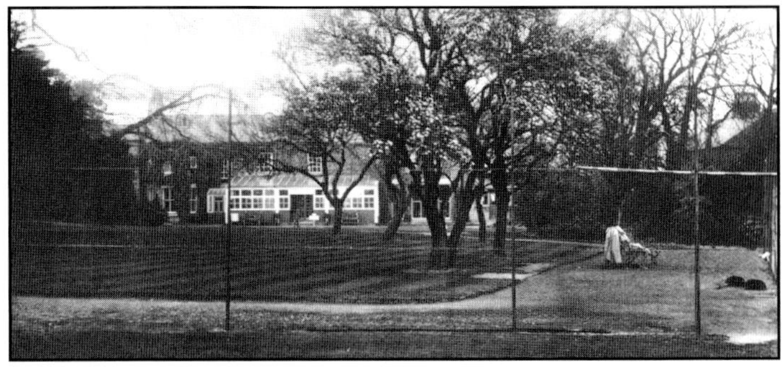

Above: *The caption on this postcard says 'Putting and croquet grounds* Victory Hall ***Upton****'. Originally called* The Elms, *a large house with grounds on the corner of Upton Road and Salacre Lane Upton Village, it was bought by public subscription for £2,000 in memory of those men of Upton who were killed in the First World War. A War Memorial was erected in front of the building and unveiled 22 July 1921 [see 1921]. The building opened as a sports and social centre called Victory Hall and the grounds, seen here at the back of the hall, were also used for tennis*

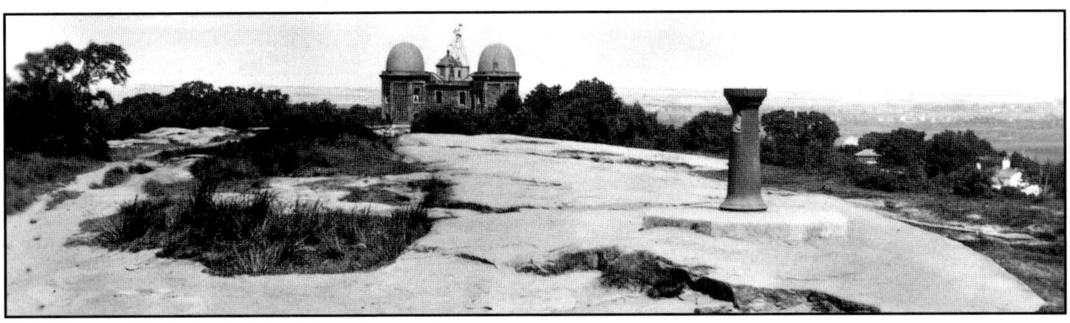

Left: ***Bidston*** *Observatory is seen on Bidston Hill with a distance guide on the right. The Observatory was built here in 1867 by the Mersey Docks and Harbour Board. In 1929 the Board and Liverpool University combined to form the Liverpool Observatory*

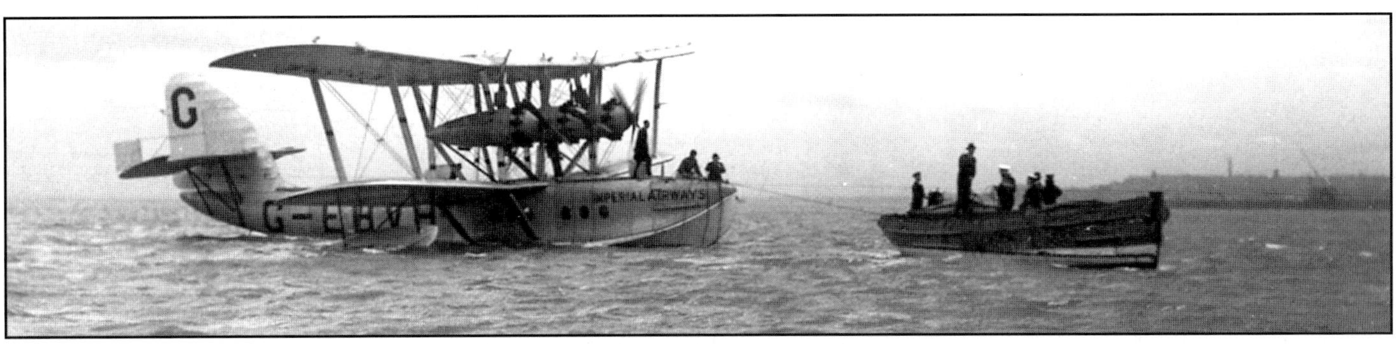

Above: *This Imperial Airways' Flying Boat* City of Athens *is seen being towed by a launch loaned by White Star Line on the River Mersey September 1928. It was operated from 'The Liverpool Marine Aerodrome' off* **Rock Ferry** *by Mersey Docks and Harbour Board - this experimental flight to Belfast was the only known service. The Short S8 Calcutta flying boat G-EBVH seen here had a crew of two and could carry up to 15 passengers***.** *The inaugural flight on Saturday 22 September 1928 carried 12 distinguished guests who were treated to a Civic Luncheon on arrival at Belfast. The first week went successfully so it was decided to continue into a second week. However, the aircraft was damaged and eventually returned to Southampton for repairs, after which it operated on the Channel Islands service - so came to an end this experimental service*

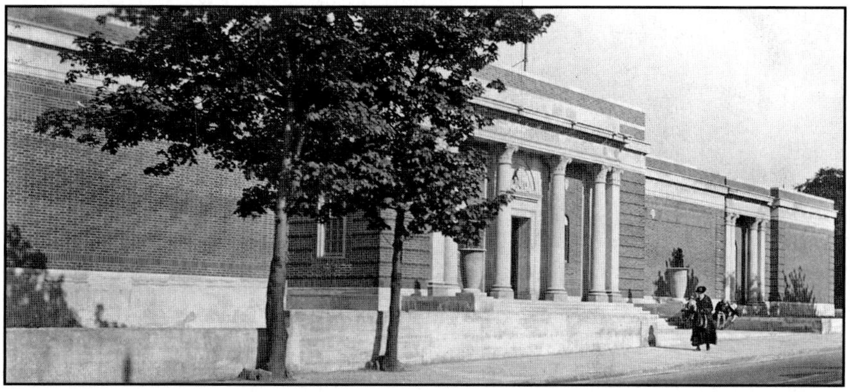

Above: *The Williamson Art Gallery opened in Slatey Road* ***Birkenhead*** *1 December 1928. It was named after John Williamson, a former Commissioner for Birkenhead and shipowner who left £20,000 in his will for the erection of a museum and art gallery. This was to be paid on the death of his son. His son died four years after his father and left a further £20,000 towards the project*

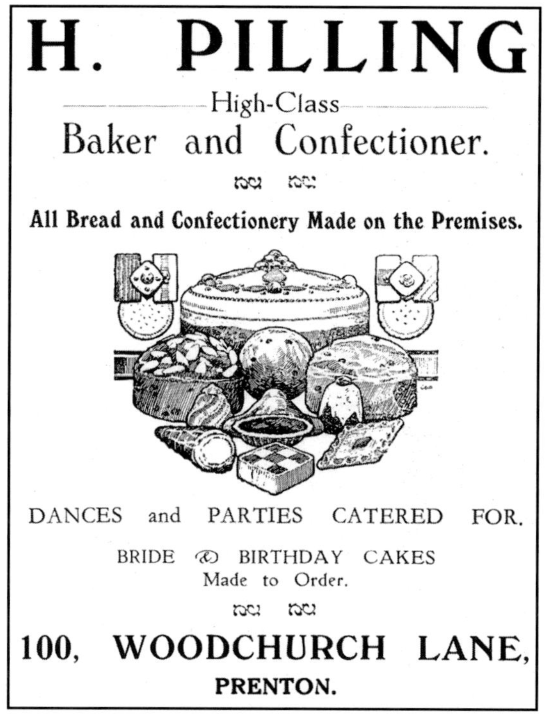

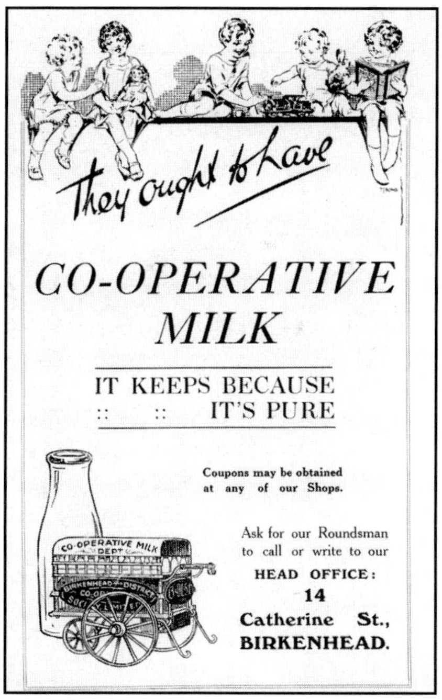

Left: *This advert was before the Birkenhead Co-op milk production moved to a new dairy in* ***Prenton*** *[see 1931]*

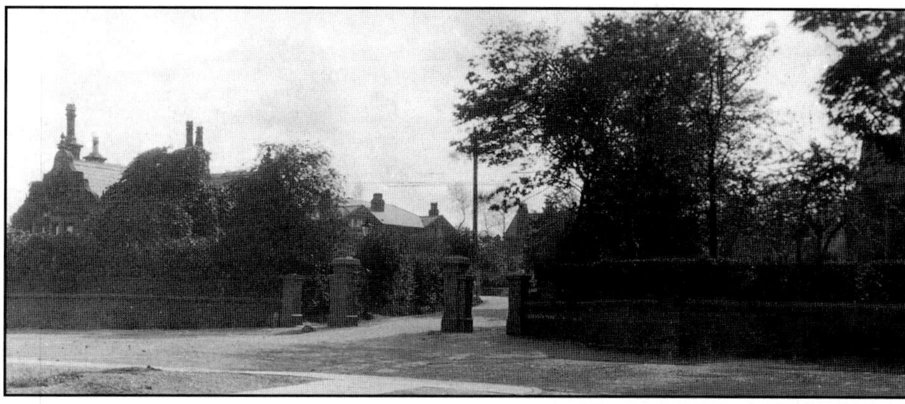

Above: *Egerton Park gates in Old Chester Road* ***Rock Ferry*** *are seen on this postcard of 1928 - 100 years after the park was laid out. Some of the houses in this enclosed Victorian estate suffered bomb damage during the Second World War and have been replaced with modern houses*

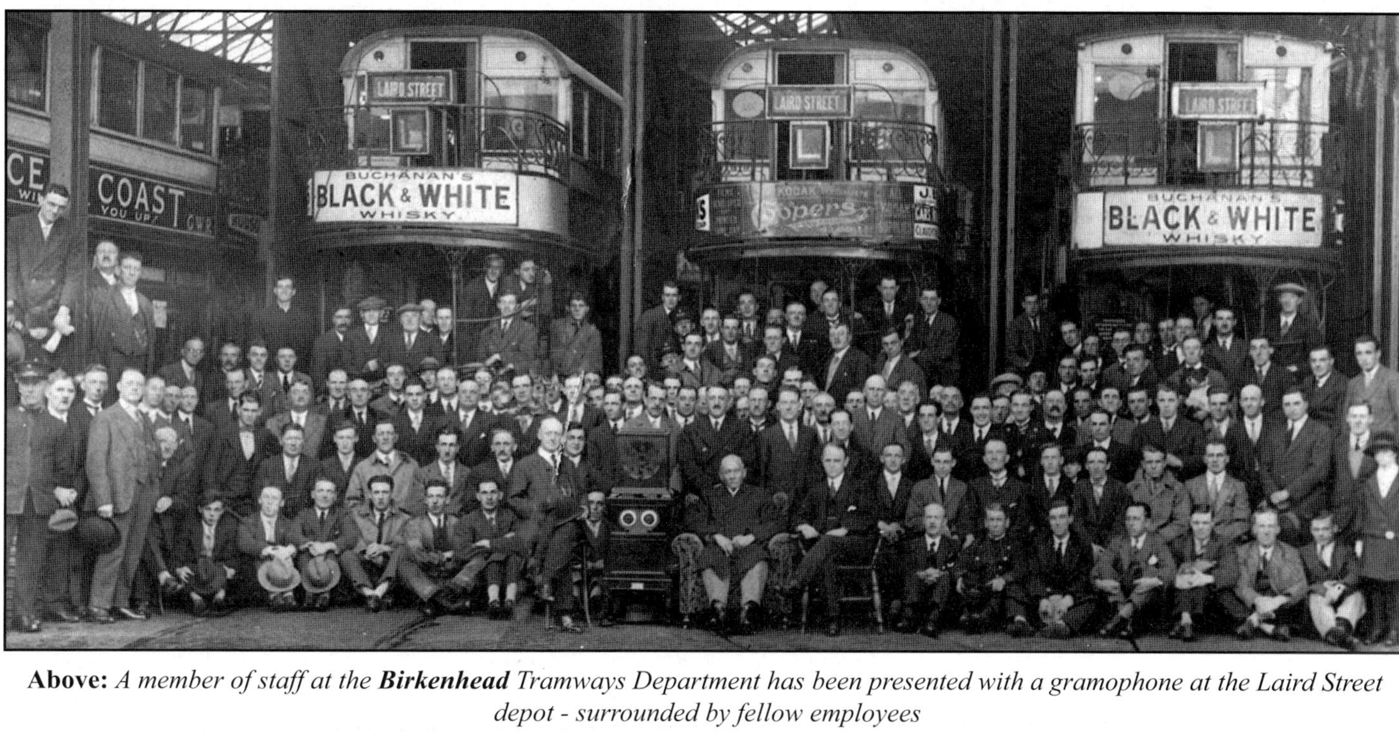

Above: *A member of staff at the* ***Birkenhead*** *Tramways Department has been presented with a gramophone at the Laird Street depot - surrounded by fellow employees*

1929

– **Bidston** Observatory merged with Liverpool University Tidal Institute[WPPB]

– **Birkenhead** Library, built in 1909, was demolished to make way for the Mersey Tunnel approach roads

– **Upton** Cricket Club acquired the land behind their pavilion [they became members of the Merseyside Competition in 1941][SOUV]

– *Bidston Court*, a large Victorian mansion in Vyner Road **Bidston,** owned by Ernest Royden, was taken down and moved 'brick by brick' to its new home at **Frankby** on an estate of 150 acres purchased by Ernest Royden in 1925. The building, which took over three years to move, was then named *Hillbark* after the building it replaced

– Kingsley Preparatory School opened in Ford Road **Upton**[SUAH]

– A new bandstand was erected in **Birkenhead** Park and the old cast iron one removed, being resited in Mersey Park **Tranmere**[TPG] [see 1902 and 1955]

– Cole Street school opened in **Birkenhead**

– New Out-Patients Department opened at the **Birkenhead** General Hospital - cost £20,000[SOUV]

– Birkenhead YWCA entertained 50 Polish Girl Guides at their Fernlea Hall who used it as their 'camping site' for the Jamboree[SOUV]

Feb 28 New buildings opened at the **Birkenhead** Girls' Secondary School[PROG]

July 31 World Jamboree of Boy Scouts opened at **Arrowe** Park - some 50,000 boy Scouts gathered here from 31 July to 13 August [see photos]. Holding the World Scout Jamboree at Arrowe Park caused the Birkenhead Police a great deal of extra and arduous work - to alleviate some of the pressure a strong detachment of Police from **Liverpool** was sent to help out[MQP]

Aug 1 Prince of Wales arrived at the Arrowe Park Jamboree via **Hooton** Aerodrome

Oct 21 Bus service between **New Brighton** and **New Ferry** commenced

Nov 29 New Health Clinic opened in North **Birkenhead**[SOUV]

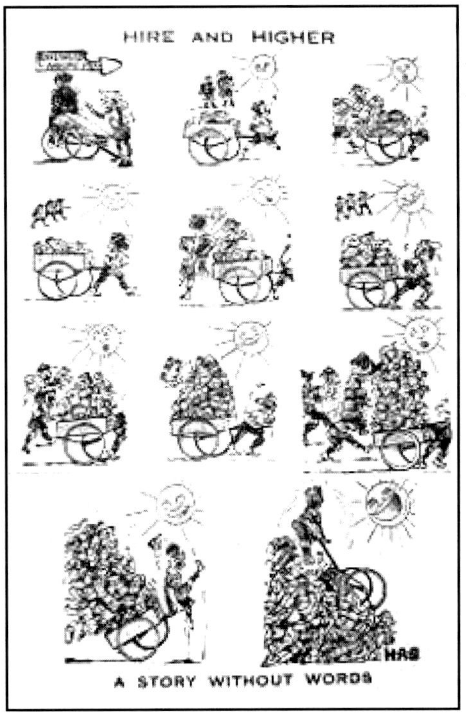

Left: *This postcard was published especially for the Arrowe Park Scout Jamboree by the* Birkenhead News

WORLD SCOUT JAMBOREE AT ARROWE PARK

The venue of ***Arrowe*** *Park was chosen for the 1929 International Jamboree as it was the 21st Anniversary of the inaugural meeting of the Boy Scout Movement at the YMCA Grange Road* ***Birkenhead*** *on 24 January 1908 [see 1910]. Birkenhead Corporation had recently purchased Arrowe Hall which was an old country house with 425 acres and was four miles from Woodside Ferry with connection to* ***Liverpool*** *[most scouts from abroad came by sea] and Woodside Railway Station on the LM&S and GW Joint Railways. The number of Scouts expected was 50,000 - half being from 65 overseas countries. Arrowe Park was divided into eight sub-camps each consisting of 3,000 to 4,000 Scouts with a mixture of home, Commonwealth and foreign. There were two Auxiliary Camps at Overchurch and Upton each with 9,000 to 10,000 Scouts. Each Scout Troop was expected to entertain the other Scouts and visitors either within their 'village' or in the main arena [in the far distance in the photo below]. There were 320,000 visitors over the two weeks who paid 1/- [5p] - those in uniform were free*

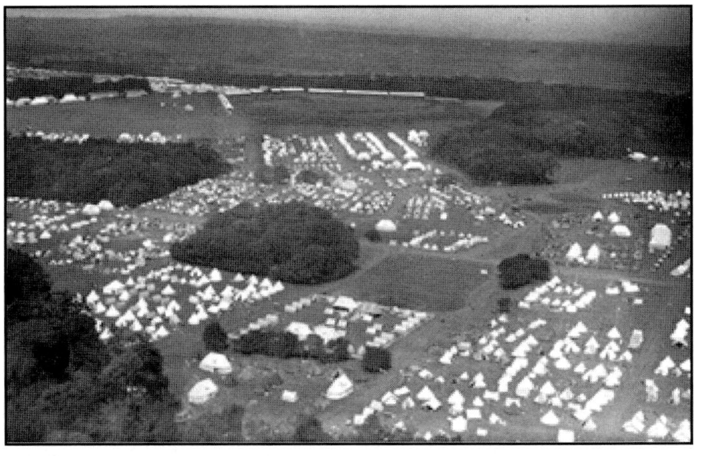

Above: *This air-view of the World Scout Jamboree at Arrowe Park which ran from 31 July 1929 for two weeks shows part of the area set aside for camp sites. Each country had its own enclosed area*

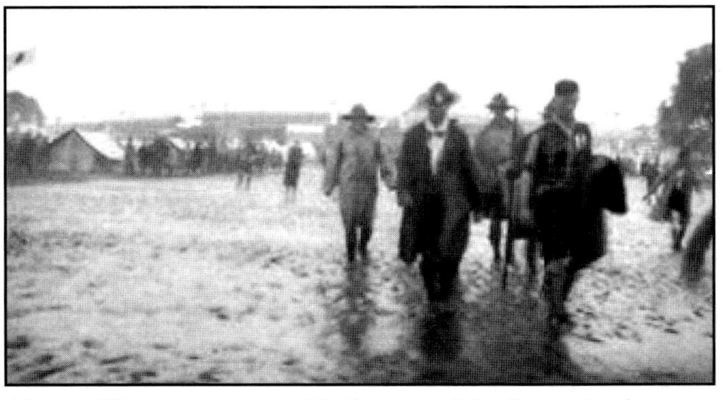

Above: *The most memorable feature of the Scout Jamboree at* ***Arrowe*** *Park - was the rain. According to the author's mother, who was a visitor, they re-named it 'mudboree'*

Right: *Scouts are seen on the platform of* ***Upton*** *Station, before making their way to Arrowe Park for the Scout Jamboree. This was the nearest station to* ***Arrowe*** *Park being 1.25 miles across the fields*

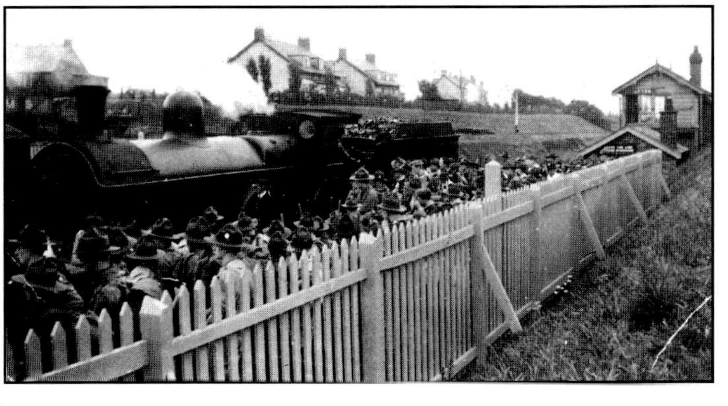

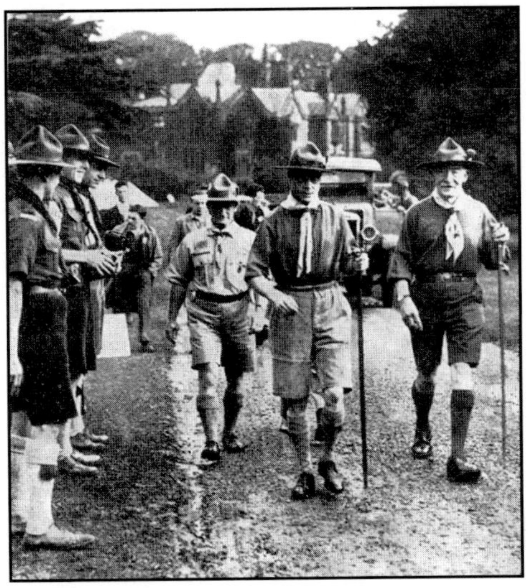

Right: *Prince of Wales with the Chief Scout Baden Powell - **Arrowe** Hall is in the background*

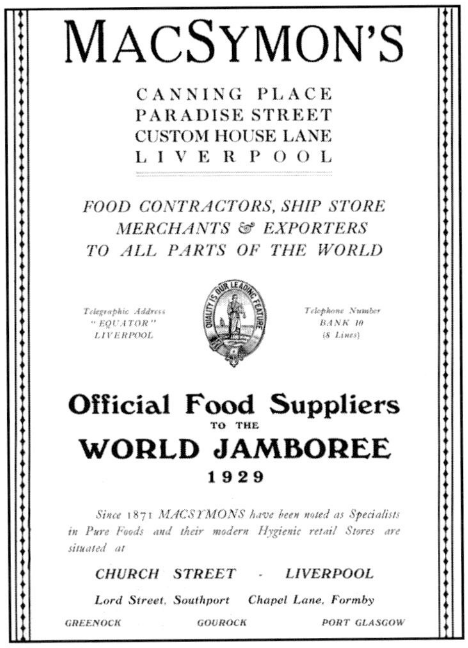

Right: *This was an advert for MacSymon's of Liverpool who were the official food suppliers to the World Scout Jamboree at **Arrowe** Park [see below]*

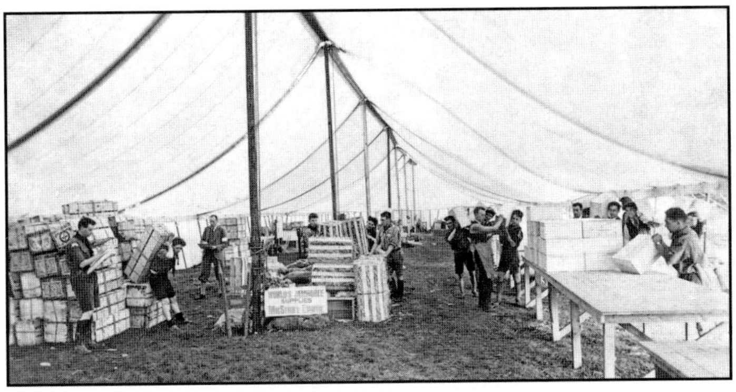

Left: *This main supply marquee pictured was an advertising postcard for MacSymon's [see above] - it measured 200ft. x 60ft. with over 50 tons of food passing through here daily for the 14 days of the event. The following are total amounts of food consumed over the two weeks:- 42,000 tins of sardines; 10 tons of onions; 25 tons of cabbage; 13 tons of rice; 10 tons of coffee; 9 tons of beans; 17 tons of jam; 15 tons of butter; 1,200 gallons of milk and 750,000 1lb loaves of bread*

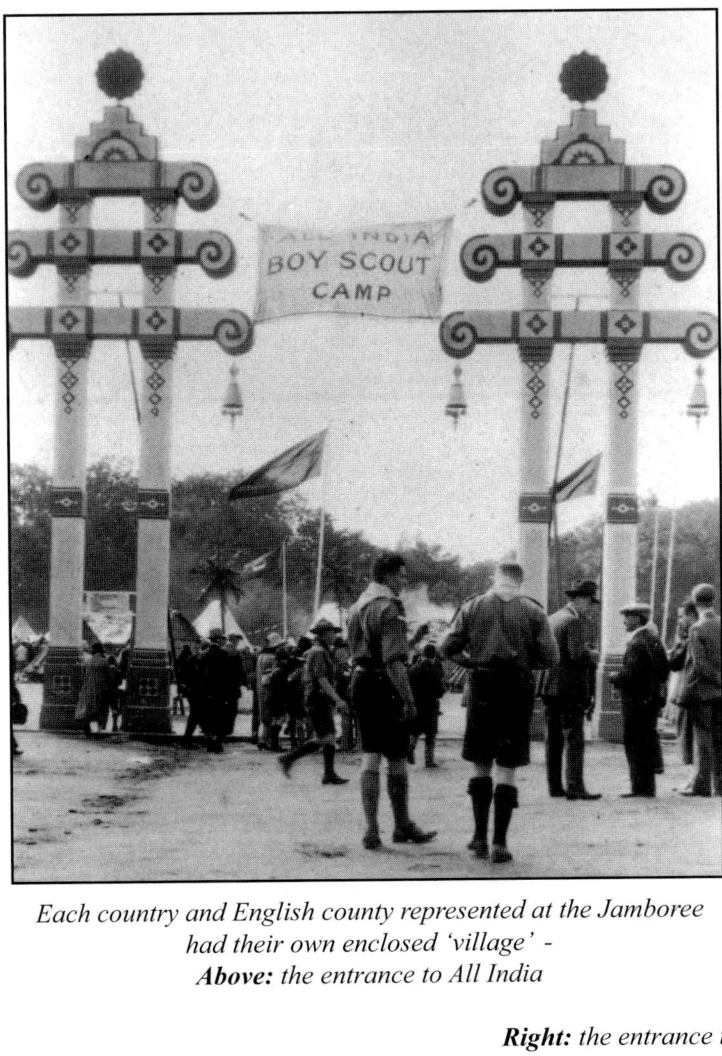

Each country and English county represented at the Jamboree had their own enclosed 'village' -
***Above:** the entrance to All India*

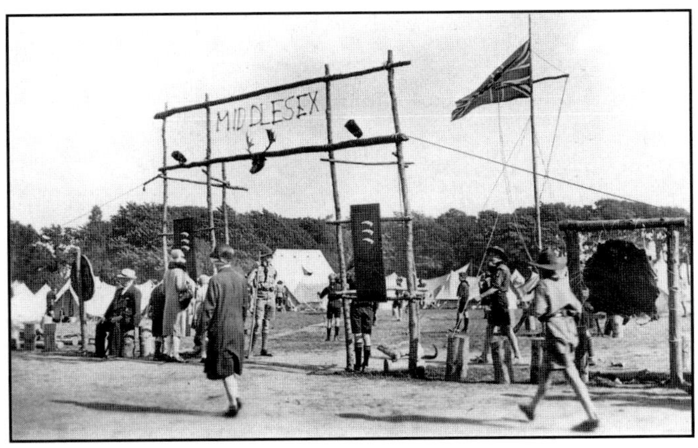

***Above:** The entrance to Middlesex*

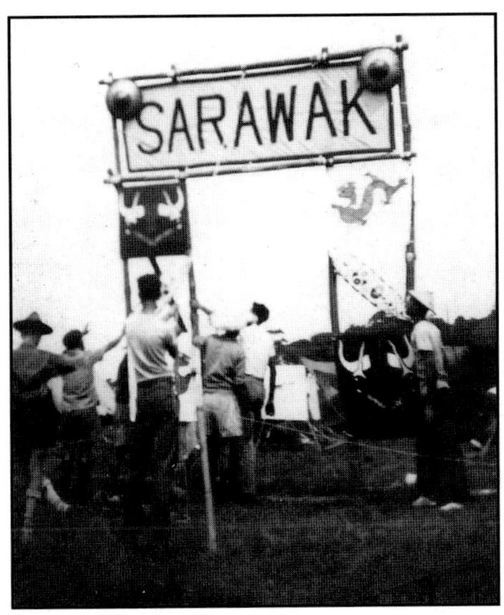

***Right:** the entrance to Sarawak*

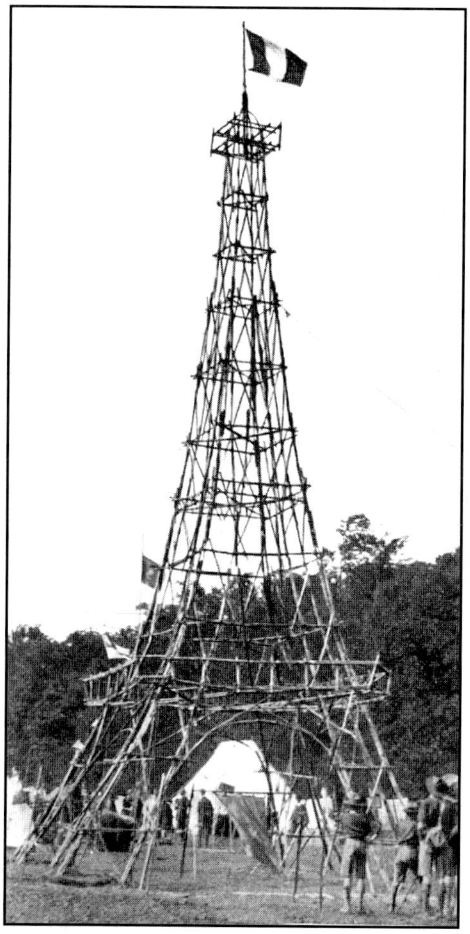

Right: *This advert for the Birkenhead Co-op Society was featured in the* Daily Arrowe *newspaper. They were advertising their shop within the Market shopping area at* ***Arrowe*** *Park and also their store in Grange Road* ***Birkenhead***

Left: *One of the outstanding features of the Arrowe Park Jamboree was the French Scouts' 'Eiffel Tower which was built entirely of Scout Staves and stood over 50 feet high*

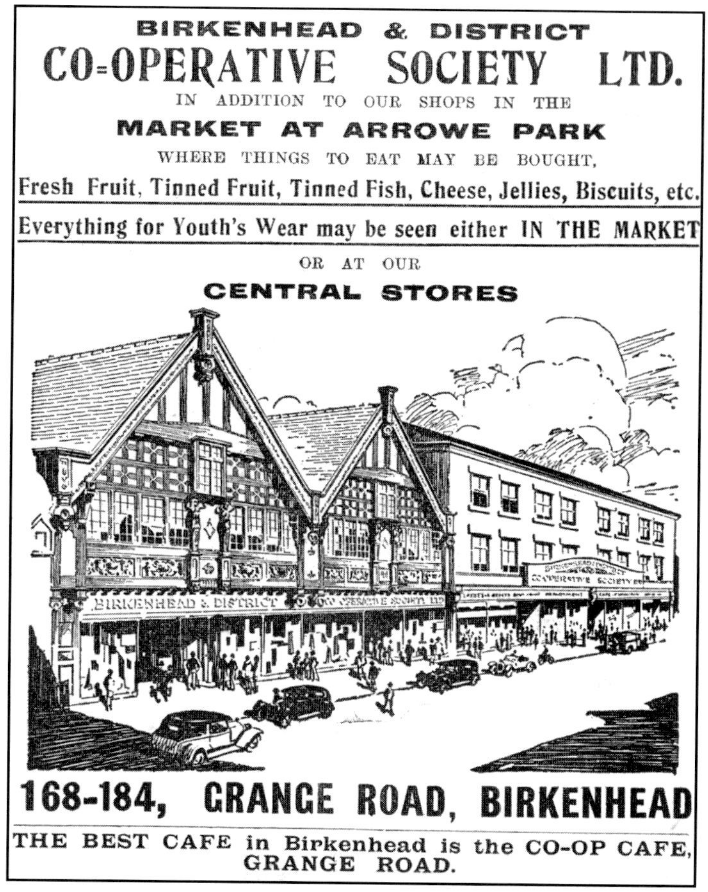

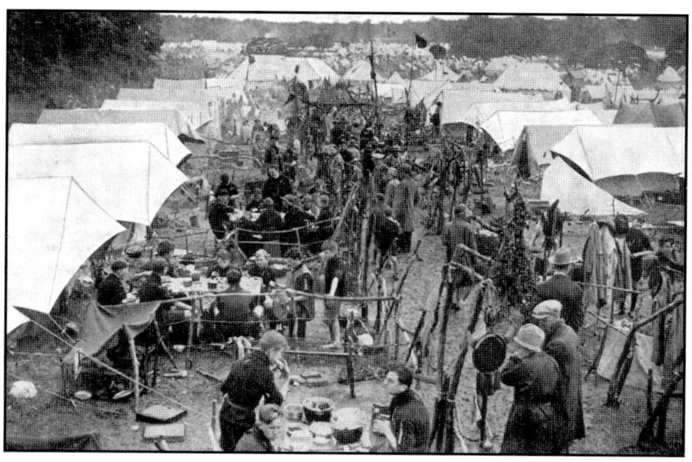

Left: *Lunch-time at one of the sub-camps with troops eating in the allocated space in front of their tents. The general public, seen here and below were allowed in from 12 noon each day - with over 320,000 of them paying 1/- [5p] entrance over the 14 days*

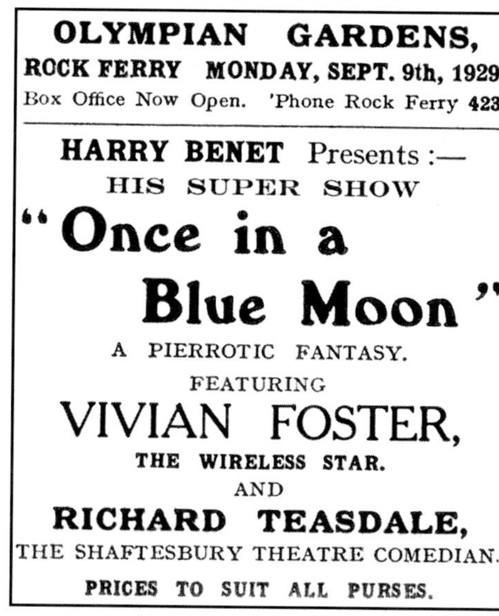

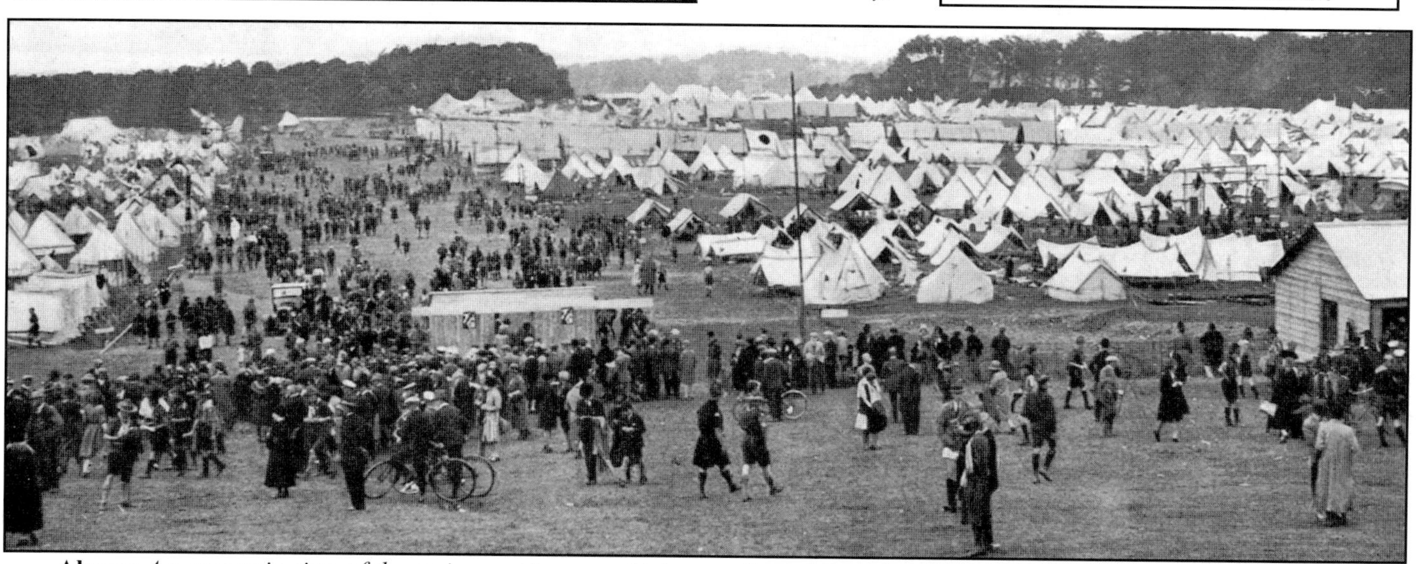

Above: *A panoramic view of the main camping area At* ***Arrowe*** *Park taken after noon when the visitors were allowed in*

1930

– Workhouse taken over by Cheshire County Council - renamed **Clatterbridge** (County) General Hospital

– The Road Traffic Act of 1930 gave a grant to all Police Forces to purchase and maintain motor vehicles for traffic duties. **Birkenhead** bought three new motor cycle combinations for traffic patrol, transferring six policemen from other duties[MQP]

– Holy Cross Roman Catholic Church opened in Hoylake Road **Birkenhead** [see 1959][DOS]

– **Birkenhead** YWCA found a hole in their garden in The Woodlands 27 feet deep which interested archaeologists but it was soon filled in with 12 tons of spoil from the Mersey Tunnel[SOUV]

– Carlton Players first performed in **Birkenhead** [then known as the Carlton Amateur Dramatic Society]

Sept 30 Death announced of FE Smith, Earl of **Birkenhead,** aged 59 - brilliant Statesman, Lawyer and Orator[OIH]

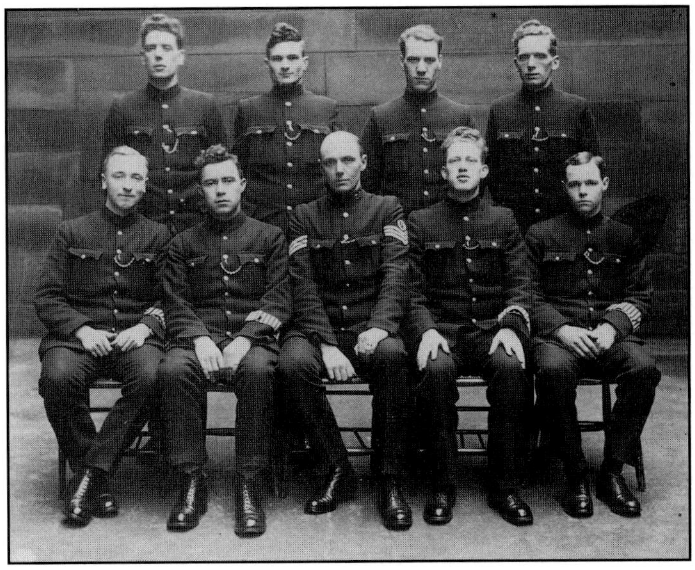

Above: *Members of the* ***Birkenhead*** *Police Force taken under the Town Hall building in Mortimer Street c1930:- JM Inglis; GD Green; JGR Beerdecker; J Howard KW Fenwell; D MacDonald; Sgt Morris; Petatt; TR Appleton*

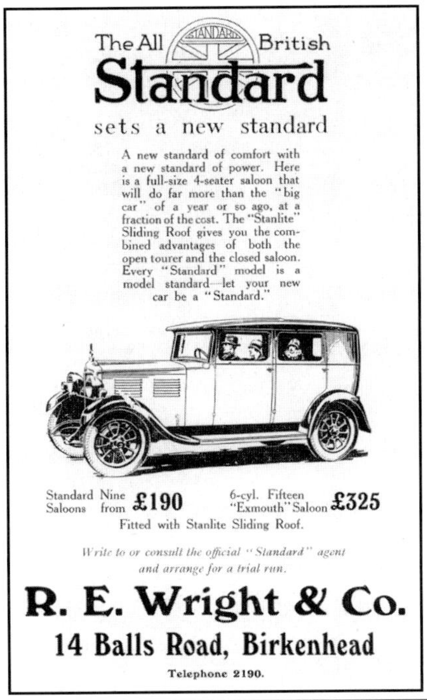

Left: *This advert was for RE Wright & Co, 14 Balls Road* ***Birkenhead*** *who were agents for the 'All British Standard' - prices from £190 to £325*

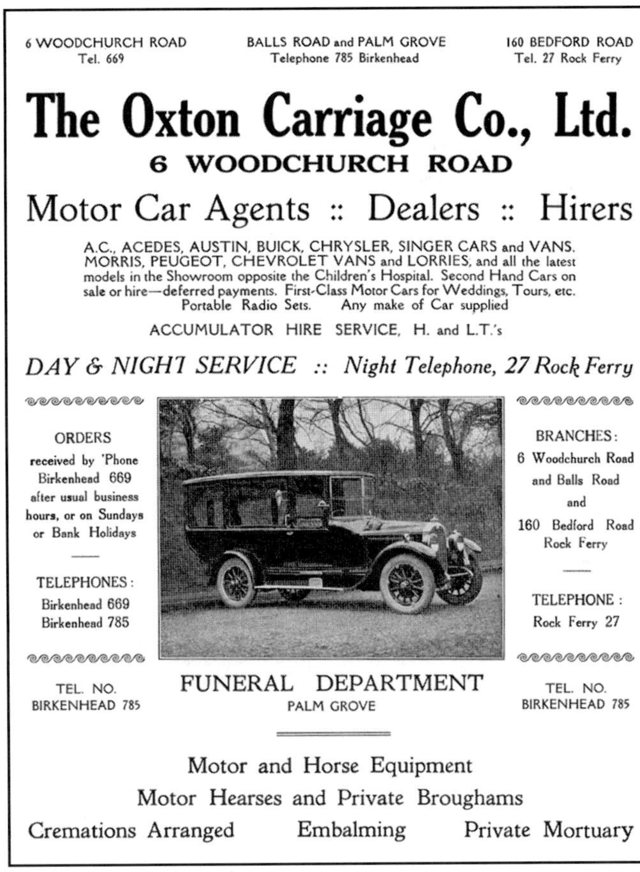

Below: *Seen in* ***New Ferry****, this Crosville Daimler single-decker Reg No. FM1883, was operating on the seasonal route between Rock Ferry Pier and Raby Mere which started 4 June 1924 and ended in 1938*[WCB]

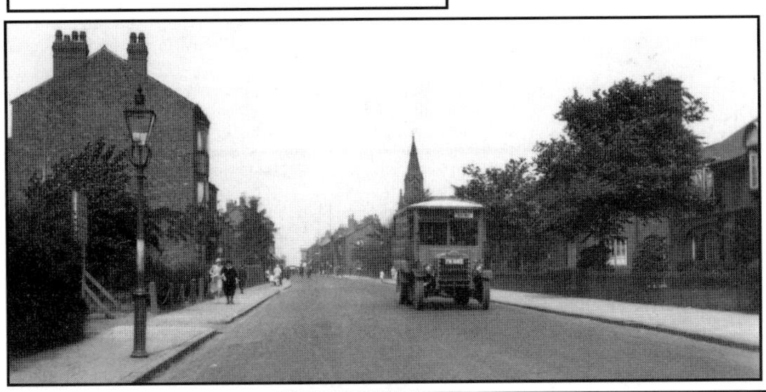

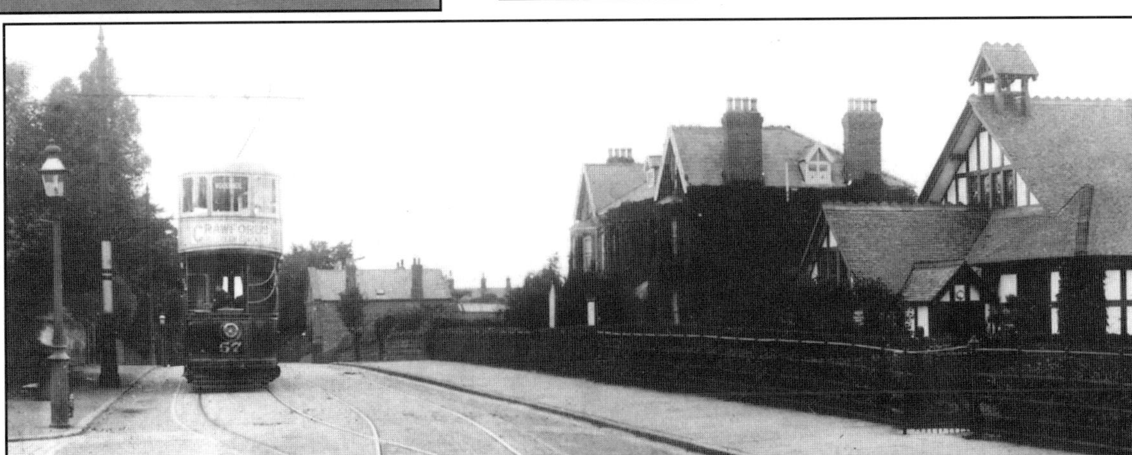

Right: *The No.57* ***Birkenhead*** *Corporation tram on the Circle Route is seen in Shrewsbury Road passing All Saint's Church on the right*

1931

– *Overdale*, a house in Beresford Road **Oxton** owned by Graham White MP, was presented to Birkenhead School and used to house Junior School [see photo this page - also 1899 Holy Name Church][BSPH]

– Duke of Kent visited Cammell Laird shipyard **Birkenhead** and laid the keel of HMS *Achillies*[MOI]

– **Arrowe** Park opened to the public - a statue in the form of a scout was unveiled in the main drive near the entrance to Arrowe Hall to commemorate the Jamboree [see 1929 and 1944]

– **Thornton Hough** Women's Institute opened[YW8]

Mar 3 Bascule bridge replaced swing bridge between East and West Floats at Duke Street **Birkenhead**

Mar 10 Polling day for **Upton** who decided to join **Birkenhead** instead of **Wallasey**

Apr 14 *Argyle Theatre* **Birkenhead** became the first music hall in the country to broadcast live on BBC radio[RP]

July Birkenhead and District Co-operative Society opened their new dairy on Swan Hill Woodchurch Road **Prenton** [see photo next page][SOUV]

July 30 **Arrowe** Park Golf Course opened

Sept 26 Wirral Grammar School for Boys and Girls **Bebington** - both opened [see photos]

Dec 27 The **New Ferry** to Woodside tram route closed[BET]

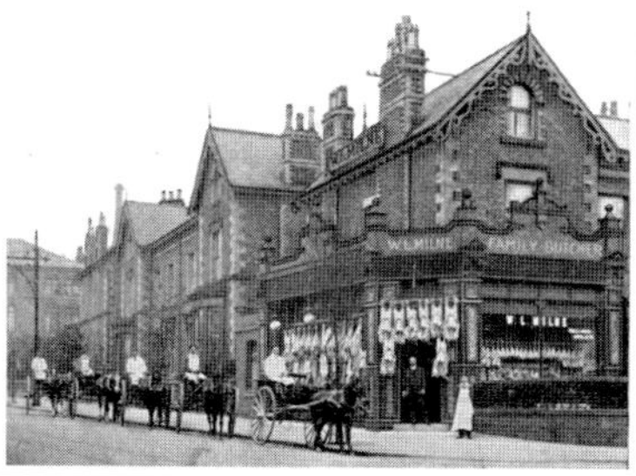

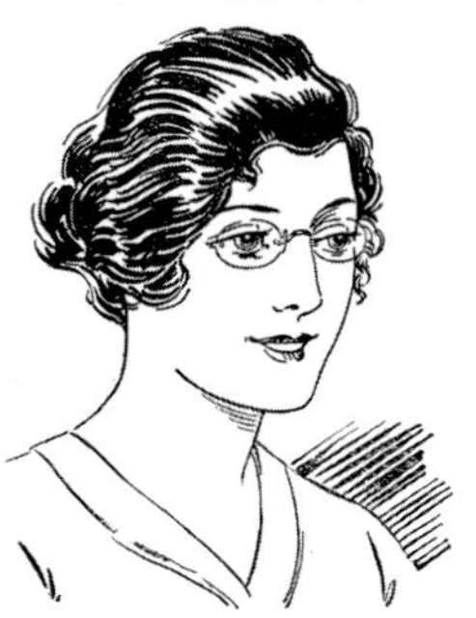

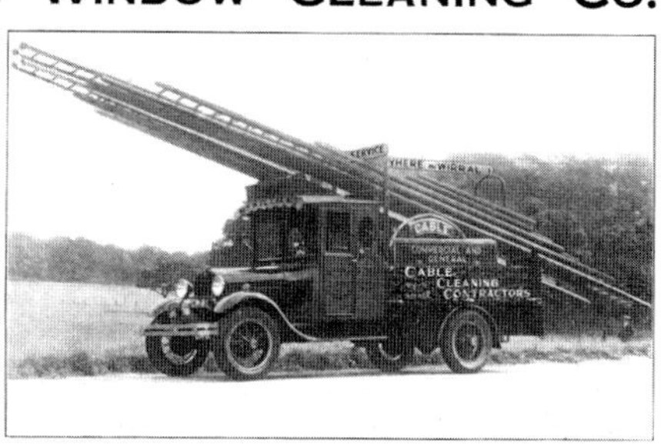

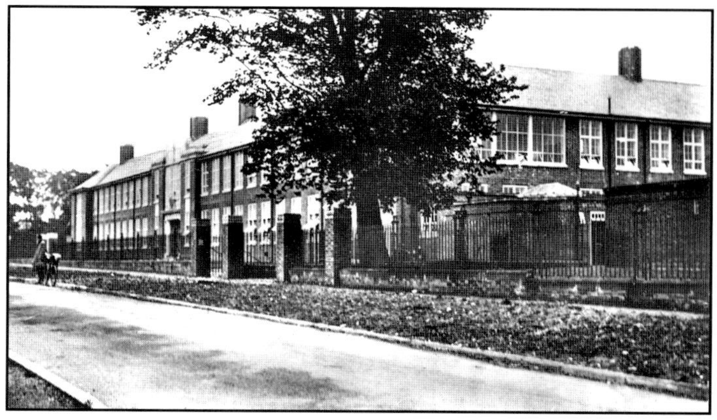

Above: *Bebington County School for Boys - the name of the school changed in 1936 to Wirral Grammar School for Boys - was built and opened in Cross Lane* ***Bebington*** *at the same time as the girls' school in Heath Road [see below]. Originally the Council had bought five acres of land for £1,750 in 1925. However, with the purchase of additional land off William Hope, a Liverpool Merchant, the site for the two schools was then 22 acres (some years later further land was purchased from Lever Brothers). Both schools were officially opened by the Lord Lieutenant of Cheshire, Brigadier-General Sir William Bromley Davenport on 26 September 1931. Built at a cost of £100,000 for 450 boys aged 10 to 19. The design and building materials were almost the same as used on the girls' school with buildings of red sandstone brick, main entrance of Portland stone and a green slate roof. At the time the schools opened, they were surrounded by countryside with the nearest bus stop being in Lower Bebington Village*

Below: *Originally called Bebington County School but changed in 1936 to Wirral Grammar School for Girls it was opened in Heath Road* ***Bebington*** *on 26 September 1931 - the same time as Bebington County School for Boys around the corner in Cross Lane [see above]. Built at a cost of £90,000 it was intended to accommodate a maximum of 420 girls*

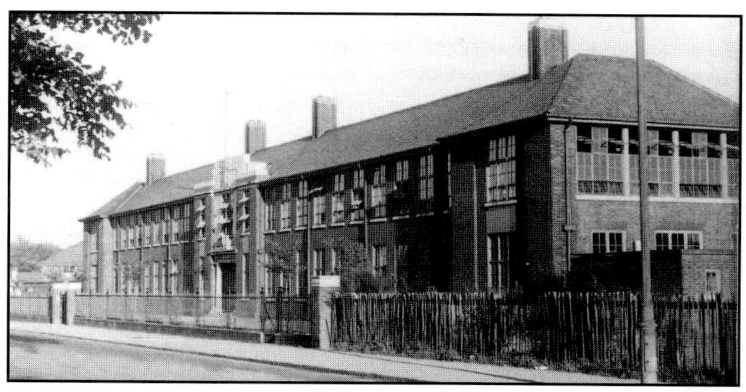

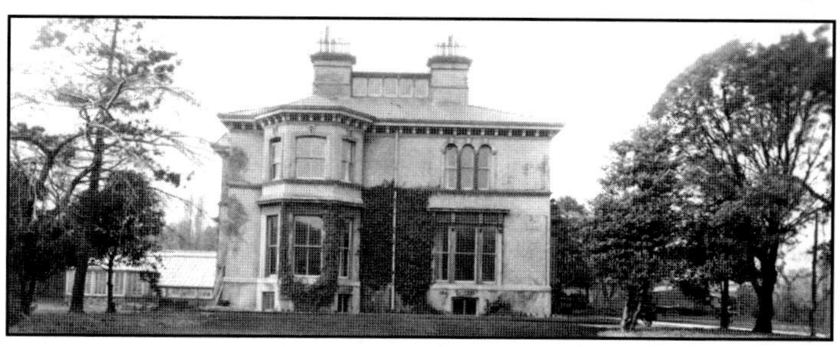

Above: Overdale, *a prominent house on the corner of Bidston Road and Beresford Road* ***Oxton*** *was donated to Birkenhead School by the Rt Hon. H Graham White - Birkenhead MP and Old Boy of the school - it was used then and is still used today to house Junior School*[BSPH]

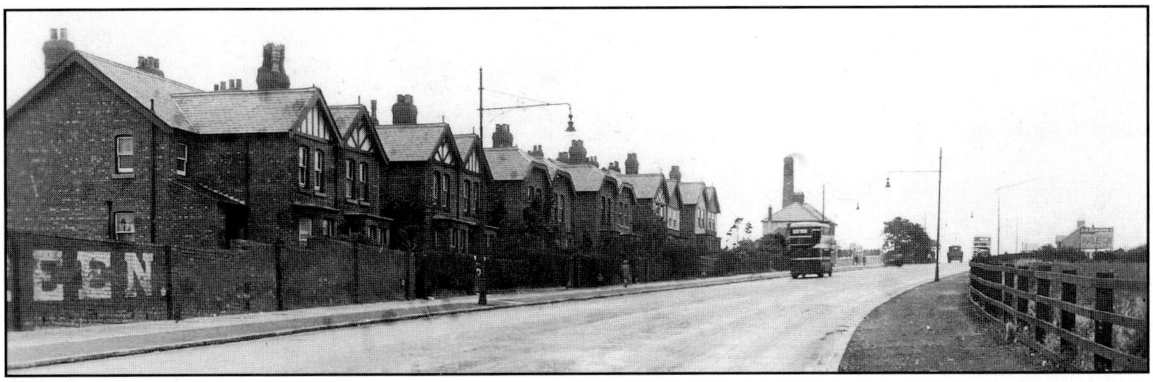

Left: *This part of Woodchurch Road* **Prenton** *was known as Swan Hill - two buses are about to pass each other by the entrance to the new Birkenhead Co-op Dairy [see below] with the Birkenhead Brickworks chimney seen above the bus*

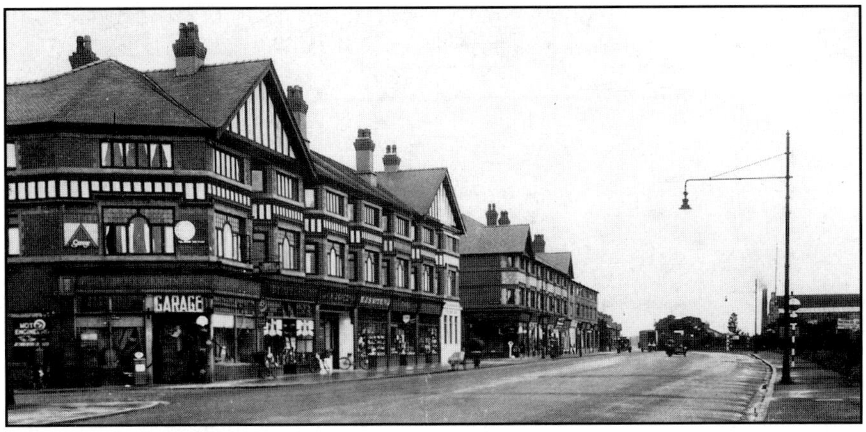

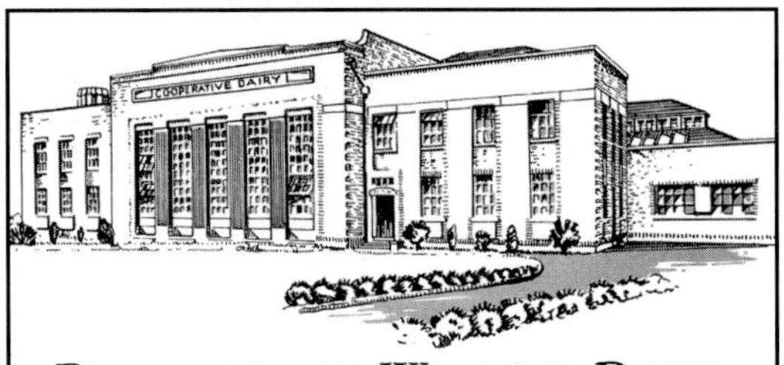

BIRKENHEAD'S WONDER DAIRY

Above: *Birkenhead & District Co-operative Society new Wonder Dairy opened on Swan Hill Woodchurch Road* **Prenton** *July 1931 [see above]*

Above: *This 1931 postcard is looking down Woodchurch Road* **Prenton** *towards Arrowe Park. Hughes & Watts - Motor Engineers are on the right with the chimney of the Birkenhead Brickworks beyond [see 1953]. Elm Road North is on the left with shops as numbered then but since changed: No.2 Lowe & Powell - Motor Engineers with petrol pumps; No.4 John Irwin - Grocers; No.6 Henry Jones - Butcher; No.8 Helen Smith - Chandler; No.10 Miss Annie Noble - Confectioner; No.12 Mrs MC Fairburn - Stationer; No.14 Lloyds Bank. Curzon Road then: No.16. Chas H Wright - Chemist (weighing machine outside); No.18 Miss Ada Midley - Milliner; No.20 Frank Goldstone - Stationer; No.22 Heaney & Co - Electrician; No.24 Hartley's Creamery; No.26 Harold W Rotheram - Fishmonger; sub branch District Bank; No.28 Miss Lilian Banks - Milliner*

Right: *Looking down Storeton Road* **Prenton** *towards* **Bebington** *with the* Halfway House *on the right [see 1889] - which is so named as it was halfway between Woodside Birkenhead and Woodchurch - part of Martin's Bank is on the extreme left with the Woodchurch Lane Post Office next door run by Robert Hislop who was also a Confectioner. The Post Office moved to the corner of Elm Road after 4 May 1943. The shop beyond was jointly run by Ada Serves - Milliner and ET Selves - Boot Repairer. The sign the other side of Woodchcurch Lane says "For Sale this Valuable Corner Plot - Apply Hancock Birkenhead"*

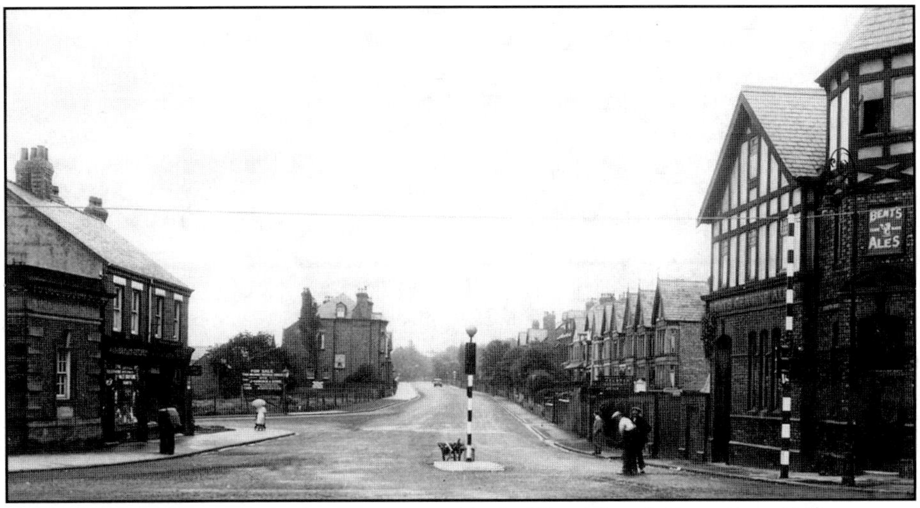

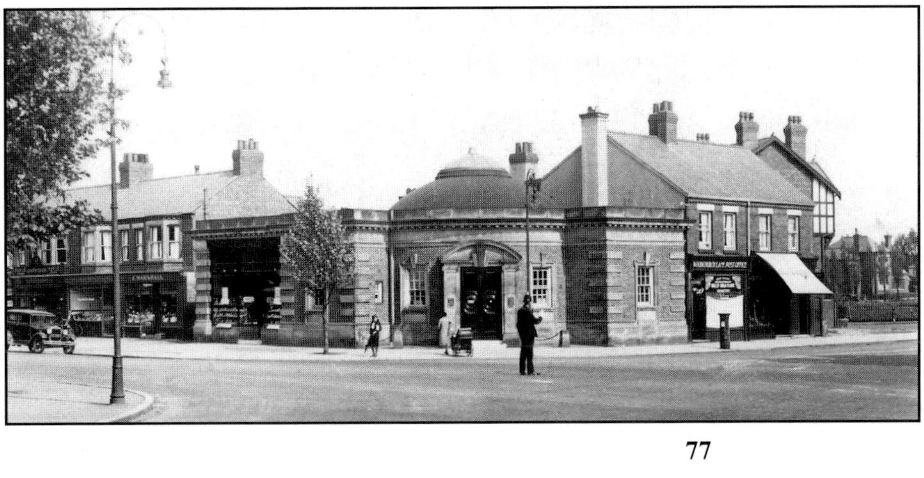

Left: *Woodchurch Lane Post Office, seen in the previous picture, is on the right next to the shop with the awning. The policeman in the middle of the road is standing in front of the single-storey* **Prenton** *branch of Martin's Bank [this building has lost its charm due to a recent metal and glass second floor extension]. To the left of the small tree at No.289 was George Lunt & Sons - Baker; 287 was John Marshall - Fruiterer & Greengrocer; 285 was William Amery - Fishmonger and 283 SC Barnes - Confectioner*

1932

– **Brimstage** Village Hall erected on the site of the Red Cat Inn[YW8]

– **New Ferry** baths opened - cost £12,000 [see photo]

– Holt Hill Convent **Tranmere** closed its boarding school in order to provide more accommodation for the day school which became a Direct Grant Grammar School[DoS]

– The *Prenton Hotel*, Borough Road **Prenton** was built to replace the *Old Feathers* which was demolished to make way for the Mersey Tunnel - it was later to be renamed *The Prenton Park* [see photo]

April 9 **Overchurch** Scout Hut opened

Aug 10 **Frankby** Hall Estate which comprised 810 acres of land in **Frankby, Greasby** and **Newton** was up for auction. Frankby Hall was withdrawn at £5,000 - but bought the following year for £12,000 by Wallasey Corporation for use as a cemetery

Oct 31 ***Birkenhead*** *Hippodrome Theatre*, Grange Road re-opened [see poster this page]

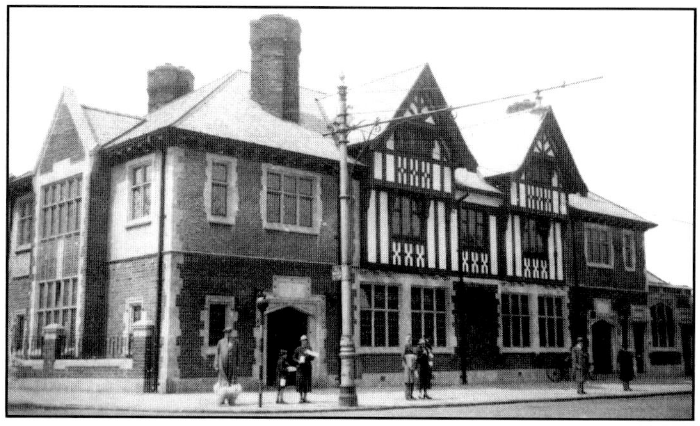

Above: The Prenton Hotel *was opened on the corner of Borough Road and Prenton Road West* **Prenton** *opposite Tranmere Rovers' ground - it took its licence from the Old Feathers pub which was demolished to make way for the new Mersey Tunnel approach roads - it was later re-named the* Prenton Park Hotel

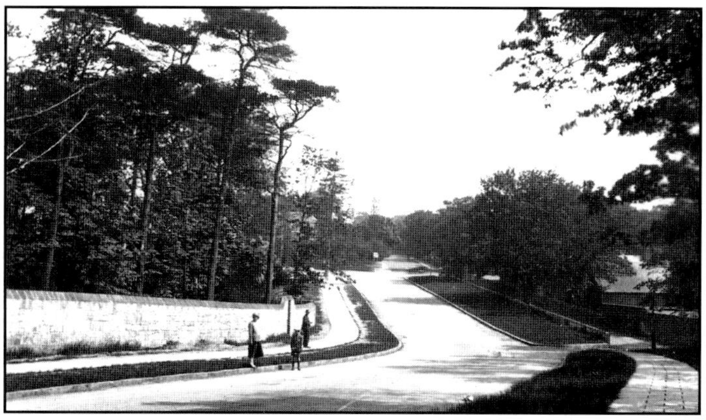

Above: *Kings Lane* **Bebington,** *looking up the hill towards its junction with Old Chester Road. The road was widened in 1922, ready for houses to be built either side [compare photo of Kings Lane looking behind the photographer - see 1920]*

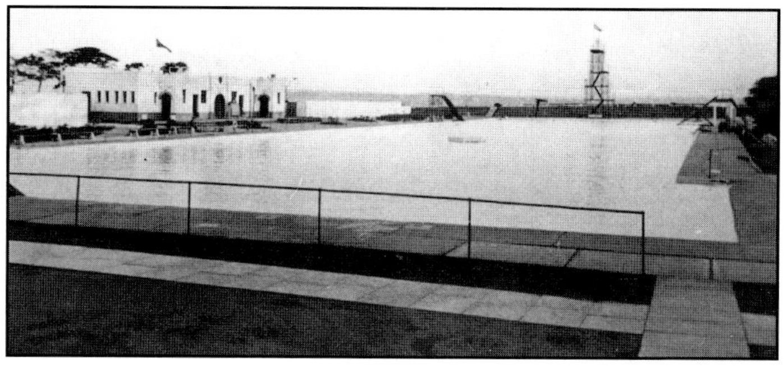

Above: ***New Ferry*** *Baths pictured before they opened - the diving board was three metres high [see also 1952]*

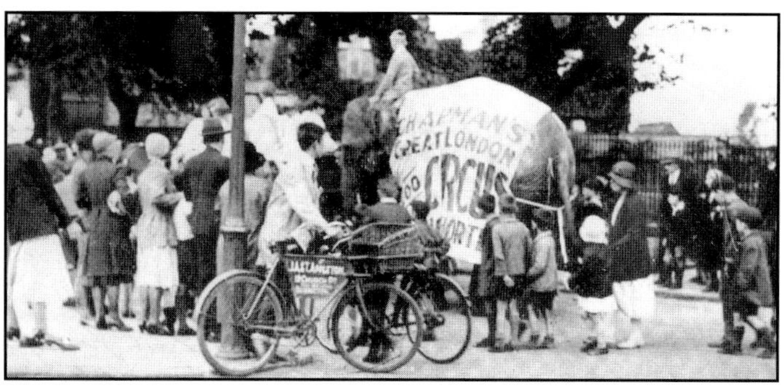

Left: *A crowd has gathered to see an elephant from "Chapman's Great London Zoo Circus" who advertised that the Circus is in town [see also 1939 for the circus tiger]*

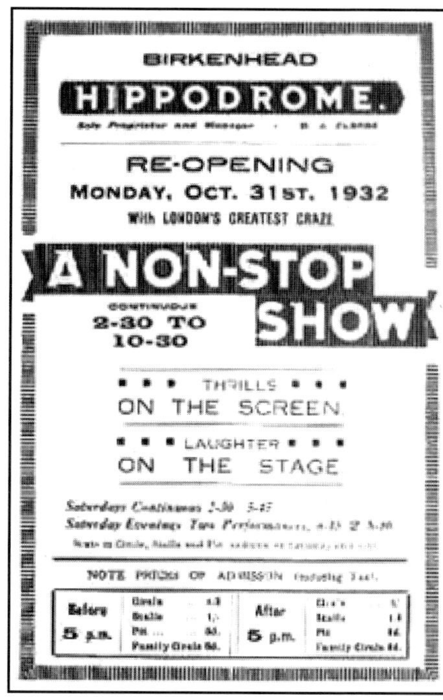

Above: *This advert was for the re-opening of the* **Birkenhead** *Hippodrome Theatre 31 October 1932 - within 18 months they had sold out to Birkenhead Co-op who were to build their new store on the site*

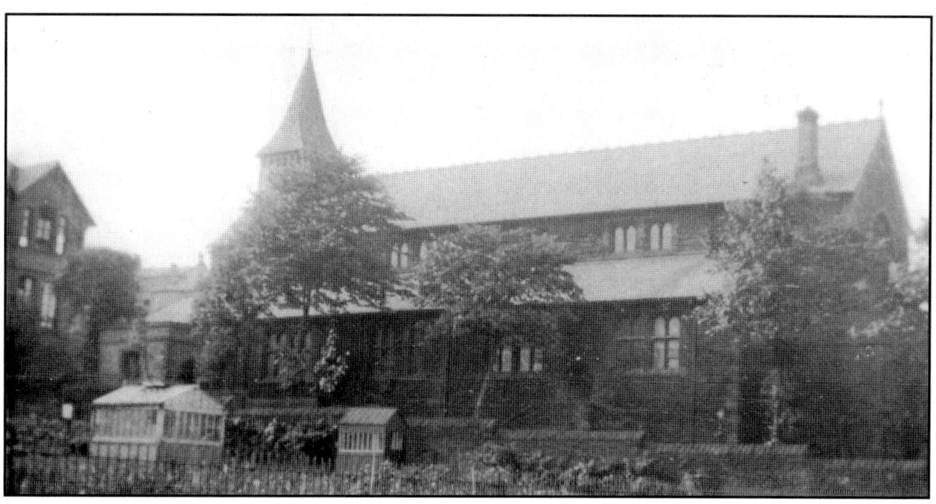

Left: *This 1932 postcard shows St Luke's Church in Old Chester Road, Lower* ***Tranmere*** *which was consecrated on St Luke's Day 18 October 1881. The school attached to the Church opened 24 May 1884*

1933

– **Birkenhead** Police took over the **Upton** District from Cheshire including Upton Police Station. Due to the increased area, police boxes were erected at Sparks Lane, **Barnston**; Vyner Road, **Bidston**; Pine Walks **Prenton** and Overchurch Road, **Saughall Massie**[MQP]

– Grange Secondary School opened in Tollemache Road **Birkenhead [see 1943]**

Feb 28 **Birkenhead** Corporation ferry boat *Bidston* made its first sailing

Mar 27 Byrne Avenue Baths **Rock Ferry** opened[PROG] The Baths when opened were described as amongst the finest in the country. The main bath hall was 75ft. long x 35ft. wide with a balcony which seated 300 people [the Birkenhead Philharmonic Society performed concerts here with the acoustics found to be very suitable]; the smaller bath hall was 75ft. x 30ft. - in the first year there were 273,000 bathers here [see 1956]

Apr 28 **Bidston** Dock opened at the extreme end of the West Float on Bidston Moss at a cost of £700,000[SOUV] [see 1958]

Apr 28 Borough of Birkenhead borders extended to include: **Arrowe, Upton,Woodchurch, Noctorum** and parts of **Bidston**[SOUV]

Aug First Birkenhead and District Annual Sheep Dog Trials held in Rectory Fields **Woodchurch**

Sept St Anselm' College for boys opened in Manor Hill **Birkenhead**

Sept 12 The *Southern Cross,* a Mission ship was launched at Cammell Laird - built for the Melanesian Mission it was dedicated by the Bishop of Liverpool

W. R. MILLETT & CO.,

Tel.: B'head 63. 13 Hamilton Square, Birkenhead.

PEATCOAL BRIQUETTES

The New Economical Fuel Invention.

20 cwt. (about 1,500)	@ 50/-	per ton delivered in bags.
10 cwt. (about 750)	@ 52/6	,, ,, ,,
5 cwt. (about 375)	@ 55/-	,, ,, ,,
1 cwt. (about 75)	@ 60/-	,, ,, ,,

They are bright and clean to handle and give no abnoxious fumes, last longer than the ordinary Briquette and do not crumble in the fire.

FREE SAMPLE AT ABOVE ADDRESS.

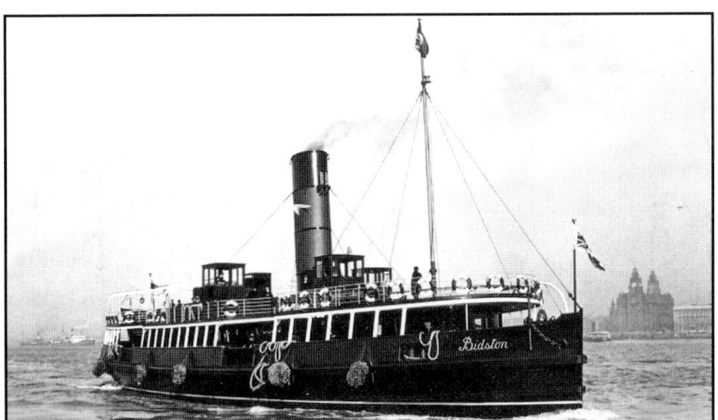

***Above:* Birkenhead** *Corporation ferry boat* Bidston *is pictured prior to beginning its first sailing 28 February 1933*

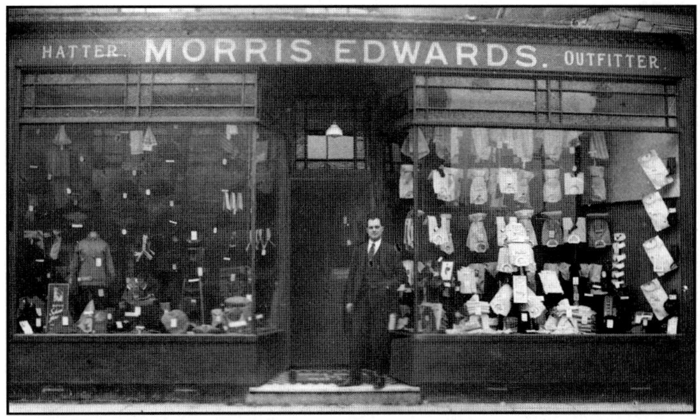

Above: *Morris Edwards pictured outside his shop at 5 Well Lane **Rock Ferry** which opened in 1927. The seventh child of a farming family from Llangwn North Wales, he came to work at Allansons, Grange Road **Birkenhead** after army service during the First World War. In 1923 he opened his first gents' outfitters at 290, Old Chester Road, later selling ladies' clothes here and gents' at 5 Well Lane. Together with his two sons he would later establish other gentlemen's outfitters at **New Ferry** and **Heswall**. During this period shops lined long stretches of Old Chester Road and New Chester Road, social structures were different. People like Mr Edwards were familiar figures, forming a strong part of the framework of society and commerce - keeping money within the area of those that spent it. Economic fortunes were also different. Well Lane had a photographer who also had premises in Bold Street Liverpool, at the corner of Bedford Road and New Chester Road was an antique shop described as one of the best in England and in 1927, 2,800,000 people travelled on the Rock Ferry steamer [see below, 1938 and 1952]*

Below: *Successive Merit Awards in the London Window Dressing Competition, for displays like this one in Morris Edwards' Well Lane branch, featuring a chameleon, prompted a Saville Row trade paper to write of Morris Edwards "the good taste and refinement displayed is indicative of an establishment of the very best description" [see above, 1938 & 1952]*

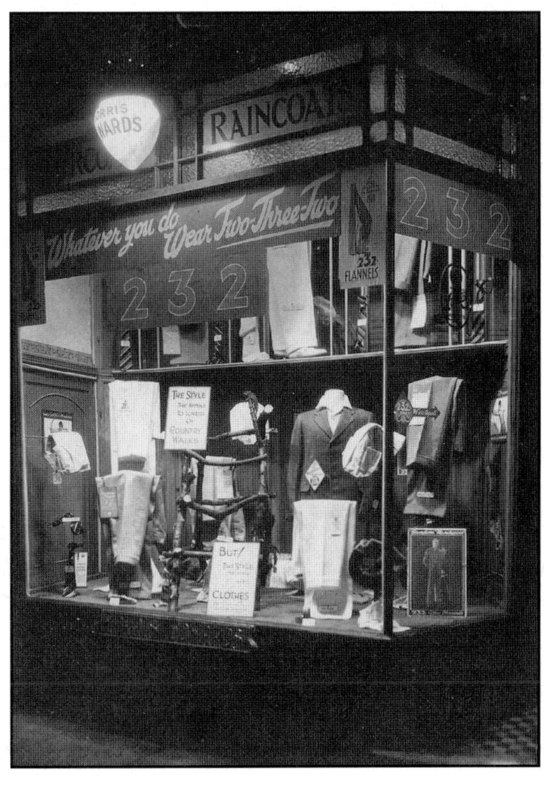

– New road safety measures introduced including 'Belisha Beacons', traffic lights and the 30 mph speed limit

– Two parcels of land between Osmaston Road and Glenavon Road **Prenton** were purchased by Higher **Tranmere** High School for Girls

– YMCA moved from Grange Road to Whetstone Lane **Birkenhead**

– **Landican** Cemetery opened in Arrowe Park Road

Mar 10 Last performance at the **Birkenhead** Hippodrome Theatre, Grange Road - bought by Birkenhead Co-op, who demolished it and erected a new building on the site[PROG]

Mar 16 Submarine *Sealion* launched at Cammell Laird **Birkenhead**[MOI]

Mar 31 Good Friday. 66,500 pay to walk through the new Mersey Road Tunnel for charity prior to being opened by the King with Queen Mary on 18 July [see photos on this and next page]

May 12 Destroyer HMS *Fearless* launched at Cammell Laird, **Birkenhead**[MOI]

June 29 Destroyer HMS *Foresight* launched at Cammell Laird, **Birkenhead**[MOI]

July 18 Queensway Mersey Tunnel opened by King George V and Queen Mary [see photo and article this and next page]
They also opened the new library in Borough Road **Birkenhead** - this was their last official engagement so they left for **Rock Ferry** Station where they departed the Borough [see article this page and photo next page]

Sept 29 The tram route, which ran from Woodside **Birkenhead** to Atherton Road, **Hr Tranmere**, closed[BET]

Nov 4 St John The Evangelist RC Church Bebington Road **New Ferry** opened[DoS]

MERSEY TUNNEL - OPENED 18 JULY 1934

*Following a committee being set up in 1922 to decide between a bridge or tunnel to link **Birkenhead** and **Liverpool** - the latter was chosen and the ratepayers of Birkenhead, Liverpool and Bootle decided by Poll in favour of the project. In August 1925 an Act of Parliament was passed, which granted a capital contribution of £2,500,000 towards the costs of construction and the charging of tolls was permitted. Work started the Liverpool side of the River Mersey in December 1925 and Birkenhead March 1926. Two pilot headings were driven from each side of the river, one above the other. When they met mid-river in April 1928, the two tunnels were broken out into one, taking the form of a large iron tube. The tube was bisected with the top half carrying the roadway. A branch tunnel was constructed at either end [only the Liverpool branch tunnel is used today]. The Tunnel, which cost £8 million was opened by King George V on 18 July 1934 and named 'Queensway' in honour of Queen Mary. Initially the tunnel was under-used but by the 1960s the Tunnel could not cope with the traffic - so a new one was constructed from Liverpool to Wallasey, work commencing January 1966. The Queen opened the new tunnel 24 June 1971, naming it 'Kingsway'.*

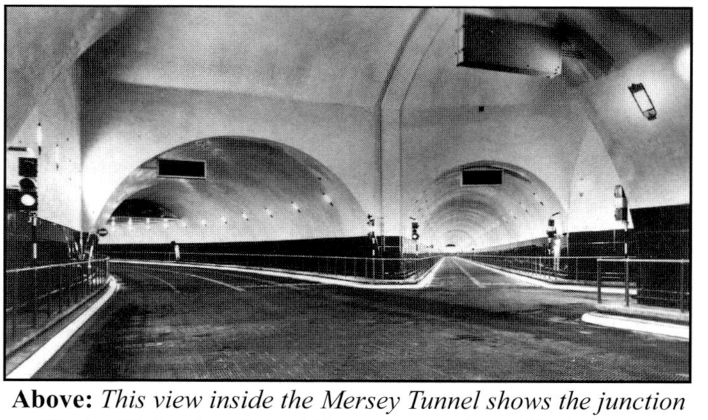

Above: *This view inside the Mersey Tunnel shows the junction with the **Birkenhead** Dock Branch exit, the traffic being controlled by traffic lights - this is no longer used [see 1956]*

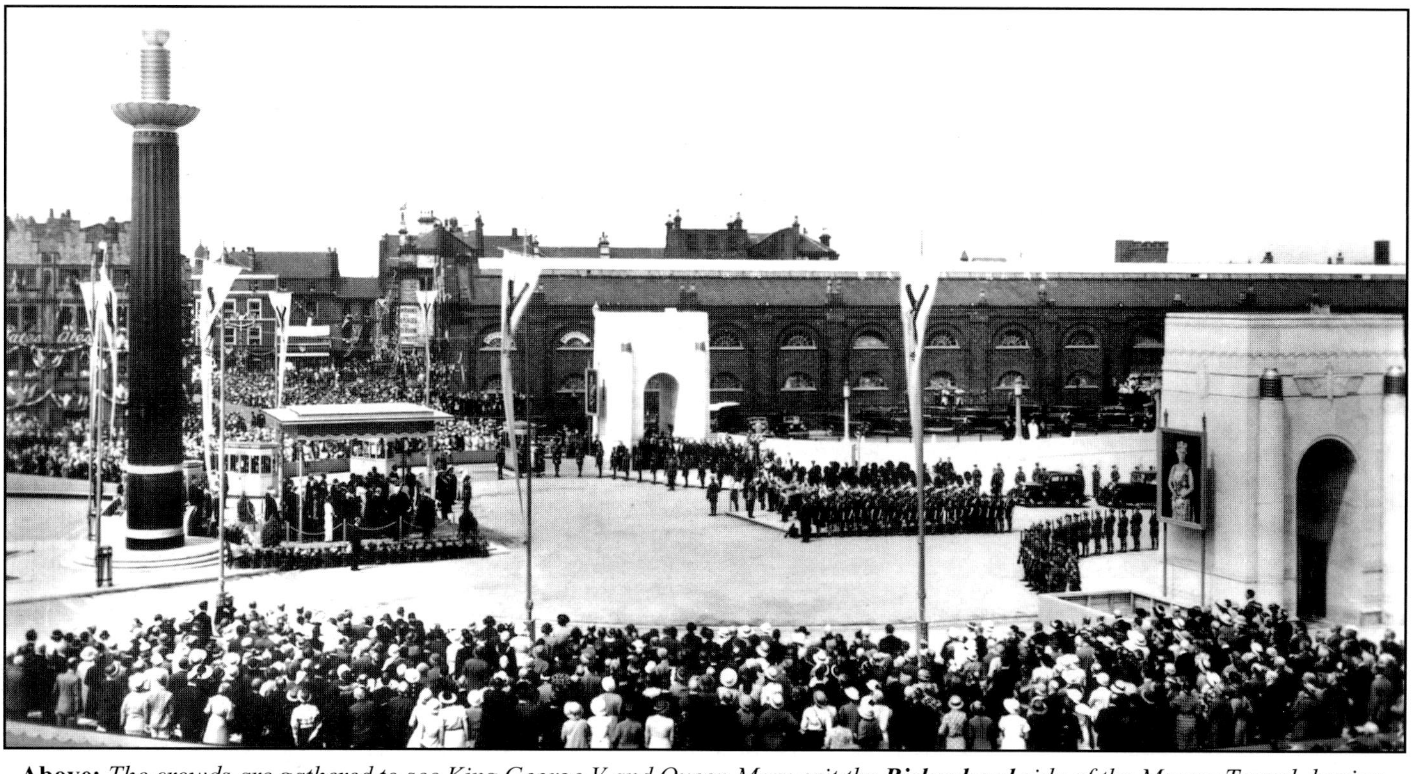

Above: *The crowds are gathered to see King George V and Queen Mary exit the **Birkenhead** side of the Mersey Tunnel, having officially opened it in **Liverpool.** The Royal Party alighted at the dias in front of the column where the Mayor and Mayoress of Birkenhead were presented to the King and Queen who in turn presented several of those involved in the project. Within five minutes the Royals were travelling along Borough Road to open the new library [see next page]*

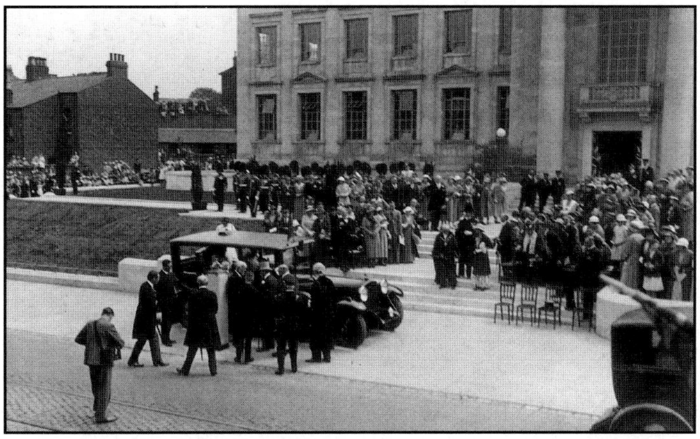

Above: *The King and Queen are seen outside the new Library in Borough Road* ***Birkenhead****. The King has just moved a switch on the white post by the Royal car which caused the Union Jacks either side of the main entrance to drop - which meant that the Library was officially opened. Beyond the Royal car is the Band of HM Coldstream Guards who played a selection of music prior to the arrival of their Majesties. Within five minutes of arriving the Royal Party was proceeding via Borough Road, Bedford Drive, Bedford Avenue, Bedford Road to* ***Rock Ferry*** *Station, where they departed the Borough*

Right: *This was an advert for Cycle dealer R Edmunds of 9 Whetstone Lane - over 70 years later the firm is still trading from the same address*

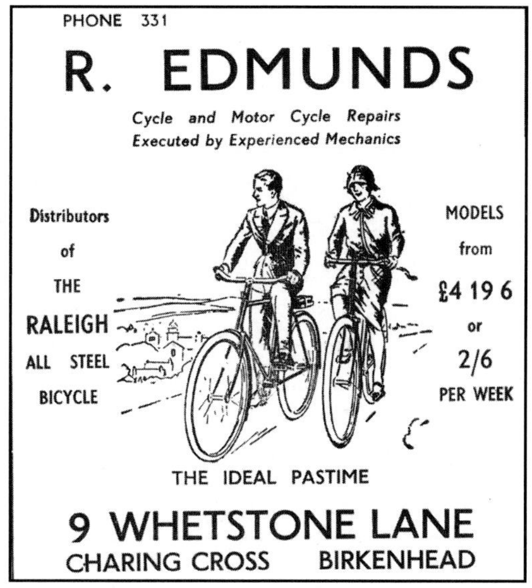

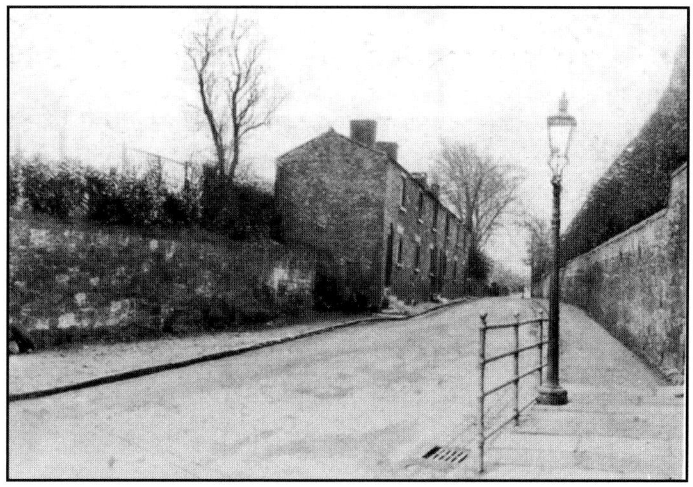

Above: *This view looking up Heath Road from Lower* ***Bebington*** *Village shows how narrow the road was before the cottages were demolished and the road widened*

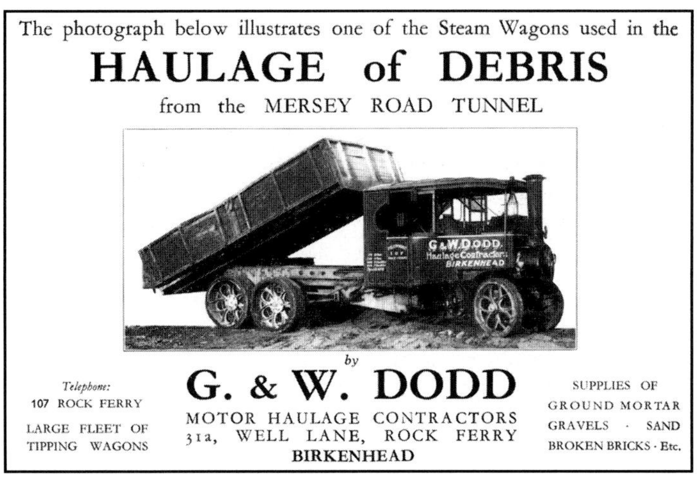

Left: *This was an advert for G & W Dodd of Well Lane,* ***Rock Ferry*** *who were one of the haulage contractors employed to remove debris from the tunnel, using their fleet of steam wagons - one is pictured. The total amount of rock and gravel excavated and removed was 1,200,000 tons*

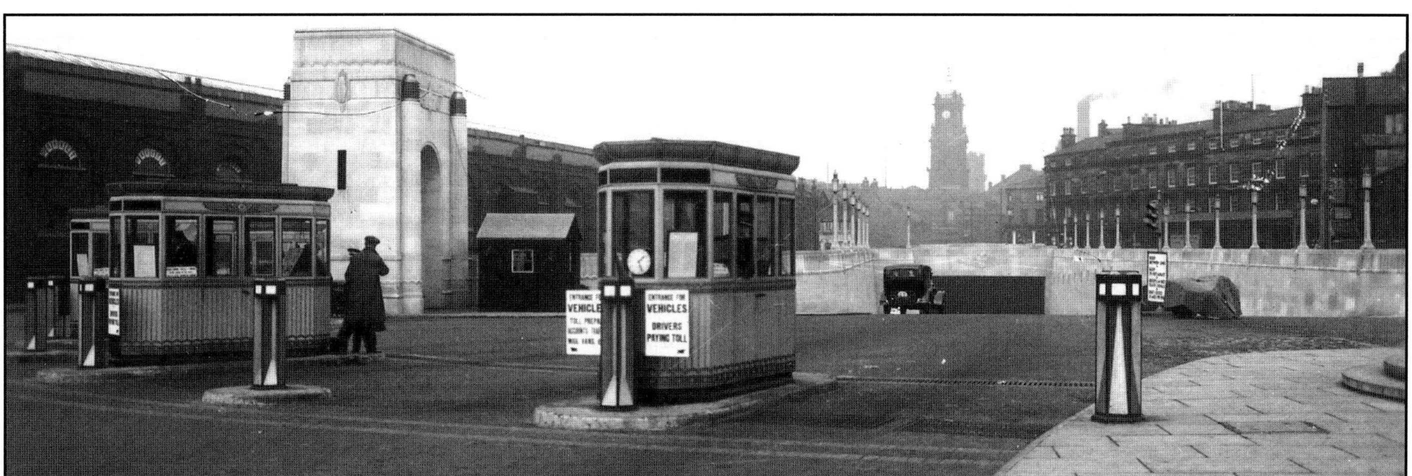

Above:- *A car is seen about to enter the Mersey Tunnel having paid a toll at one of the Toll Booths. Some interesting facts:- in 1959 the toll for a Pedal Bicycle (with rider) 3d [1p]; Pedal Bicycle (with rider) and side-car 6d [2p]; Motor cars per vehicle 1/6d [9p] plus 2d for each passenger over 14 and 1d for those under 14; Tractors 1/- & with trailer 1/6d; breakdown charges for a Bicycle 2/-, a car 5/-, all other vehicles £2 per hour minimum charge 10/-; for each 6 inches or fractions thereof of excess height (probably roof rack) 6d [the toll booth operators almost needed a maths degree!]. Speeds in the slow lane were between 6 and 21 mph - in the fast lane between 21 and 30 mph In the first year of operation 3 million vehicles used the tunnel - rising to 11 million by 1959 and 17 million by 1968. The traffic was eased when the new Kingsway tunnel opened in 1971*

1935

– **Birkenhead** Co-op Society opened new premises in Grange Road on the site of the Hippodrome Theatre [see 1934]

– New houses on the Townfield Estate, Townfield Lane **Bebington** built by G Brereton offered for sale from £650 to £825[SOUV] [see advert next page]

– Boulton's Sunshine Villas have eight developments on Wirral from £550 to £975

– Nine hole municipal golf course opened at Brackenwood **Bebington** [see photo]

Mar 2 **Birkenhead** Municipal Exhibition held at the Drill Hall, Grange Road West - the object of the exhibition was to enable every department of the Corporation to illustrate to the residents of the Borough, the progress they had made over a long period of years [see Revo advert][SOUV]

May **Tranmere** Cross rediscovered being used as a sun dial in the grounds of Tranmere Hall Farm - having disappeared in 1862 [see also 1937][SOUV]

May 6 King George V Silver Jubilee

June **Birkenhead** Police had to deal with a disturbance between dock labourers and 'blackshirts' (Fascists) in Park Street[MQP]

Sept 25 **Birkenhead** Town Council rejected a proposal that a Corporation Bus service should operate through the Mersey Tunnel [see 1956]

Nov The Borough Police Court in **Birkenhead** Town Hall was gutted by fire[NEWS]

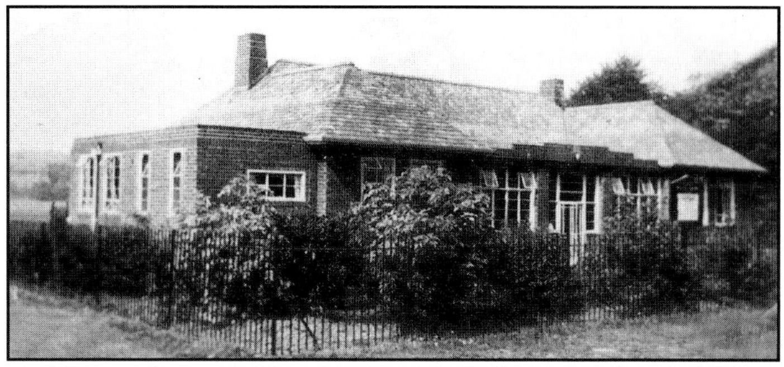

Above: *Due to an increasing population - the demand for welfare services was greater than ever. In 1935 this new Maternity and Child Welfare Centre was opened in* ***New Ferry*** *Park and was claimed to be one of the most up-to-date in the country. The scheme provided ante-natal and post-natal care and treatment; an ear, nose and throat clinic; dental treatment for expectant and nursing mothers and children; orthopaedic clinic; toddlers' clinic; treatment of defective vision; free supply of milk and food to necessitous mothers and a massage and remedial exercises department. A home help service had been in operation for many years*

Below: *St Andrew's Church is seen in the distance in Church Road Lower* ***Bebington*** *with a Birkenhead Corporation bus by Edgeworth Road*

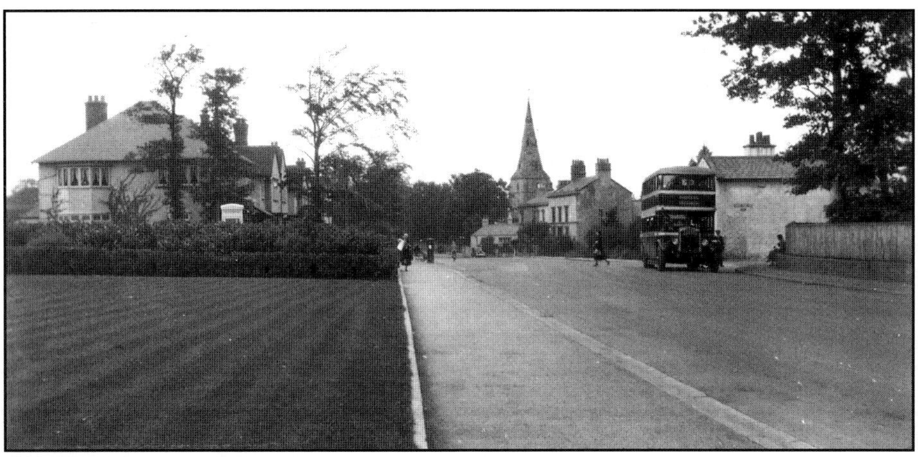

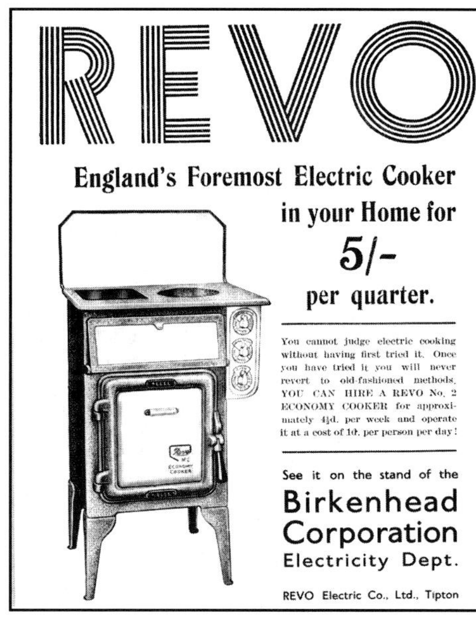

Above: *Revo Cookers could be bought from the* ***Birkenhead*** *Corporation Electricity Department*

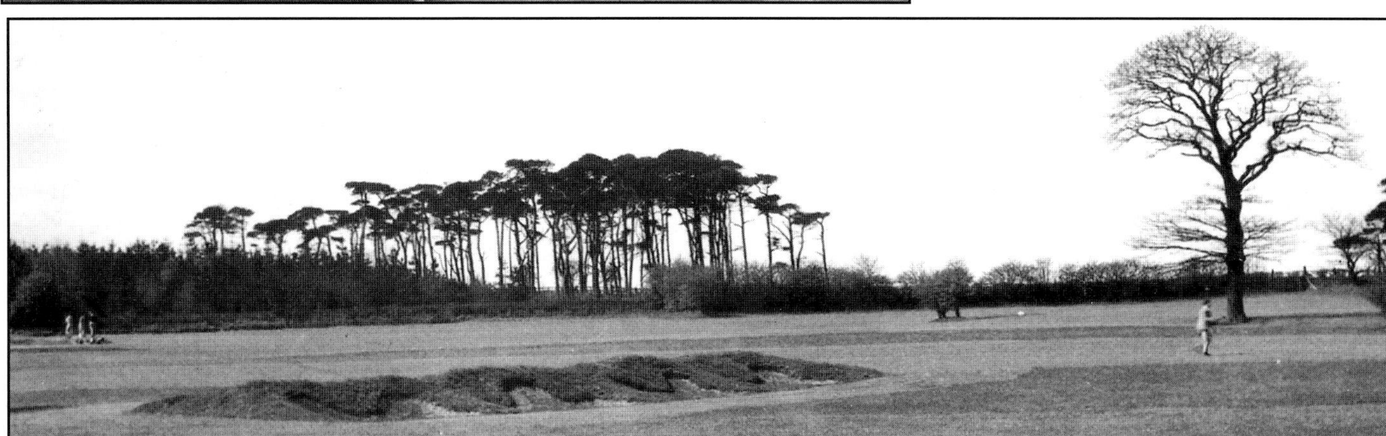

Above: *Following the closure of Bebington Golf Club, Town Lane* ***Bebington*** *in 1935, the greens were moved to Arrowe Park and the members joined the new nine hole Brackenwood Golf Club, Hr Bebington, using a room in* Brackenwood House *[see 1939] as the clubhouse. A Ladies Golf Club was formed here in 1936. In 1939 the house was taken over by the military, the fairways ploughed up and vegetables grown for the war effort - the course was re-instated in 1946. By 1954,* Brackenwood House *had become unstable due to dry rot so the clubhouse moved to the former stables to the* Brackenwood House. *The Golf Club bought Needlewood Farm from Lord Leverhulme in the 1970s and extended the course to 18 holes, opening in 1976*

1936

– St Stephen's new Church Hall, **Prenton** opened - built at a cost of £3,300, it replaced the original one which had been the temporary church from 1894 to 1897[SOUV]

– St Philip's Church opened at **Storeton**. It was decided to build a Parochial Hall which could accommodate up to 250 people - following the proposed housing development of Storeton and surrounding area by the Leverhulme Estate Office. Three acres of land had been set aside for the project which meant that if a larger Church was needed, there was sufficient land to build a new Church with the Church Hall already in place. The Second World War intervened and the development never took place. However, the Storeton Mission, with the assistance of the Diocesan Board of Finance, purchased the freehold in 1940. Services continued until 1977 and in 1984 was sold for private development. The Church retained a plot of land which was let for grazing - in event of the redevelopment of the village, the Church would still have an interest

– First edition of the ***Bebington** News*[FB]

– ***Tranmere** New Hall*, which stood in the angle between Greenway Road and Prenton Road East, was demolished[SOT]

Jan 20 **King George V died**

June Work started on the new *Ritz* cinema in **Birkenhead**

Sept 2 **Upton** Library opened [see photo next page]

Dec 11 **King Edward VIII abdicates**

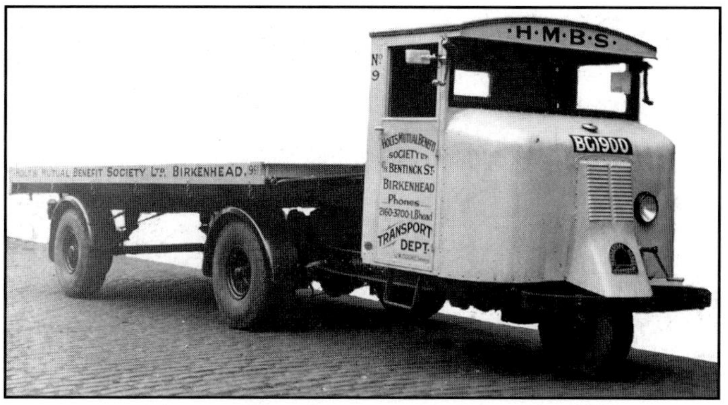

Above: *The Scammell Mechanical Horse was introduced in the early 1930s. It only had one wheel at the front which made it easy to manouevre around busy streets and was economical to run - note the starting handle. It is seen here before being delivered to HMBS - Holt's Mutual Benefit Society Ltd, Bentinck Street* ***Birkenhead***

Right: *Boulton's builders were based at Old Chester Road* ***Rock Ferry*** *- they advertised 'Sunshine Villas' at eight developments across Wirral which could be rented from 13/7 per week [75p]*

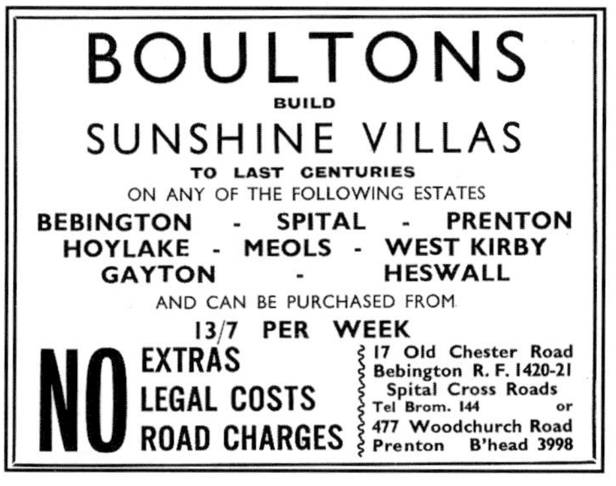

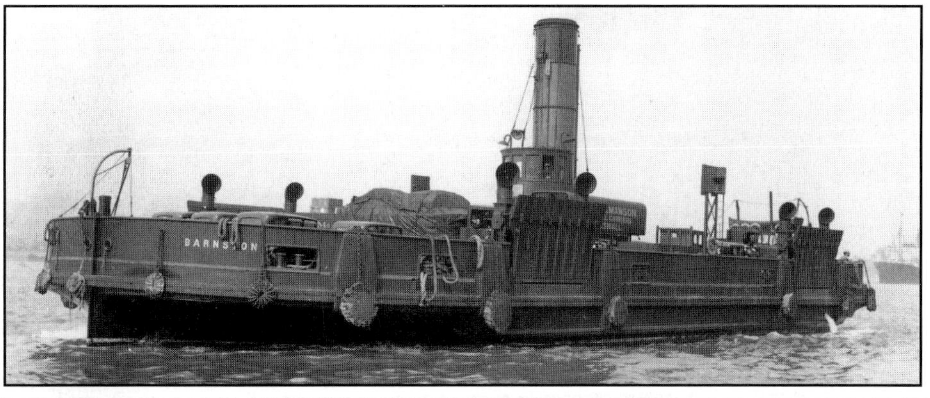

Left: *The Birkenhead Corporation Luggage Boat* Barnston *is seen in the River Mersey where she transported vehicles between* ***Birkenhead*** *to* ***Liverpool****. When she was launched in 1921 there was a great demand for her services until the Mersey Road Tunnel opened in 1934*

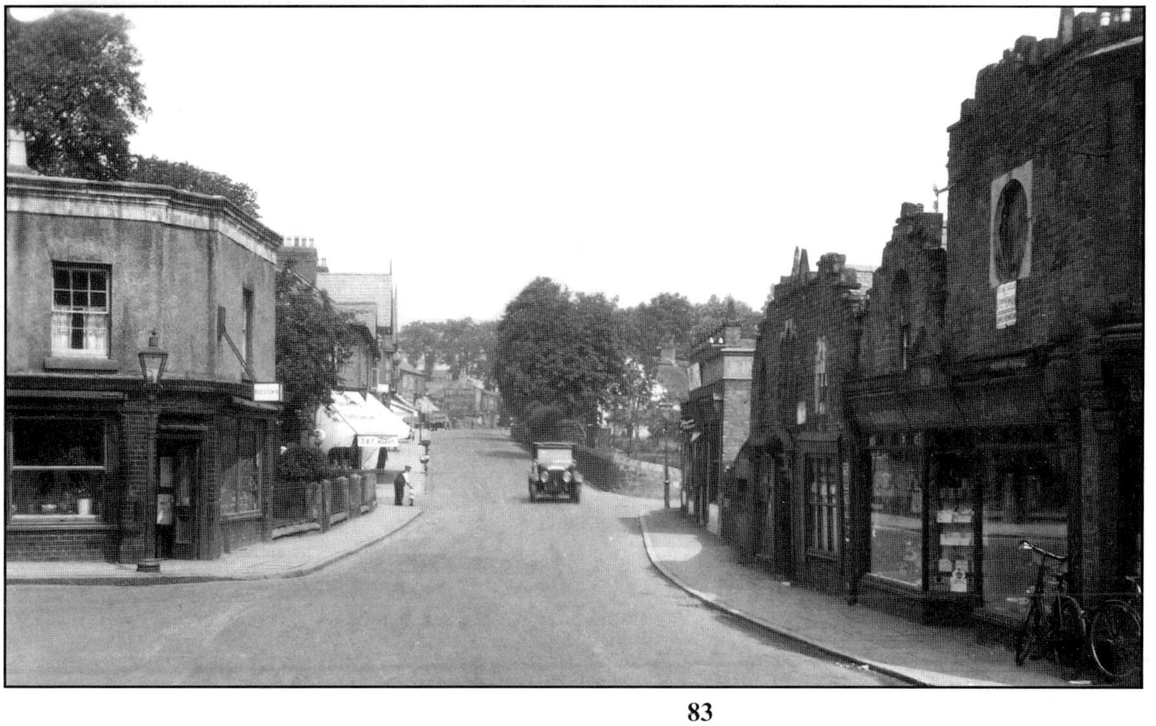

Left: *The Grove is to the right of the car which is travelling down The Village Lower* ***Bebington*** *with Heath Road on the left. The near buildings were demolished 1964-5 and the road widened, with the original fountain dating back to 1863 being re-instated in 1996 from its temporary home of 93 years in Mayer Park [see 1903]*

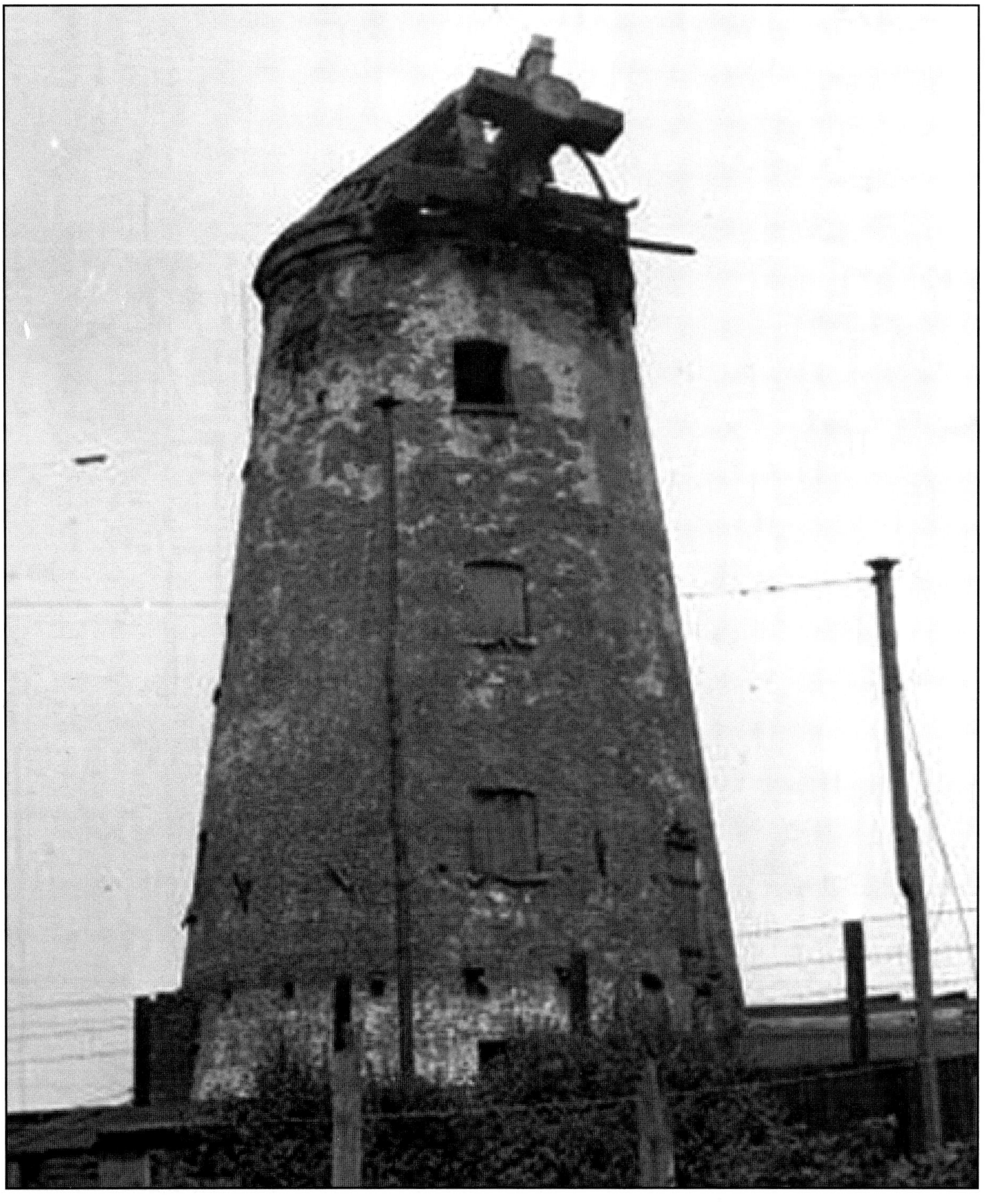

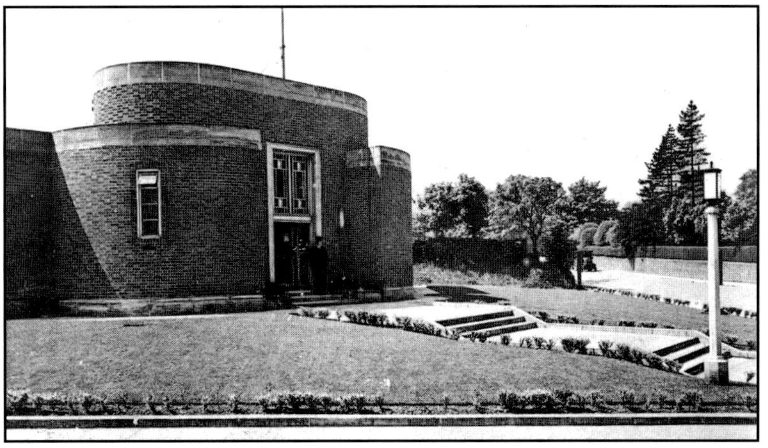

Above: *Higher* ***Bebington*** *Tower Mill, which was a landmark for over 150 years, is seen in School Lane. It was diagonally opposite the old school, in a state of neglect and without its sails. This mill dates back to the early 19th century and operated until the beginning of the 20th century. The sails were deemed unsafe and were taken down during the First World War. It was used for storing machinery and during the Second World War used as a look-out post. In 1963 it was listed as "a building of special architectural and historic interest" - but despite this, was demolished c1971 and houses built on the site[see also 1906]*

Above: *The newly opened* ***Upton*** *Public Library is seen here in Upton Road with a Commissionaire in uniform and flat cap standing by the entrance. Opened 2 September 1936, it was built by JA Milestone & Son Ltd of Wallasey at a cost of £6,200*

1937

– The *Arrowe Park Hotel* replaced *Horse & Jockey Inn* at **Woodchurch** [see photo next page][WTDW]

– Tutty's store in Oxton Road **Birkenhead** taken over by Rostances

– *Swan Hotel* Holm Lane **Oxton** rebuilt

– YMCA sold their premises in Grange Road **Birkenhead** to British Home Stores and started to build their new premises in Whetstone Lane[SOUV]

– The Birkenhead Photographic Association, who had been affiliated to the YMCA decided to sever connections when the YMCA sold their premises - this was done in a spirit of goodwill [see 1884][SOUV]

Feb 12 The 1,316 seater *Regal Cinema* opened (later *Essoldo*) in Bebington Road **Rock Ferry**

Apr 13 Aircraft carrier *Ark Royal* launched at Cammell Laird **Birkenhead** – she was the first ship to be designed and built as an aircraft carrier [see photo]

May 10 King George V Memorial unveiled adjoining Central Library Borough Road **Birkenhead** [see photo 1934]

May 12 King George VI crowned - see Grange Road decorated for the occasion on the next page

July 15 Jubilee Week - Scout Show at St Anselm's College Hall **Birkenhead**[PROG]

July 17 Last **Birkenhead** electric tram ran on the Circle Route[BET]

Oct **Tranmere** Cross re-erected in Victoria Park [see photo next page, 1862 and 1935][SOUV]

Oct 4 The new *Ritz Cinema* between Claughton Road and Oliver Street **Birkenhead** was opened by Gracie Fields as the "Showpiece of the North" [see 1958][PROG]

Oct 4 Week long "Geneva at **Birkenhead** International Week" held in the Town Hall

Oct 17 Bruce Ismay died (White Star Line)

Sept 28 **Bebington** received its Royal Charter

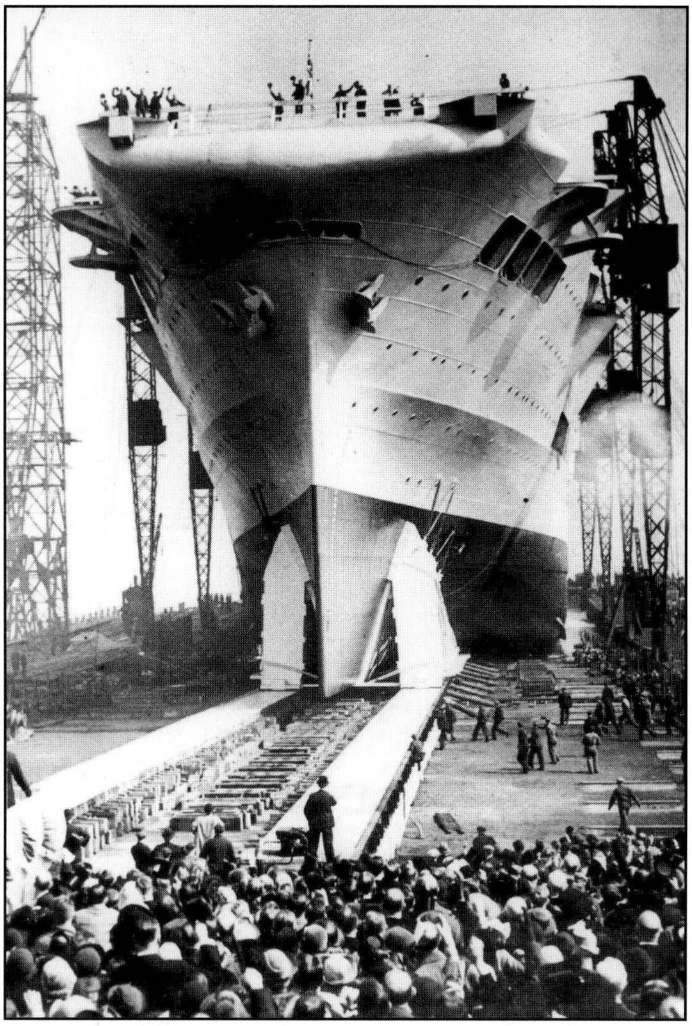

Above: *The* Ark Royal *was launched at Cammell Laird* ***Birkenhead*** *on 13 April 1937 - she was the first ship to be designed and built as an aircraft carrier, carrying up to 60 aircraft including Blackburn Skuas and Fairey Swordfish. She was fitted out just before war broke out in September 1939 and took part in several battles including tracking down the* Graf Spee *and the sinking of the* Bismarck. *She was torpedoed off Gibralta 13 November 1941 and sank*

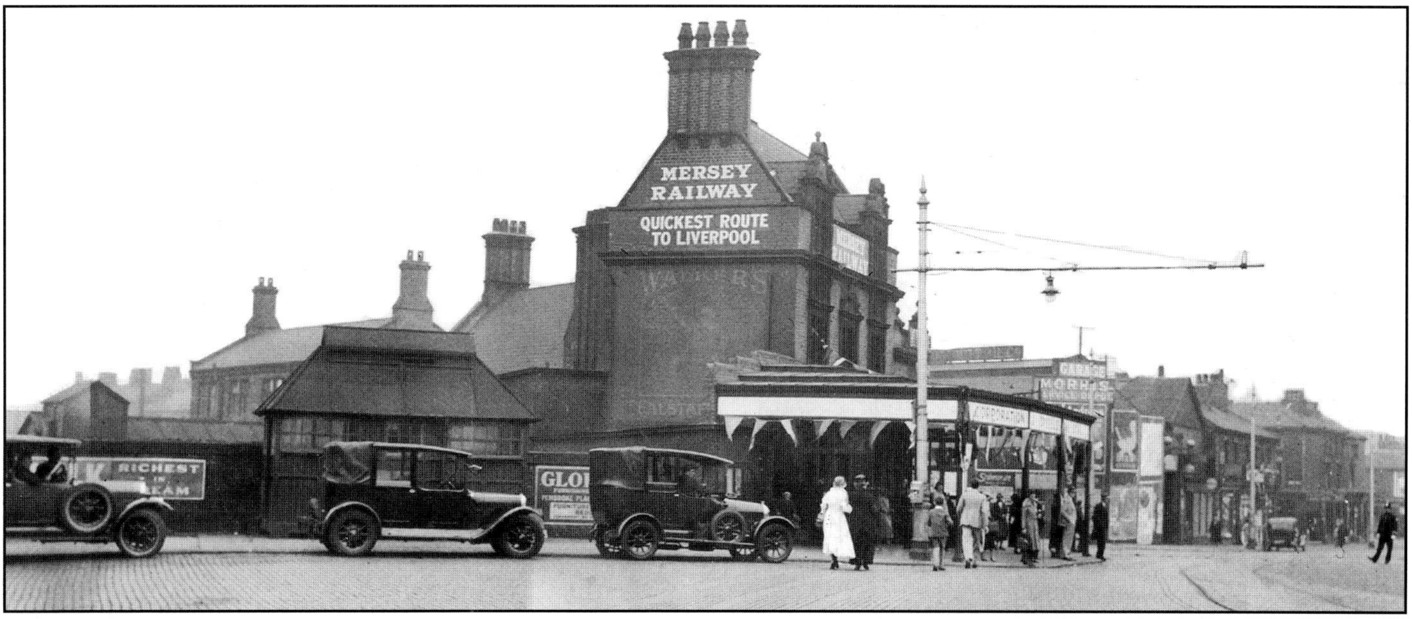

Above: *The taxis were waiting outside Central Station for custom in Borough Road* ***Birkenhead*** *- an advert for Mersey Railway on top of the station building describes it as the "Quickest Route to Liverpool" [compared to the Mersey ferries]. A policeman is seen to the right on duty in the middle of Borough Road facing Argyle Street South*

1937 continued

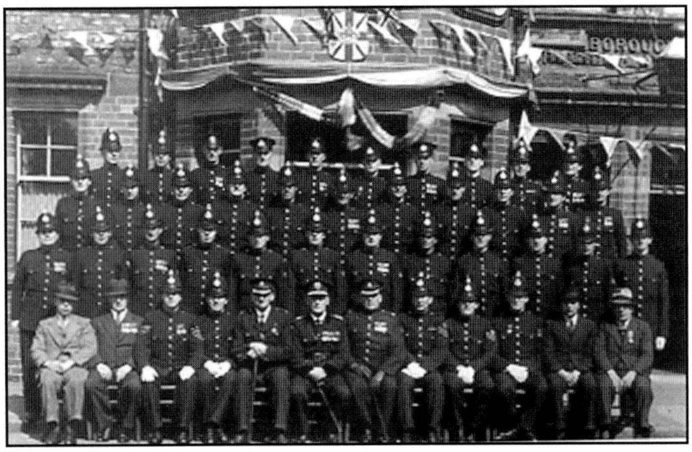

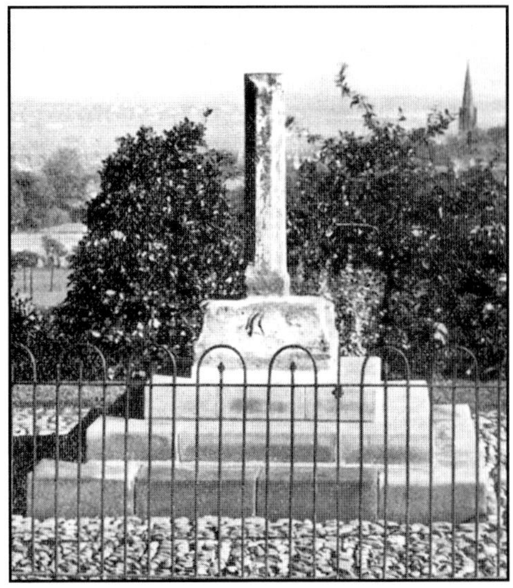

Right: *Tranmere Cross, which was lost in 1862, was found in 1935 and seen here re-erected in Victoria Park* **Tranmere** *[see 1862]*

Above: *This group of policemen are pictured outside Slatey Road Police Station with the flags celebrating the Coronation of King George VI. The station, which opened in 1902, was destroyed by bombing 29 September 1940 [see photo 1940]*

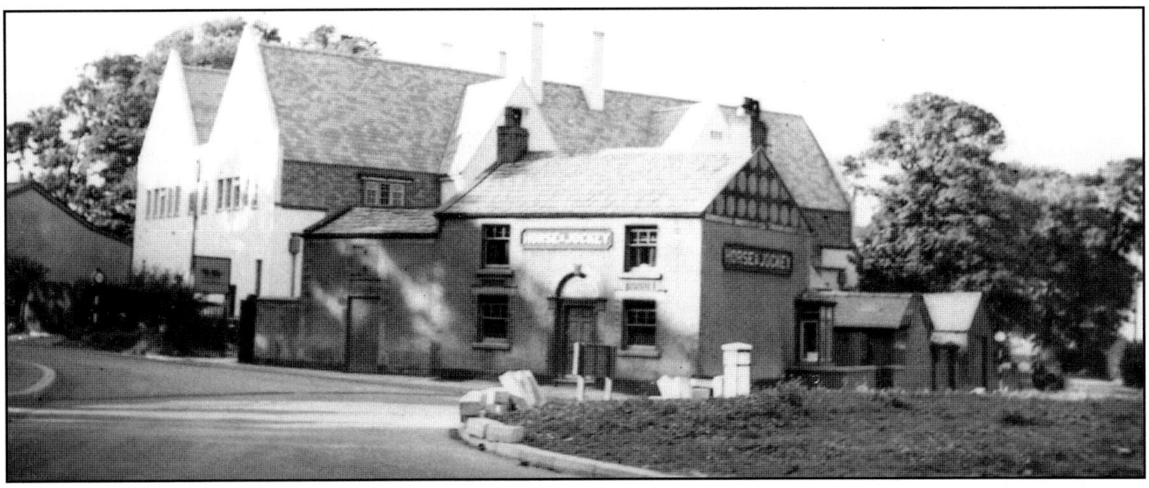

Left: *The* Horse & Jockey Inn *is seen in front of the new* **Arrowe** Park Hotel. *The licence changed overnight from the old to the new with the* Horse & Jockey Inn *being demolished [see 1907] - the site is now the area in front of the Arrowe Park Hotel. The road layout changed with the roundabout being installed*

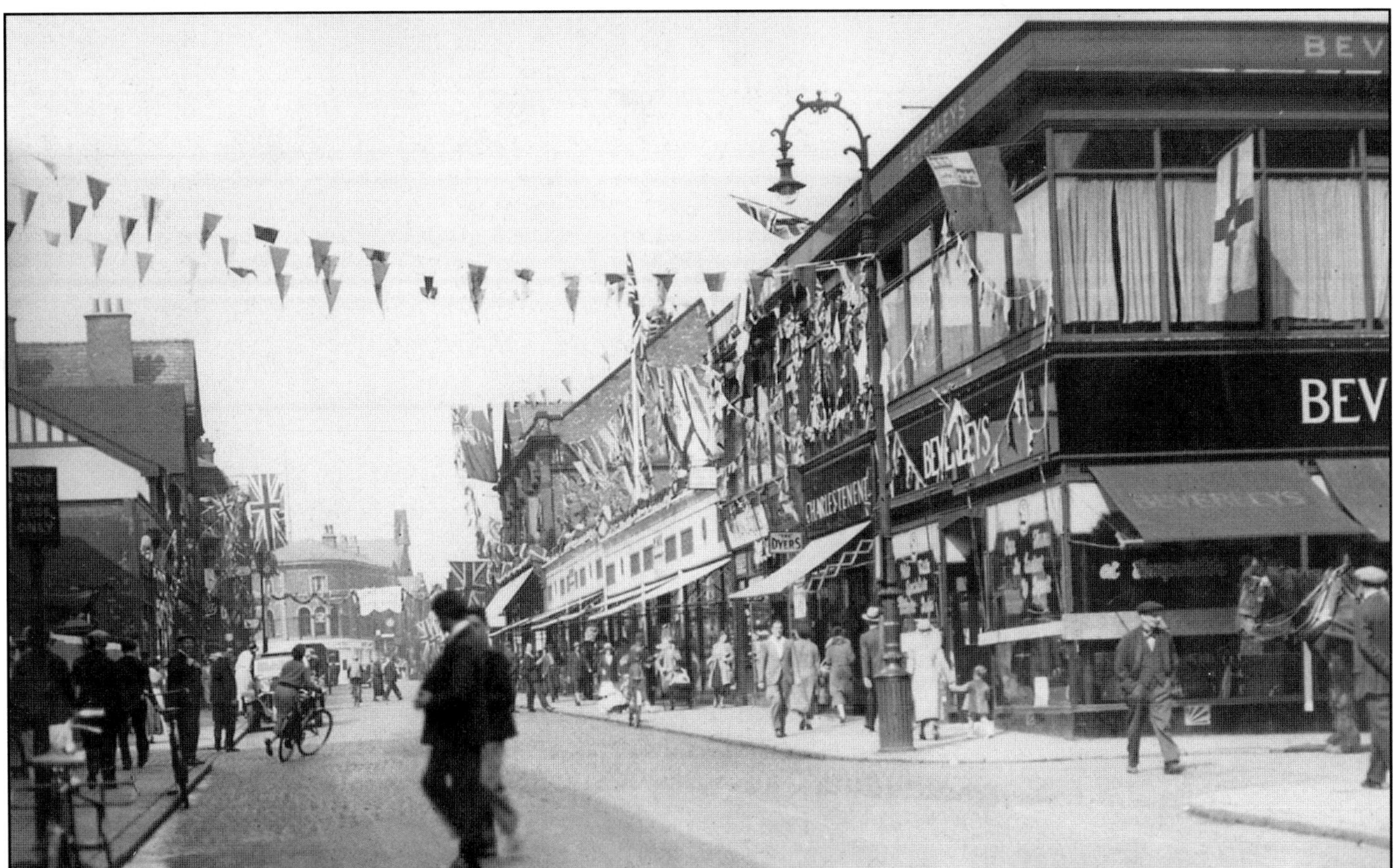

Above: *Grange Road* **Birkenhead** *is decorated for the Coronation of King Gearge VI - Beverley's Home Furnishing shop is seen on the right at the junction of Catherine Street and in the distance Robb Bros Drapers etc at Nos, 230-246*

1938

– **Birkenhead** Fire Station Whetstone Lane was extended to include married quarters

– The **Upton** by-pass [Arrowe Park Road] was built easing the congestion in Rake Lane

– St Stephen's Church **Prenton** - new Vicarage acquired replacing the one in Acrefield Road[SOUV]

Feb 4 New YMCA building opened in Whetstone Lane **Birkenhead** built by Lloyd & Cross and opened by the Earl of Shrewsbury

May 30 New *Gaumont Cinema* opened Park Road East **Birkenhead** showing 'I See Ice' starring George Formby[GB]

June 29 The launch of the submarine *Thetis* from Cammell Laird **Birkenhead** [see photo next page]

July 28 The 34,000 ton Cunard liner SS *Mauretania* launched at Cammell Laird **Birkenhead** [see photo next page][MOI]

Oct 6 Overchurch Primary School Moreton Road **Upton** opened

Right: *David Evans is advertising properties for sale or rent at: Manor Hill* ***Claughton*** *- described as "The most favoured position in Merseyside"; Carlett Park Estate - "in the delightful village of* ***Eastham****"; Ford Hill Estate "On the Western slopes of* ***Bidston*** *Hill - a noteable Wirral beauty spot"*

THREE

Attractive Estates

WITH UNEQUALLED CHARM & FACILITIES.

Manor Hill Estate

CLAUGHTON, BIRKENHEAD

THE MOST FAVOURED POSITION ON MERSEYSIDE

Convenient to Trains (Park Station), Trams, 'Buses, Excellent Shops, Schools, Parks.

FIFTEEN MINUTES FROM CENTRE OF LIVERPOOL.

Carlett Park Estate

BEBINGTON

Situate in the delightful village of Eastham,

BEAUTIFUL WOODLAND COUNTRY

Houses overlooking the river.

Excellent Bus services to all parts

Ford Hill Estate

BIDSTON

On the Western slopes of Bidston Hill.

A NOTED WIRRAL BEAUTY SPOT

Magnificent situation.

Both beautiful and convenient.

Houses to be Sold or Let

WE HAVE A REPUTATION EXTENDING OVER 35 YEARS FOR GOOD MATERIALS, SOUND CONSTRUCTION, DISTINCTIVE DESIGN.

Freehold Land. Garage Space to each House. Clean Concrete Roads.

Inspect these Estates and obtain Particulars from

The Hamilton Estates Ltd., or

DAVID EVANS & SON,

8, HAMILTON SQUARE, BIRKENHEAD.

Telephone **391**

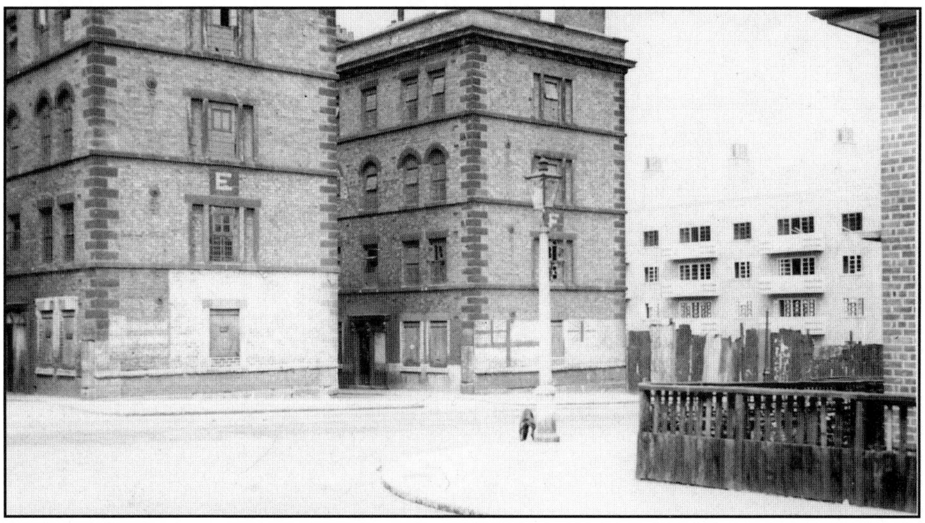

Above: *This 'old and new' photograph taken from Townsend Road shows the old Dock cottages on the left and the almost complete Ilchester Square flats on the right - both empty. Blocks E & F (letters on end of blocks) were among the first to be built in 1844. There were four or five 'houses' in each block - each house had eight flats. All the Dock Cottages had been demolished by 1939. The Ilchester Square flats did not last as long - being demolished in 1972*

Tailoring Dept.

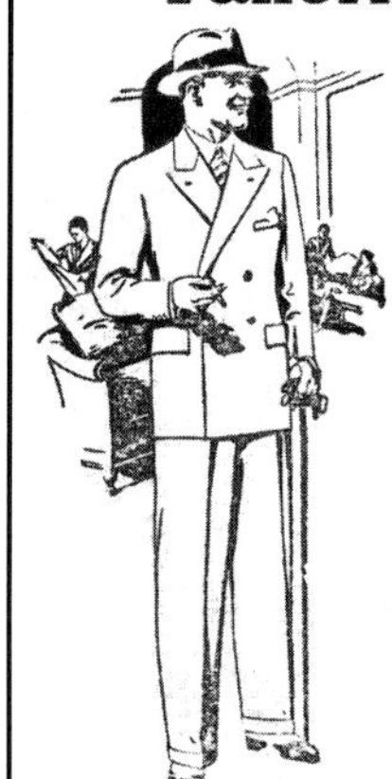

Don't make do with "READY MADE" and "NEAREST TO YOUR SIZE" SUIT when you can have one made exactly to your own measurements and style for the same cost at MORRIS EDWARDS, price:

50/- to £5-5-0

Personal attention to ensure correct balance and perfect fitting. Order your next suit FROM

Morris Edwards

(Tailor of Distinctive Clothes)

BEBINGTON ROAD, NEW FERRY.

WELL LANE, ROCK FERRY.

Open till 10 p.m. all Christmas week.
Keen prices. Phone 300 & 772. Cash Trade.

Above: *This advert was for Morris Edwards, Gentleman's Outfitters, who then had shops in* ***Rock Ferry*** *and* ***New Ferry*** *between 1935-41. The Rock Ferry branch opened in Well Lane in 1927 [see also 1933]. However, this building was destroyed following a bombing raid 12/13 March 1941. The building remained derelict until 1949 when it was purchased by Mr Trafford, who opened an optician's shop. The New Ferry branch opened in Bebington Road in 1935, finally closing in 2007 [see also 1933 and 1952]*

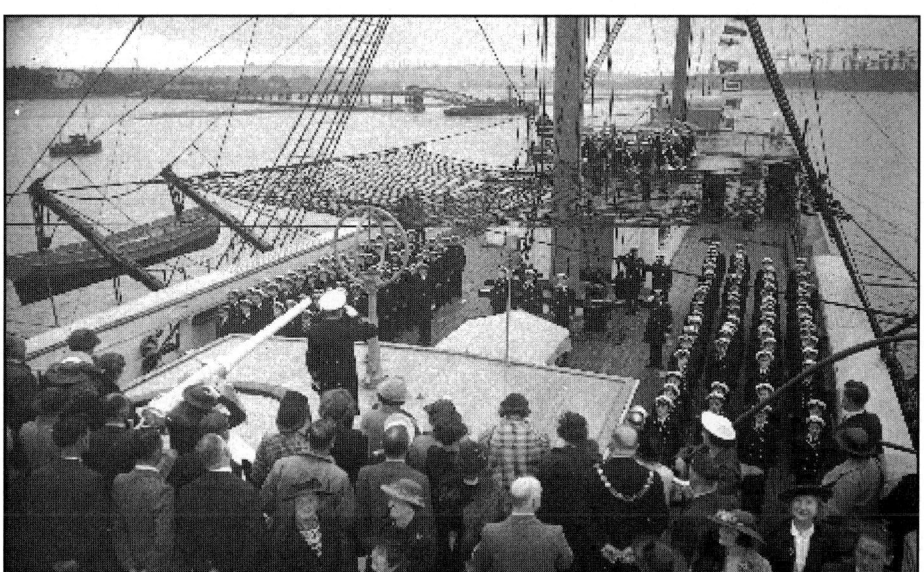

Left: *A view aboard the HMC* **Conway** *moored off* ***Rock Ferry*** *where the Mayor of Birkenhead looks on with parents and friends of the boys, who are being put through their paces. Rock Ferry Pier is seen in the background*

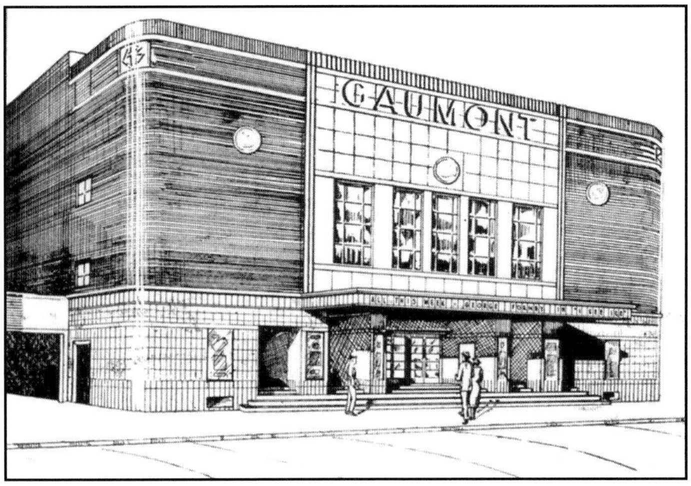

Above: *This sketch was in the opening brochure for the* Gaumont Cinema *in Park Road East,* ***Birkenhead*** *[see advert opposite]. It was originally the* Park Cinema *which closed on 21 January 1937 and was rebuilt at a cost of £40,000, with seating for 1,697. The cinema closed 4 January 1964, re-opening the same year as a Bingo and Social Club*[SSW1]

Right: *This was the first page of the Souvenir Brochure for the gala opening of the* Gaumont Cinema *in Park Road East,* ***Birkenhead*** *by the Mayor, Alderman C McVey with the star of the film, Miss Nova Pilbeam, on 30 May 1938 The film was the premier provincial presentation of* I See Ice *with George Formby [see sketch opposite]*[SSW1]

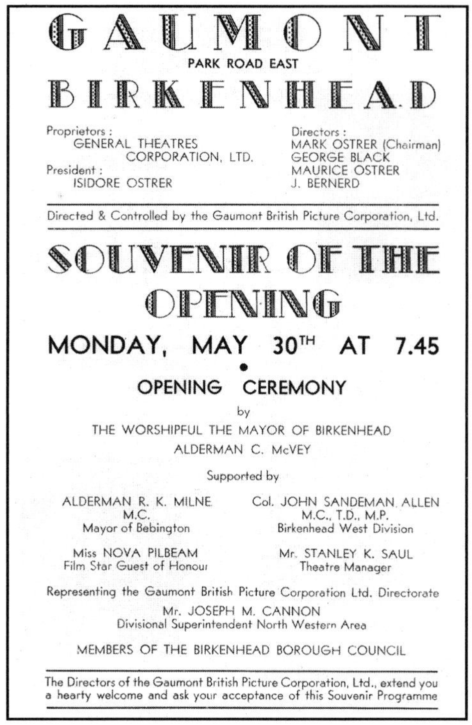
GAUMONT
PARK ROAD EAST
BIRKENHEAD

Proprietors :
GENERAL THEATRES CORPORATION, LTD.
President :
ISIDORE OSTRER

Directors :
MARK OSTRER (Chairman)
GEORGE BLACK
MAURICE OSTRER
J. BERNERD

Directed & Controlled by the Gaumont British Picture Corporation, Ltd.

SOUVENIR OF THE OPENING

MONDAY, MAY 30TH AT 7.45

•

OPENING CEREMONY

by

THE WORSHIPFUL THE MAYOR OF BIRKENHEAD
ALDERMAN C. McVEY

Supported by

ALDERMAN R. K. MILNE M.C.
Mayor of Bebington

Col. JOHN SANDEMAN ALLEN M.C., T.D., M.P.
Birkenhead West Division

Miss NOVA PILBEAM
Film Star Guest of Honour

Mr. STANLEY K. SAUL
Theatre Manager

Representing the Gaumont British Picture Corporation Ltd. Directorate
Mr. JOSEPH M. CANNON
Divisional Superintendent North Western Area

MEMBERS OF THE BIRKENHEAD BOROUGH COUNCIL

The Directors of the Gaumont British Picture Corporation, Ltd., extend you a hearty welcome and ask your acceptance of this Souvenir Programme

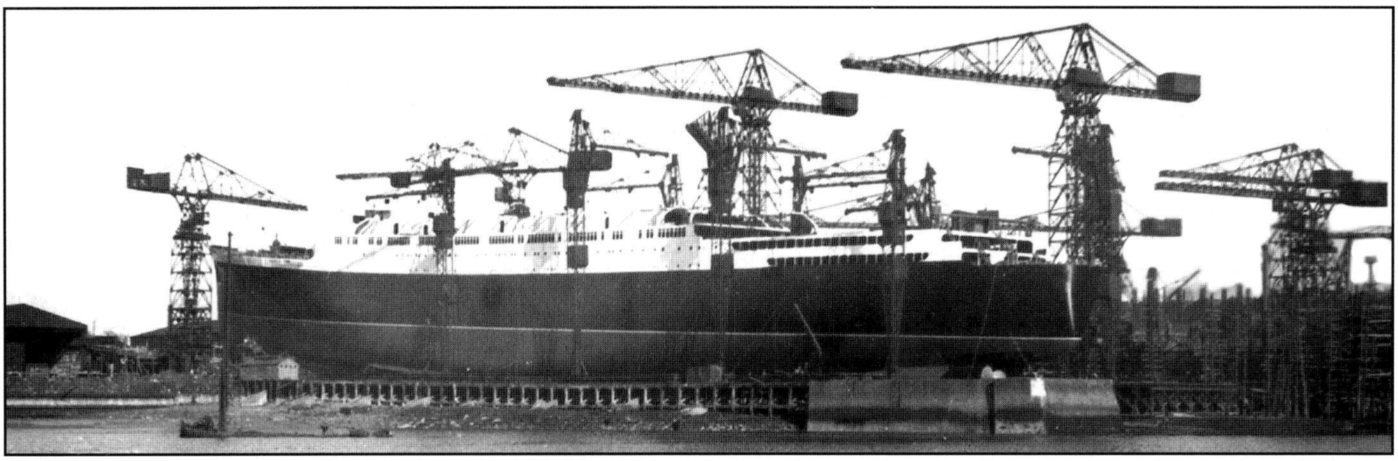

Above: *The Cunard White Star liner* Mauretania *is seen in the Cammell Laird shipyard* ***Birkenhead*** *ready for launching on 28 July 1938 - which was said to be the greatest day in the history of Cammell Laird. She was then the largest ship ever built in an English shipyard and although not a warship, she played an important role during the Second World War, successfully carrying some 335,000 troops over half a million miles. She was eventually scrapped in 1965*

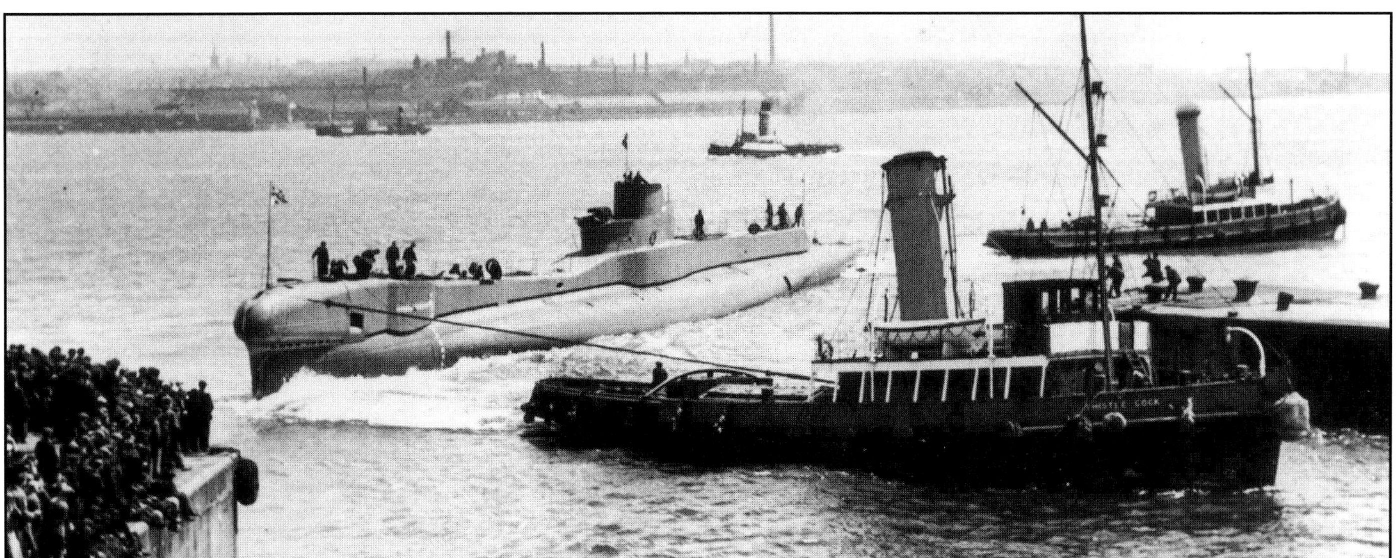

Above: *HMS* Thetis *is pictured in the River Mersey having just been launched at Cammell Laird* ***Birkenhead****. She sank in Liverpool Bay off Anglesey 1 June 1939 with the loss of 99 men - there were only four survivors [for more information see "The Admiralty Regrets" and "HMS Thetis - Secrets and Scandal" - Avid Publications]*

1939

– Part of St Catherines Hospital in Church Road **Tranmere** became a military hospital

– By 1939 the workhouse at **Clatterbridge** had been redeveloped as a hospital

Mar 20 *Central Hotel* Clifton Crescent [opposite Central Station] **Birkenhead** opened

May 3 *Prince of Wales* launched at Cammell Laird **Birkenhead**

June 1 Submarine *Thetis* sank on trials, 99 died with only four survivers [see photo on previous page]

June 17 SS *Mauretania* sailed on its maiden voyage to New York

June 19 The contents of *Redcourt* Devonshire Place **Birkenhead** sold at auction by the executors of the late Miss Alice Rae, daughter of George Rae

June 30 **Rock Ferry** ferry closed [see photo]

Sept 3 **Birkenhead** Institute evacuated to Oswestry and shared the buildings of Oswestry High School - this was not a success as only half the school went and the phoney war made it unreal and pointless. They had all returned by April 1940[SOUV]

Sept 3 WAR DECLARED

Sept 3 **Birkenhead** Police Force declared that following the outbreak of war and the introduction of the 'black-out', an increasing number of accidents were reported involving vehicles[MQP]

Nov 13 *Palace Cinema* New Chester Road **Rock Ferry** re-opened with the film 'Stagecoach'

Dec **Higher Tranmere** High School for Girls closed due to the school being compelled to evacuate to Dolgelley, North Wales[SOUV]

Dec 1 **Birkenhead** General Hospital new Coronation wing opened by Lord Leverhulme - built at a cost of £25,000[SOUV]

Dec 15 Mr Robert Smith's two sons gifted an ambulance to the **Birkenhead** Red Cross Society in his memory

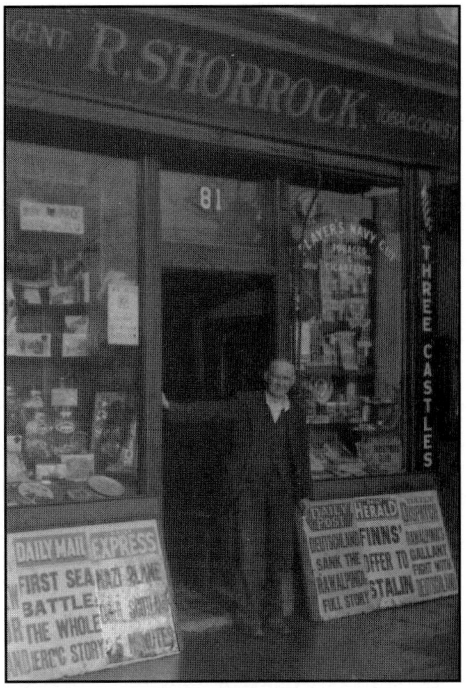

Right: *This peaceful photograph of Mr Shorrock outside his shop at 81 New Ferry Road* ***New Ferry*** *is put into perspective when you read the newspaper bill boards - including: "Deutschland sank the* Rawalpindi *- full story". There were only 17 survivors from the* Rawalpindi *out of 300 crew*

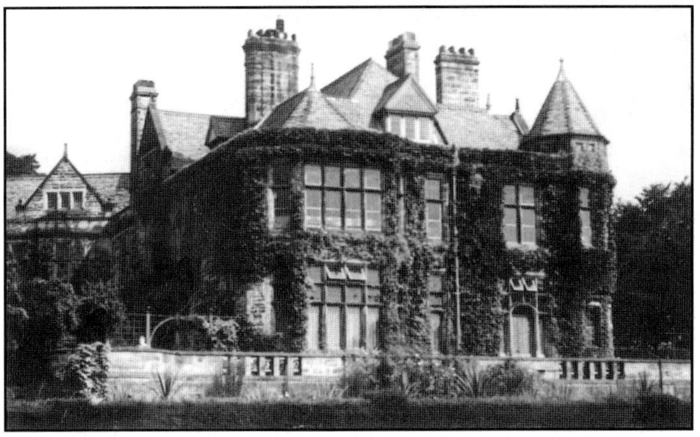

Above: Brackenwood House, *Bracken Lane* ***Bebington*** *was built in 1885 for John Evans (Evans Medical). It was purchased in 1920 by the Bebington Urban Council and used as offices. Brackenwood Golf Club used one of their rooms as a clubhouse [see 1935]. During the war it was used as a First Aid Centre. Due to dry rot it was demolished 1958*

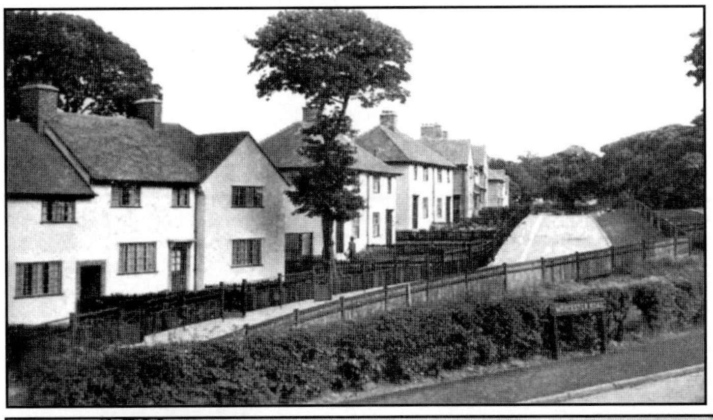

Left: *The houses seen in Worcester Road* ***Birkenhead*** *were built on one of the pre-war council estates erected in Birkenhead. Boundary Road is seen on the right parallel with the white Worcester Road [see 1901 for the cottages that once stood there]*

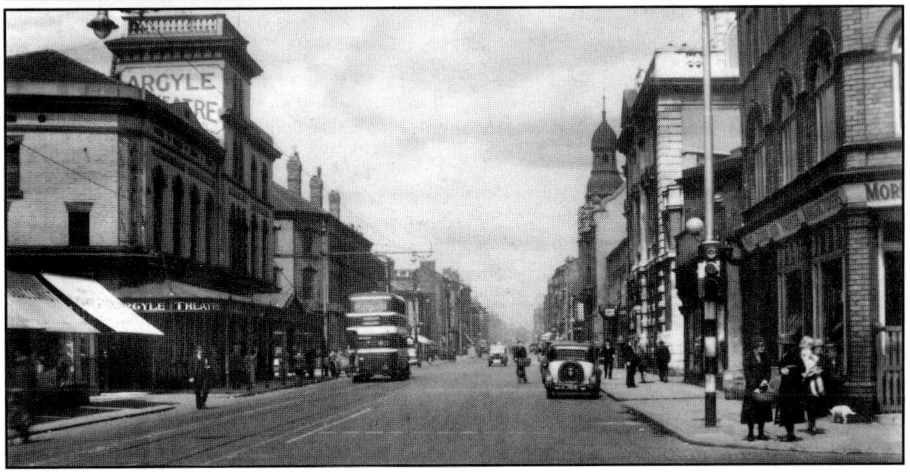

Left: *The bus on the left is passing the* Argyle Theatre *in Argyle Street* ***Birkenhead.*** *This theatre was opened here in 1868 and over the years, under the leadership of Dennis Clarke, became one of the leading theatres outside London. It was the first theatre to show moving pictures outside London and in 1931 became the first theatre to broadcast live on the radio. More fame followed when they were the first to broadcast direct to USA. Many stars appeared here over the years - that came to an end on 21 September 1940 when the theatre was destroyed [see 1940]*

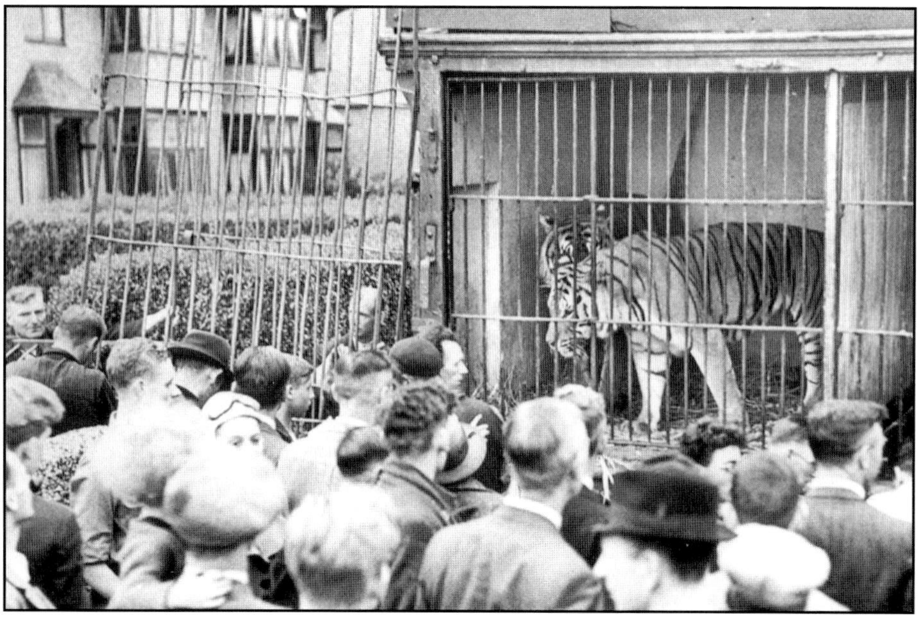

Left: *On 27 June 1939, Chapmans' Travelling Zoo & Circus were performing in Tranmere Rovers' car park. One of the circus hands was distracted when the two tigers Romeo and Bengal were returning from their performance via a cage tunnel and escaped. One of them wandered into the big top but was soon captured and returned to the cage. The other one leapt the hawthorn hedge into Borough Road. He lay down in the garden of No. 749 but was aroused when a police van and circus hands arrived, so set off across a few gardens. At No. 745 it was persuaded into the garage and when the doors were closed it soon fell asleep. The trainer coaxed Romeo into the cage tunnel which led to the travelling cage where he joined Bengal. They were back in time for the evening performance which went ahead as if nothing had happened!*

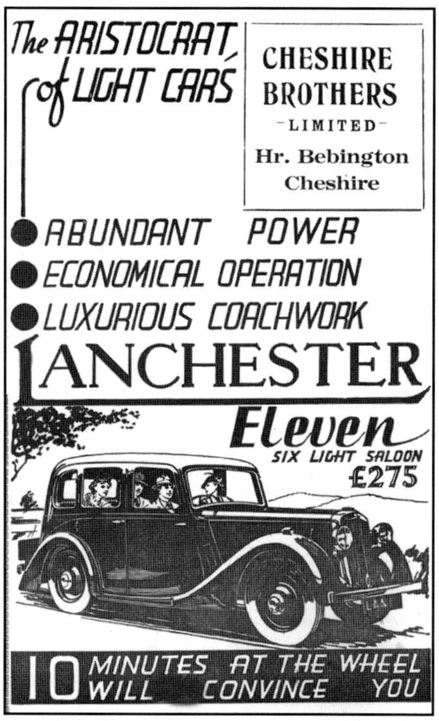

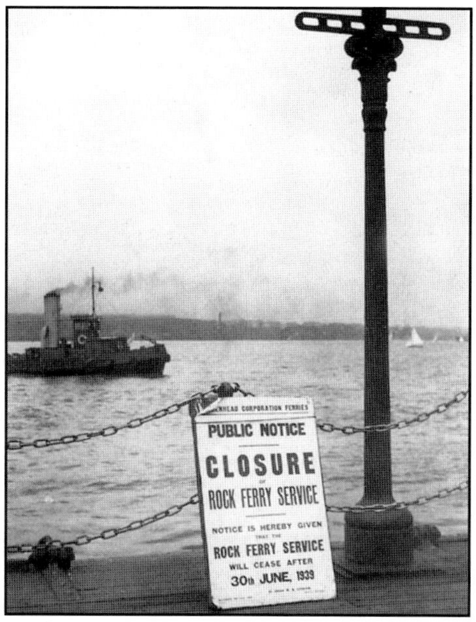

Above: *Notice of closure of the Rock Ferry ferry service displayed on* ***Rock Ferry*** *stage 30 June 1939*

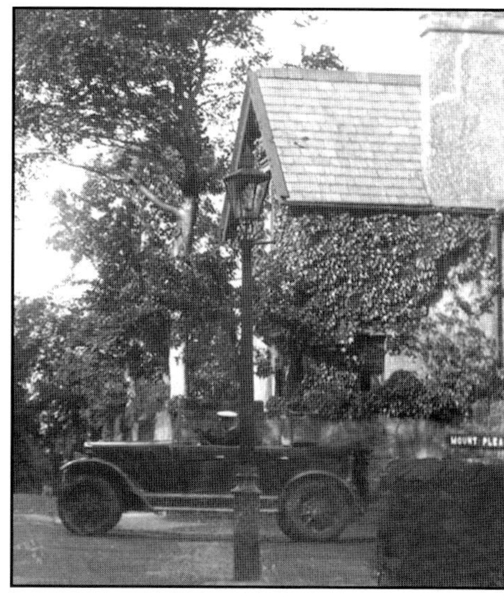

Above: *This open-top tourer is coming out of Mount Pleasant* ***Oxton*** *into Rose Mount. The charming ivy-covered house on the right is Rosemount Cottage*

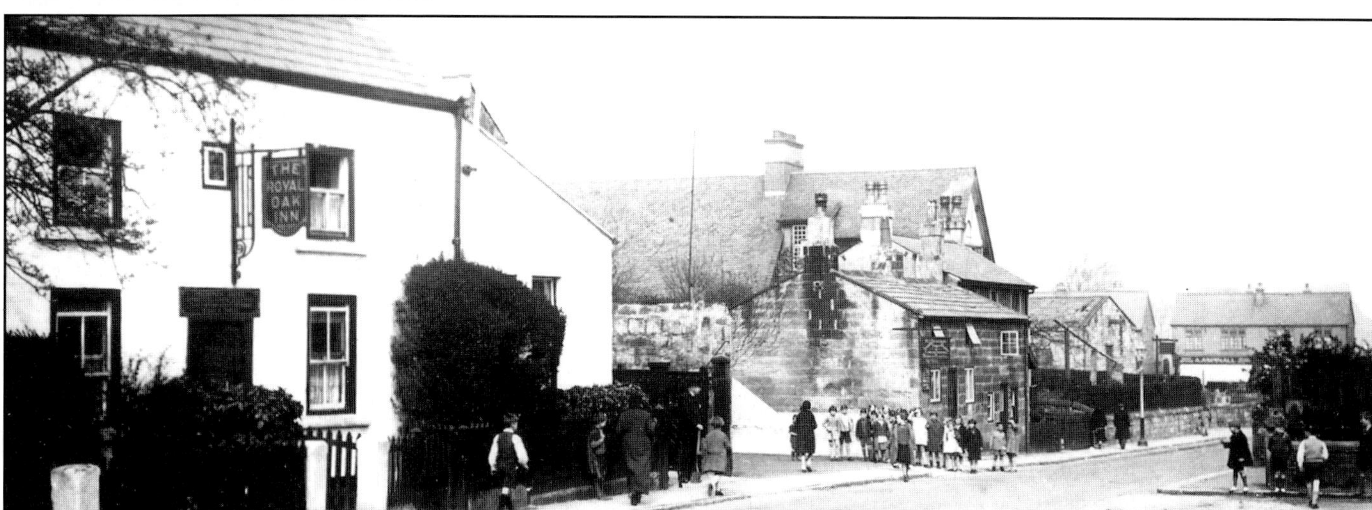

Above: *This pre-war photograph looking down Village Road Higher* ***Bebington*** *shows* The Royal Oak Inn *on the left, which dated back to 1739 and only had a beer licence. It was bought by Birkenhead Brewery who later transferred the licence from here to the new pub* The Acorn *in Teehey Lane just around the corner [see 1958]. The old* Royal Oak *building was then converted into offices. The shops on the right in the distance were in Teehey Lane*

1940

– **Wallasey** Corporation, opened new cemetery at **Frankby**

– Railings around **Birkenhead** Park salvaged for war effort[BAW]

– **Birkenhead** YWCA's premises in The Woodlands were taken over for use as a shelter for bombed and homeless people - the YWCA moved to 6 Caroline Place and the residents joined together in finding temporary accommodation[SOUV]

– The two Russian guns, presented to the town by the War Office in 1857, were removed from Cannon Hill in **Birkenhead** Park and sent for scrap[TPG]

– **Birkenhead** Park housed a searchlight battery, barrage balloon site and public air-raid shelters[TPG]

May 10 Evacuation of Dunkirk commenced

June Evacuees from Guernsey arrive at **Irby**[WHF]

July 23 LDV became known as Home Guard[BAW]

Aug 5 Our Lady of Pity RC Church opened in Mill Lane **Greasby**[DoS] [see 1952]

Aug 9 First bombs dropped on Merseyside fell on **Prenton**[BAW]

Aug 9 Due to the large number of sightseers curious to see the damage caused by the bombing, a cordon was placed around **Prenton** only allowing access to residents[BAW]

Aug 29 King George and Queen Elizabeth visit Cammell Laird **Birkenhead**[BAW]

Sept 21 *Argyle Theatre* **Birkenhead** suffered a direct hit during bombing raid and was destroyed [see photos][BAW]

Sept 29 Slatey Road Police station **Birkenhead** suffered bomb damage and was later demolished [see photo this page - also 1937][BAW]

Sept 29 Allansons' store Grange Road **Birkenhead** damaged by incendiary bomb[BAW]

Oct 8 German Junkers bomber plane shot down near **Bromborough** Dock[BAW]

Nov 5 Two day visit of King George and Queen Elizabeth visit bombed areas in **Wallasey** and **Birkenhead**[AW]

Nov 6 King George and Queen Mary visited the **Birkenhead** General Hospital to inspect the new Coronation Wing[SOUV]

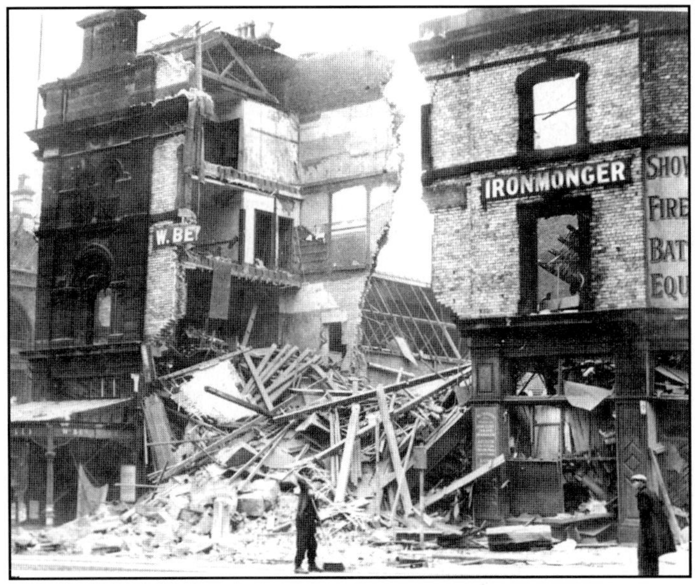

Above: *This was the result of a bombing raid on* ***Birkenhead*** *1/2 October 1940 when the centre part of William Bernard's Ironmongers shop collapsed in Hamilton Street*

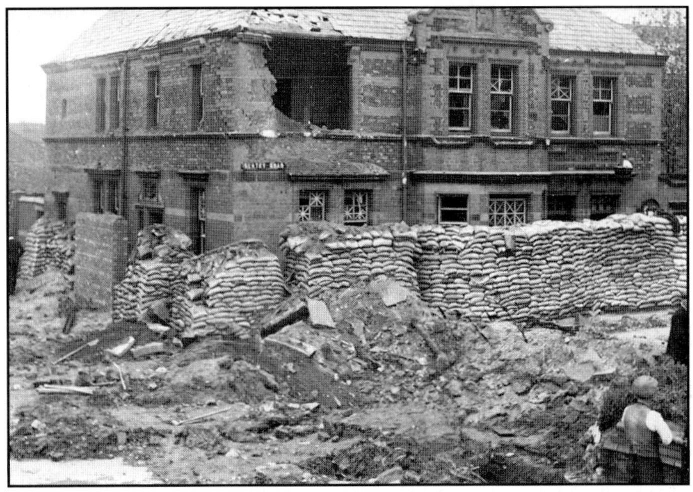

Above: *Slatey Road Police Station* ***Birkenhead*** *on the corner of Mather Road was so badly damaged by bombing on 29 September, it was later demolished - part of the site is now the car park for the Williamson Art Gallery, which was to the right [see also 1937]*[BAW]

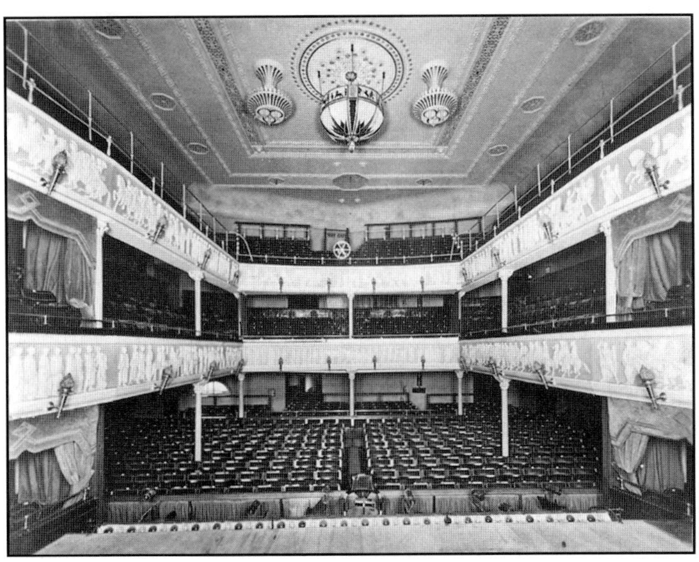

Above: *The interior of the Argyle Theatre, Argyle Street* ***Birkenhead*** *seen before it was destroyed by fire following a fierce air-raid 26 September 1940 [see photo on right]*

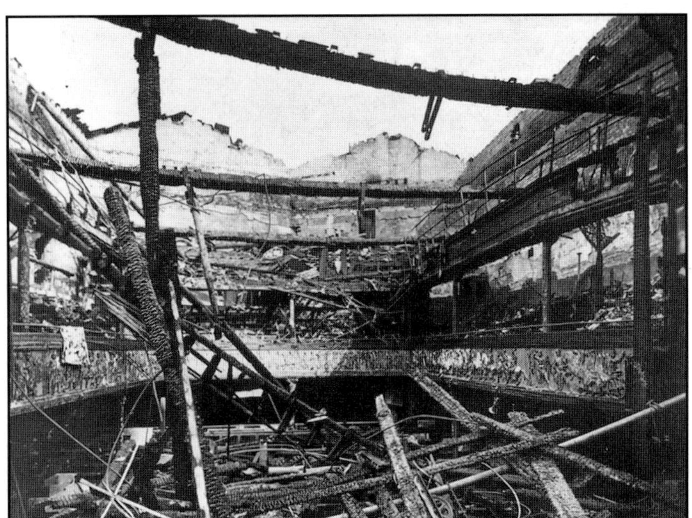

Above: *The interior of the Argyle Theatre, Argyle Street* ***Birkenhead*** *seen after it was destroyed by fire following a fierce air-raid 21 September 1940 [see photo on left from same position]*

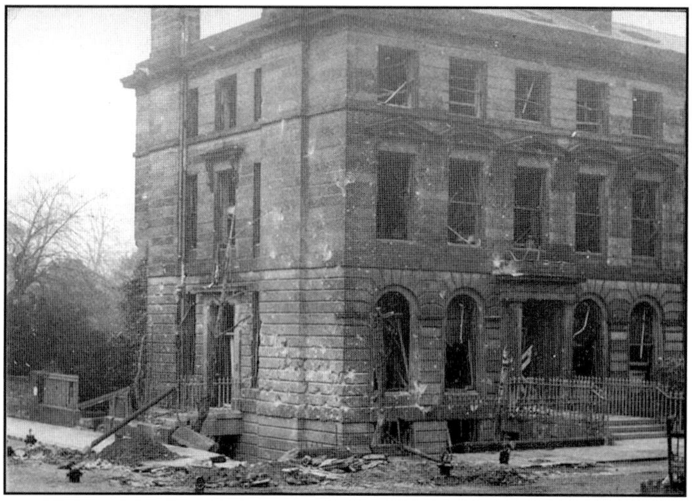

Above: *This building in St Aidan's Terrace* ***Claughton*** *is still intact despite all the windows having been blown out in an air raid on 21 December 1940*

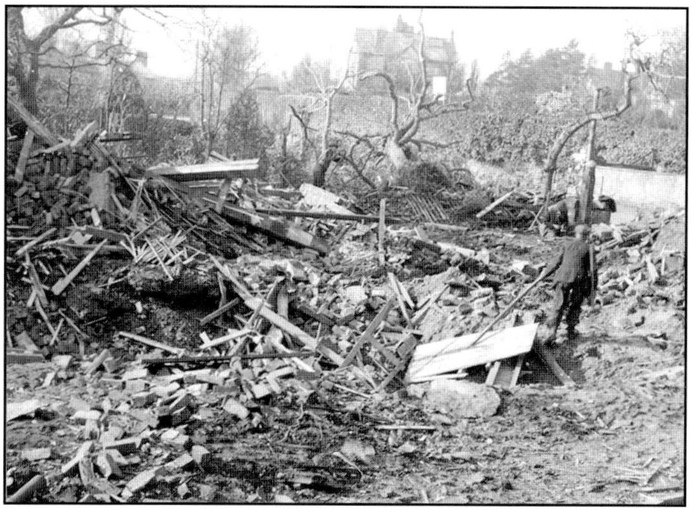

Above: *This devastation in Willowbank Road* ***Tranmere*** *was caused on 17 September 1940*

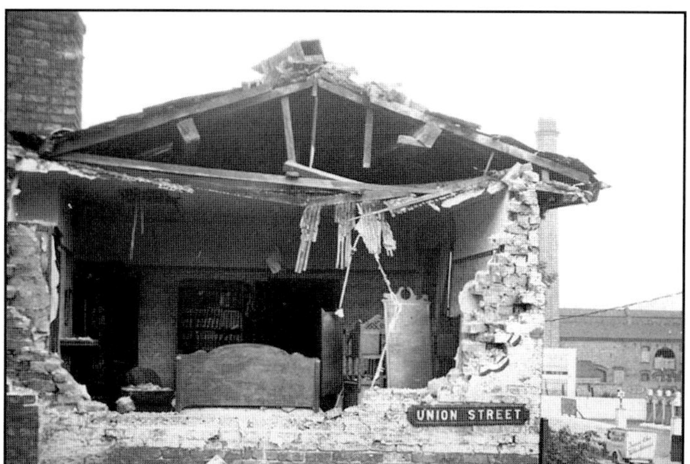

Above: *The street sign for Union Street* ***Birkenhead*** *has not been damaged following an air raid on 21 September - however, the side of the house has been blown away leaving a 'doll's house' view of the bedroom*

Right: *These houses in Hawthorne Road* ***Tranmere*** *suffered from a bombing raid on 17 September 1940*

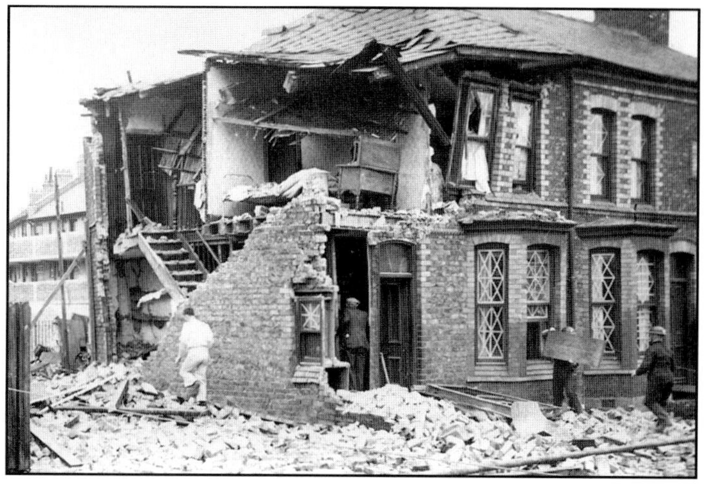

Above: *Despite the devastation to this house in Patten Street* ***Birkenhead*** *on 31 August, most of the windows which had been taped were not broken*

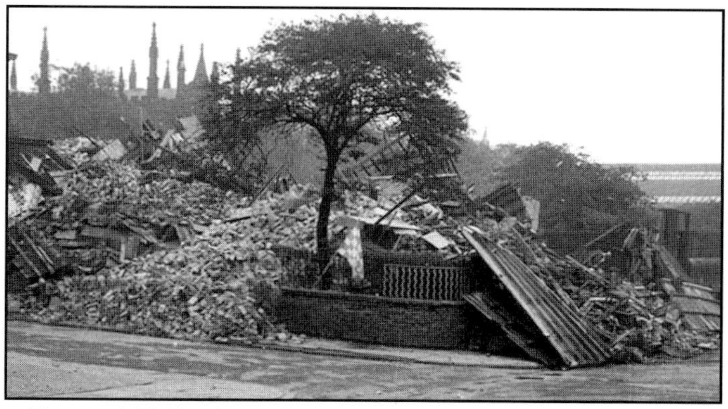

Above: *200 bombers attacked Merseyside on 31 August - this was the damage caused in Priory Street* ***Birkenhead***[BAW]

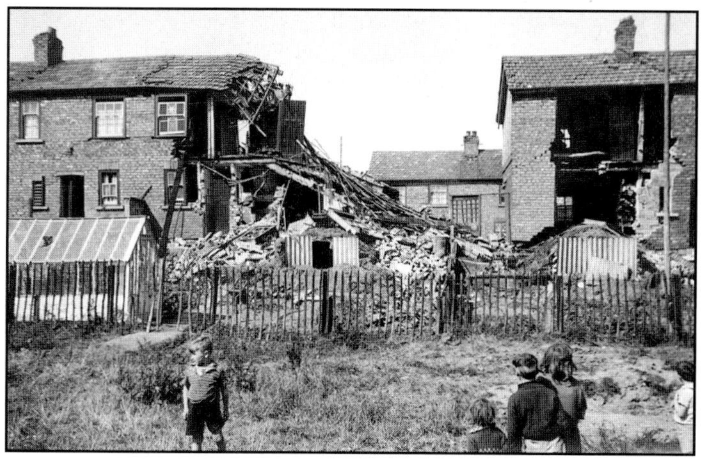

Above: *The two Anderson shelters in the back gardens of the houses damaged in Proctor Road* ***Rock Ferry*** *4 September are undamaged - despite part of the building falling on them*[BAW]

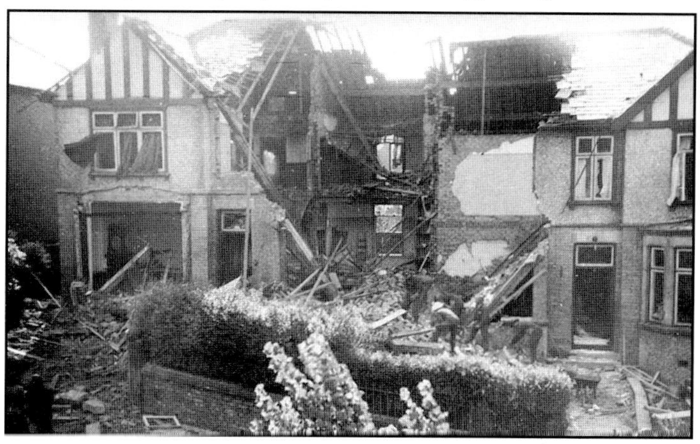

1941

Mar 9 A land mine destroyed Claughton Higher grade School on Borough Road **Birkenhead** [see also 1954][BAW]

Mar 12 On the night of 12/13 March 288 were killed and 275 seriously wounded in **Birkenhead's** worst raid of the war - including one at the the *Carnarvon Castle* Bidston Road **Oxton** which was destroyed due to a land mine falling behind the pub [see two photos][BAW]

Mar 12 A land mine destroyed **Higher Tranmere** High School for Girls in Clarence Road which had been taken over by the army - 30 to 40 personnel were buried many killed - the school never re-opened[SOUV]

Mar 12 Incendiary bombs destroyed the Old School Room and Headmaster's House **Bidston** [see 1922][BAW]

Apr 25 Winston Churchill paid surprise visit to **Birkenhead** and **Wallasey**[BAW]

May 1 For seven days Merseyside was bombed - known as the 'May Blitz'. Although Liverpool took the brunt of the bombing, **Birkenhead, Bebington, Oxton, Claughton, Prenton, Tranmere, Rock Ferry** and **Upton** all suffered. Although the bombing was more intense than in March, there were fewer casualties, as more people took cover in the shelters

May 21 The training ship HMS *Conway,* which was moored in the Mersey off **Rock Ferry,** left her moorings and sailed to the safer waters of the the Menai Straits (see 1939 & also 1953)[YWPH]

July 21 **Birkenhead** luggage ferry service discontinued

Aug 18 All fire Brigades nationalised[TM]

Nov 13 Built by **Birkenhead** shipbuilder Cammell Laird, the aircraft carrier *Ark Royal* was torpedoed and sunk off Gibraltar [see 1937]

Dec 10 The *Prince of Wales* a Cammell Laird, **Birkenhead** built Battleship was torpedoed and sunk off Malaya

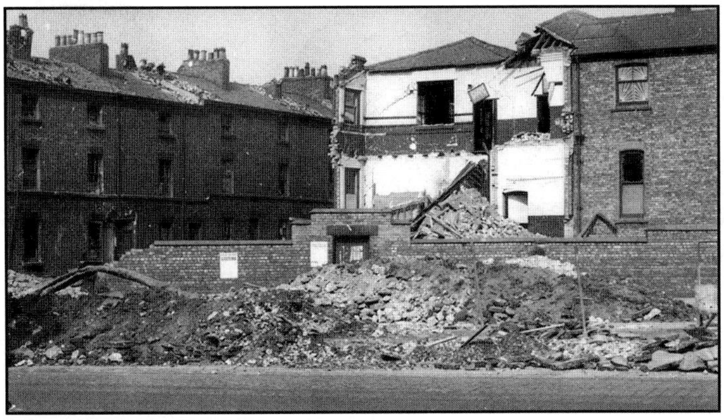

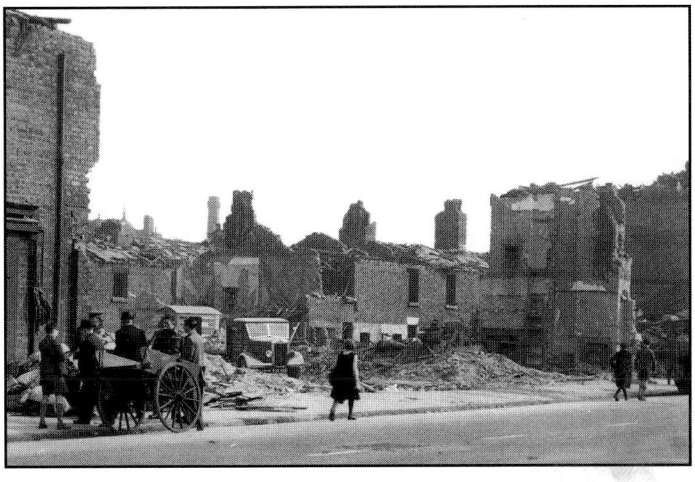

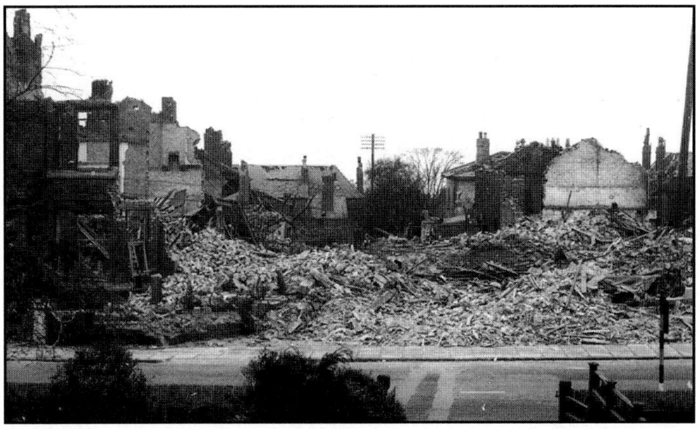

Above: *Only rubble was left after a land mine destroyed the Carnarvon Castle pub on Bidston Road* ***Oxton*** *13/14 March - one person was killed [see below and 1956][BAW]*

Below: *A different view of the damage caused in the photo above - looking towards St Saviour's Church* ***Oxton*** *[see 1948][BAW]*

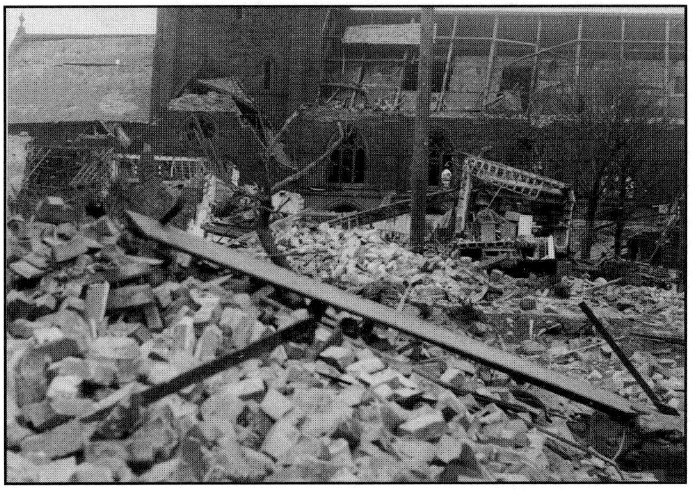

Left: *The damage caused to St Werburgh's School in Wilbraham Street is seen from Borough Road* ***Birkenhead*** *following a raid on the night of 12/13 March 1941*

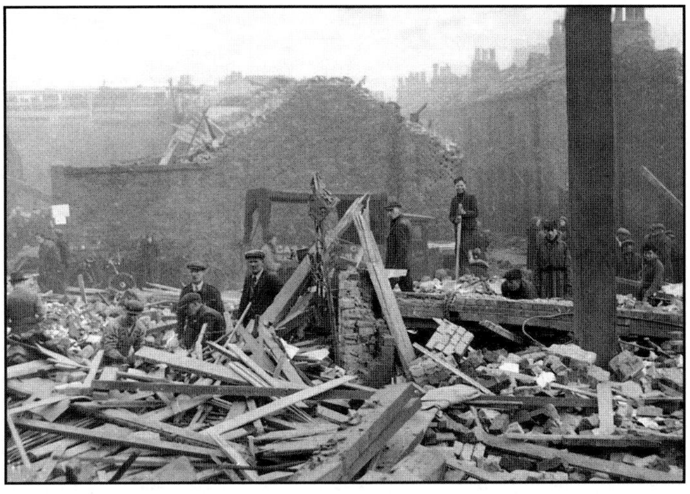

Above: *The rescue men take a break from sifting through the rubble in Livingstone Street* ***Birkenhead*** *following the raid on 13/14 March - this was to be Birkenhead's worst raid with over 288 killed and 275 injured*

Left: *This was the view of Lansdowne Road off Laird Street* ***Birkenhead*** *when all the rubble from the demolished houses had been cleared away following the air raid on 12/13 March*

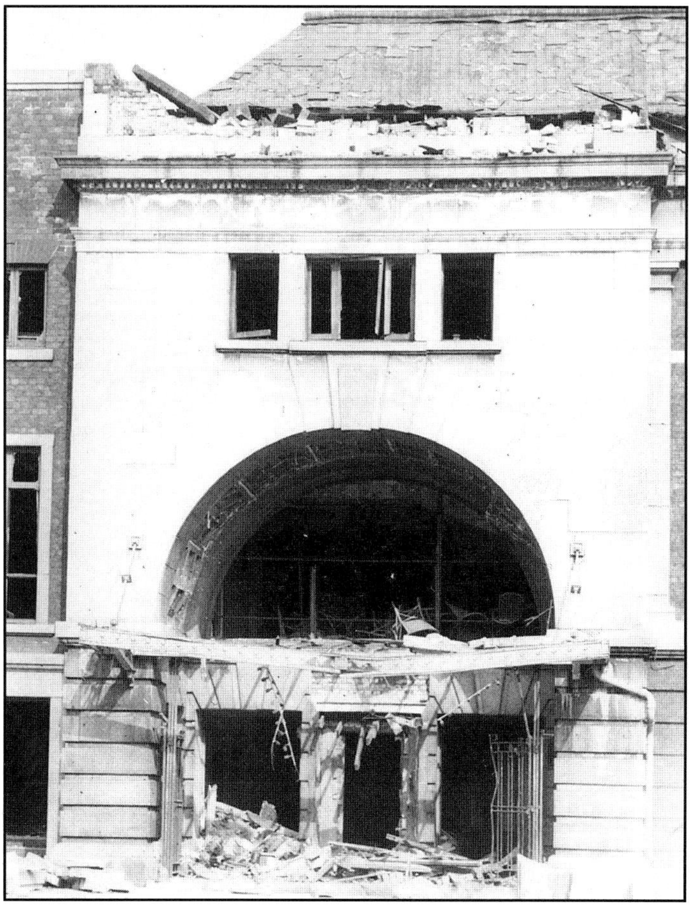

Left: *The* Avenue Cinema *at the junction of Bidston Avenue and Norman Street* ***Birkenhead*** *showing damage to the front of the building following the air raid on 12/13 March. The foundations were deemed unsafe so the building was demolished. The site was later occupied by the* The Avenue - *a Birkenhead Brewery pub* [see 1958]

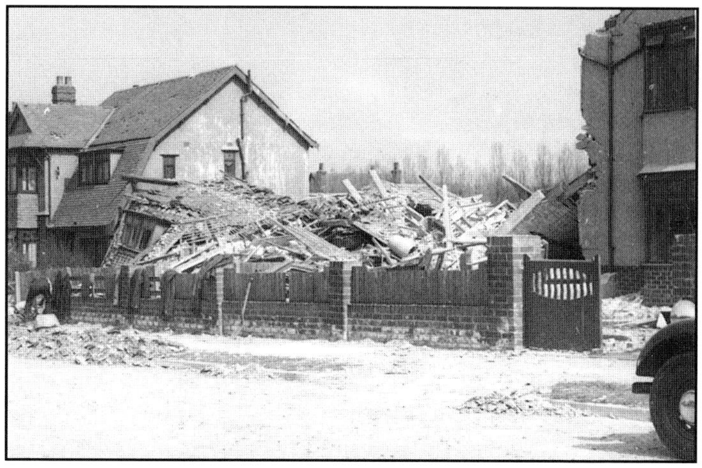

Above: *This was all that was left of the houses at Nos. 30, 32 and 34 Heath Drive* ***Upton*** *following an air raid on 1/2 May 1941. A crater was made by an unexploded bomb between Nos. 32 and 34. The bomb was not visible so no precautions were taken. However, the following evening the bomb exploded, causing the devastion seen above. Amazingly there were no serious casualties but an incredible escape. As soon as the bomb exploded, a man at No. 34 dived under the table which protected him from the collapsed house - he was later dug out alive*[BAW]

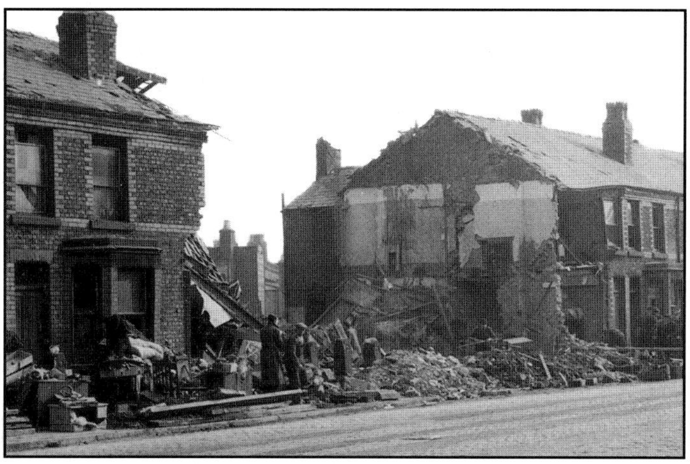

Above: *This was 62 to 68 Laird Street* ***Birkenhead*** *following an air raid on 12/13 March. Some furniture has been rescued from the house on the left and awaiting removal to safer premises*

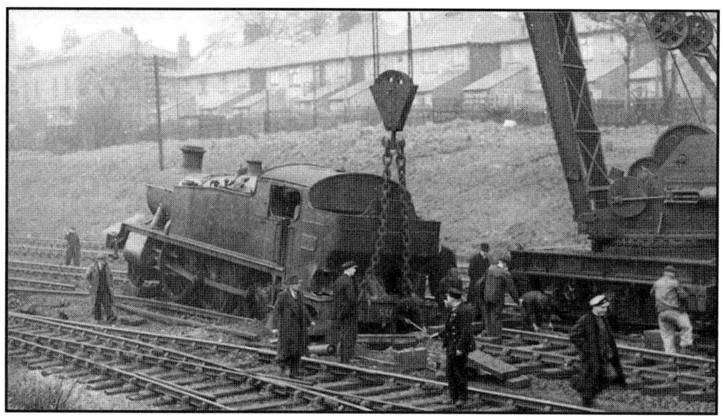

Above: *It must have been a large explosion that moved this railway engine off the track near Highfield Road Rock Ferry on 1 May 1941*

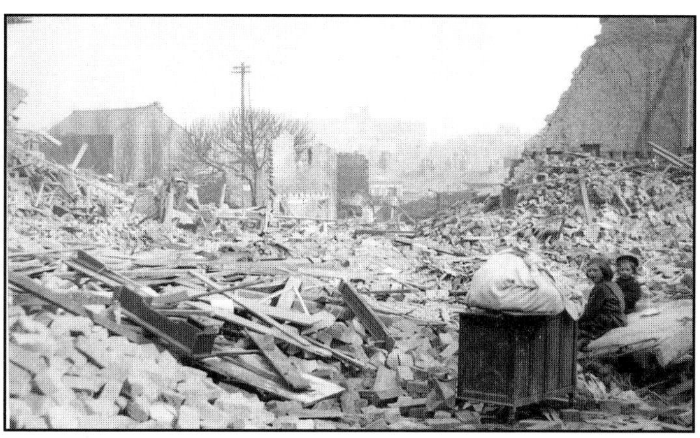

Above: *The two girls on the right are waiting with all that seems to have been rescued following a land mine devastating Carnforth Street* ***Birkenhead*** *on 12/13 March 1941*

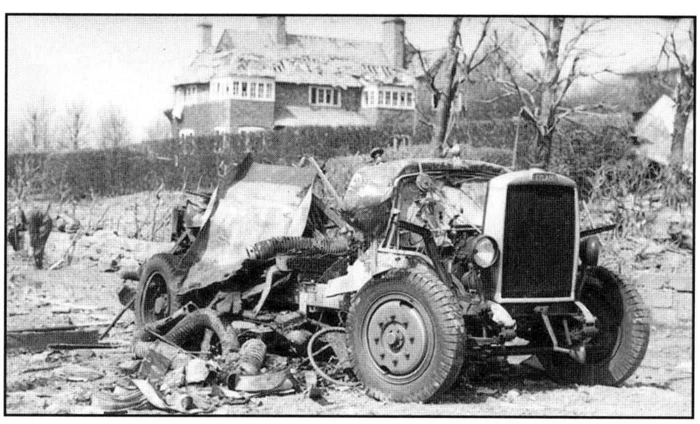

Above: *This was all that was left of a fire engine in Golf Links Road* ***Prenton*** *following a raid on 2/3 May 1941 in which one of the crew lost his life and several others were injured*[BAW]

1942

– The Birkenhead YWCA rented No. 249 Grange Road **Birkenhead** for the duration of the war, opening at lunch time to workers from offices, shops, Civil Defence workers, NFS etc[SOUV]

– Ships with supplies for the invasion of North Africa including munitions, tanks etc were despached mainly from **Birkenhead** Docks - as were those that carried supplies to the beleaguered Malta

– A Relief Hospital at *Arrowe Hall* **Arrowe** Park was prepared, to take the strain off the Municipal, General and Children's Hospitals[SOUV] [see 1927]

Jan **Birkenhead** was the top area nationwide for collecting waste paper[BAW]

Jan Mr George Arnold Cherry was appointed as **Birkenhead** Transport Manager - his name was painted on the side of Corporation buses for years

Jan 10 Last bomb fell on Merseyside[BAW]

Jan 19 Alderman GA Solly died - a former Mayor, he had been involved in the public life of **Birkenhead** Borough for over 60 years

Mar National Warship Week. Towns in Wirral to sponsor warships:- **Birkenhead** raised over £1,500,000 for HMS *Charybdis*; **Bebington** raised £236,000 for HMS Sabre

Apr 18 Lord Woolton, Minister of Food, visited **Bebington.** He opened the cooking depot in Acre Lane which was to provide meal services on a substantial scale in an emergency. He then opened the Victoria British Restaurant in Higher **Bebington**

May 3 Death of Mr AK Bulley founder of **Ness** Gardens

June 21 The **Birkenhead** Home Guard - the 4th Cheshire Battalion held a Drumhead Service at Birkenhead Park

Aug 3 The Home Guard Athletic Sports meeting was held at Tranmere Rovers ground **Prenton** - this drew a big Bank Holiday crowd. Teams taking part included: the Birkenhead ARP Wardens, the Borough Police, ATC, NFS, Old Soldiers, Tranmere Rovers etc

Aug Seaman's Hostel in Watson Street **Birkenhead** opened by the Mayor

Sept 13 St Peter's Church Rock Ferry celebrated its centenary [services were held at that time at their daughter Church St Barnabas due to bomb damage at St Peter's] - but for the occasion two tons of rubble and broken masonry were removed) [see photo][SOUV]

Oct 14 A Spitfire on a test flight from Hawarden crashed into the south east corner of Birkenhead Park - the pilot had baled out[TPG]

Nov 7 'RAF in Action' Exhibition held at the Williamson Art Gallery Slatey Road **Birkenhead**

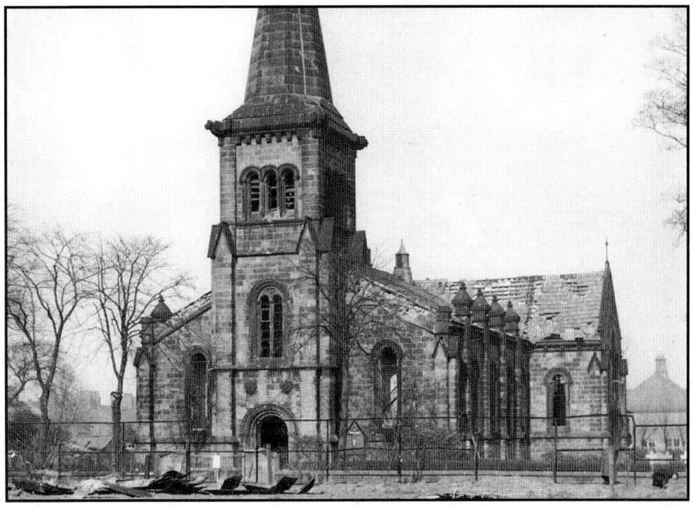

Above: *St Peter's Church* **Rock Ferry** *celebrated its centenary on 13 September but due to bomb damage on 12/13 March 1941 (see above), services were held then at their daughter Church St Barnabas. However, for the occasion two tons of rubble and broken masonry were removed and the services were held in St Peter's Church*

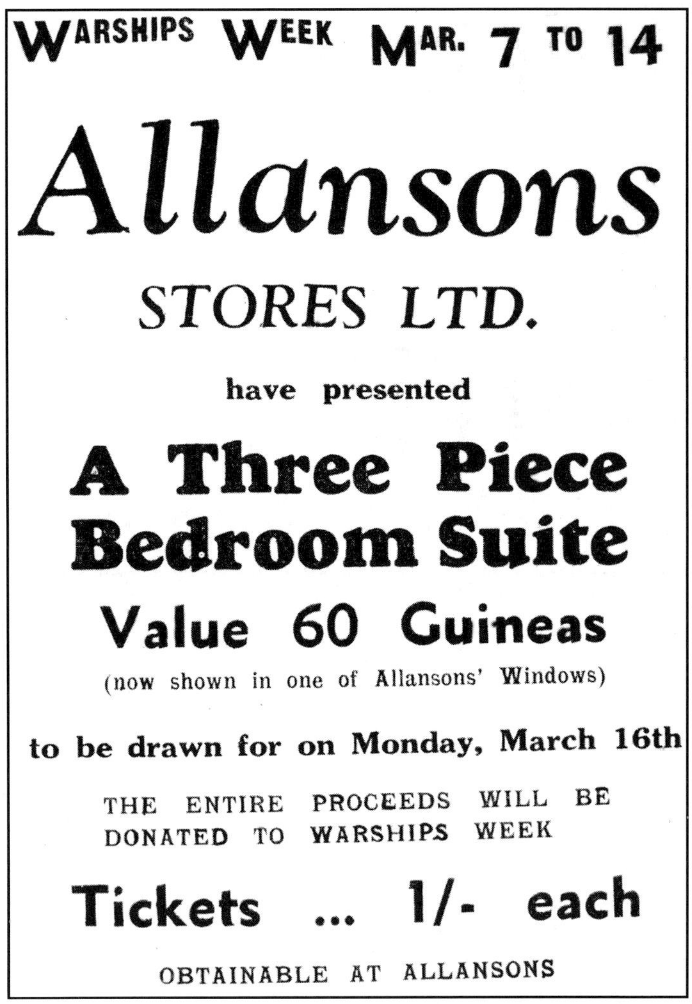

Above: *This was the contribution of Allansons Store of Grange Road* **Birkenhead** *towards Birkenhead's 'Warship Week' target of £1 million - from 7 to 14 March 1942. The town was the best in the country when it achieved this in only one day. The final total was £1,507,858 which not only paid for the adopted warship* Charybdis *but also for fitting it out*

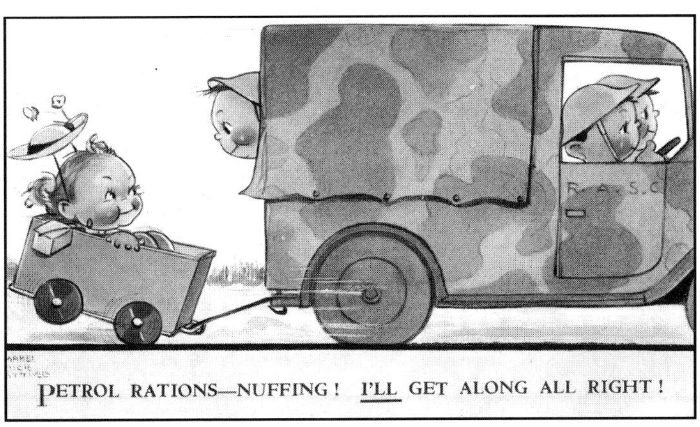

1943

Aug 4 St John The Evangelist RC Church Bebington Road **New Ferry** consecrated by Bishop Moriarty[DOS]

July 30 boys and masters from Birkenhead School spent a month potato picking in Knutsford - to help the war effort[BSPH]

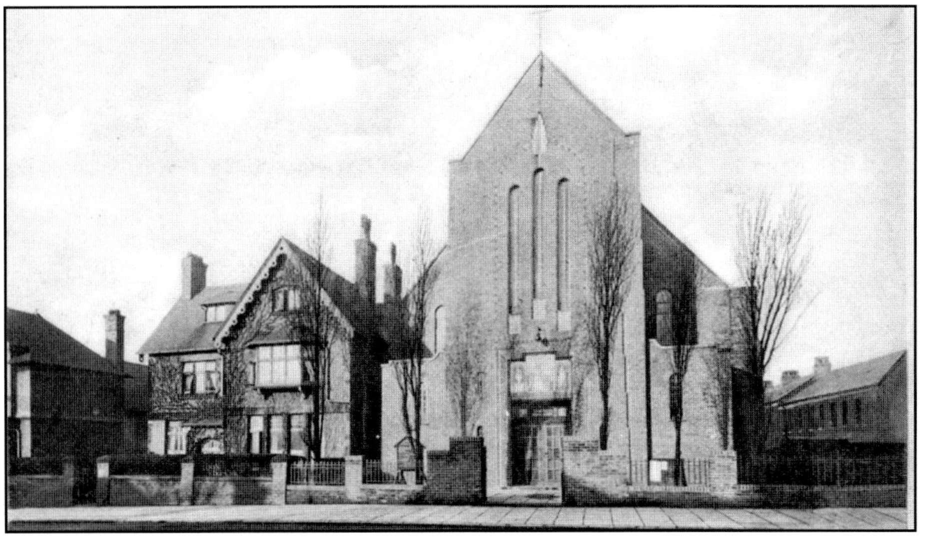

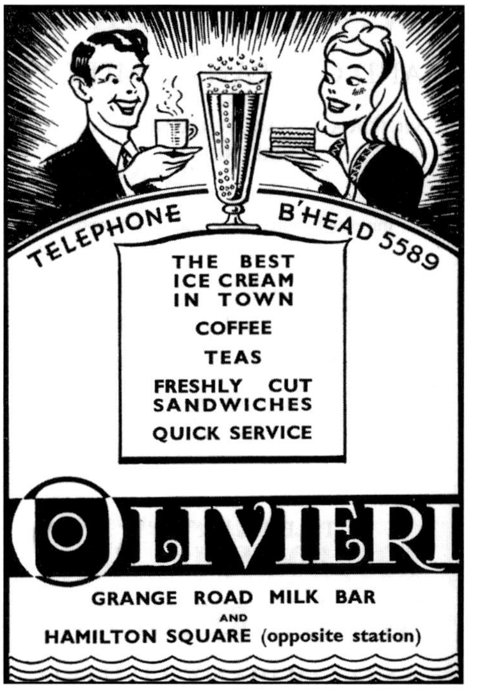

Above: *St John the Evangelist Roman Catholic Church is seen in Bebington Road* ***New Ferry.*** *This spacious, airy Church which was free from pillars, was opened in November 1934 and consecrated August 1943*

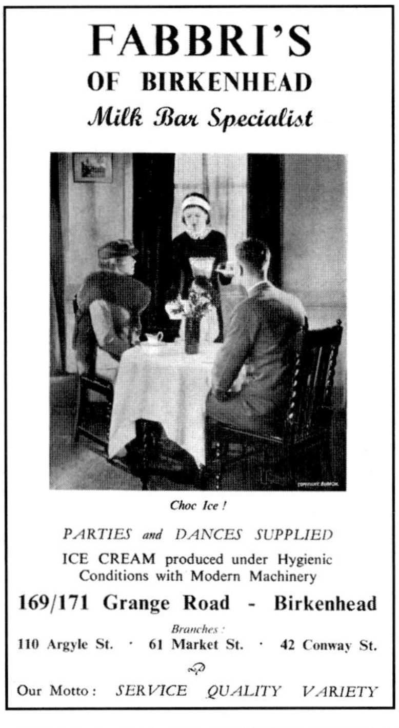

Right: *This postcard and the one on the previous page were both by the children's artist Mabel Lucie Attwell, using petrol rationing as one theme and a boy friend in the forces returning home as the other*

Below: *Tollemache School in Upton Road* ***Bidston*** *Accommodated 480 boys and 480 girls - opened in 1933. It survived the bombing raids on Birkenhead coming out relatively unscathed. When Birkenhead Institute closed, the school relocated here. It closed in the 1990s with the buildings here demolished. Wilfred Owen Drive now occupies the site [named after the famous First World War poet who was an old boy of Birkenhead Institute]*

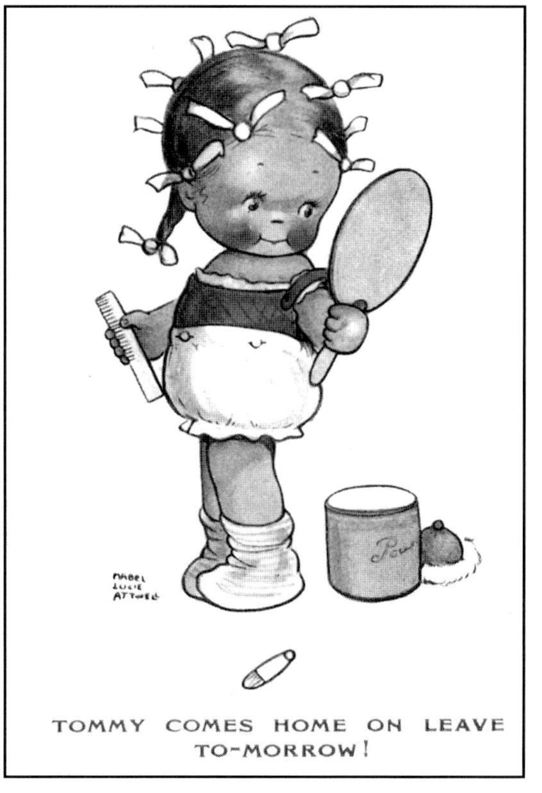

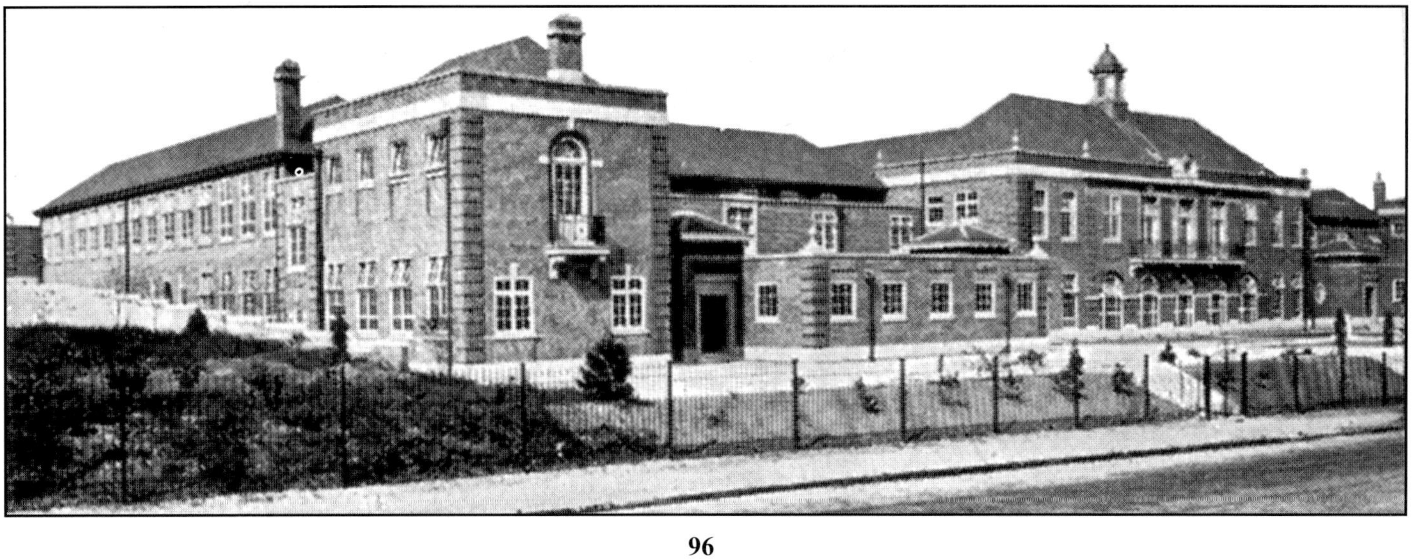

1944

– An emergency hospital had been established on agricultural land adjoining Clatterbridge Hospital. Completed in two stages, the first, a line of wooden hutment wards and an operating theatre/x-ray block completed in 1940 and in 1941 a line of brick hutment wards. In 1944 the emergency hospital was evacuated of its patients and handed over to the American Military Authorities [they thought the casualties following the 'D' Day invasion would have been greater than they were - hence the extra precautions]. They occupied it for less than a year and in 1946 the brick hutment wards were handed back to the General Hospital while the concrete hutments were used firstly as a prisoner-of-war camp and then the headquarters of various territorial army units. In March 1951 the whole of the American hospital site and buildings were acquired by the Ministry of Health from the war department - the site now occupied a total of 67 acres [see 1945]

– Wirral Ladies Golf Club **Bidston,** was earmarked as a transit camp where 10,000 American troops were to live under canvas for six weeks prior to departing to take part in the 'D' Day Invasion of Normandy[WLGC]

Mar 11 Grange Presbyterian Church of England opened in King's Road **Bebington**. Due to the lack of building materials during the war the building was pre-fabricated and with furnishings only cost £300, which was raised on the opening day [see also 1950][SOUV]

Sept 17 'Battle of Britain Sunday' - a service was held at the *Savoy Cinema* in Argyle Street **Birkenhead** - presided over by the Mayor of Birkenhead Alderman TH Heron

Dec 3 The Mayor of **Birkenhead**, accompanied by Colonel Hodson DSO, MC took the salute at the stand-down Parade in Birkenhead of the 4th Cheshire Battalion Home Guard. In the evening the Mayor attended, together with 400 men of the 132nd Rocket Anti-Aircraft Battery, a Hot-Pot Supper and Smoking Concert at the Grange Road British Restaurant. The **Bebington** Home Guard stand-down of the 21st Cheshire Battalion and the 214th (102nd Cheshire) AA Battery - was taken at the *Rialto Cinema.* They had a short service followed by a march to Lady Lever Art Gallery for the final salute

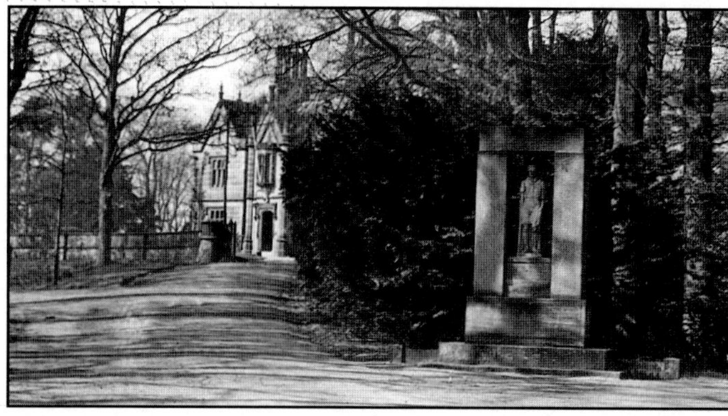

Above: *The monument and statue to commemorate the World Scout Jamboree, held here at* **Arrowe** *Park in 1929, is standing near the entrance gates to Arrowe Hall (seen on the left). They were later moved to the entrance to the Arrowe Park Hospital*

Below: *This was one of many slogans used on the reverse side of postcards during the war to encourage everybody to invest in savings*

"KEEP SAVING FOR A RAINY DAY"

We saved to win the war,
Our efforts must not cease;
By saving more and more,
We'll surely win the peace!

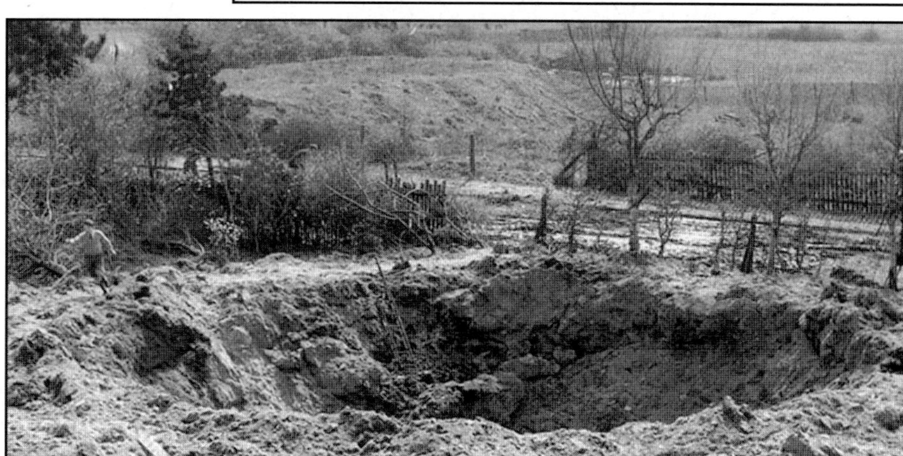

Above: *This was the damage caused by a bomb which fell in land off Golf Links Road* **Prenton** *on 2 May 1941. Because most of the man power was used to demolish unsafe houses and repair those that could be saved, craters like this were often not filled in until after the war*

1945

– Work started on building the Mountwood Estate in **Birkenhead** including bungalows for 'aged persons'

– **Birkenhead** Dockers took part in the National strike to increase their daily pay of 16/- by 9/- shillings plus a reduction of hours from 44 to 40. After six weeks of striking they received an extra 3/- but no reduction in working hours

– St Anselm's College, Manor Hill, **Birkenhead** became a Direct Grant Grammar School[DOS]

May 3 **Germany surrenders**

May 7 **Birkenhead** Town Station closed[RSoW]

May 8 **VE (Victory in Europe) Day**
Many celebrations were held including street parties. The Town Hall Hamilton Square **Birkenhead** was illuminated with over 6,000 lights

May 14 Over 3,500 spectators witnessed a Charity Cricket match at **Oxton** between the Lord Mayor of Liverpool's Empire XI and the Mayor of Birkenhead's Merseyside XI. The players included:- Herbert Sutcliffe, Charles S Dempster, Eddie Paynter, Charlie Hallows,and Learie Constantine - as an added attraction, a helicopter - 'the wingless wonder' was flown over the field for several minutes during the tea interval by the Chief Test Pilot for Martin Hearn Ltd, Major JH Cordes, then landed on the pitch[BAW]

Aug 9 **Atom bomb dropped on Nagasaki**

Aug 14 **Japan surrenders to the Allies**

Aug 15 **VJ (Victory in Japan) Day - the end of the war** celebrations were held across the Borough - floodlights on public buildings - the main one being on **Birkenhead** Town Hall - bonfires, parades etc - a large 'V' for victory sign was erected in Hamilton Square Gardens

Nov 12 Grange Presbyterian Church of England **Bebington** obtained land at the junction of Kings Lane and Kings Road on which to build a new church[SOUV]

Nov 29 Isle of Man ferry *King Orry* was launched at Cammell Laird **Birkenhead**

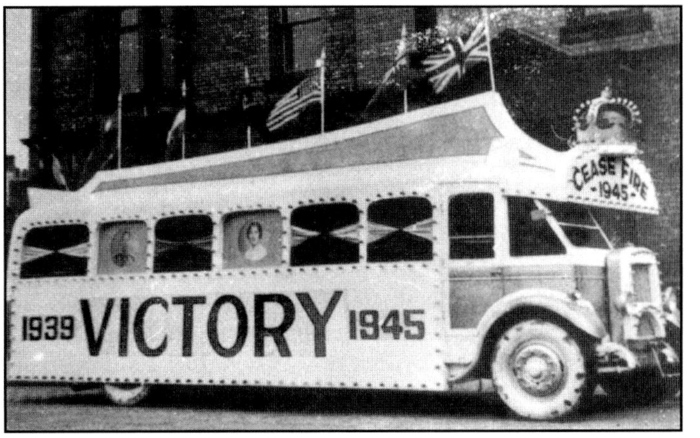

Above: *At the end of the Second World War, this* ***Birkenhead*** *Corporation single-decker bus, which had come into service in 1930, was converted into an illuminated 'Victory' celebration bus*

Below: An emergency hospital had been established on agricultural land adjoining **Clatterbridge** Hospital. Completed in two stages, the first, a line of wooden hutment wards and an operating theatre/x-ray block completed in 1940 (rows of buildings on right with dark roofs) and in 1941 a line of brick hutment wards (rows of buildings with light coloured roofs). In 1944 the emergency hospital was evacuated of its patients and handed over to the American Military Authorities (they thought the casualties following the 'D' Day invasion would have been greater than they were - hence the extra precautions). They occupied it for less than a year and in 1946 the brick hutment wards were handed back to the General Hospital while the concrete hutments were used firstly as a prisoner-of-war camp and then the headquarters of various territorial army units. In March 1951 the whole of the American hospital site and buildings were acquired by the Ministry of Health from the war department - the site now occupied a total of 67 acres. The original buildings are top centre/right

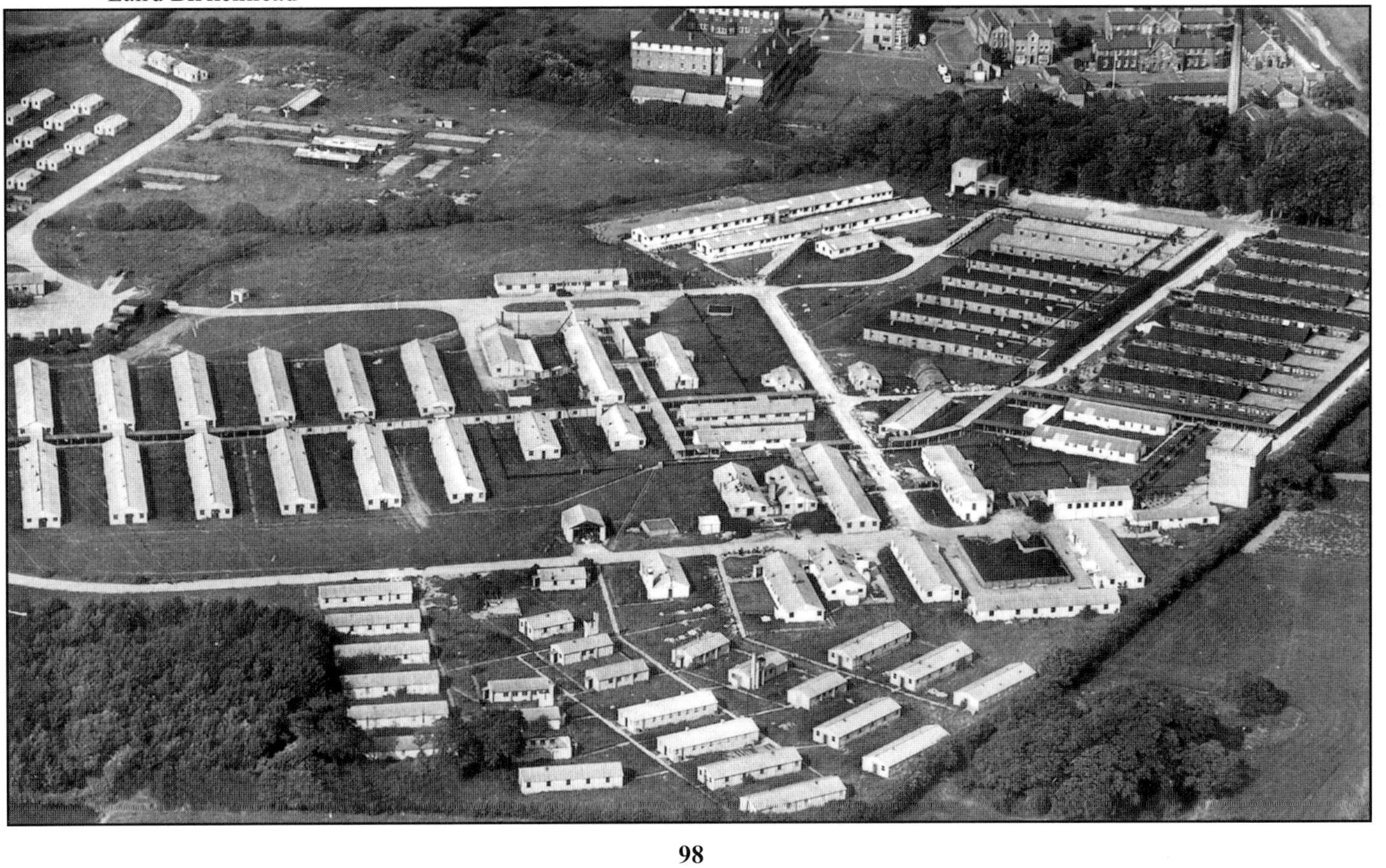

1946

– Vernon's Industries erected purpose-built industrial units in Valley Road **Birkenhead** [see advert for Vernon's Toys this page - also 1952]

– Launch of the Great Western's Ship *St David* at Cammell Laird **Birkenhead** - this was the 14th GWR ship built at the Birkenhead shipyard

June The One O'Clock Gun, which was sited at Morpeth Pier **Birkenhead**, started firing again having stopped in 1939. It finally ceased firing 18 July 1969 [see also 1867]

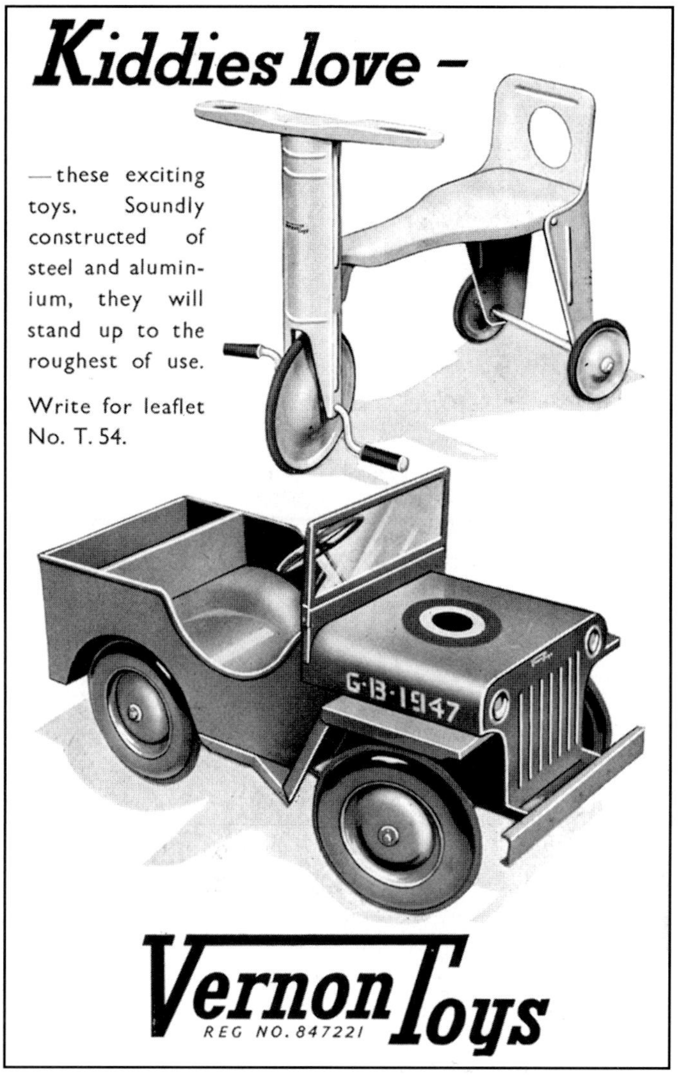

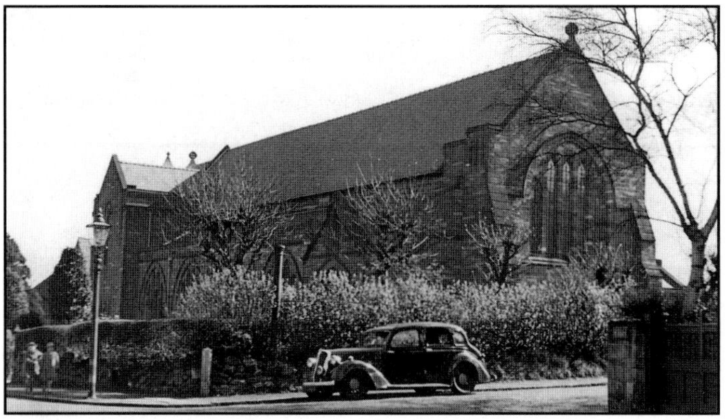

Above: *behind the car in Reservoir Road at the junction of Prenton Lane* ***Prenton*** *is St Stephen's Church. Despite the Church Council deciding in 1946 that the following year a Jubilee Appeal of up to £5,000 to build the Church tower, that was originally designed but never built - the Church today still has no tower*

Below: *Despite the post war rationing and shortages of raw materials - this 1946 advert for Watson's Garage in Hamilton Street gives the impression that there were no such problems*

Above Right: *Vernon's Industries erected purpose-built industrial units in Valley Road* ***Birkenhead****. Despite the shortage of raw materials one of the ventures was to build large children's toys in the form of a three-wheeler scooter and a pedal car Jeep. These were very popular, particularly for export. King Farouk of Egypt was reputed to have bought one of the pedal cars for his children*

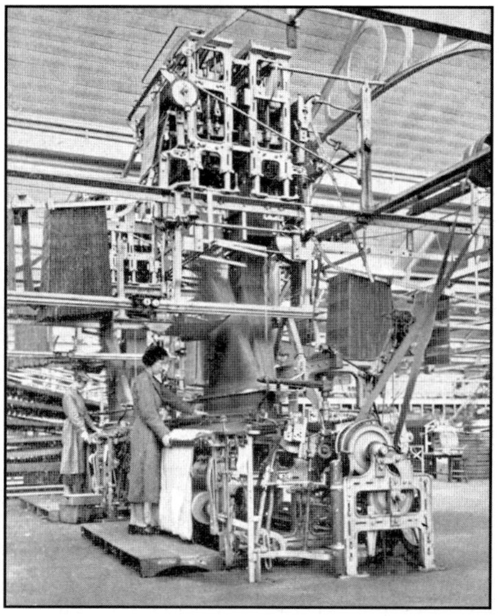

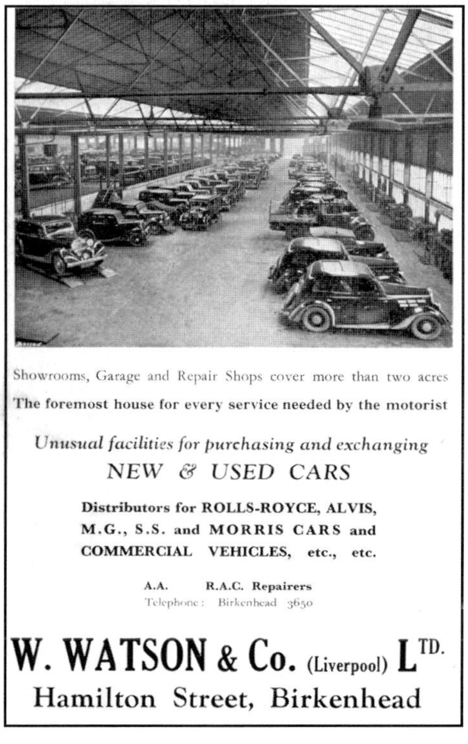

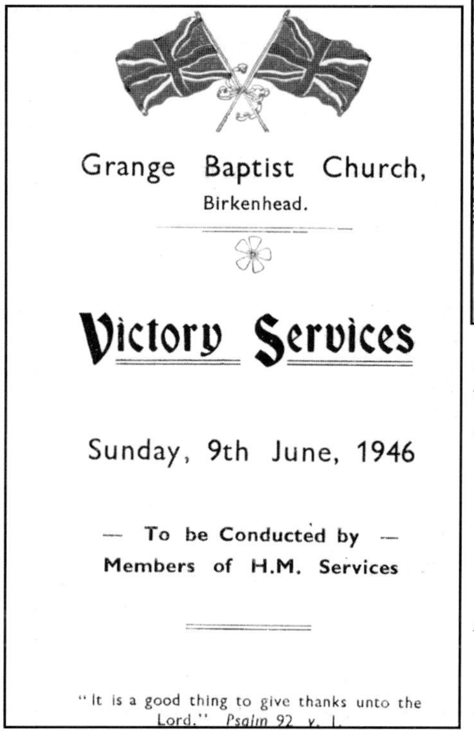

Above: *This complicated looking machine was for tapestry weaving used by Arthur H Lee & Sons. Founded in 1888, they moved to Stanley Road* ***Birkenhead*** *in 1908 where they produced high quality hand-woven and machine woven tapestries for royalty, luxury liners, stately homes and export. Between the wars was its most prosperous when they employed some 400 people. Escalating costs and not willing to compromise on quality they closed in 1970*[TTM]

1947

– The County Borough of **Birkenhead** produced an outline plan for the town [see artist's drawing][OP]

– **Arrowe** Park Golf Course used for the qualifying rounds of the British Open[BCSB]

– The famous spire of the Wesley Church, Church Road, Higher **Tranmere** was removed as it had become dangerous following a bomb blast during the war [see 1907]

Jan The *Ritz* Cinema re-opened in **Birkenhead** having been repaired following bomb damage [see 1954]

Oct Building commenced on the **Woodchurch** Estate

Nov 20 Royal Wedding of Princess Elizabeth to Prince Philip

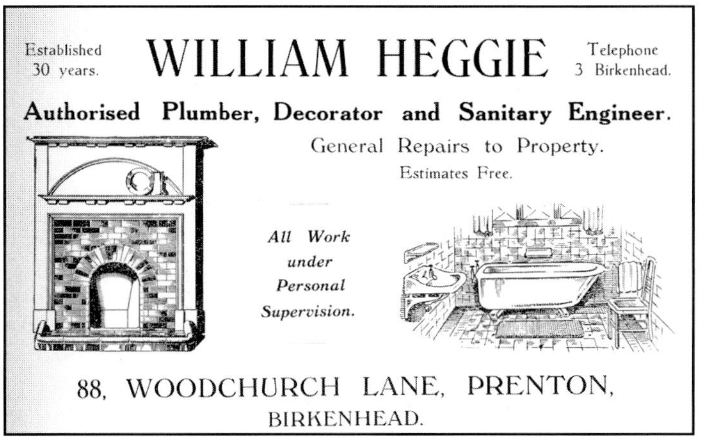

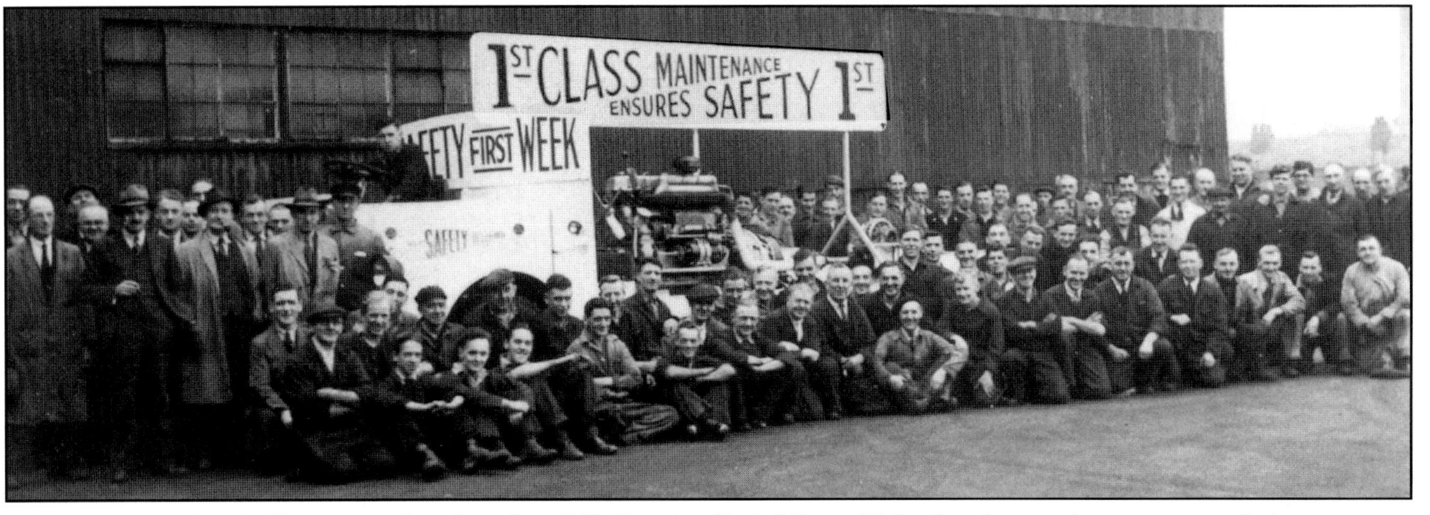

Above: *This group of workers from PSI Chassis of Laird Street* ***Birkenhead*** are posing to promote their 'Safety First Week' - October 1947

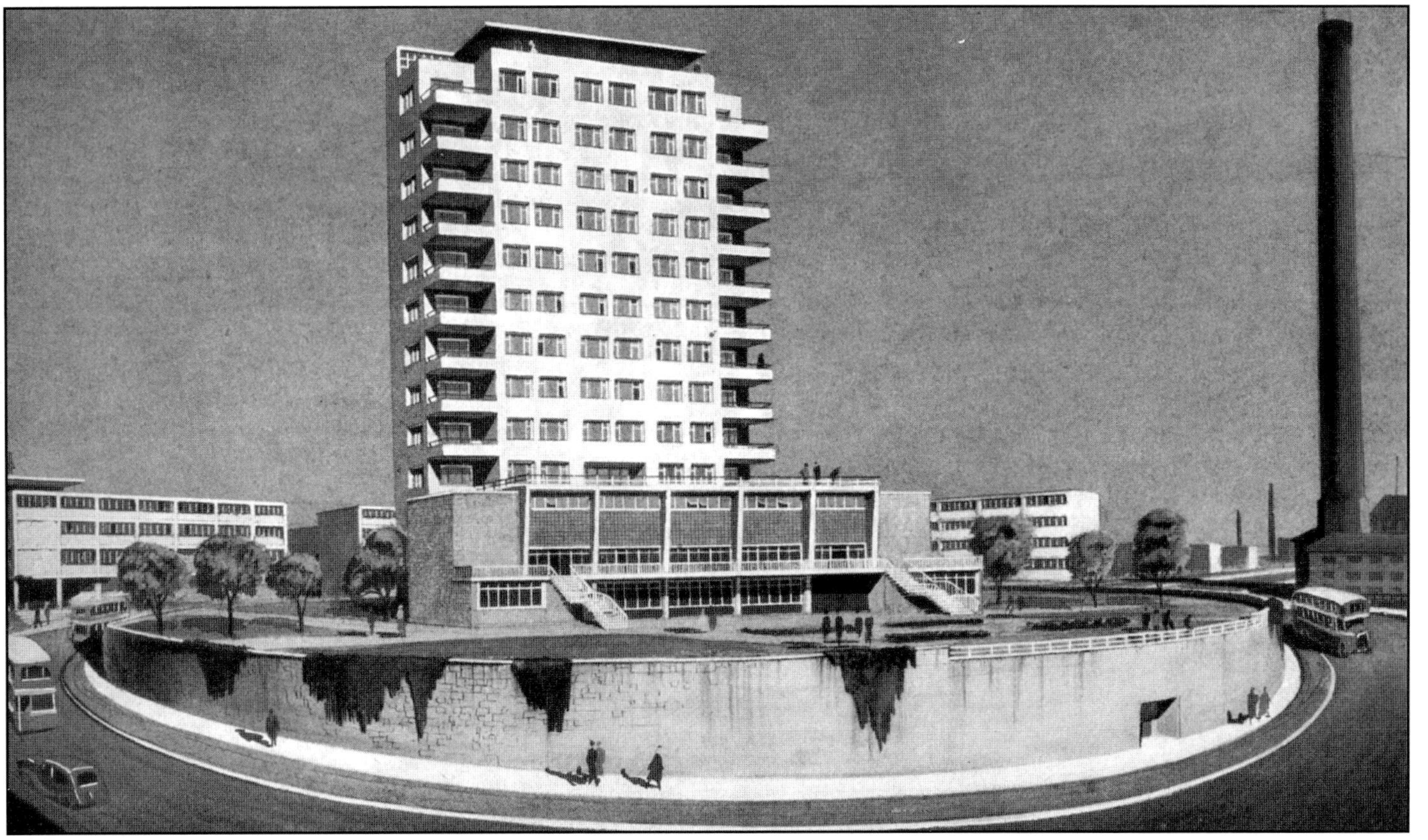

Above: *In 1947 the County Borough of* ***Birkenhead*** *produced an outline plan for the town. This was an opportunity to repair the damage caused by extensive bombing to the town during the war. This was a suggested plan for a new* Woodside Hotel *which abutted the main line railway terminus - and would be the Western end of the European railway system following the construction of a Channel Tunnel*

1948

– **Oxton** Cricket Club bought 2.66 acres adjoining the third XI ground off the Earl of Shrewsbury for £4,000[SOUV]

– Wine Merchants Mackie & Gladstone of Birkenhead (founded 1836) was taken over by **Birkenhead** Brewery - they had owned about 40 off-licence shops[BB] [see 1958]

Apr 1 Denationalisation of the Fire Brigade Service. Re-established under Local Authority control[FPH]

July 5 **Birkenhead** Fire Service & Ambulance Service combine – Fire Brigade personnel increased to 122 who were then employed on a 60 hour week[FPH]

July 14 Last service of the Grange Road Presbyterian Church of England **Birkenhead** in its centenary year - the church financed a new Church i in **Bebington**[see photo][SOUV]

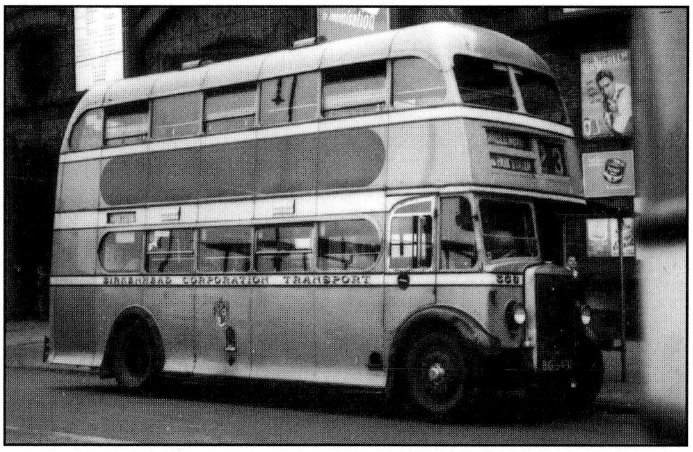

Above: *This No.23 bus, which is destined for Hurrell Road via Park Station, is standing at Woodside terminus outside Woodside Station - an advert for Brylcreem featuring Dennis Compton, the England cricketer, is seen to the right of the bus*

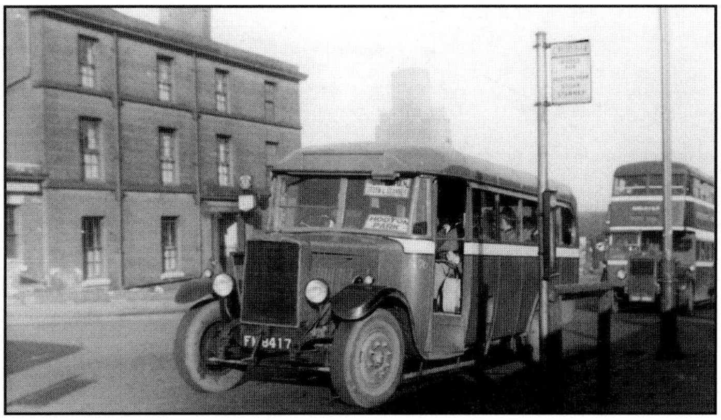

Above: *The Hooton-bound Crosville Leyland Cub 26 seater single-decker bus, which came into service in 1932, is seen waiting at Woodside* ***Birkenhead*** *with the* Woodside Hotel *in the background*

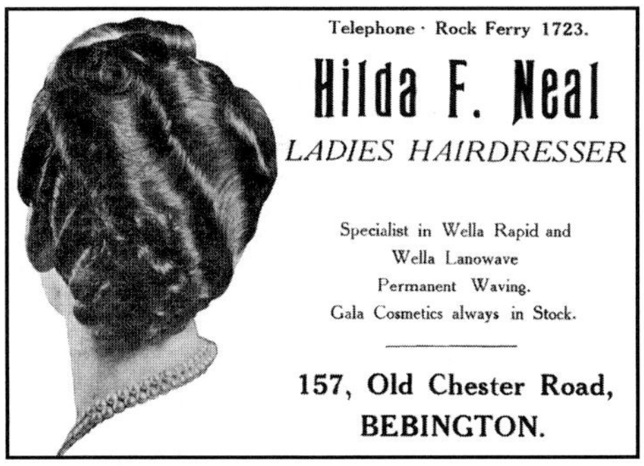

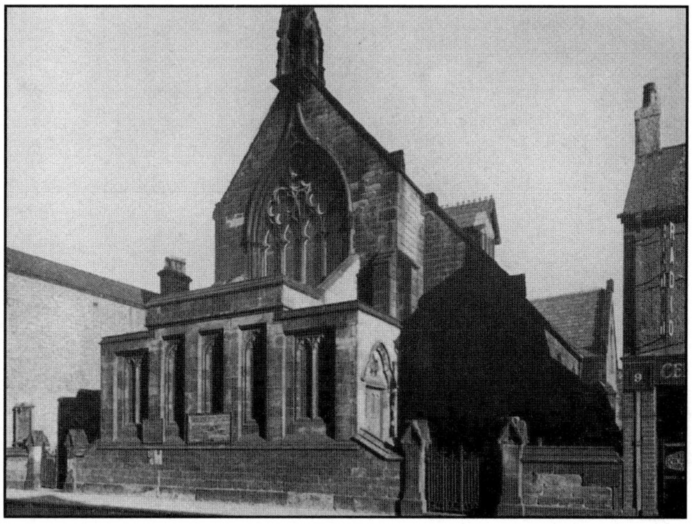

Above: *Grange Road Presbyterian Church of England* ***Birkenhead*** *in its final, centenary year - the Church helped to finance the new Church being built at* ***Bebington*** *and was thus called 'Grange' Presbyterian Church [see 1950] - this building was bought by the Birkenhead Repertory Theatre Ltd and is still used today as the* Little Theatre[SOUV]

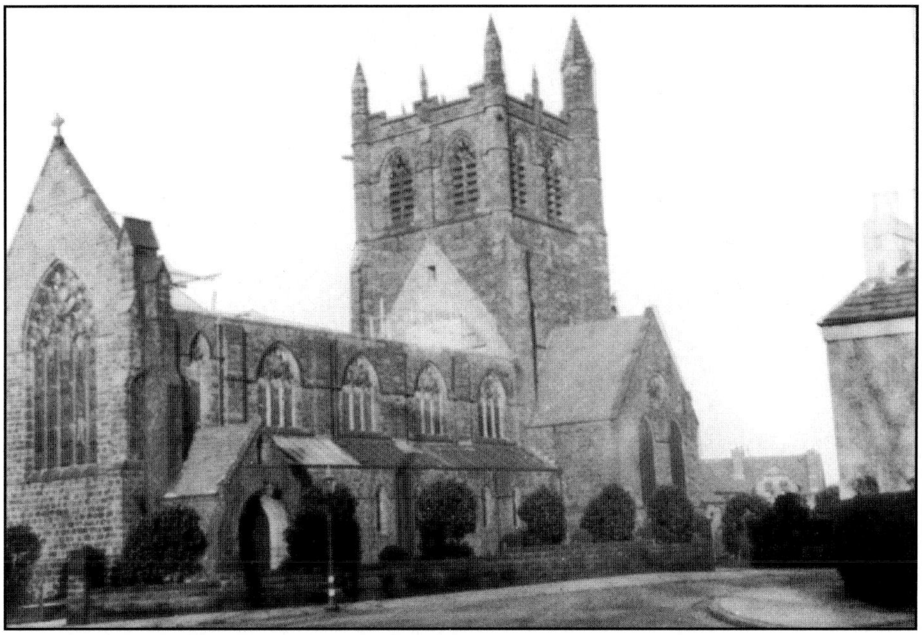

Left: *St Saviour's Church is seen without its roof in Gerald Road,* ***Oxton*** *looking from Bidston Road. The damage to the Church was caused by a land mine falling behind the* Carnarvon Castle *in Bidston Road on 13/14 March 1941 [see 1941]. Besides damaging the roof of the Church, the North Aisle and memorial windows also suffered. Due to a shortage of building materials, a temporary corrugated iron roof was used to keep the bad weather out. However, if rain fell during the service, the noise of the rain on the corrugated iron roof made so much noise that it was often difficult to hear the organ playing and even more difficult to hear the sermon*

1949

– **Bebington** Dramatic Society celebrated its 25th anniversary with the play *Miss Elizabeth Bennett* by AA Milne [a play from 'Pride & Prejudice'] at the YMCA Theatre **Birkenhead**[Prog]

– The century-old business of Ryalls & Jones was incorporated into the music house of Rushworth & Dreaper [see photo and advert]

– The new Clatterbridge hospital Restaurant opened - had been converted from the former hospital chapel [see photo]

May 6 First council house on the **Woodchurch** Estate formarlly opened [see also 1956]

July 16 Fo: one week - "**Birkenhead** for Britain" Industrial Exhibition held at the Drill Hall Grange Road West[SOUV]

Aug Extension to the Shrewsbury Lawn Tennis Club's pavilion in Shrewsbury Road **Oxton** - it had originally been a hen-house[BLTC]

Sept 29 Building work commenced on the **Birkenhead** Technical College in Borough Road [see 1950]

Oct 15 Foundation stone laid for the new Grange Presbyterian Church, Church Road Higher **Bebington**[SOUV]

Nov 21 Royal film performance at Ritz Theatre **Birkenhead** showing The Forsyte Saga. The band & trumpeters of the 22nd Cheshire Regiment provided live music

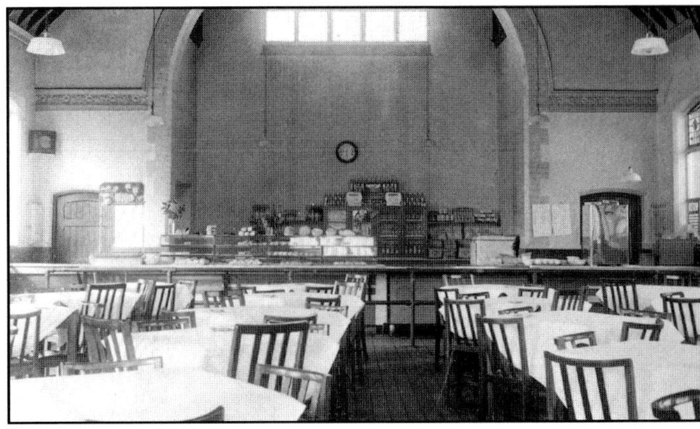

Above: *The* ***Clatterbridge*** *Hospital restaurant was opened by actress Barbara Mullen who was appearing at The* Liverpool Empire *Theatre. It had been converted from the former hospital chapel and provided service for over 20 years. The nurses' dining room opened in 1959*

Right: *Perry's business of sailmaking and ship's chandler was founded in 1804, one year before the Battle of Trafalgar*

ON ADMIRALTY LIST

R. PERRY & CO. LTD.

ESTABLISHED 1804

SAILMAKERS
RIGGERS and OUTFITTERS

Every Description of Canvas Work	Yacht Sails and Outfits a speciality
Awnings, Tarpaulins, Covers, etc.	Rigging and gear, hemp & wire ropes, blocks etc.

90, Church Street and 1-3 Ivy Street
Branch Works—
114, Lower George's Street, Kingstown (Co. Dublin)

Telephone: BIRKENHEAD 16 Telegrams: "PERRY SAILMAKERS, BIRKENHEAD"

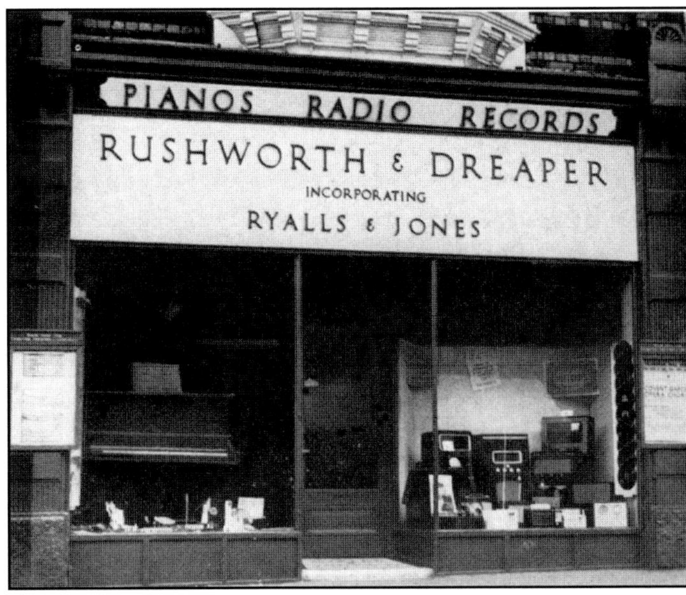

Above: *The former Ryalls & Jones shop at 251 Grange Road* ***Birkenhead*** *whose new sign advises that they have been taken over by Rushworth & Dreaper, the famous Liverpool Company, with both names on the shop sign [see advert below]. The window display seems a bit drab - but rationing was still in force*

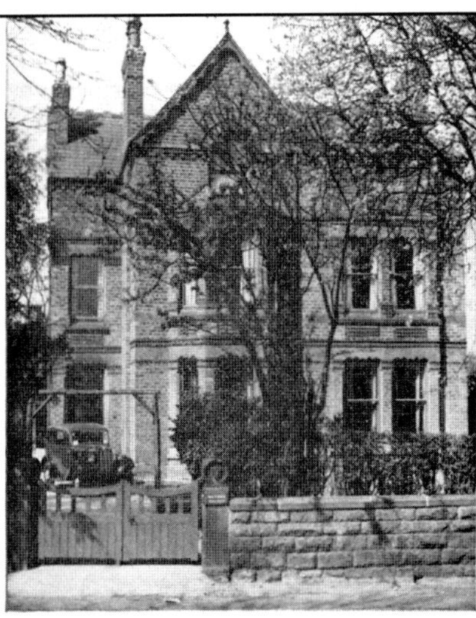

BEDFORD SCHOOL OF DANCING
46 EGERTON PARK, Bebington Road, ROCK FERRY.

Principal: REGINALD V. BIRCH.

Assistant Teachers:
Mrs. R. V. BIRCH. Miss MARY HENDERSON.
Miss LILIAN DURRANCE. Mr. W. J. SMITH.

Telephone .. .. ROCK FERRY 122.

LEFT: *The popular Bedford School of Dancing was based at 46 Egerton Park* ***Rock Ferry*** *whose principal was Reginald V Birch with four assistant teachers*

Below: *This advert for 'Birkenhead's Music Centre' referred to the shop above*

BIRKENHEAD'S MUSIC CENTRE

RUSHWORTH'S

Incorporating RYALLS & JONES LTD.

Unequalled selection . . . . . of
PIANOS
RADIO
TELEVISION
GRAMOPHONES
RECORDS MUSIC
VIOLINS . BAND
INSTRUMENTS
ETC.

for . . . . . .
EVERYTHING
MUSICAL

EASY PAYMENTS
arranged

251 GRANGE RD.
BIRKENHEAD · Telephone 1723

1950

– A new tide predictor which included all the latest developments was installed at **Bidston** Observatory[SOUV]

– **Birkenhead** Brewery acquired the business of Moorhouse Bros Ltd, one of Merseyside's leading mineral water suppliers

– The original Wirral & District Association Cup, which had been lost since 1921, was found by the 1920 winners Harrowby FC and returned to the Association[WDFA]

Mar 27 Inaugural concert at the Byrne Avenue Assembly Hall **New Ferry** [Byrne Avenue Baths] with Dennis Noble, Joseph Greene and the Birkenhead Male Voice Choir[PROG]

May 3 Queen Elizabeth launched the Aircraft Carrier *Ark Royal* at Cammell Laird **Birkenhead** [see photo] and laid the foundation stone for Birkenhead Technical College in Borough Road Birkenhead [see artist's impression on next page] which was finally opened in 1955[SOUV]

Nov 11 The War Memorial Window unveiled at the **Tranmere** Congregational Church in memory of those Church members who gave their lives in the Second World War[SOUV]

Dec The first time **Birkenhead**'s senior Police Officers have their photograph taken as a group and then appears in a local newspaper

Dec 16 Grange Presbyterian Church Hall **Bebington** opened and dedicated - cost £13,000 for the building alone [see 1956][SOUV]

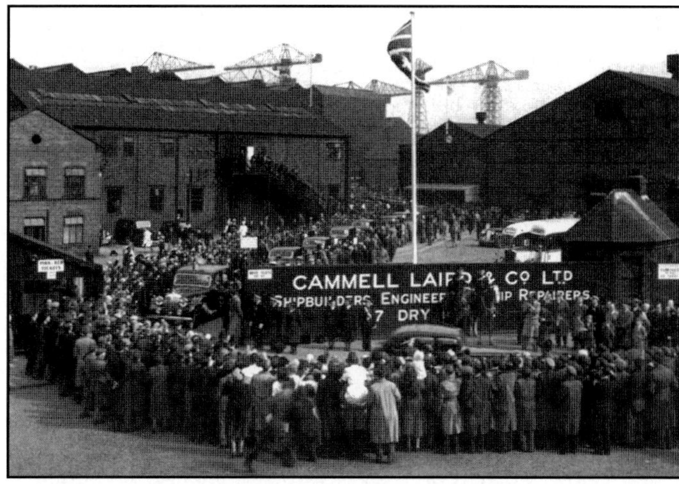

Above: *Queen Elizabeth [the Queen Mother] is seen in the Royal Car visiting Cammell Laird shipyard* **Birkenhead** *3 May 1950 - to launch the aircraft carrier* Ark Royal *[see below]*

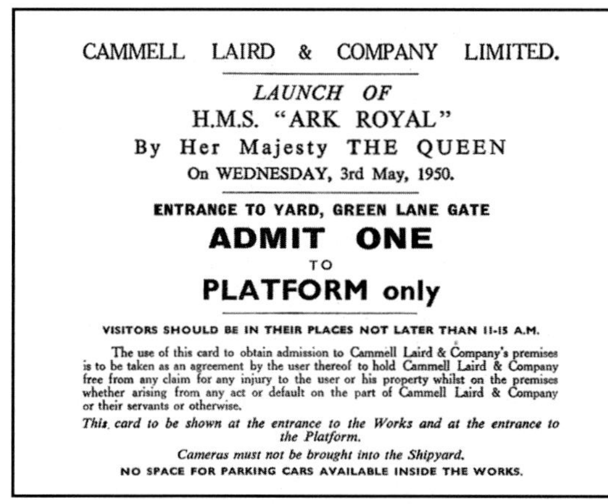

CAMMELL LAIRD & COMPANY LIMITED.

LAUNCH OF
H.M.S. "ARK ROYAL"
By Her Majesty THE QUEEN
On WEDNESDAY, 3rd May, 1950.

ENTRANCE TO YARD, GREEN LANE GATE

ADMIT ONE
TO
PLATFORM only

VISITORS SHOULD BE IN THEIR PLACES NOT LATER THAN 11-15 A.M.

The use of this card to obtain admission to Cammell Laird & Company's premises is to be taken as an agreement by the user thereof to hold Cammell Laird & Company free from any claim for any injury to the user or his property whilst on the premises whether arising from any act or default on the part of Cammell Laird & Company or their servants or otherwise.

This card to be shown at the entrance to the Works and at the entrance to the Platform.

Cameras must not be brought into the Shipyard.

NO SPACE FOR PARKING CARS AVAILABLE INSIDE THE WORKS.

Above: *This ticket was an invitation from Cammell Laird to attend the launching of the HMS* Ark Royal *by her Majesty The Queen [Mother] on 3 May 1950 [see photo above and below]*

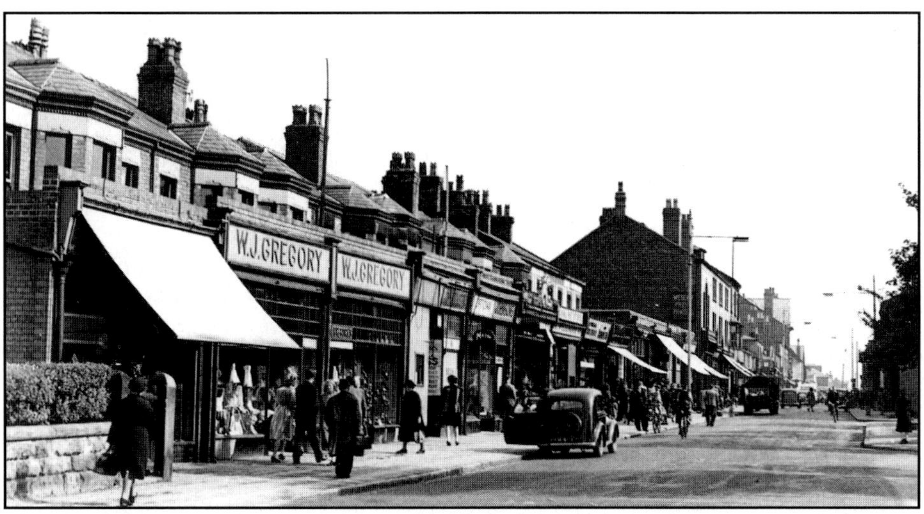

Left: *This photograph was taken in Bebington Road* **New Ferry** *and although the shop windows seem to be full, there was still rationing. These single-storey buildings were erected in the gardens of the houses behind, to take advantage of a growing population*

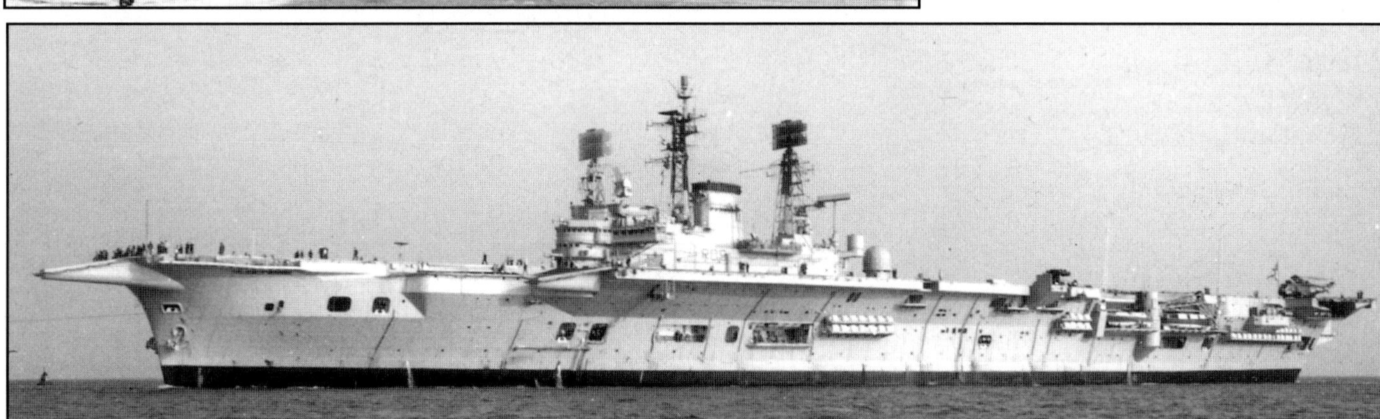

Above: *The aircraft carrier* Ark Royal *is pictured here some years after being launched by Queen Elizabeth [the Queen Mother] at Cammell Laird shipyard* **Birkenhead** *3 May 1950 [see photo above]*

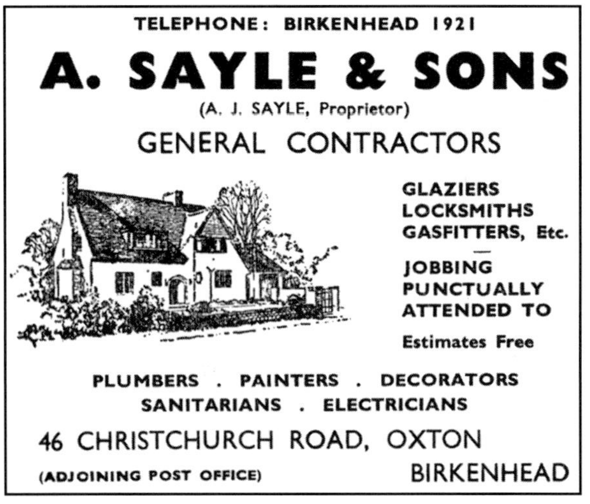

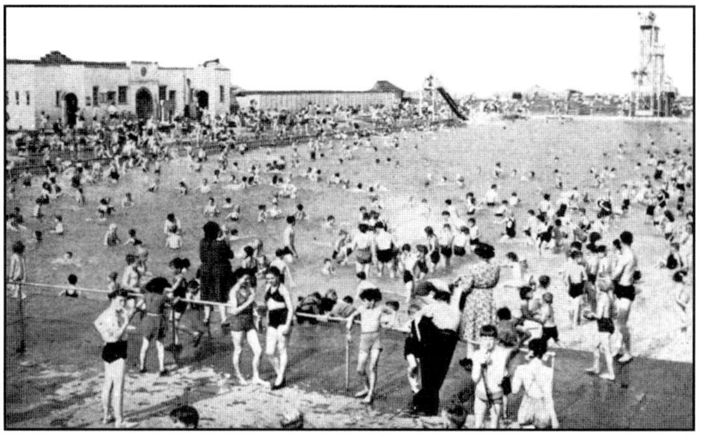

Above: ***New Ferry*** *open-air baths. Built in 1932 at a cost of £12,000 they were still very popular in 1950 - they closed in the 1970s*

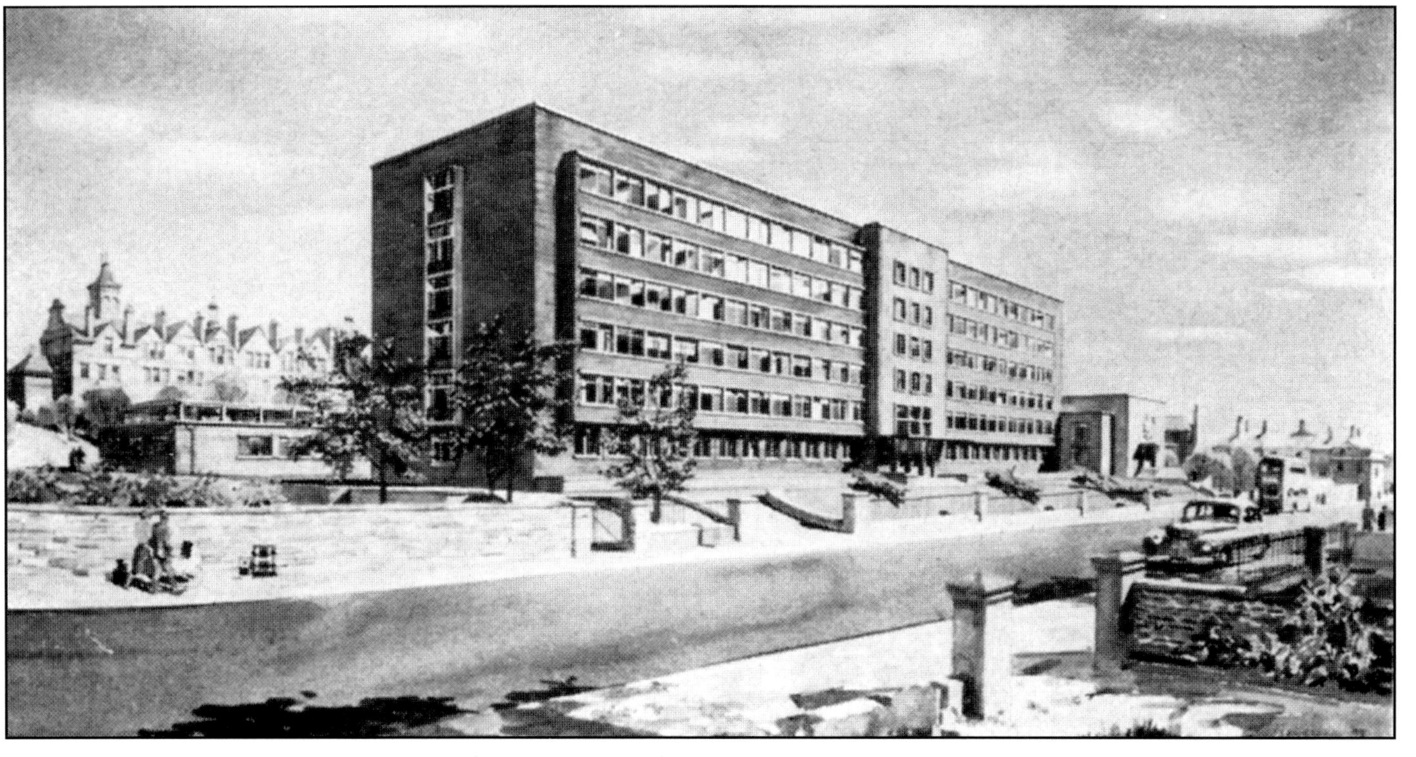

Above: *This was an artist's impression of* **Birkenhead** *Technical College in Borough Road. The foundation stone was laid by Queen Elizabeth [the Queen Mother] on 3 May 1950. Woodchurch Road Primary School is seen to the left of the college*

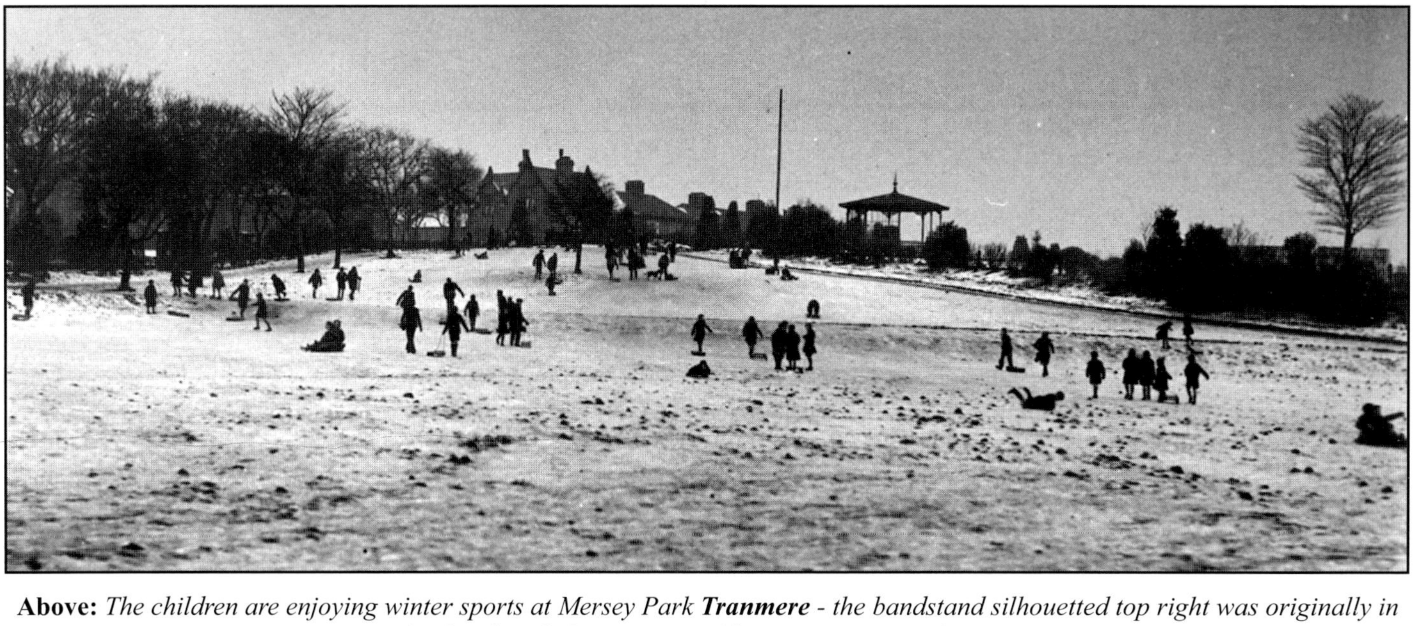

Above: *The children are enjoying winter sports at Mersey Park* ***Tranmere*** *- the bandstand silhouetted top right was originally in Birkenhead Park, but was moved here in 1929 [see also 1902]*

1951

— **Birkenhead** Co-operative Society celebrated their centenary

– **Bebington** Congregational Church formed[SOUV]

– St Anselm's College completed their building programme including an assembly hall and gymnasium - started in 1933 but delayed due to lack of funds and the outbreak of war in 1939[DoS]

Mar **Birkenhead** Amateur Operatic Society celebrated its Silver Jubilee with a performance of 'Showboat'

Apr Carlton Players of **Birkenhead** celebrated their 21st Birthday

May 12 Church of Christ **Birkenhead** dedicated their new Church in Park Road South [previously the Catholic Apostolic Church][SOUV]

May 22 First big post-war Gang Show performed for two nights at the Tower Ballroom **New Brighton**

Aug 25 The Festival of Britain **Birkenhead** Horse Show and Gymkhana was the first of 20 to be held annually at the Old Birkonian Rugby Club ground **Noctorum**[BSPH]

Sept 1 Official opening of Old Parkonian's Ground Holm Lane **Oxton** - HA Fry's Lancashire XV v LB (Losh) Smith's Cheshire XV[YWPH] [see photo]

Sept 4 Festival of Britain ship *Campania* arrived at Bidston Dock **Birkenhead** where she was open to public viewing from 5th until 14th September[FOBB] [see photo next page]

Sept 8 For two days - Scout Jamborette at **Arrowe** Park[FOBB]

Dec 3 **Storeton** Station on the Bidston to Wrexham railway line closed to passengers[PWR] [see next page]

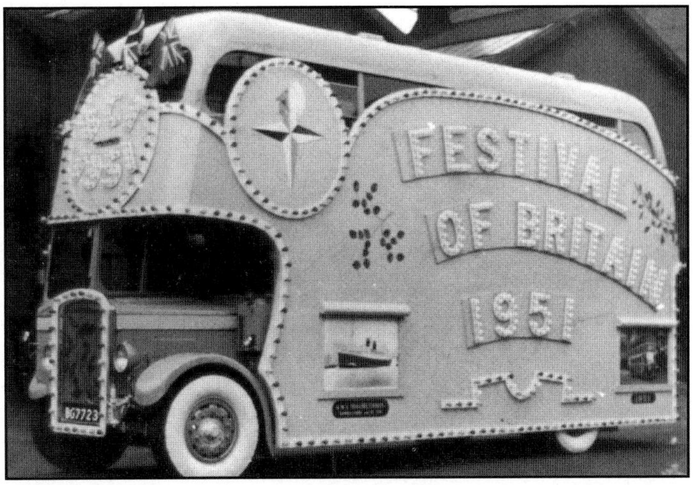

Above: *One of the ways* **Birkenhead** *celebrated the Festival of Britain was to convert a Leyland Titan TD5 bus into an illuminated Festival Bus*[TBB]

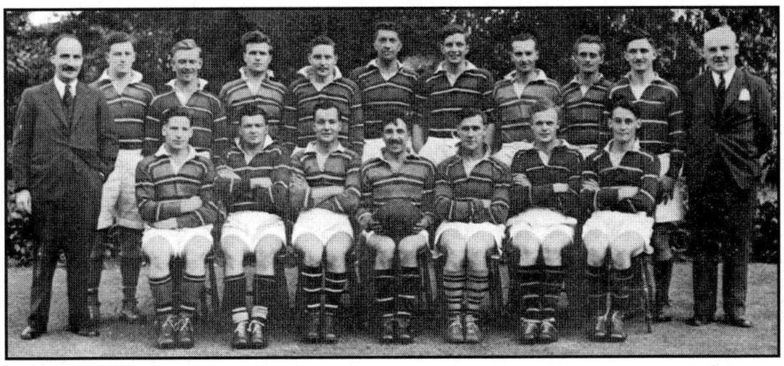

Above: *This was the Old Parkonian's Rugby XV 1950/51 whose photograph appeared in the souvenir programme on the occasion of the opening of the Old Parkonians' Association Recreation Ground in Holm Lane* **Oxton** *1 September 1951. The occasion was celebrated with a 'Grand Match' between Mr LB (Losh) Smith's Cheshire XV v Mr HA Fry's Lancashire XV. The Old Boys' Rugby Club had been formed in September 1928 followed in September 1931 by the Old Parkonians' Association*

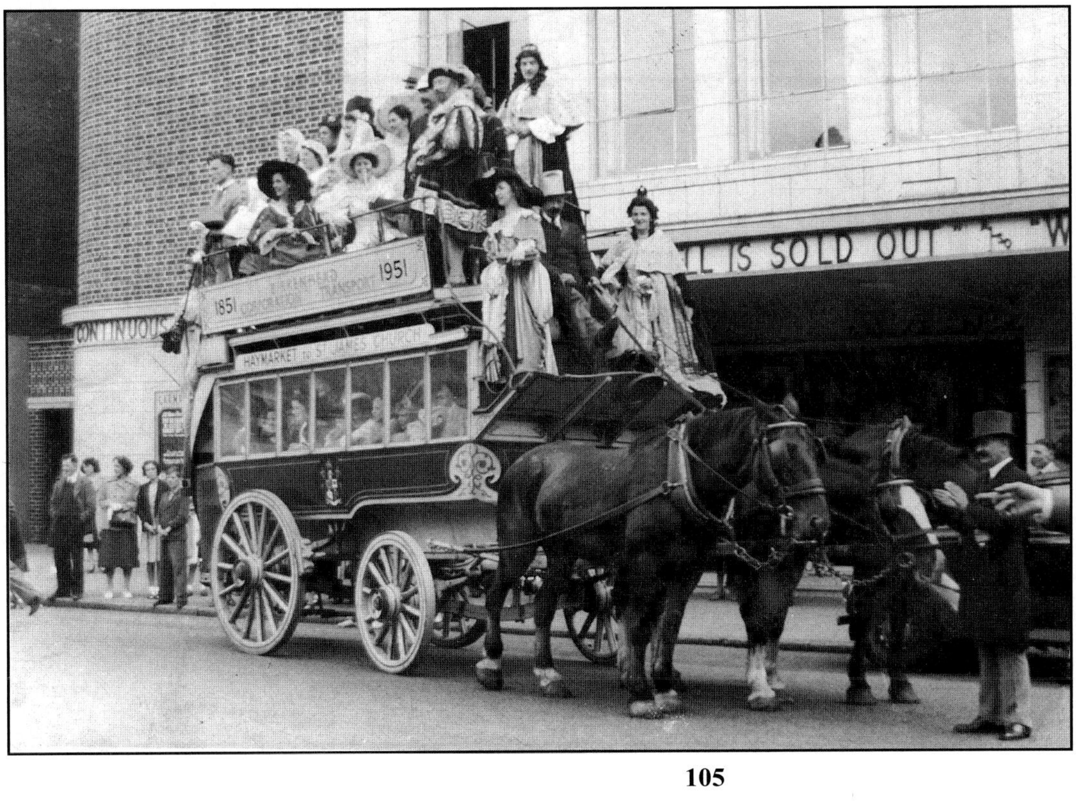

Left: *This horse-drawn covered omnibus is seen outside the* Gaumont Cinema *in Park Road East - this was to advertise the* **Birkenhead** *& District Amateur Theatre Federation performance at this cinema of "1066 and All That" - with Reginald Arkell and Alfred Reynolds. This was part of the Festival of Britain celebrations and ran from Monday 3 to Saturday 11 September*

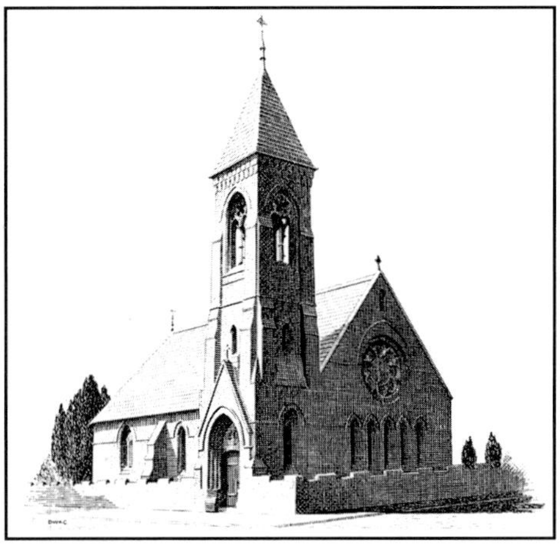

Above: *Church of Christ* **Birkenhead** *dedicated their new Church in Park Road South on May 12 1951 - it had previously been the Catholic Apostolic Church [see 1917]*

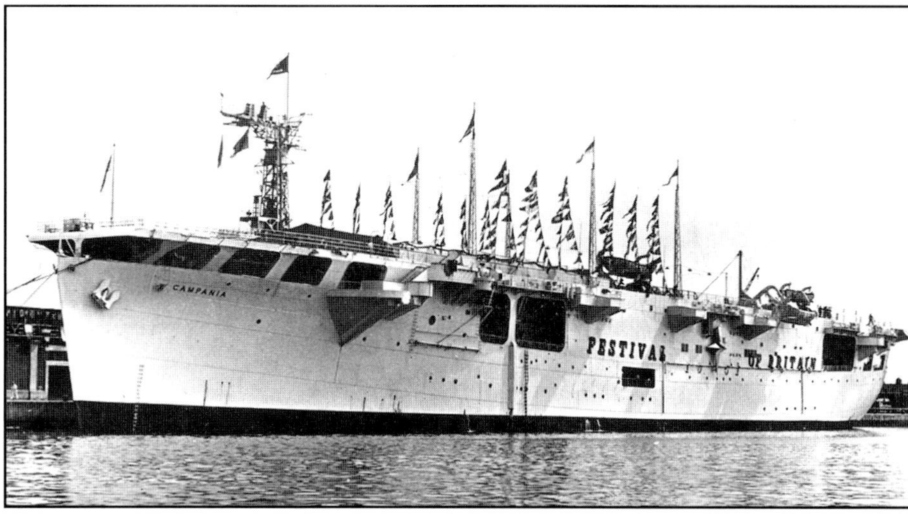

Above: *The former ferry carrier HMS* Campania *was chosen as a floating exhibition that would tour the country visiting 10 ports from May to October 1951. She visited* ***Birkenhead*** *from 4 to 14 September where the public could view her at Bidston Dock [also see below]* [YWPH]

Below: *This is how HMS* Campania *looked after she had been converted into a miniature version of the South Bank Exhibition at Cammell Laird shipyard* ***Birkenhead*** *prior to touring the country - this section of the exhibition was called "The People at Home" [also see above]*[YWPH]

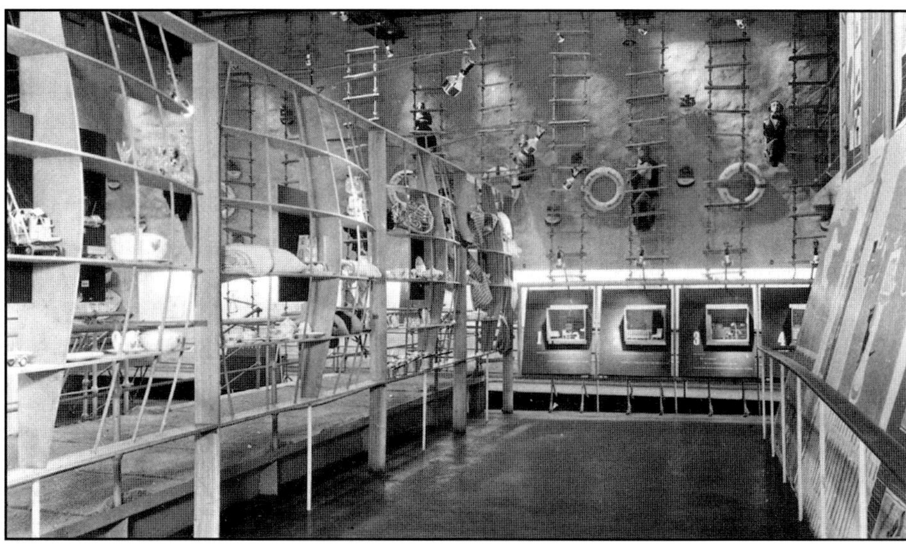

Below: Storeton [for **Barnston]** Station is seen on the **Bidston** to **Wrexham** railway line looking towards **Upton** - it opened in 1896 and this station was closed to passengers 3 December 1951[RSOW]

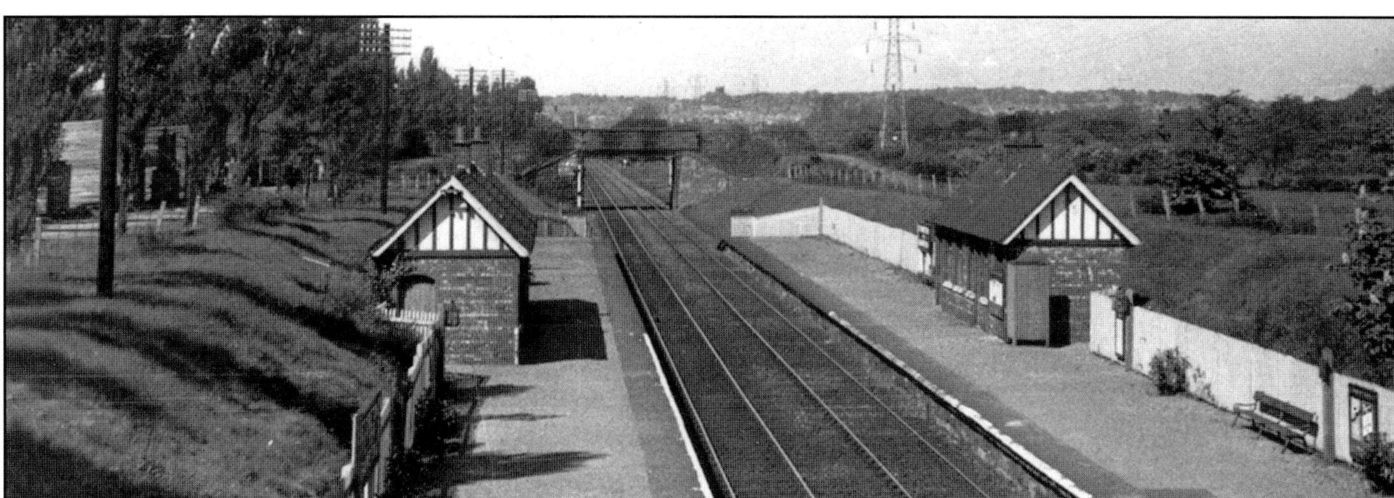

1952

– New RC Church 'Our Lady of Pity' opened in Mill Lane **Greasby**[SDYB]

– Birkenhead School's McAllester Memorial Ground, Bidston Road **Oxton** officially opened - donated by GL McAllester in memory of his brother[BSPH]

Feb 7 **King George VI dies**

Dec 8 First Japaneese ship to enter the Mersey since the war

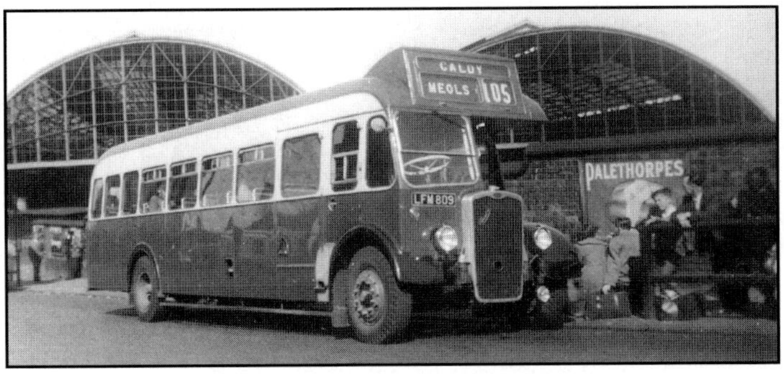

Above: *The **Meols** bound 105 single-deck bus was a 35 seater with rear entrance. It is waiting at Woodside **Birkenhead** with the station behind - this service later changed number and became the F27*

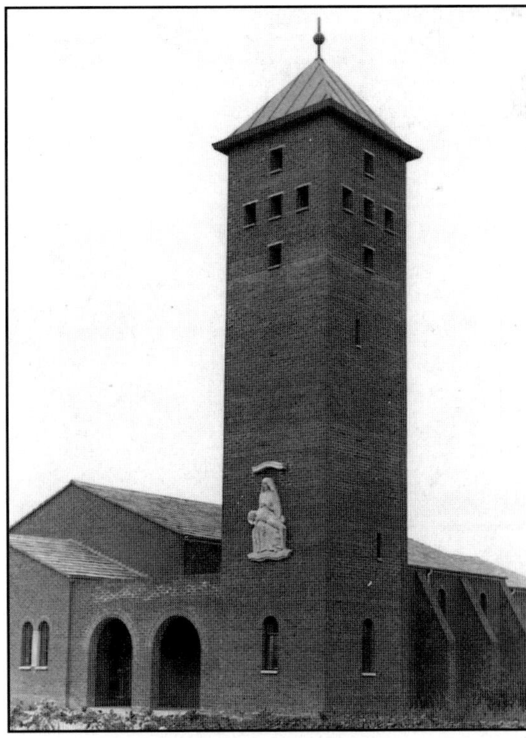

Above: *Our Lady of Pity Church seen here in Mill Lane **Greasby** was erected at a cost of £10,000 and opened in 1952. This site in Mill Lane had been purchased in 1940 and an old army hut was bought from a church in **Heswall** - it was dedicated 5 August 1940*

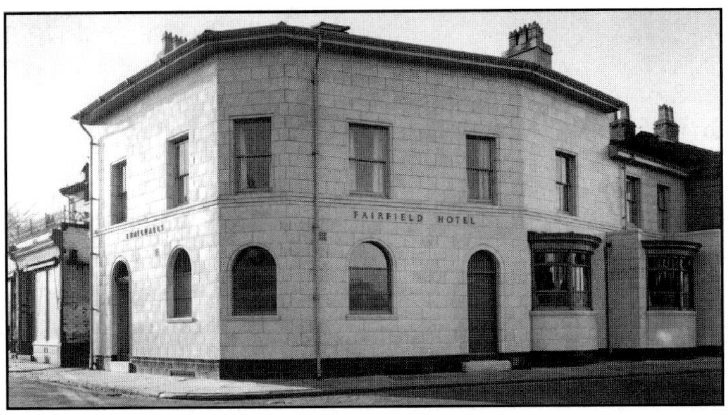

Above: *The* Fairfield Hotel, *a Threlfalls' pub on the corner of Old Chester Road and Well Lane **Tranmere,** photographed in 1952 having just been renovated*

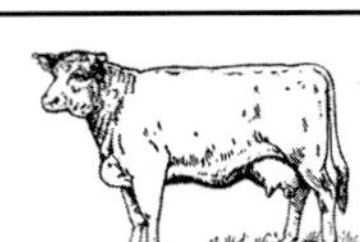

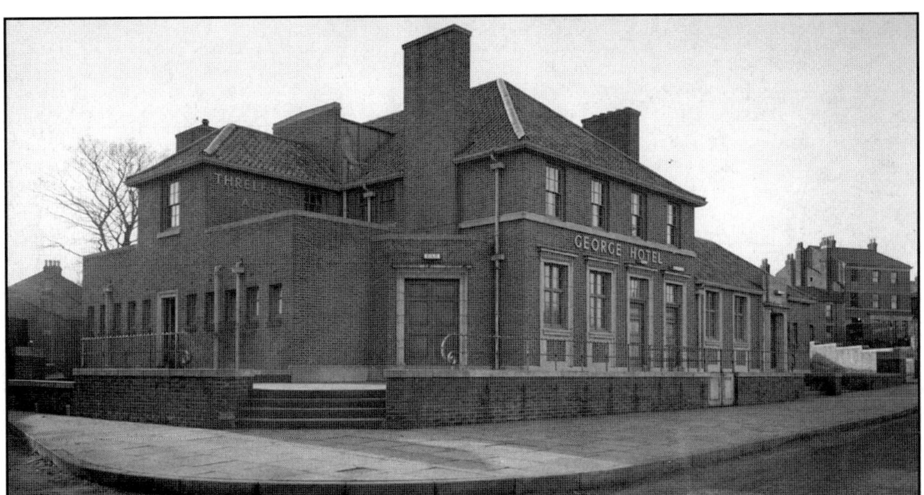

Left: *The* George Hotel 57 *Village Road Higher **Bebington** photographed the same day as the* Fairfield Hotel *above. Often known as 'Ellis's pub' after a previous landlord - it dates back to at least 1860 when John Oxton was the victualler. The Co-op store with van outside is on the right - two of their top windows have not been repaired following war damage*

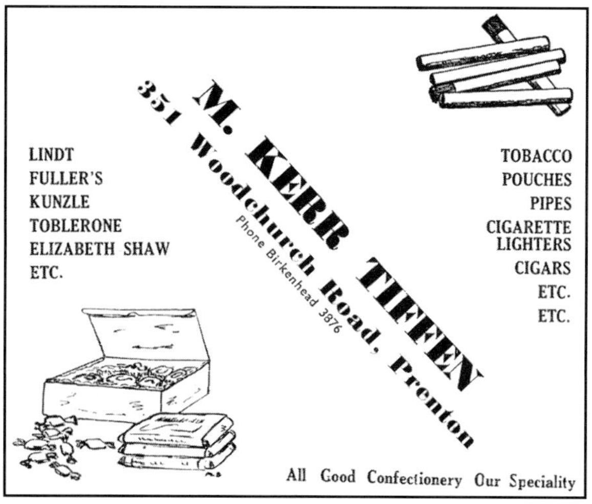

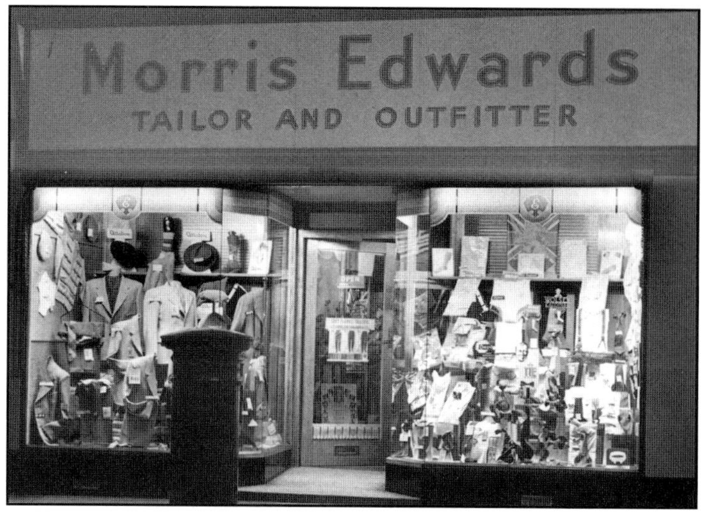

Above: *Morris Edwards, 56 Bebington Road* ***New Ferry.*** *Opened in 1935, this branch was later doubled in size, supplying many local people with wedding suits and school uniforms - but New Ferry's fortunes changed, crime rose, wealth went elsewhere and gradually independant shops disappeared, including this one in 2007*

Below: *The interior of Morris Edwards'* ***New Ferry*** *store, seen above. Mr Edwards (on the left) with his son Gordon. Mr Edwards was crippled in the 1930s and walked with the aid of sticks. However, he became Chairman of the Bebington Chamber of Trade in the 1950s when there were discussions on how to make New Ferry and Bebington shopping centres rival Birkenhead and a trade show was held at Mayer Hall. A small, well known figure at the counter of his shop and behind the wheel of his beloved Jaguar, he went on to work every day until well into his 90s. Both his sons put their whole working lives into the shops. Despite conflicting with his work, Gordon managed to become a nationally-known amateur golfer. He played off scratch for decades, with 155 Cheshire County appearances; Cheshire Stroke or Match-play Champion seven times; English Senior Amateur Champion three times and Spanish Seniors Champion 2001. He played against many well known golfers - including Gary Player also Mark James and narrowly losing to Nick Faldo in the 1975 English Amateur Championship at Lytham, having been in the lead for most of the match*

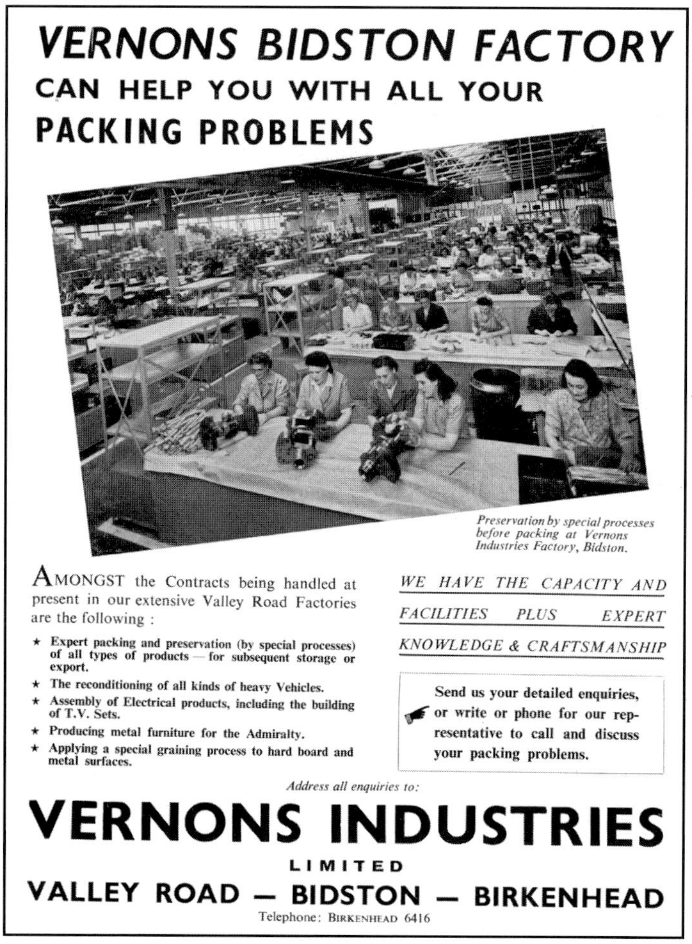

Above: *This advert featured the Vernon's packing factory in Valley Road* ***Bidston*** *which was one of the companies set up within this industrial estate, opening in 1946*

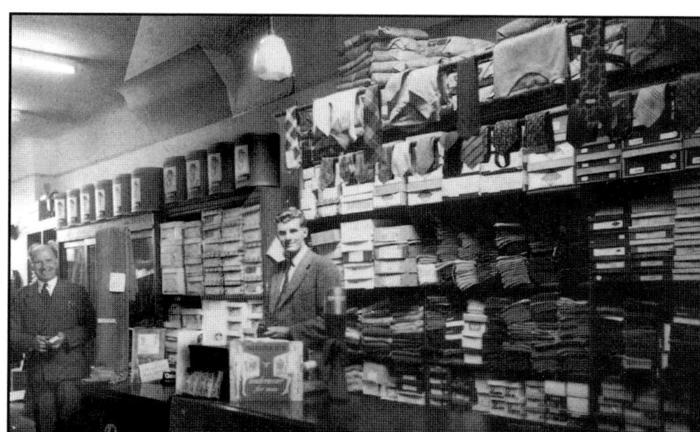

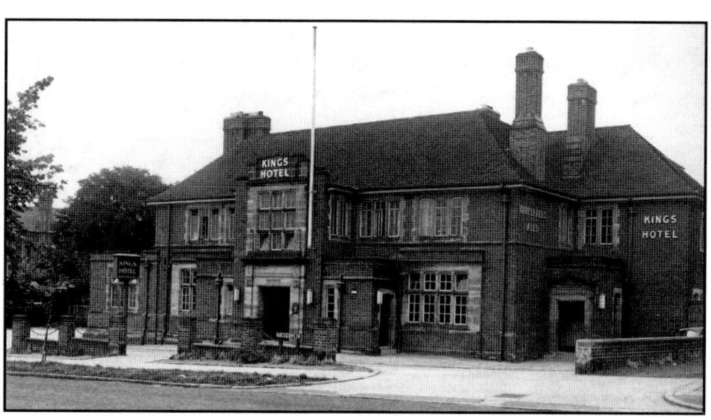

Left: *The King's Hotel pictured in King's Lane* ***Rock Ferry*** *was a Threlfall's pub built in the 1930s when King's Lane was transformed from a country lane surrounded by fields into a residential area surrounded by houses. The name King was not the Royal one but named after Colonel King, a local land owner*

1953

– Methodist Church opened in Glenavon Road **Prenton** [see photo next page]

Apr 14 Training ship HMS Conway on her way from Anglesey to be overhauled and refitted in dry dock at **Birkenhead**, slipped her moorings and became beached on the Caernarvon side of the Menai Straits close to the Suspension Bridge (see this page, also 1941)[TC]

May 30 HM Submarines *Artful* and *Seneschal* open to the public in **Birkenhead** Docks[BCSB]

May 30 Start of a week-long programme of Coronation events in **Birkenhead** including the illuminations being switched on in Hamilton Square and the decorated bus touring the town[PROG]

June 2 Queen Elizabeth II Coronation Day. Coronation Peal of Church Bells - St Mary's **Birkenhead**, St Saviour's **Oxton** and St Oswald's **Bidston**. Tea parties at children's and aged persons' homes; Coronation Fanfare at the *Gaumont Cinema*, Park Road East, illumination of public buildings, illuminated ferry services, firing of the beacon bonfire by the Birkenhead Boy Scouts Association at **Arrowe** Park [followed by Camp Fire Songs by Scouts and Guides] etc[PROG]

June 6 Final day of the Coronation Festivities with a circular Parade of decorated vehicles assembling at **Birkenhead** Park at 2pm then touring the town and arriving back, at 5.30pm[PROG] [see photos this page]

Sept 3 Centenary anniversary of the first ***Birkenhead*** *Advertiser*

Oct 30 New **Birkenhead** Police Headquarters opened in Chester Street [see 1956]

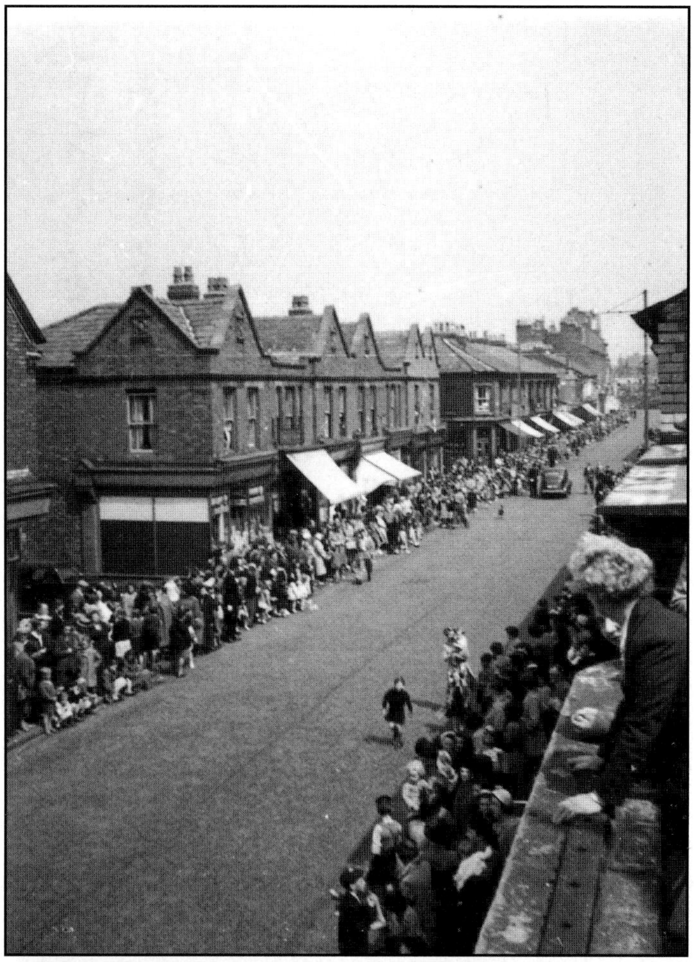

Top right: *There is hardly a viewing spot in Oxton Road* ***Birkenhead*** *- some people are even on balconies above the shops - on the final day of the Coronation Festivities where the crowd is waiting for the circular Parade of decorated vehicles which assembled at* ***Birkenhead*** *Park at 2pm then toured the town arriving back there at 5.30pm*

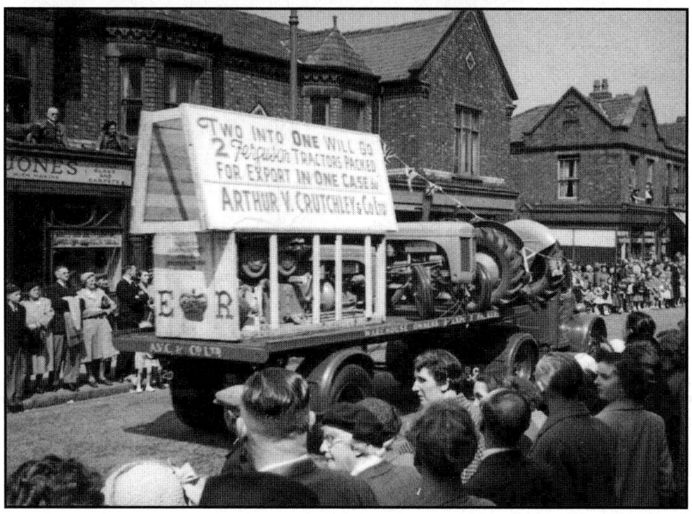

Right: *Arthur V Crutchley's lorry is taking part in* ***Birkenhead's*** *circular parade for the Coronation Festivities [see details above]. The sign on the lorry says: "Two into one will go - 2 Ferguson Tractors packed for export in one case by Arthur V Crutchley & Co Ltd"*

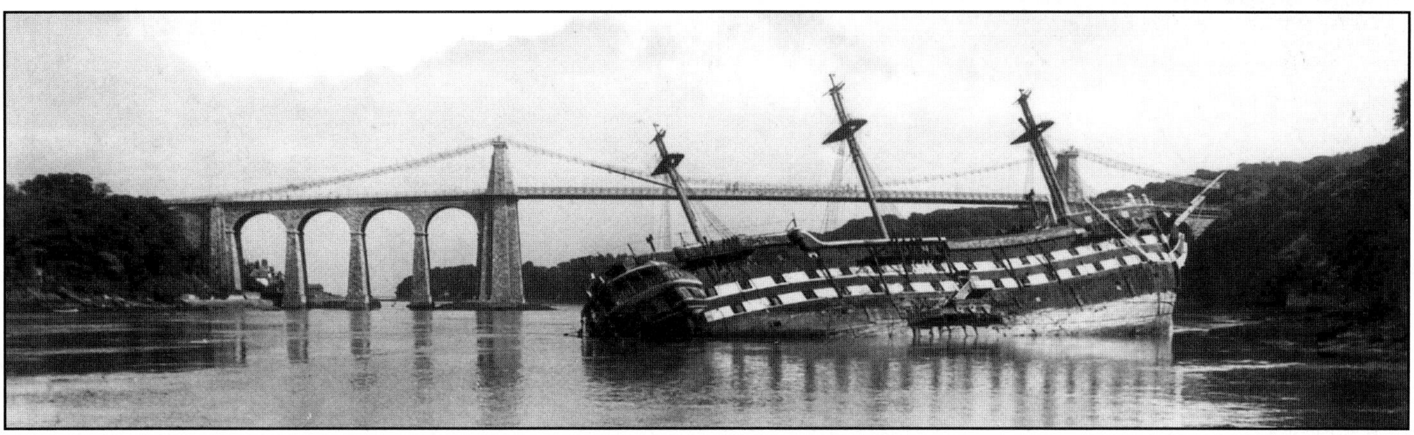

Above: *The training ship HMS Conway is seen beached and listing on the Caernarvon side of the Menai Straits with the suspension bridge in the background. Originally she was moored off* ***Rock Ferry*** *in the River Mersey but was moved to the Menai Straits in May 1942 to avoid the air raids. It was decided to move her back to the Mersey for a refit and on 14 April 1953 whilst being towed the rope broke and she became beached and was a tourist attraction for some time before being burnt out*[YWPH]

VR ER VII. GR V. GR VI.

During four reigns and almost a century our House has been proud to maintain a personal service for the discerning buyer of men's clothes. Repeat patronage has judged us to be still Monarchs in the "field of outfitting."

We confidently move forward to serve under yet another Monarch — our Gracious Elizabeth II, and join our public in wishing her a glorious and happy reign.

"LONG LIVE THE QUEEN"

HOPE & LEE LTD.

The Man's Shop

GRANGE ROAD, BIRKENHEAD

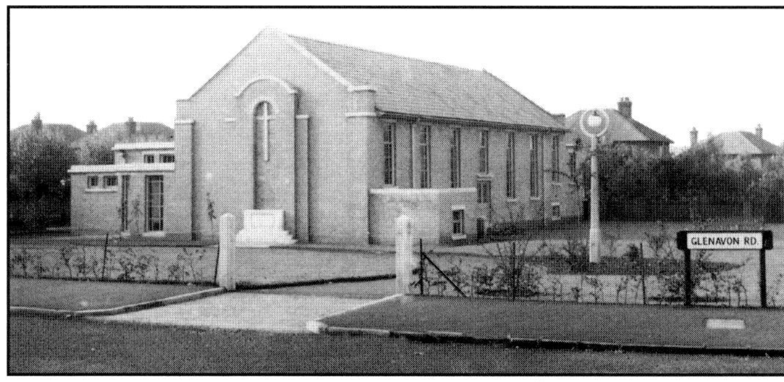

Above: *Methodist Church opened in Glenavon Road* ***Prenton*** *- seating for 250*

Everything for the HOME and the FAMILY...

ROBBS . . . the complete departmental store, where personal Service and Courteous attention are household words—and where value for money is the Supreme consideration at all times.

40 Departments

SPECIAL FEATURES

★ The Ladies HAIRDRESSING & BEAUTY SALON
★ The Ladies "JAEGER" SHOP
★ The "Wetherall" Department (in the "Robney" Gallery)
★ The OAKROOM Restaurant
Morning Coffee . Afternoon Teas
DAILY LUNCHEONS 2/9, 3/9 and 5/- or A LA CARTE

ROBBS
Birkenhead's Departmental Store
ESTABLISHED IN THE YEAR 1872

ROBB BROS LTD · CHARING X · BIRKENHEAD
TELEPHONE BIRKENHEAD 2880

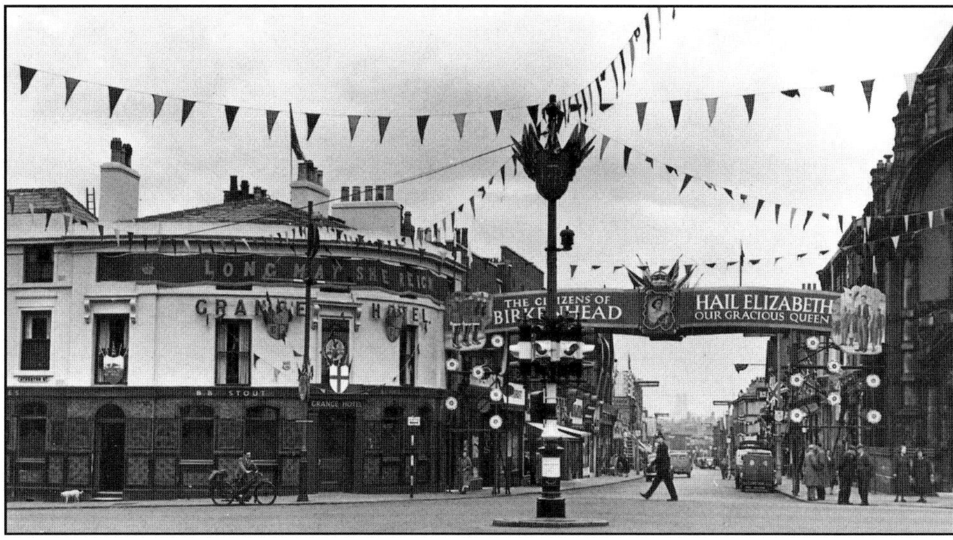

Above: *An advert for Robb Bros departmental store with over 40 departments was on the left side of Grange Road* ***Birkenhead*** *behind the policeman in the picture above right*

Above: *The top of Grange Road* ***Birkenhead*** *is festooned with bunting, shields and banners to celebrate the Coronation. The banner across the top of Grange Road says:* The Citizens of Birkenhead Hail Elizabeth our Gracious Queen *and the one above the* Grange Hotel *on the left says:* Long May She Reign. *Note the traffic lights on the pole in the centre of Charing Cross - Grange Road ahead was a one-way street*

Below: *Looking in the same direction but further down Grange Road* ***Birkenhead****, as seen above, the message on the bunting says:* Loyal Greetings From Birkenhead. *This part of Grange Road no longer exists - except for Allansons, the tall white building further down on the left which is now Beatties [see 1954]*

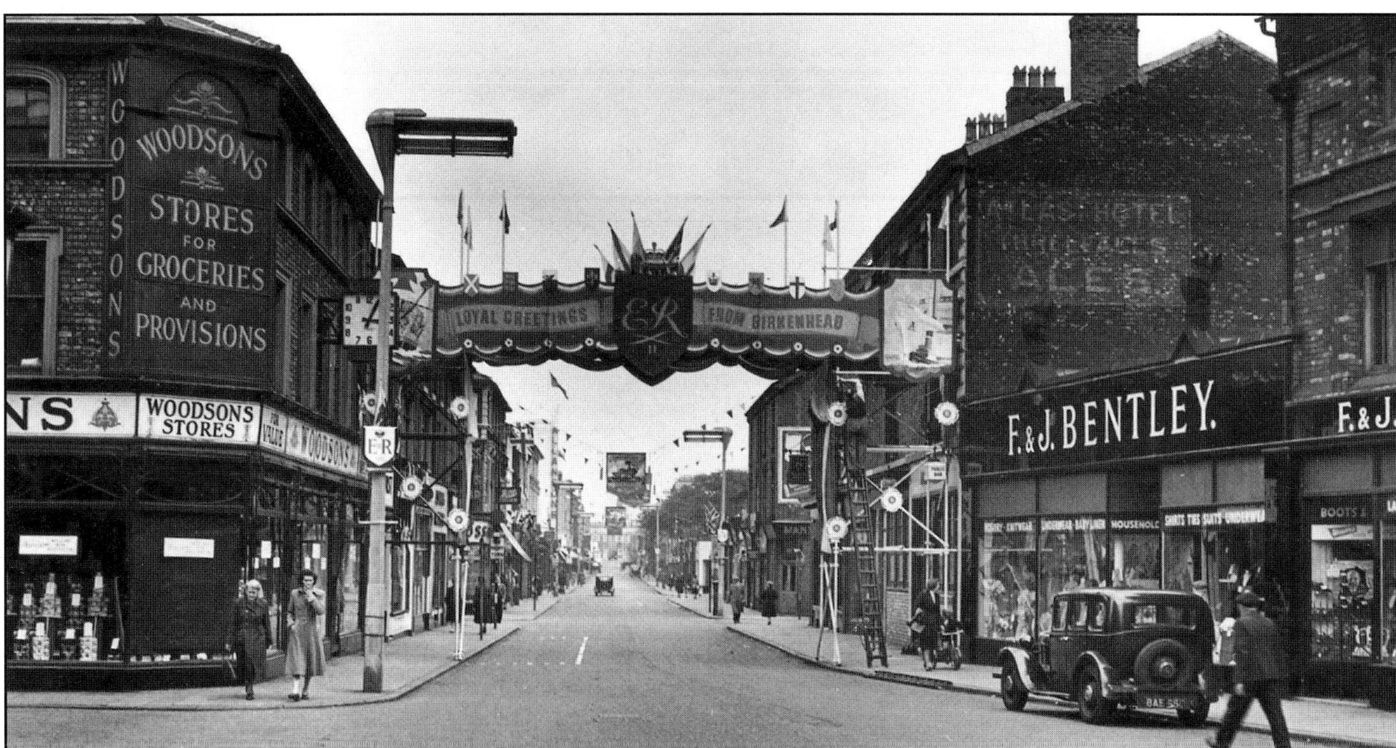

1953 continued

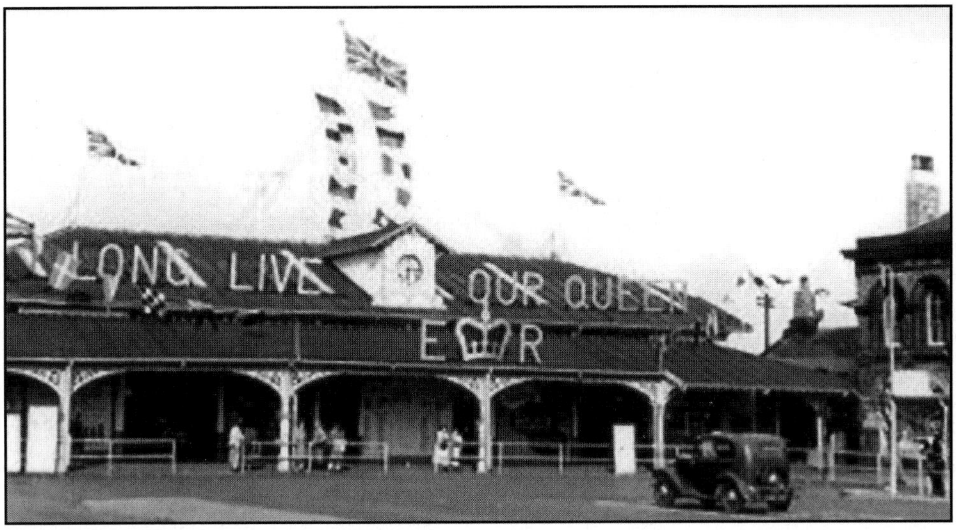

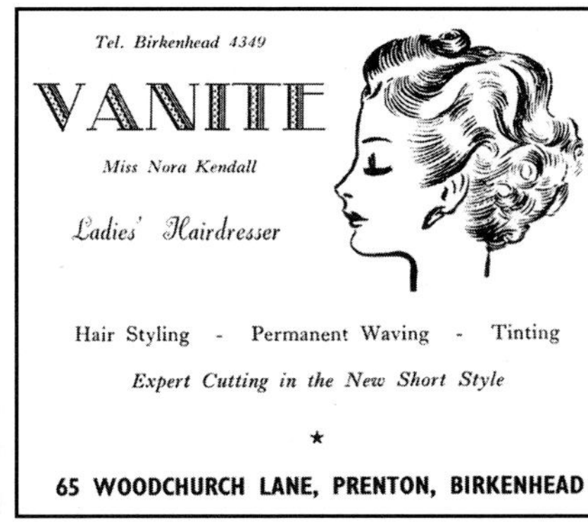

Below: *Allanson's store in Grange Road* ***Birkenhead*** *were offering:* Loyal Greetings to her Majesty Elizabeth, Our Gracious Queen - Long May She Reign

Above: *The Woodside Ferry Terminal has a number of flags flying above it and the sign:* Long Live Our Queen E R *on the roof - in preparation for the Coronation celebrations which started on 30 May through to 6 June 1953 - with Coronation Day being on 2 June*

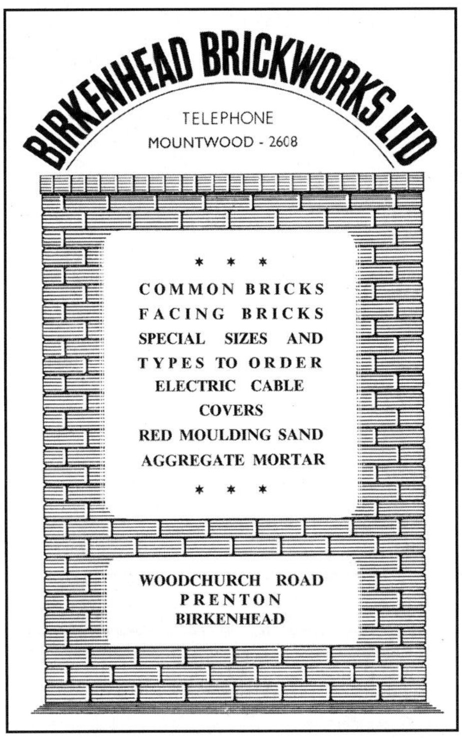

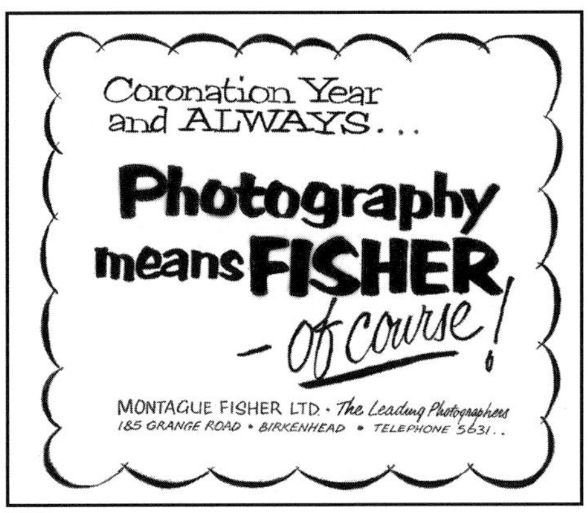

Above: *Fisher's photography shop was at 185 Grange Road* ***Birkenhead***

Left: ***Birkenhead*** *Brickworks were situated in Woodchurch Road* ***Prenton*** *[see 1931]*

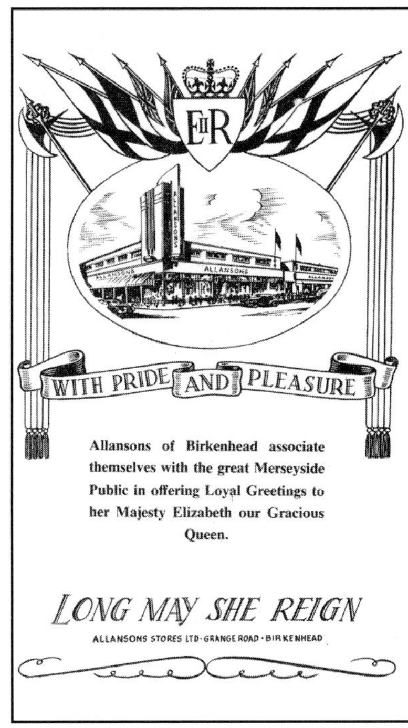

Below: *Looking across the Hamilton Square Gardens* ***Birkenhead*** *to the Town Hall, the lamp posts around the gardens were draped in flags and there was an illuminated sign* E II R *above the entrance, to celebrate the Coronation of Queen Elizabeth*

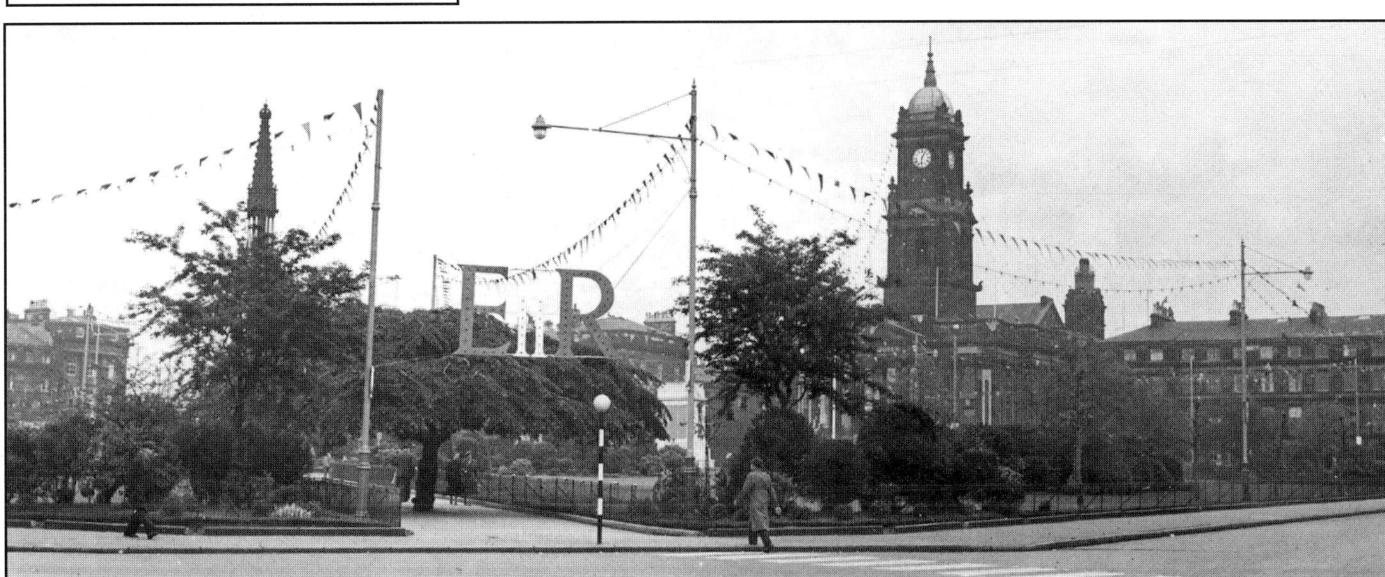

1954

– A Church maintained school opened on the site of Claughton Higher Grade School, Borough Road **Birkenhead**, which had been destroyed by a land mine [see March 1941][SOUV]

– Higher **Bebington** Branch Library opened in Bebington Road[SOUV]

– Auction of the last stock and implements of Prenton Old Hall Farm due to the farm land being developed into the **Prenton** Dell Estate[NEWS]

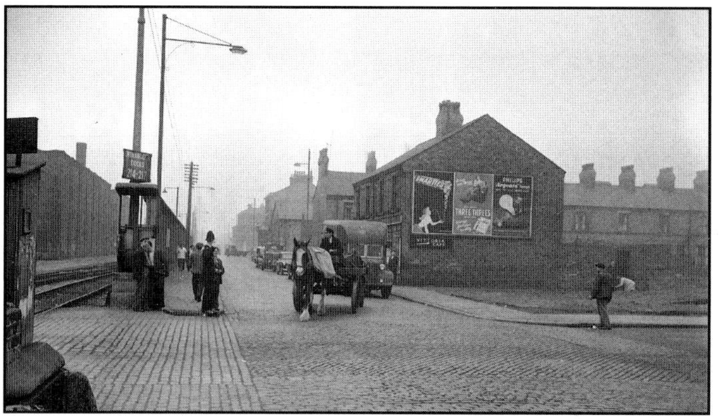

Above: *The rag and bone man in the horse-drawn cart is seen in Vittoria Street* ***Birkenhead*** *turning right past the policeman into the entrance to Docks 214 - 217. The derelict land in front of the building with the adverts for Smarties, Three & Threes Cigarettes & Philips' Lamps, was the result of bombing during the Second World War*

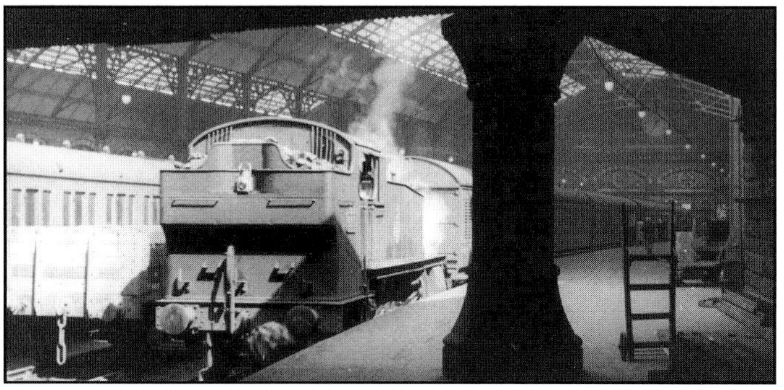

Above: *The train is standing at Woodside Station platform. The station opened here in 1878 when the* ***Chester*** *to* ***Birkenhead*** *railway was diverted from its then terminus at Monks Ferry. This was a good example of Victorian railway architecture with its graceful wrought-iron columns and arched roof with plenty of natural light. The station closed in 1967 and was later demolished*

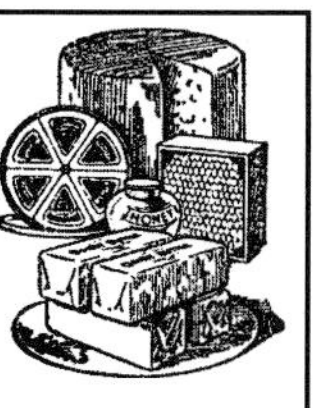

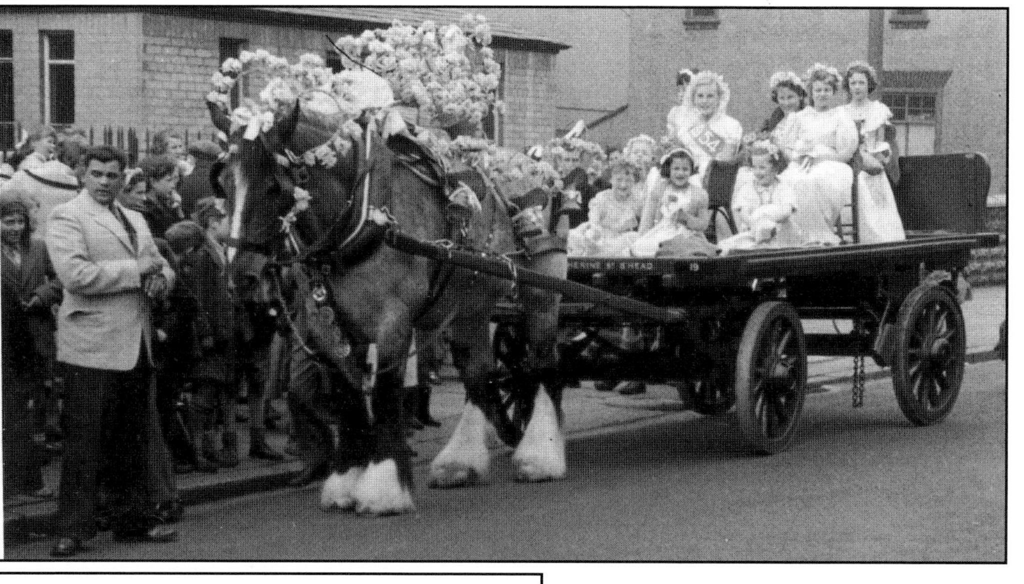

Right: *The crowds in the background are waiting for the 'Queen of 1954' [the girl with the 1954 sash] to set off with her attendants on the horse-drawn trailer which belonged to the Birkenhead Co-op whose headquarters were in Catherine Street* ***Birkenhead***

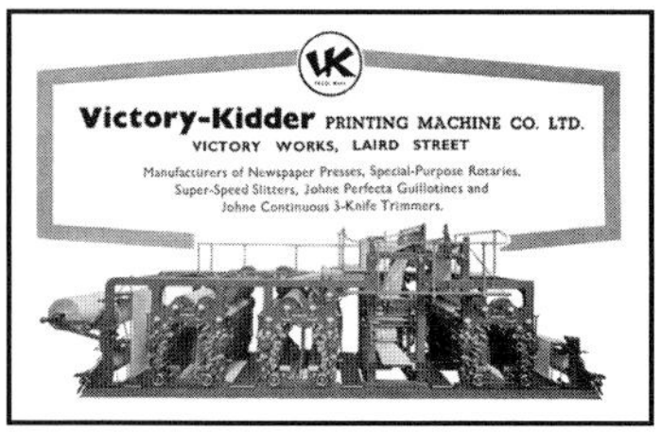

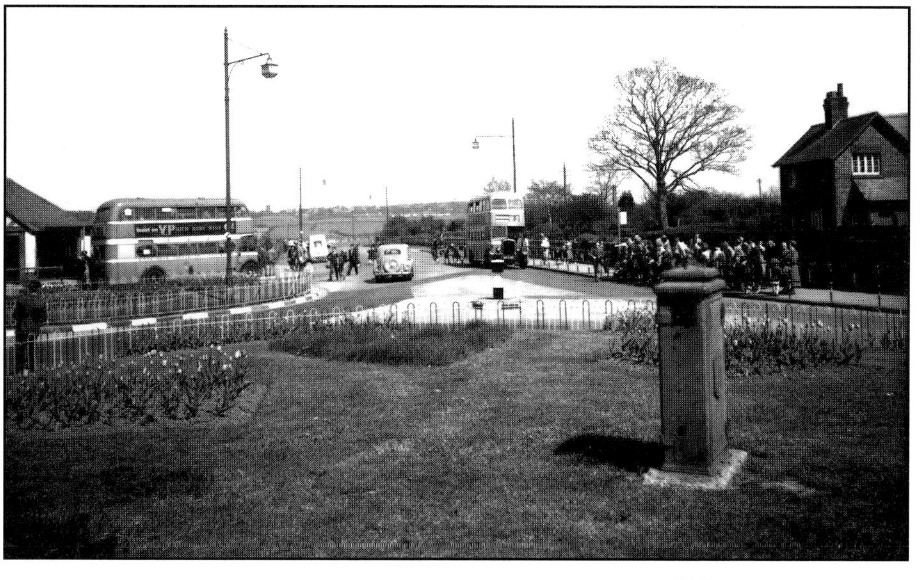

Left: *Looking from* ***Arrowe*** *Park roundabout towards* ***Oxton*** *which is on the horizon. The bus on the left is in the bus lane with shelter to the left - on the right is the No. 77 bound for Moreton*

1954 continued

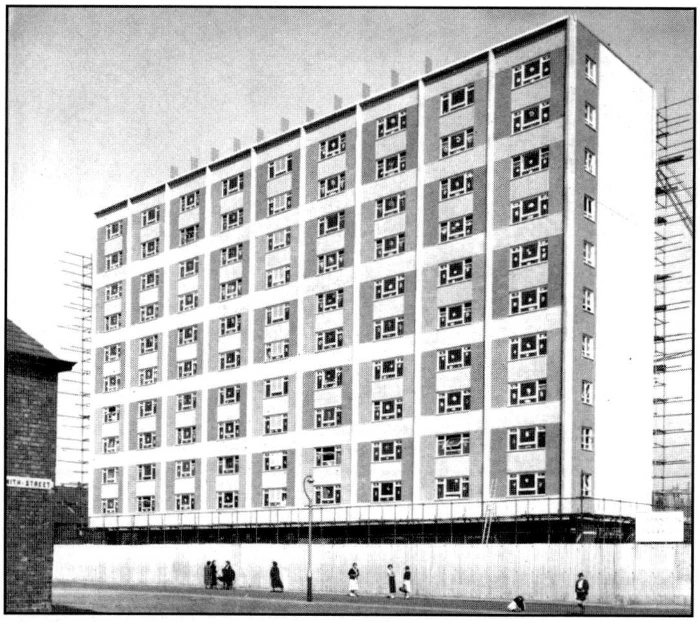

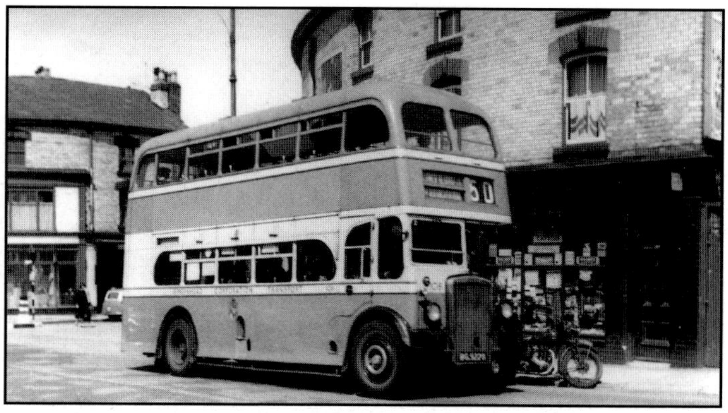

Above: *This **Birkenhead** Corporation Leyland Titan PD1 bus - fleet No. 108 - is seen outside the Post Office in Old Chester Road on the corner of St Paul's Road **Tranmere**. This bus was in service from 1946 until 1959/60*

Left: *High-rise developments of this type were one of the answers to the post-war housing crisis. This 11 storey block of flats, which is seen nearing completion, were in Beckwith Street **Birkenhead***

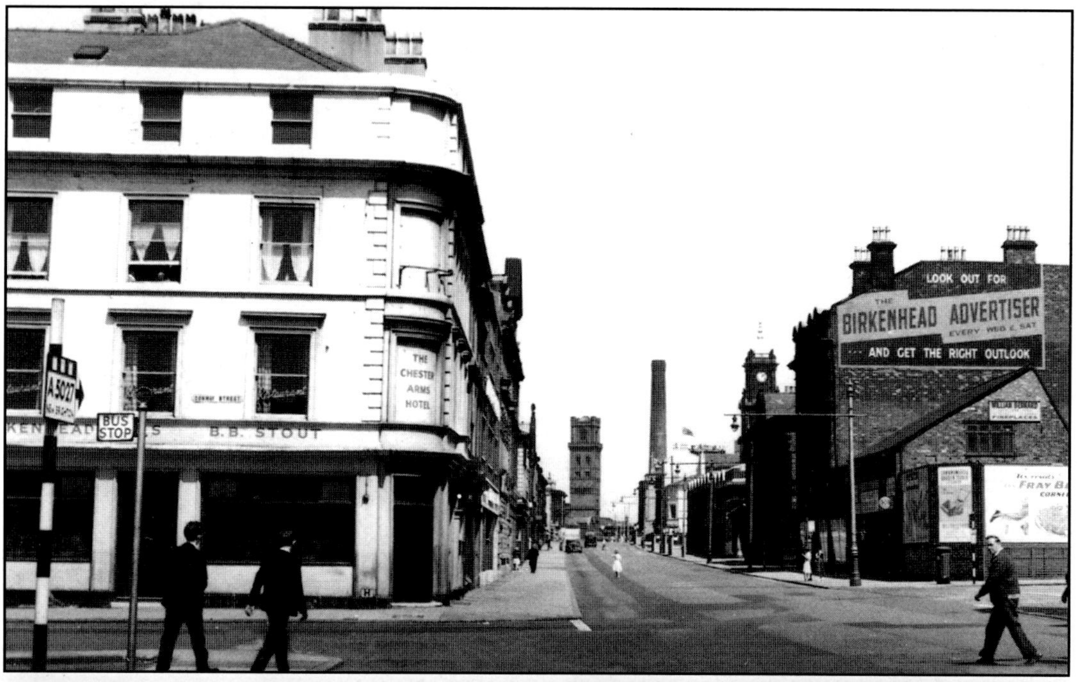

Left: *Looking down Hamilton Street **Birkenhead** - the tall square building in the distance provided the power for the hydraulic lifts at Hamilton Square Station, and to the right the domed building with the clock face is Birkenhead Town Hall.* The Chester Arms Hotel *on the left, which dated back to at least 1850 was a Birkenhead brewery pub on the corner of Hamilton Street. The building was demolished in 1971 and St Mark's House office block erected on the site*

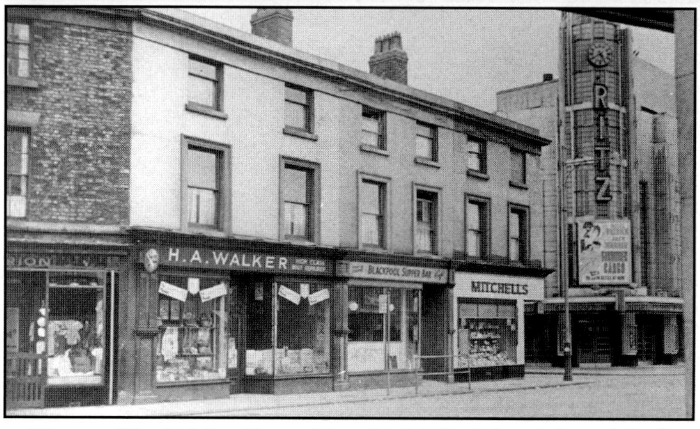

Above: *'Forbidden Cargo' in which Nigel Patrick and Jack Warner were stars was the advertised film at the* Ritz *cinema, on an island site between Claughton Road and Oliver Street **Birkenhead.** It was opened by Gracie Fields in 1937 when an estimated 75,000 fans lined the streets, causing traffic jams. The cinema was badly damaged by a bomb on 21 December 1940. Having been rebuilt it opened 13 January 1947. Its last performance as a cinema was on 5 January 1969*

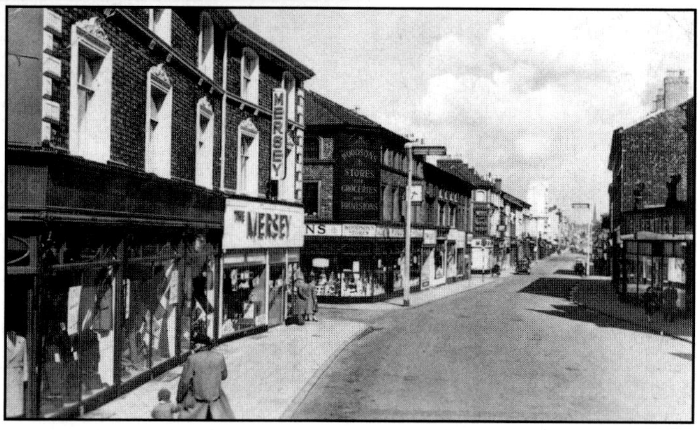

Above: *Looking down Grange Road **Birkenhead** with The Mersey furniture store and Woodson's Stores on the left either side of the junction with Milton Street and on the other side was F & J Bentley at 141-143 one selling boots and shoes and the other a pawnbroker. Allansons, the tall white building in the distance, is the only building still there today - trading as Beatties. This area is now part of Birkenhead Market*

1955

– Higher **Bebington** purpose-built branch Library opened[PROG]

Jan 8 **Birkenhead** Technical College officially opened in Borough Road [see photo]

Sep 24 The body of Alice Barton was found by three schoolboys in a Second World War pill box,between **Woodchurch** Road towards **Upton**. This case,which became known as "The Pill Box Murder", was never solved due to a series of mistakes by the police [see photo][MMB]

Nov 10 *The Brown Cow* in Bebington Road **Bebington** was the first Birkenhead Brewery pub to be opened after the war, replacing an inn of the same name[WTDW]

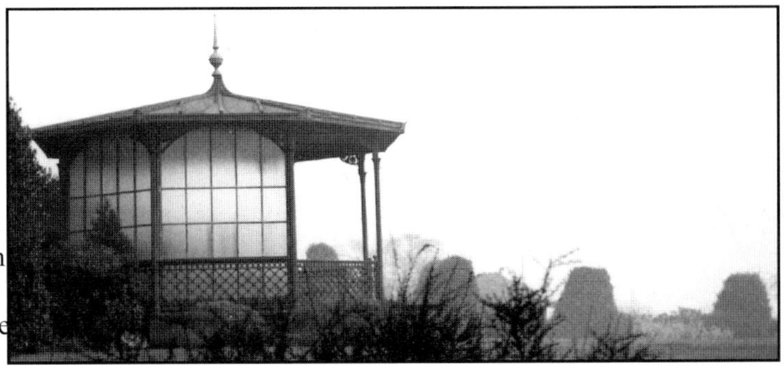

Above: *This bandstand seen in Mersey Park* ***Tranmere*** *was originally situated in Birkenhead Park - it was moved here in 1929 [see 1902]*

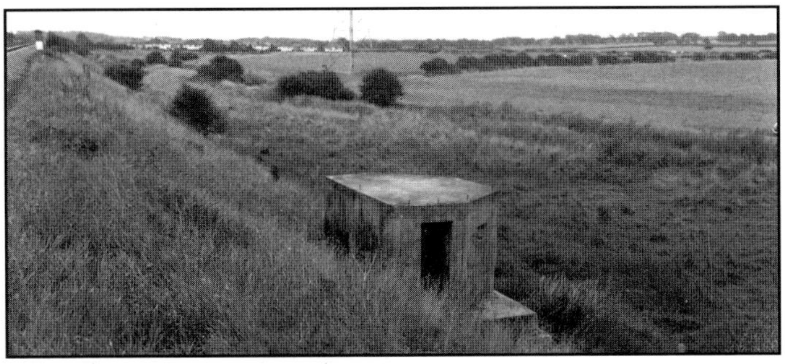

Above: *This was the pill box where Alice Barton was found brutally murdered on 24 September 1955 which was situated between* ***Prenton*** *Bridge on Woodchurch Road (seen in the distance) and* ***Upton*** *Station - on the Woodchurch side of the Bidston to Wrexham railway embankment. Following a photo of the victim superimposed on a dressed dummy, she was identified and several witnesses came forward who had seen her with her murderer. Several clues pointed to a local man but the Police wasted valuable time interviewing visiting seamen aboard the SS* Empress of France. *Her murderer was never found and the only hope now is of a deathbed confession* [MMMB]

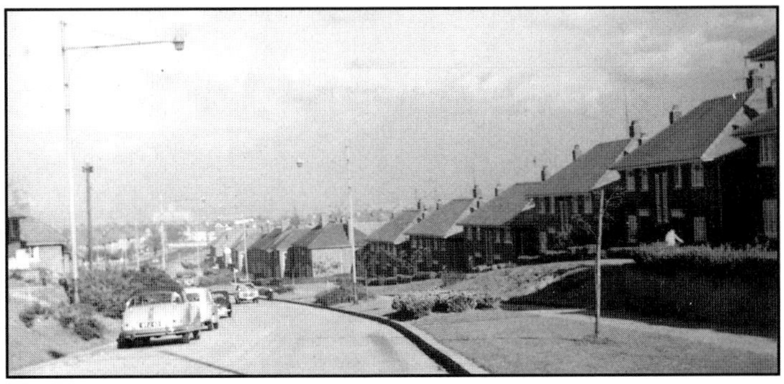

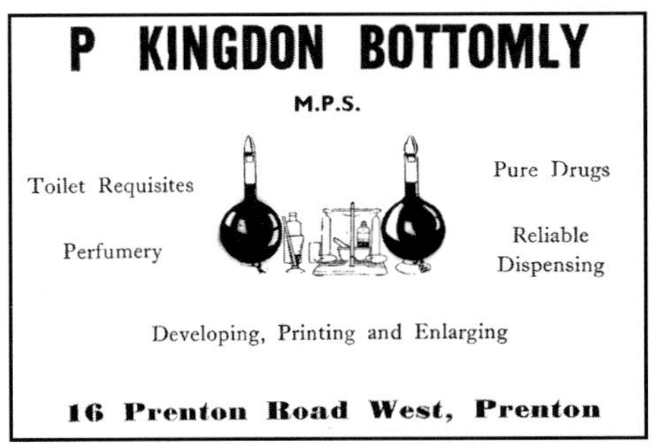

Above: *The houses seen in Mount Road were part of the Mountwood estate which was started in 1946 - at a time when garages were not included in the planning*

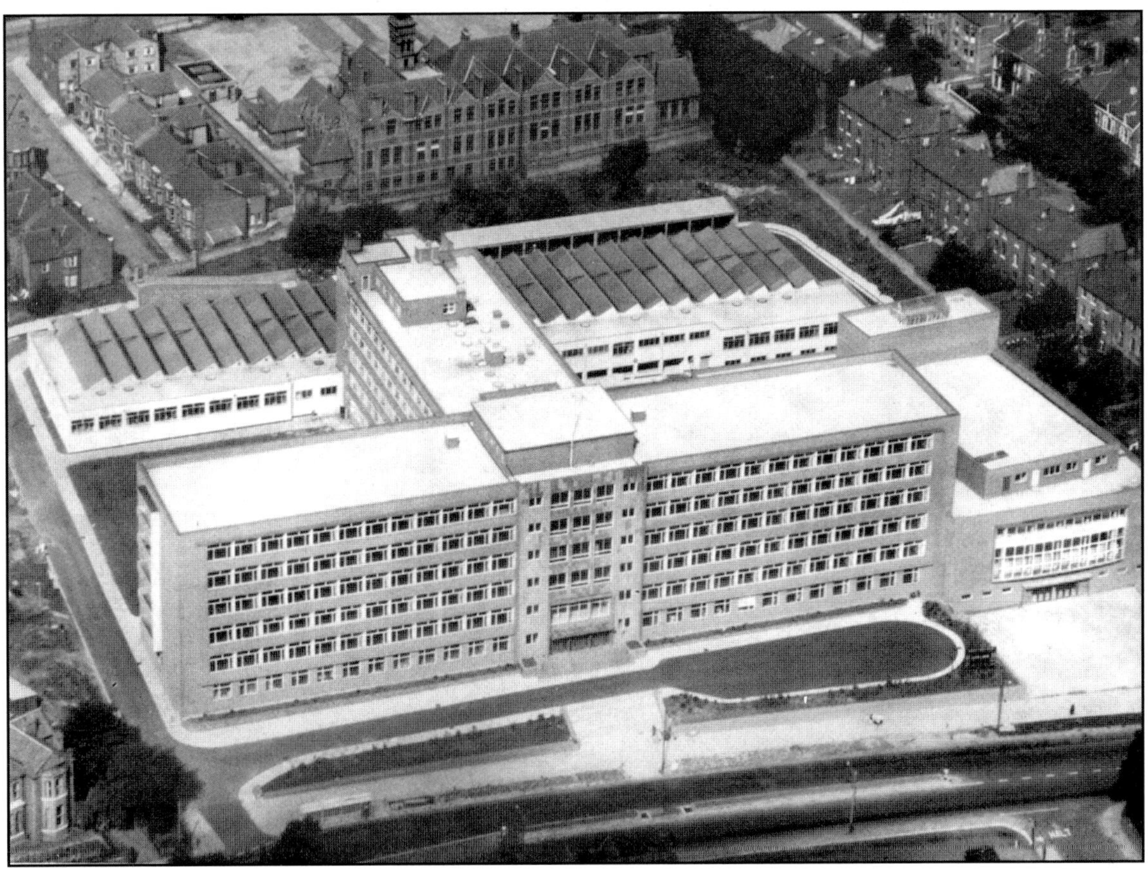

Left: *This air-view shows the 'H' shape of the* ***Birkenhead*** *Technical College in Borough Road with Woodchurch Road Primary School behind. The foundation stone was laid by Queen Elizabeth [the Queen Mother] on 3 May 1950, the same day she launched HMS* Ark Royal *[see 1950]. The building was demolished in 2005 with houses and flats built on the site*

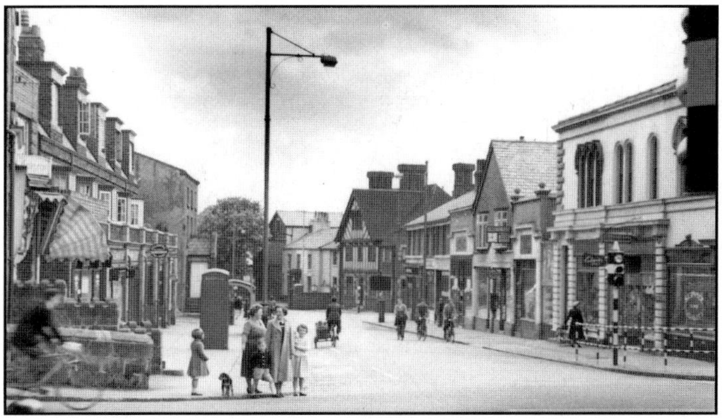

Above: *This postcard sent in 1955 was taken from the* ***Upton*** *Village traffic lights. Arrowe Park Road was to the right and built in 1938 to ease the congestion in Rake Lane. Victory Hall is seen in the far background [see 1921] - with the man on the bike cycling towards it carrying a child in a side-car*

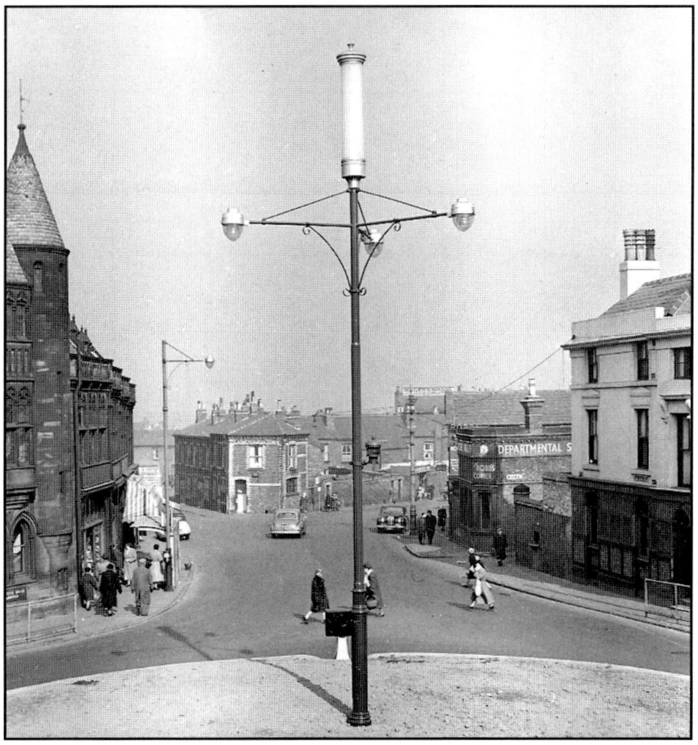

Above: *Looking down Atherton Street* ***Birkenhead*** *from Charing Cross with Exmouth Street forking off to the right. The corner of the* Grange Hotel *can be seen on the right and just beyond was a drinking fountain set into the wall. A roundabout has replaced the traffic lights [see 1953]*

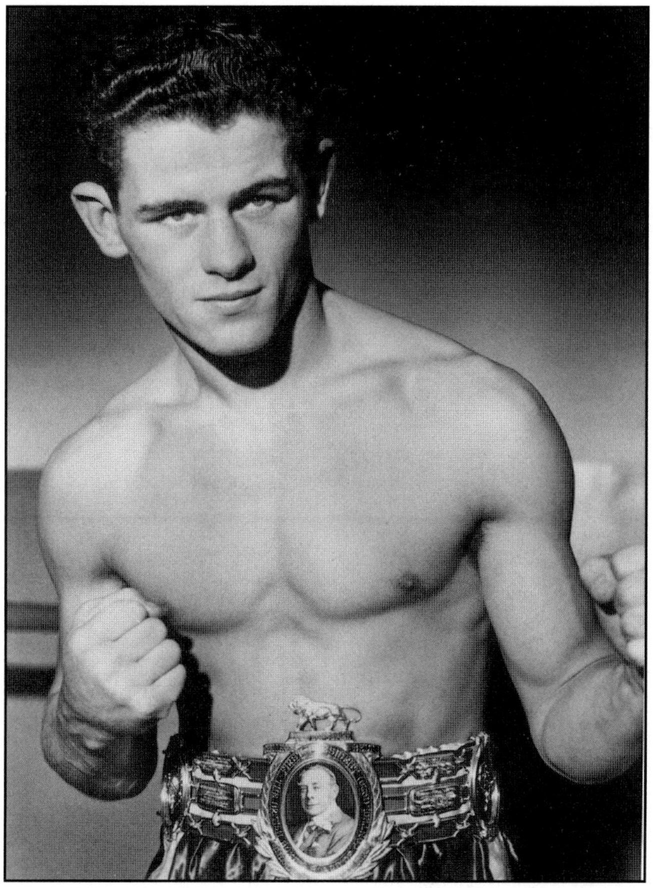

Above: *Pat McAteer, the* ***Birkenhead*** *British and British Empire Middleweight Champion was born in 1930. His first fight was in 1952 and last one 1958 - in all he had 57 professional fights - winning 49, losing 6 and drawing 2*

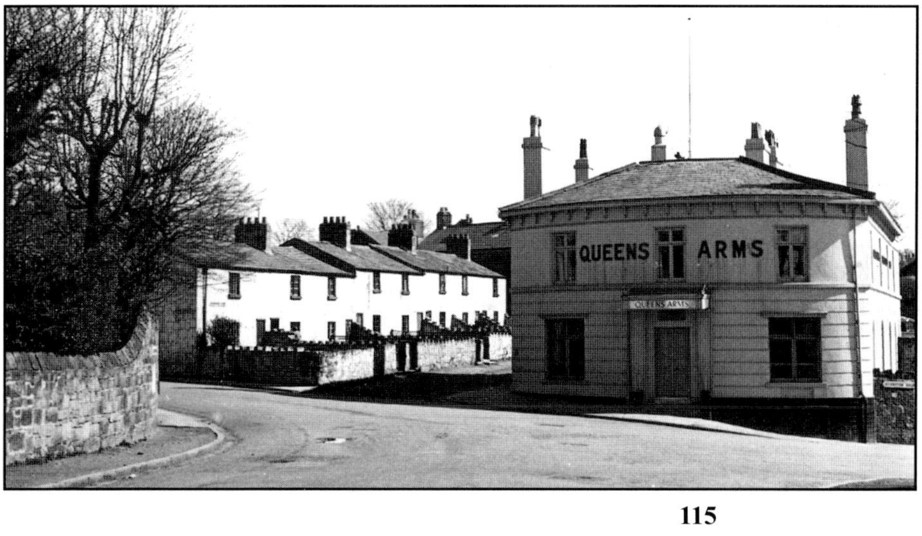

Left: *The* Queen's Arms *is seen from Ingestre Road* ***Oxton*** *with Storeton Road to the right, Rose Mount to the left and the cottages ahead, known as 'Dolly Tub Row', in Newburns Lane - named after the well known Oxton family who built them between 1840 and 1850. The* Queen's Arms Hotel *of Oxton Hill (as it was described in the 1860s) dates back to at least 1853 when the proprietor was Thomas Hughes*

1956

– Extension to the **Birkenhead** Police Headquarters in Chester Street was opened[SOUV] [see next page]

– The family firms of the Willmers and Harams, who owned the two newspapers in **Birkenhead**, the *Birkenhead News* and the *Birkenhead Advertiser*, merged and formed a new group called Willmer Brothers & Haram Ltd. Their publications consisting of the *Birkenhead News and Advertiser*, published on Saturday and Wednesday; the ***Ellesmere Port*** *News and Advertiser*, published on Thursday; the ***Hoylake*** *News and Advertiser,* published on Friday and the ***Bebington*** *News and Advertiser* published on Saturday[FB]

May 14 Night ferry service discontinued - replaced same day with a night bus service through the Mersey Tunnel

Nov The Birkenhead Brewery pub *The Carnarvon Castle*, re-opened in Bidston Road **Oxton** [see photo on next page]**,** replacing the original one which was destroyed by a land mine [see 1941][BAW]

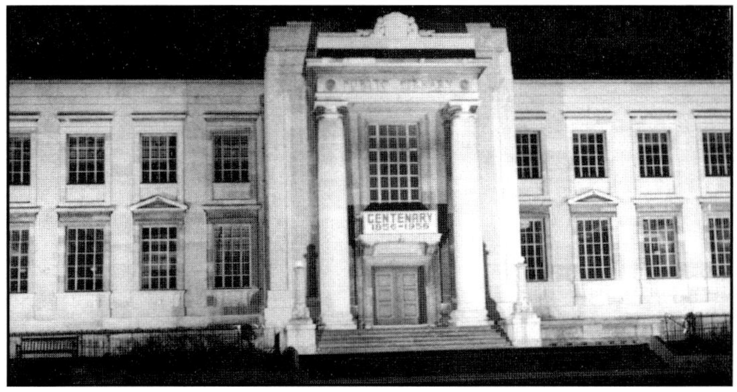

Above: *The banner above the main entrance to the Central Library, Borough Road* ***Birkenhead,*** *celebrated the centenary of the first library in Birkenhead in 1856*

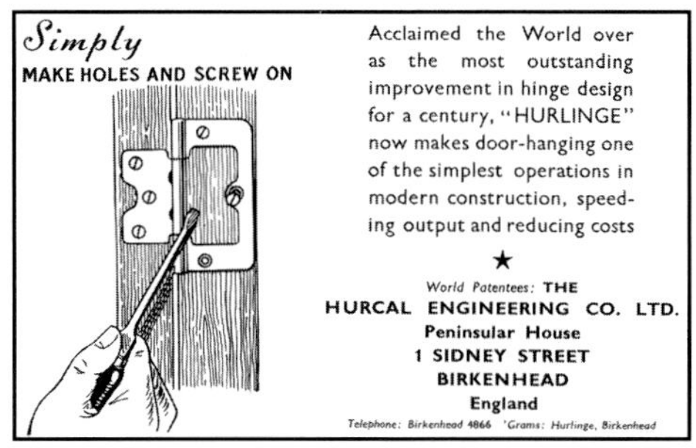

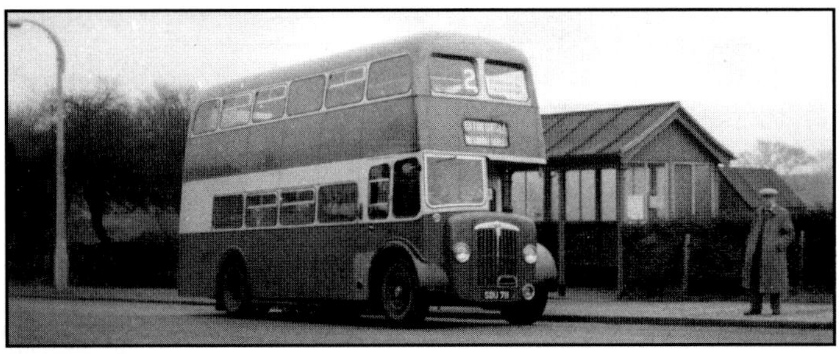

Above: *This Daimler 66 seater bus with a Willowbrook body is seen on the No. 2 route at* ***Claughton*** *Village. It was on trial to Birkenhead Transport but was not successful as none of these buses were ever purchased*

Right: *Byrne Avenue Baths, built in 1933, was described in 1957 as "one of the finest establishments of its kind in the North of England". There were two swimming baths 75 x 30 ft and 75x 35 ft (this one suited for water polo). In the winter months the larger pool was converted into an Assembly Hall seating 1,000 people or accommodating 400 for dancing*

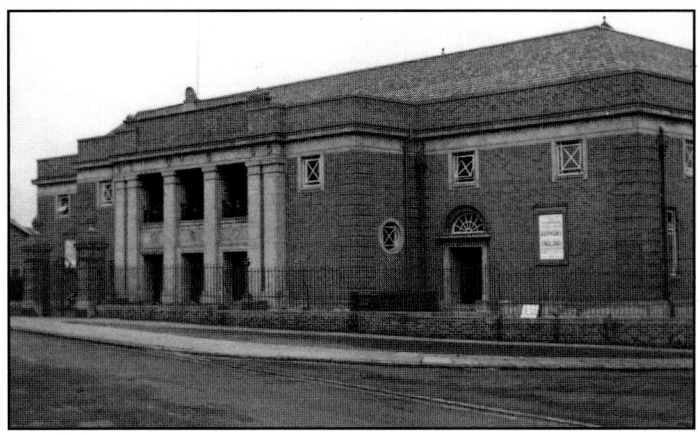

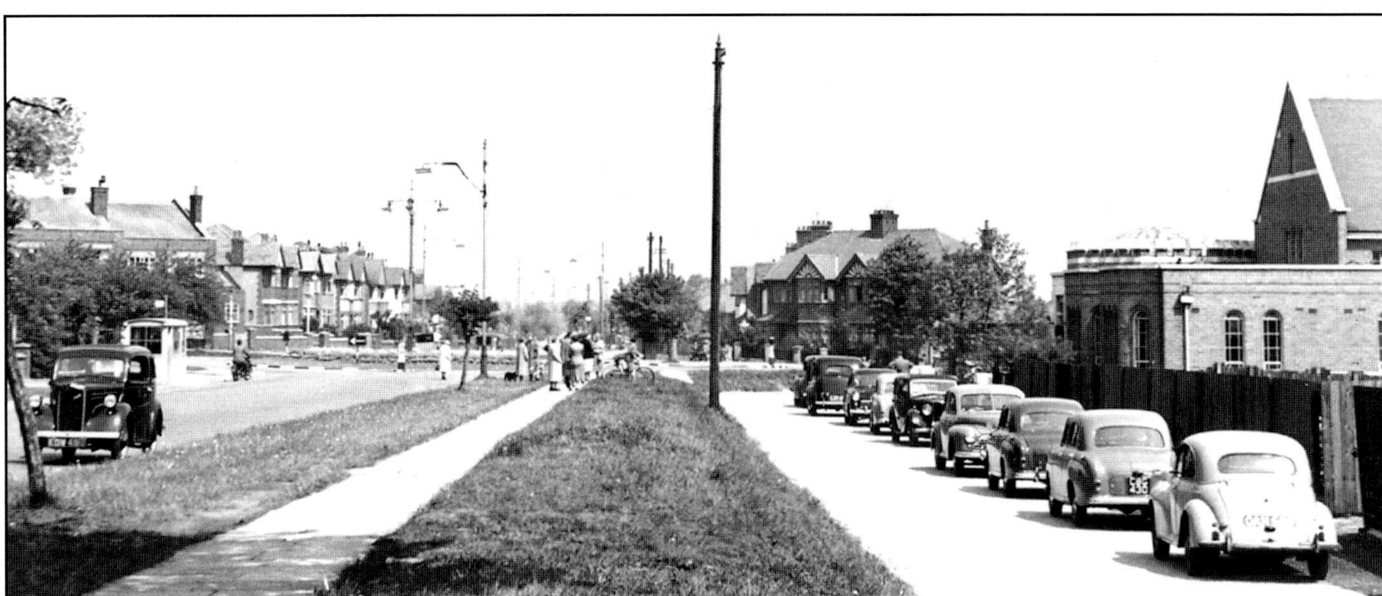

Above: *Looking along Kings Road* ***Bebington*** *towards the roundabout with Broadway to the left and and Kings Lane on the right. Grange Presbyterian Church of England can be seen on the right behind the cars. It was named after the Grange Road Presbyterian Church of England* ***Birkenhead*** *whose last service had been held 14 July 1948 in its centenary year - the Grange Church helped to finance this Church which opened here 16 December 1950*

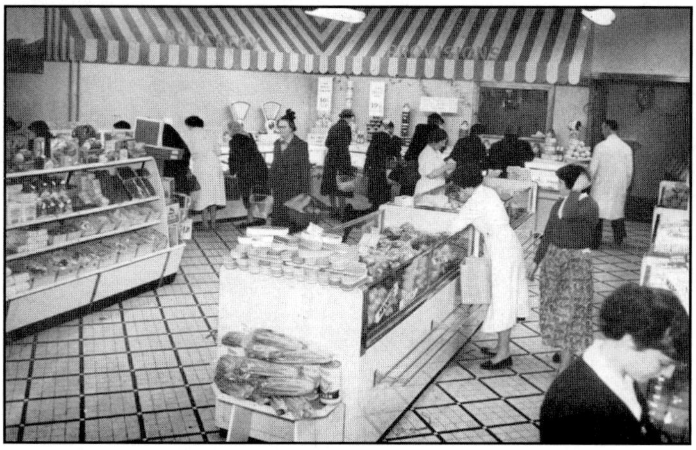

Above: *In 1956 this **Birkenhead** Co-op Society self-service store in Grange Road was considered the most up-to-date of its time*

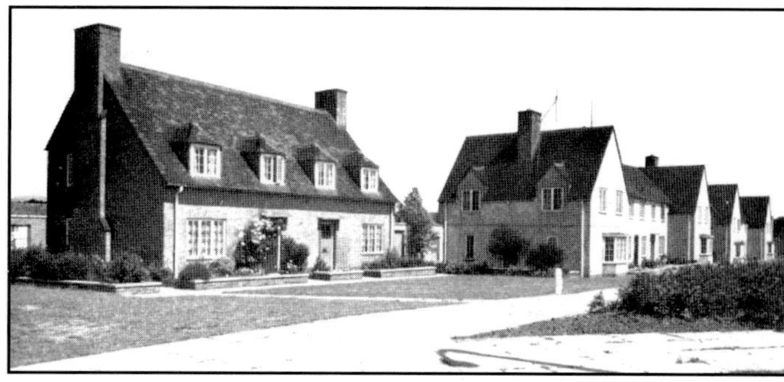

Above: *These well designed houses were built on **Birkenhead** Corporation's Woodchurch Estate. Started in 1948, the first house opened in 1949 and the Estate was awarded a Diploma by the Ministry of Health in 1950. By 1956 over 3,000 houses had been occupied*[SOUV]

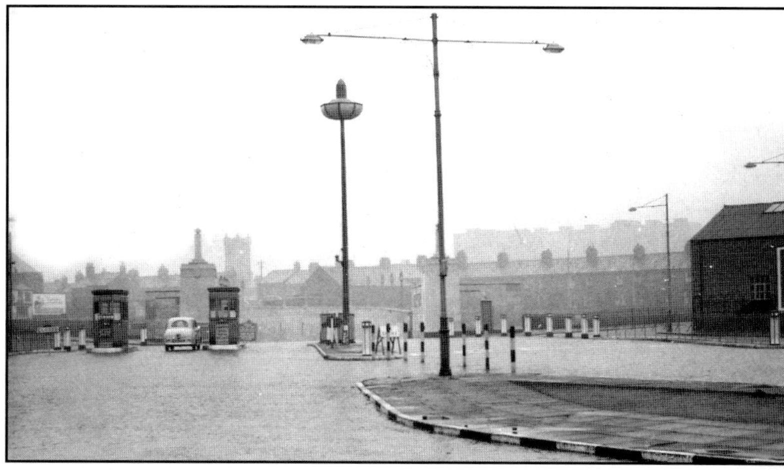

Above: *This was the **Birkenhead** Dock entrance to the Queensway Mersey Tunnel in Rendel Street - it has not been used by the public for a number of years*

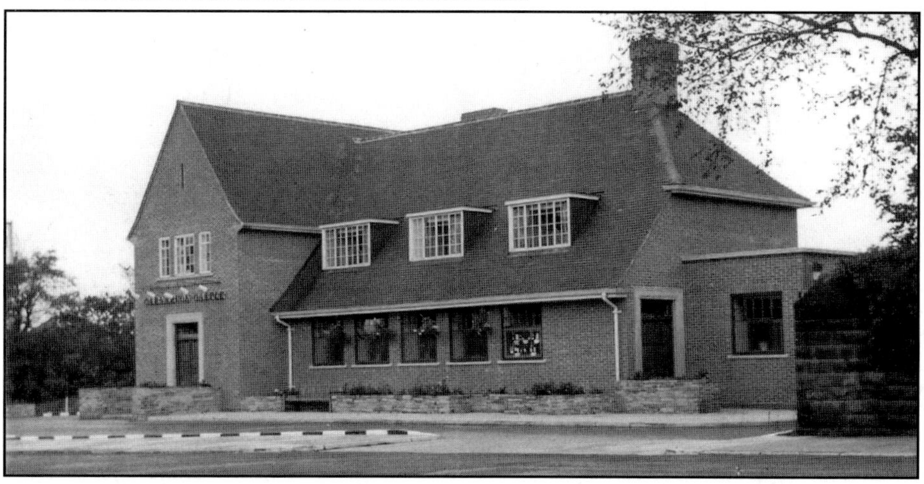

Above: *The* Carnarvon Castle *pub in Bidston Road **Oxton** is pictured here just after opening in November 1956. This Birkenhead Brewery pub, which replaced the original one which dated back to at least 1850, was destroyed by a land mine 12/13 March 1941 - it also damaged St Saviour's Church part of whose wall can just be seen on the right [see 1913 & 1941]*

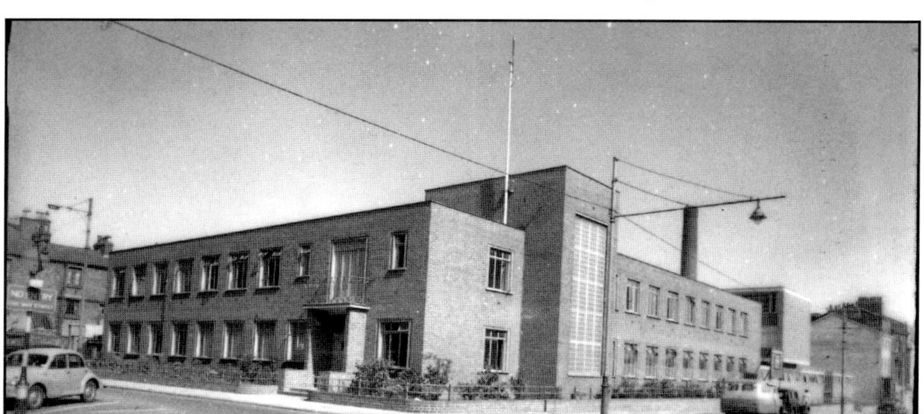

Left: *This was the new **Birkenhead** Police Headquarters which was officially opened in Chester Street in 1953 and an extension completed in 1956*

1957

– Foundation stone laid for St Mary's new Church Hall in **Upton**[SUAH]

– First stage of the new **Bebington** Town Hall opened [the new Civic Centre complex including the Library was opened in 1971]

Feb 22 The Scout Movement's Jubilee and the centenary of Baden-Powell's birth in 1857, was celebrated with a service for Scouts and Guides at St Saviour's Church **Oxton** and Birkenhead School Chapel[SOUV]

July 13 Exhibition camps were held to celebrate the jubilee year for Scouting at three venues:- **Arrowe** Park, Borough Road and Ashville Road **Birkenhead**[SOUV]

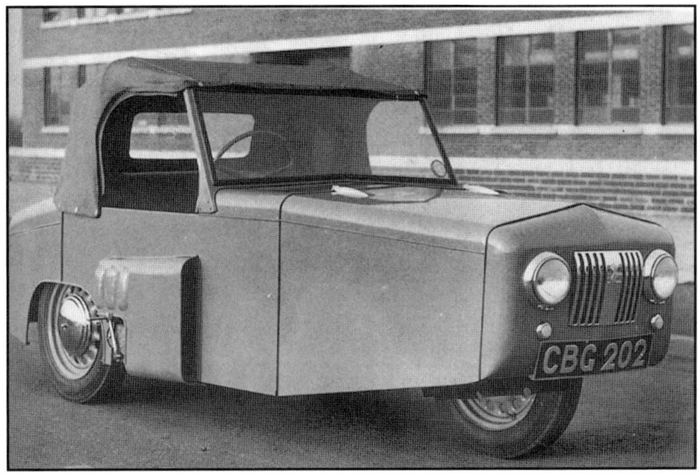

Above: *This Gordon three-wheeler vehicle was built at the Vernon's factory in Valley Road* ***Birkenhead*** *which opened in 1946 [see 1946]. The reason such vehicles were popular in the fifties was not the sporty detachable roof but they only needed a motor cycle licence and with petrol in short supply, they were very economical*

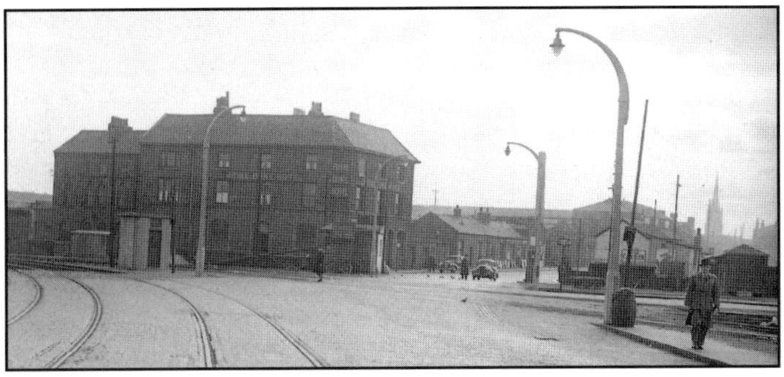

Above: *The* Royal Duke Hotel *seen ahead is at the junction of Duke Street* ***Birkenhead*** *on the right and Corporation Road on the left. The railway lines indicate the Dock Railway was still operating*

Below: *The Dell Primary School is seen on the left in The Dell* ***New Ferry***

Right: *Air view of Fender County Primary School New Hey Road* ***Woodchurch***

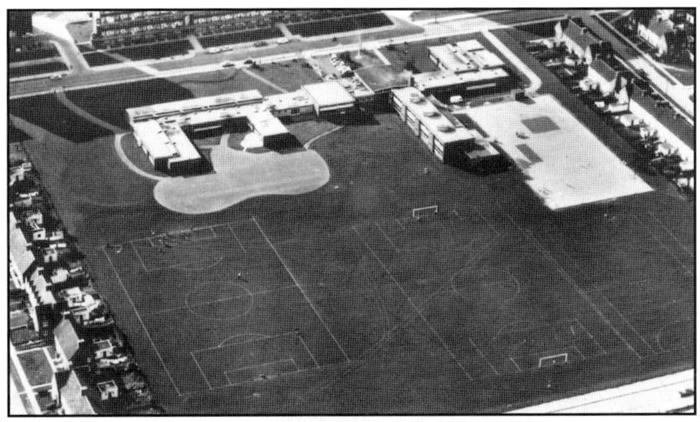

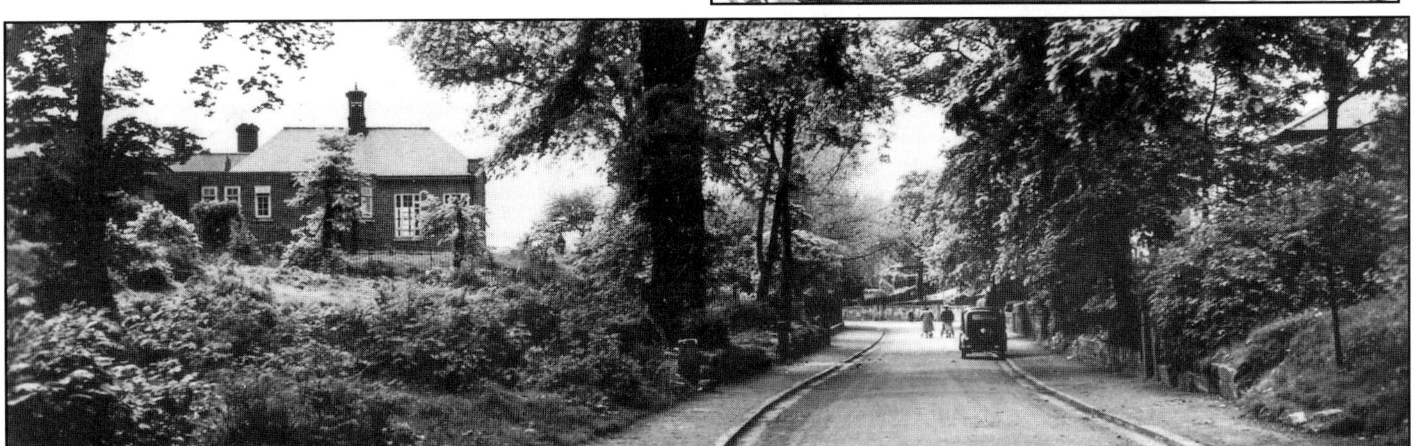

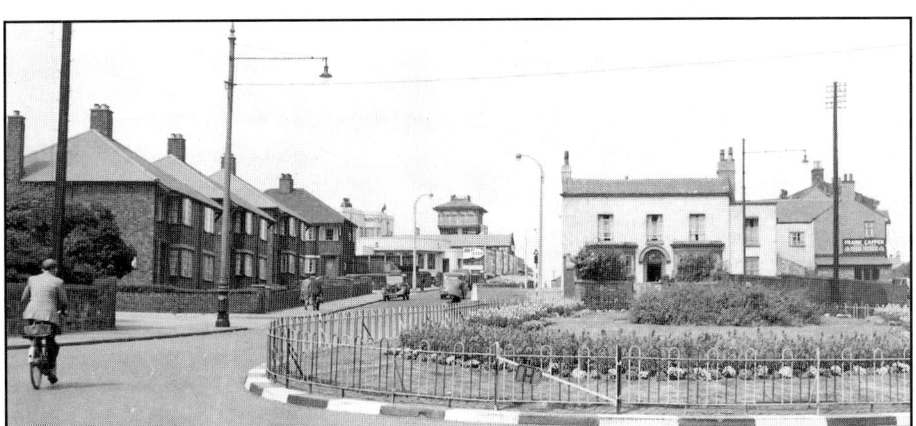

Left: *Looking up Greenway Road Higher* ***Tranmere*** *from the Mount Road roundabout, the first road on the left by the lamp post is Everest Road - the next road on the left by the car is Mallory Road and Irvine Road is off Borough Road by Tranmere Rovers. These were so named following the death on Everest of Birkenhead men George Mallory and Andrew (Sandy) Irvine in 1924. The Tranmere Water Tower seen above the other buildings has since been demolished*

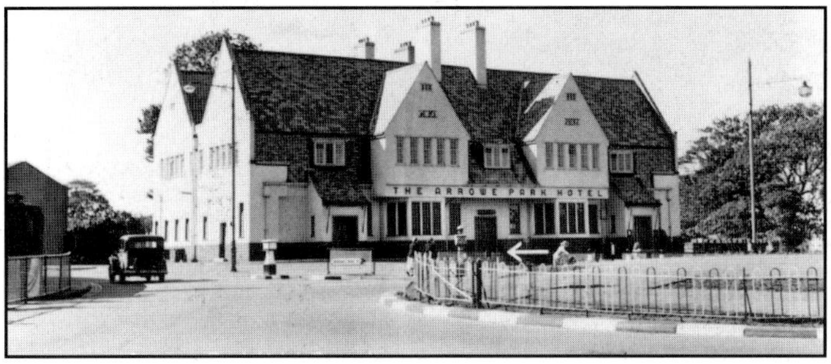

Above: *The Arrowe Park Hotel was opened at* ***Woodchurch*** *in 1937, replacing the* Horse and Jockey Inn *[see 1907]. The road to the left was Arrowe Park Road, the main road to Upton*

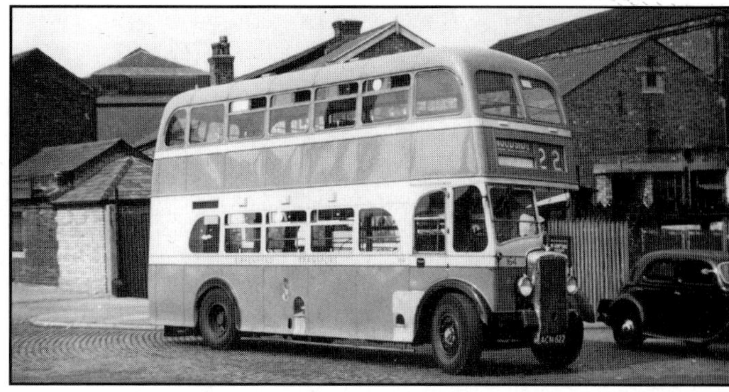

Above: *This Daimler CVG6 Reg No. ACM 622 came into service in 1949 and was withdrawn between 1963/65. Pictured at Woodside it was on the No. 22 route to* **Moreton** *Shore*

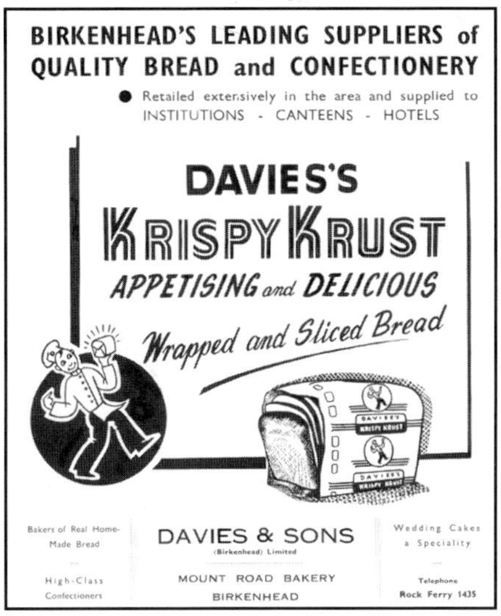

Right: ***Birkenhead*** *North Station is seen from the Stanley Road Bridge looking towards Birkenhead Park and Liverpool. It was originally named Birkenhead Docks Station, opening in 1878 and connecting with West Kirby*

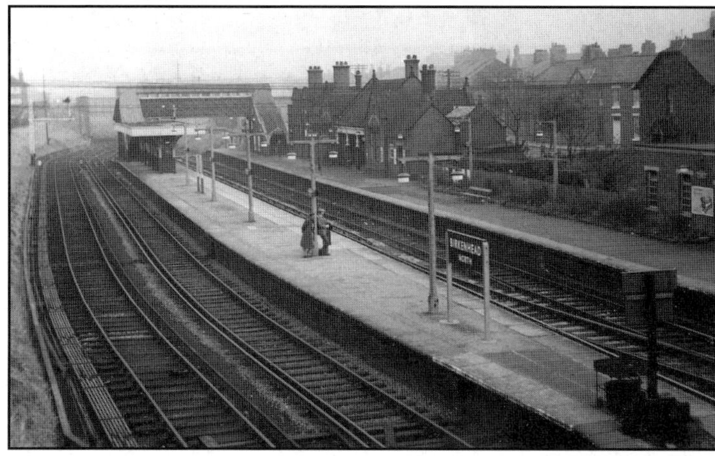

Above: *This advert describes Davies's Krispy Krust bread as being "appetising and delicious" - produced at their Mount Road Bakery Higher* ***Tranmere****, they distributed their quality bread and confectionery throughout the Borough to retail shops, institutions, canteens and hotels*

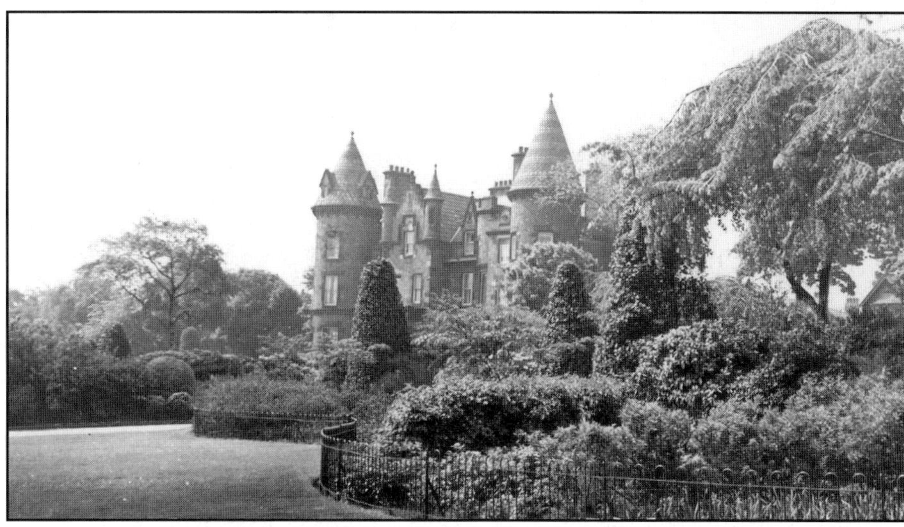

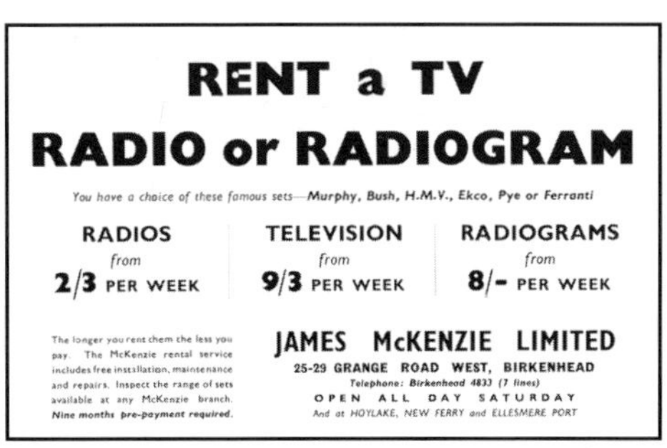

Above: The Towers *are pictured in Victoria Park* **Tranmere**. *This French style chateau was built in the 1860s by a Victor Poutz and then called* Arudy. ***Birkenhead*** *Corporation purchased the chateau and land, opening it to the public in 1901, naming it in memory of Queen Victoria who died the same year. During the First and Second World Wars it housed Belgian refugees and was later converted into flats. This delightful building was demolished c.1965 and replaced with a building that lacks character [also see below]*

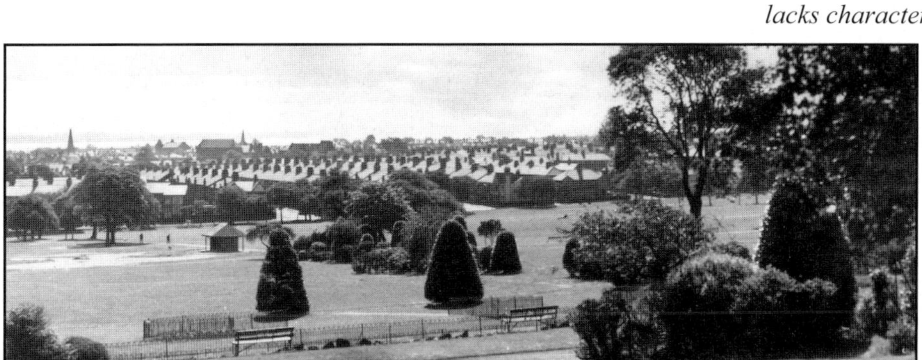

Left: *A view also in Victoria Park but looking across the well maintained open area towards* ***Liverpool***

1958

– Wirral Mineral Water Works taken over by **Birkenhead** Brewery[BB]

– Birkenhead Brewery purchased land inTeehey Lane to built a new pub called *The Acorn.* It was to replace the *Royal Oak* in Village Road [see below]

– **Birkenhead** Brewery's *The Avenue*, Norman Street opened [see below] - it was built on the site of the *Avenue Cinema* which was demolished following bombing [see 1941]. The licence came from the *Canada Hotel* and the *Boar's Head,* both blitzed during the War[WTDW]

– The first multi-storey flats in **Birkenhead**, Eldon Gardens and Oak Gardens, were opened [see photo next page][SOUV]

Nov 9 St Michael's and All Saints Church, Carlton Road **Birkenhead** held its last service. St Michael's Institute, built on adjoining land in 1924, was retained by Christ Church for a number of years as a youth centre [it was finally sold in 1969][SOUV]

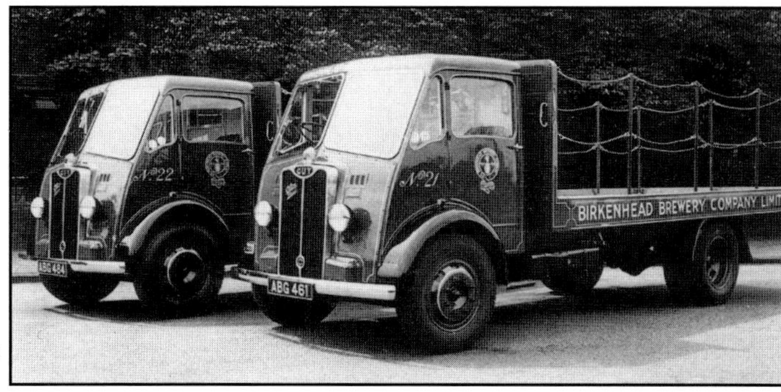

Above: *These two brand new Guy, Diesel, five ton wagons had the* ***Birkenhead*** *Brewery sign on the wagon and logo on the door.*

Below: *This wagon, similar to the two above was ordered by Mackie & Gladstone, who had been bought out by* ***Birkenhead*** *Brewery in 1948*

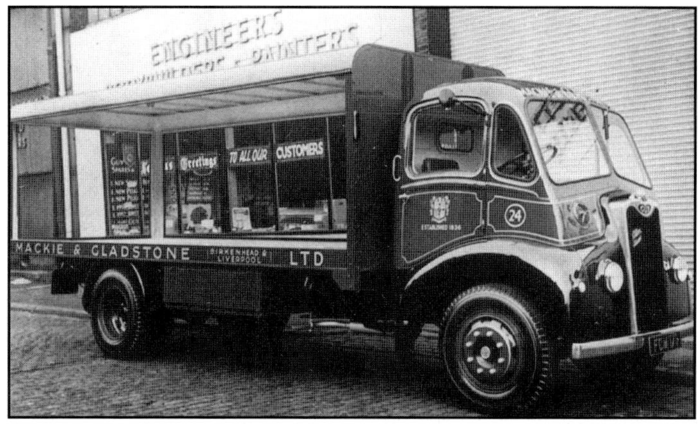

Below: *This Birkenhead Brewery sign which stood on a site at the corner of Village Road and Teehey Lane* ***Bebington*** *advised of:-* 'The Acorn' - These premises are being constructed by the Birkenhead Brewery Co Ltd and will replace the 'Royal Oak' in Village Road, on completion. *When* The Acorn *was completed and ready for opening, the* Royal Oak *closed at normal time on its last night and the licence transferred to* The Acorn *which opened the following morning at the normal opening time - hence the licence was not lost*

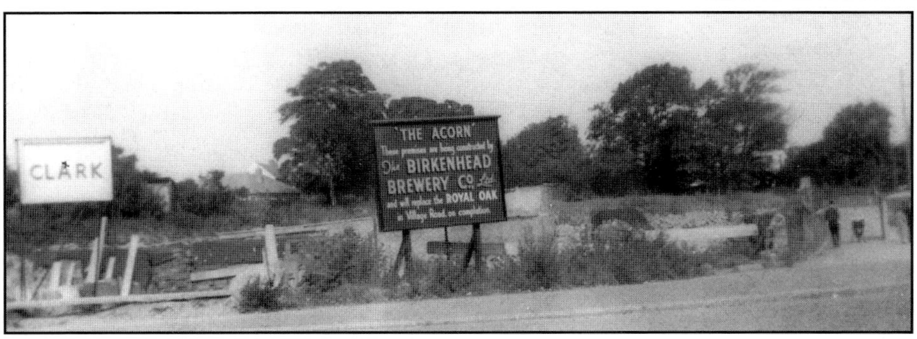

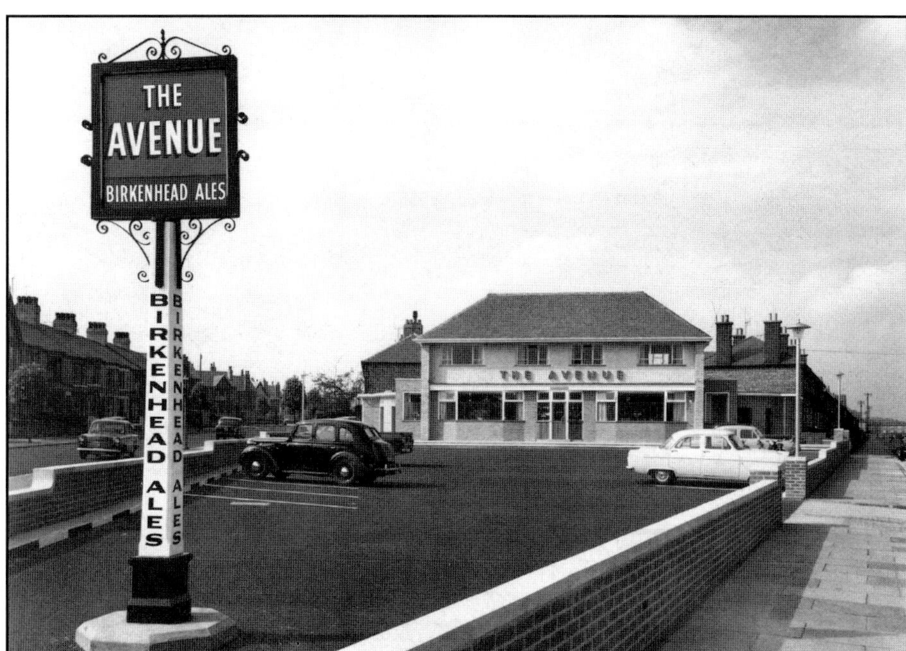

Right: The Avenue, *a Birkenhead Brewery pub seen recently opened at the junction of Norman Street and Bidston Avenue* ***Birkenhead****, took the licence from the* Canada Hotel *and the* Boar's Head *- both blitzed during the war. This pub was so named as* The Avenue *Cinema originally stood on this site - but following damage caused during an air raid on 12/13 March 1941, the foundations were deemed unsafe so the building was demolished [see 1941]*

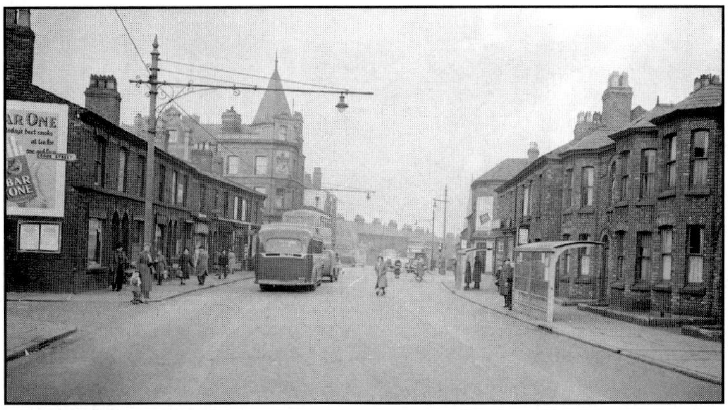

Above: *The buses on the left were travelling along Borough Road towards* ***Birkenhead*** *Fire Station (the building with the spire - see close-up this page) which was on the corner of Whetstone Lane. The Fire Station and all the buildings on the right have since been demolished*

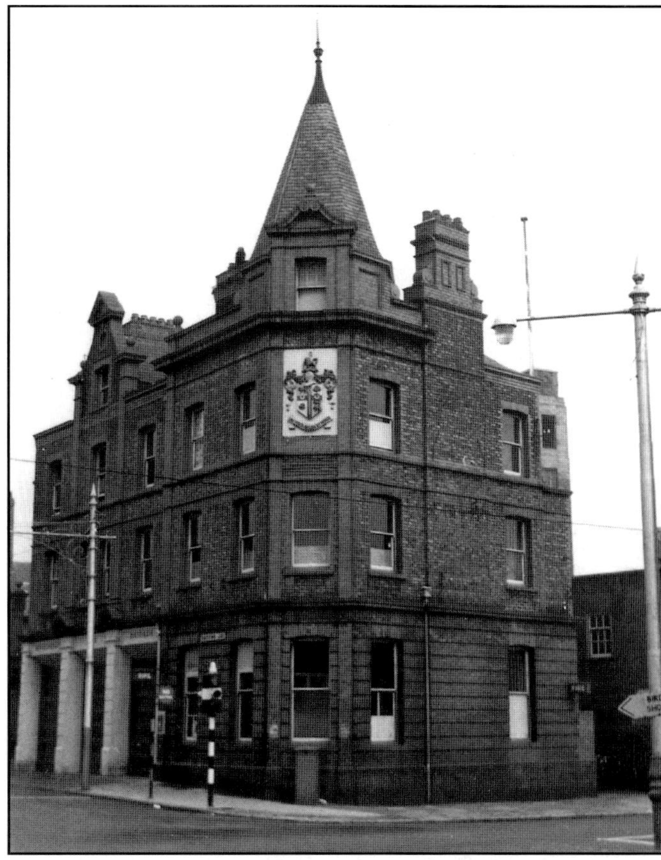

Above: *The* ***Birkenhead*** *Fire Station opened here at the junction of Borough Road and Whetstone Lane in 1895 - replacing the one at* ***Tranmere*** *which then closed down. Firemen became resident at this station in 1938. All fire brigades were nationalised in 1941 and de-nationalised in 1948 - in the same year the Ambulance Service was combined with the Fire Brigade*[FPH]

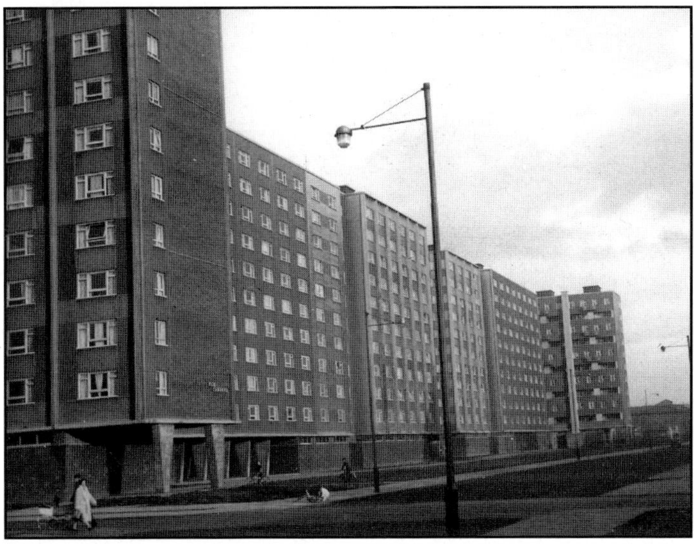

Above: *Eldon Gardens were opened here in 1958 - they were one of the Borough's first 11 storey block of flats accommodating 240 families. They were built to aleviate the acute housing problem post Second World War*

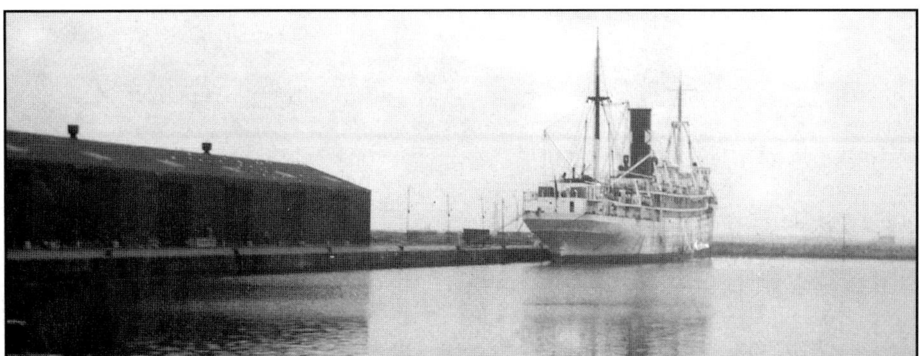

Above: *This ship is seen berthed in Bidston Dock* ***Birkenhead*** *which was the final expansion of the Birkenhead Dock Estate - opening in 1933 [see below]*

Right: *This was the Iron Ore Berth at Bidston Dock* ***Birkenhead*** *with the* Zinnia, *registered in North Shields, alongside. Two electrically operated travelling transporters were installed which could lift 6.5 tons in one go into the hoppers which was then transferred into wagons. There was a direct connection from here by rail to the John Summers & Sons steel works at Hawarden Bridge. Two ships were able to berth alongside at the same time. [The dock was no longer required and has recently been filled in]*[SOUV]

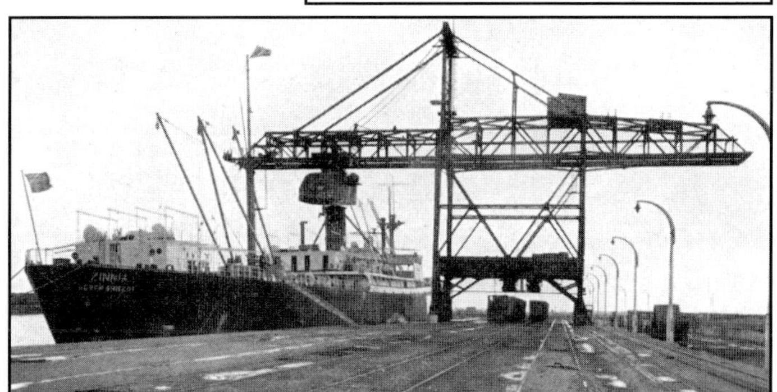

1959

– Holy Cross Catholic Church opened in Hoylake Road **Bidston** [see photo]

Spring It was announced that **Birkenhead** Corporation ferries *Hinderton* (1925) and *Thurstaston* (1930) were to be replaced [see 1960]

June 23 The Queen Mother launched the Union-Castle passenger ship *Windsor Castle* at Cammell laird [see photo below]

Oct 2 Owen Owen Supermarket was opened by the Mayor of Birkenhead in Grange Road **Birkenhead** [see advert next page][SOUV]

Oct 10 St Mary's new Church Hall opened in **Upton**[SUAH]

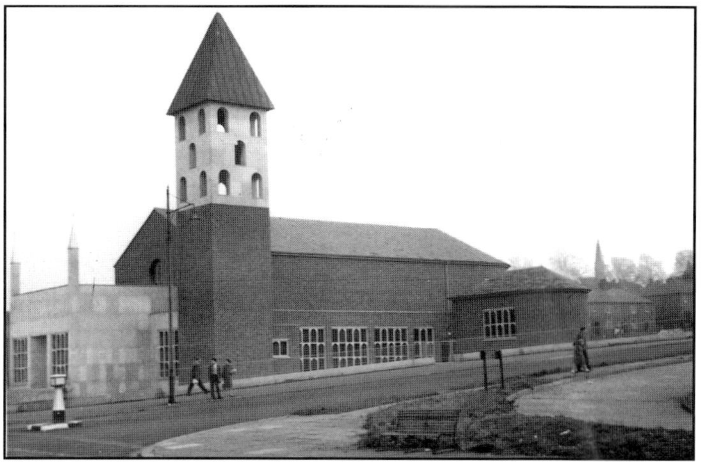

Above: *Holy Cross Catholic Church opened in Hoylake Road* ***Bidston*** *in 1959 at the junction with Worcester Road*

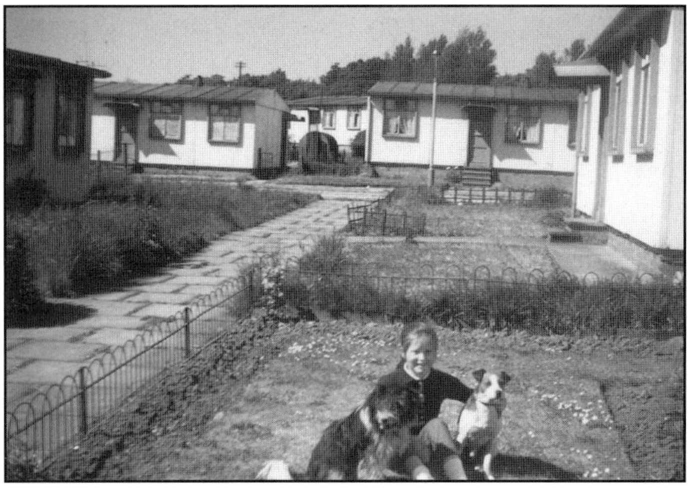

Above: *The pre-fabricated houses (known as pre-fabs) behind the girl were in Molyneux Road on the* ***Upton/Greasby*** *border between Greasby Road and Arrowe Park Road [Frankby Close and Molyneux Close occupy the site today]. These were built after the war to overcome the national housing shortage with a ten year life-span. However many survived over 30 years* [YWPH]

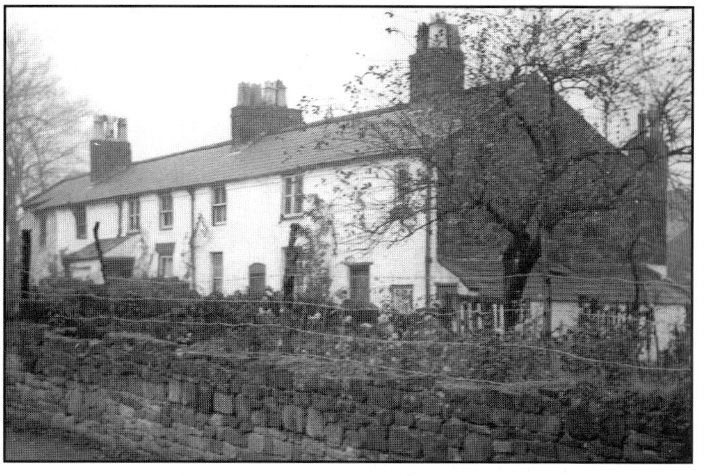

Above: *Church Terrace cottages in Pool Lane* **Woodchurch** *were owned by the Woodchurch Parish Church. Demolished in 1962, Meadowside School later built on the site*

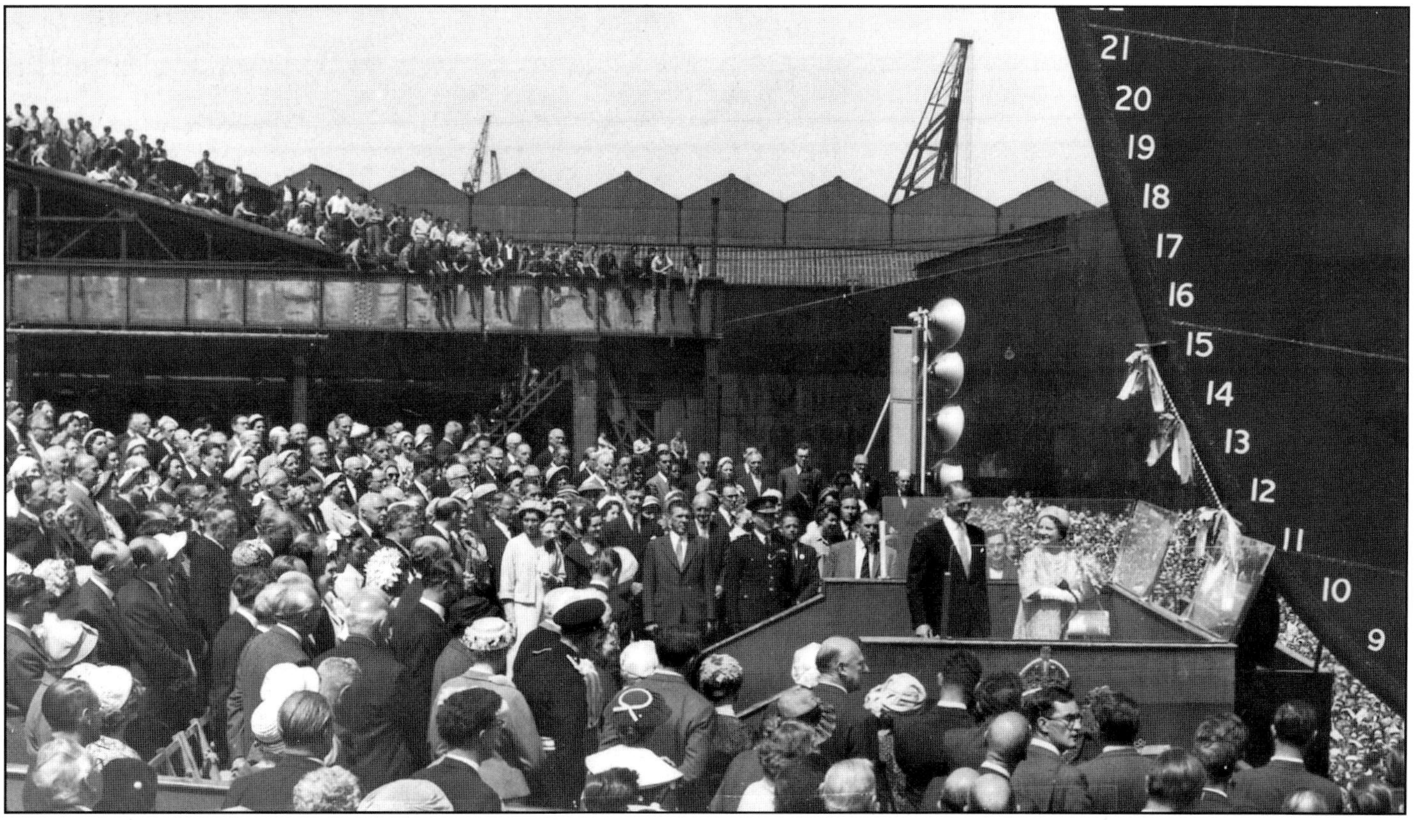

Below: *The Queen Mother is seen launching the* Windsor Castle *23 June 1959. Built by Cammell Laird - at 36,000 tonnes, she was the last big passenger ship to be built on Merseyside. She was the biggest and most famous of the Union-Castle mailships that sailed between Southampton and the Cape*

1959 continued

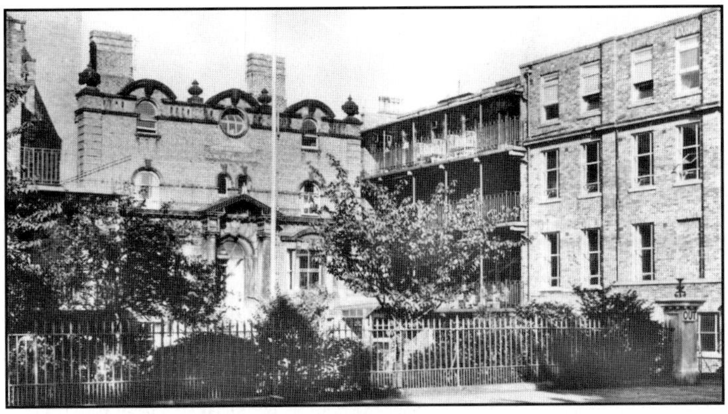

Above: *This was the view of the* ***Birkenhead*** *General Hospital [formerly the Borough Hospital] from Park Road North. The hospital was closed down when the hospital service on Wirral was centralised at Arrowe Park in 1982*

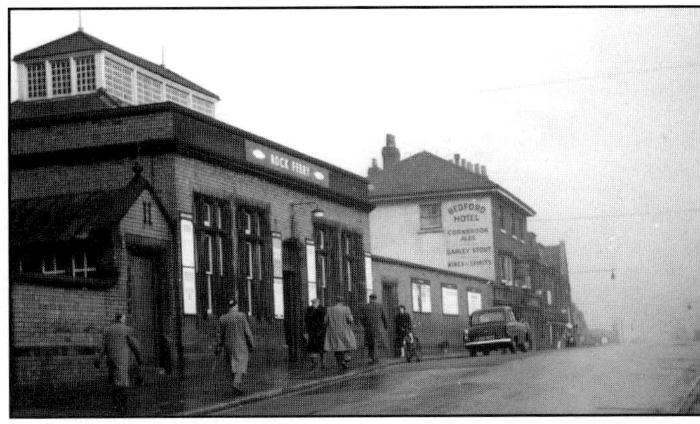

Above: ***Rock Ferry*** *Station opened here in 1862 on the* ***Birkenhead*** *to* ***Chester*** *line. It also served passengers to* ***Liverpool*** *on the Mersey Railway. The original station was on the south side of Bedford Road and was replaced by the present station in 1891*[RSoW]

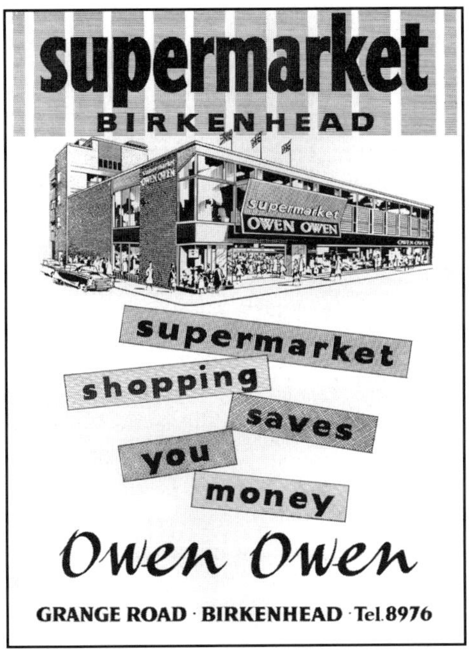

Above: *Owen Owen opened their store in Grange Road* ***Birkenhead*** *2 October 1959 by the Mayor of Birkenhead*

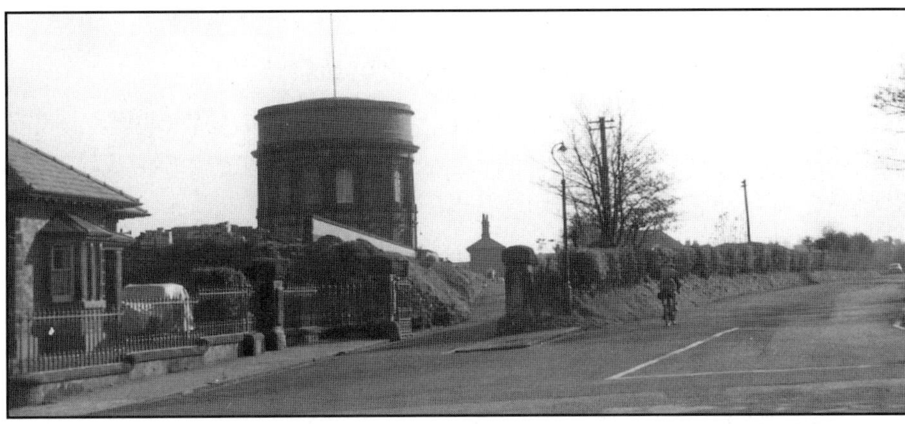

Above: *Looking along Bidston Road* ***Bidston,*** *Flaybrick Waterworks, pictured on the left, was opened in 1865*[YWPH]

Right: *Looking down Church Road Lower* ***Bebington*** *- the shops on the right were those on the left in the photo below. The second shop from the left was a branch of Moody's Wine Stores [see 1904]*

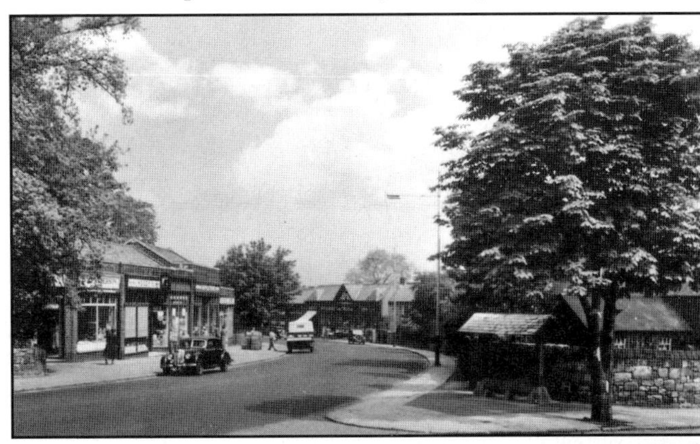

Below: *Looking up Church Road Lower* ***Bebington*** *with Bromborough Road off to the left. Behind the wall on the right was Bebington Hall. The site is now occupied by a row of shops and a supermarket with the Town Hall and Civic Centre behind*

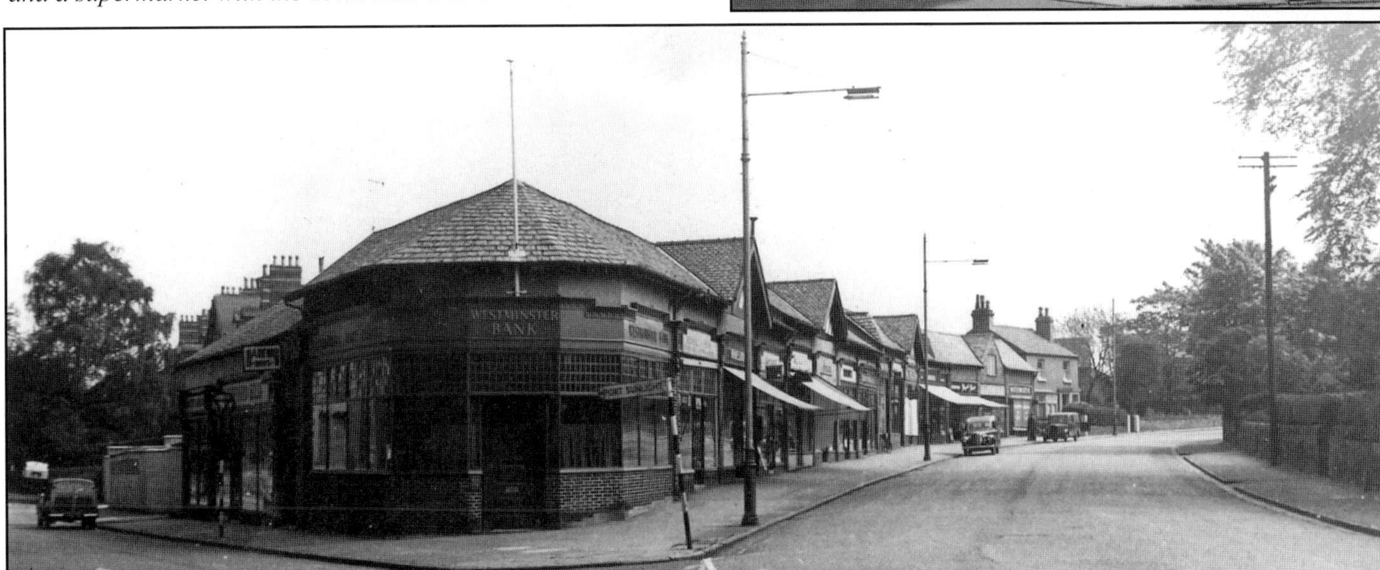

1960

– Extensive structural alterations took place at Mayer Library **Bebington** to provide new reference facilities[PROG]

Jan 30 **Birkenhead** Diesel ferry boat *Mountwood* commissioned - 464 tons and could accommodate 1,200 passengers. Her claim to fame was that she was the boat used in the film *Ferry Cross The Mersey* and also for the song of the same name by Gerry and the Pacemakers. Her sister ship *Woodchurch was* also commissioned in 1960 [see photo]

April 8. The new extension and alterations to the Oxton Cricket Club Pavilion were officially opened - this included the installation of electricity with the quaint gas lighting disappearing![SOUV]

Apr 12 Shrewsbury Lawn Tennis Club, Shrewsbury Road Oxton (founded in 1892) - became Birkenhead Lawn Tennis Club[BLTC]

May 15 Birkenhead Corporation ferry boat *Woodchurch* was built at Dartmouth [see below] . She has since been renamed *Snowdrop*

June The crude oil terminal opened at Tranmere - a joint venture between the Mersey Docks and Harbour Board and Shell Refining Company[SO]

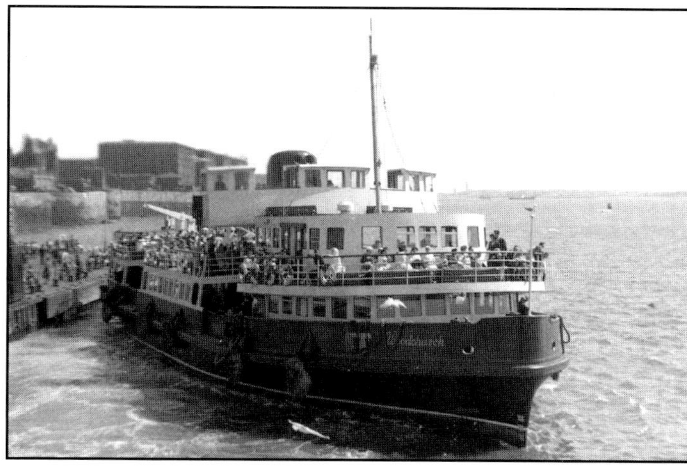

Above *The* ***Birkenhead*** *Diesel ferry boat* Woodchurch, *seen leaving Woodside Landing Stage, was commissioned in 1960, being the sister ship to the* Mountwood. *They were 464 tons and could accommodate 1,200 passengers, being the first motor vessels in the Birkenhead fleet*

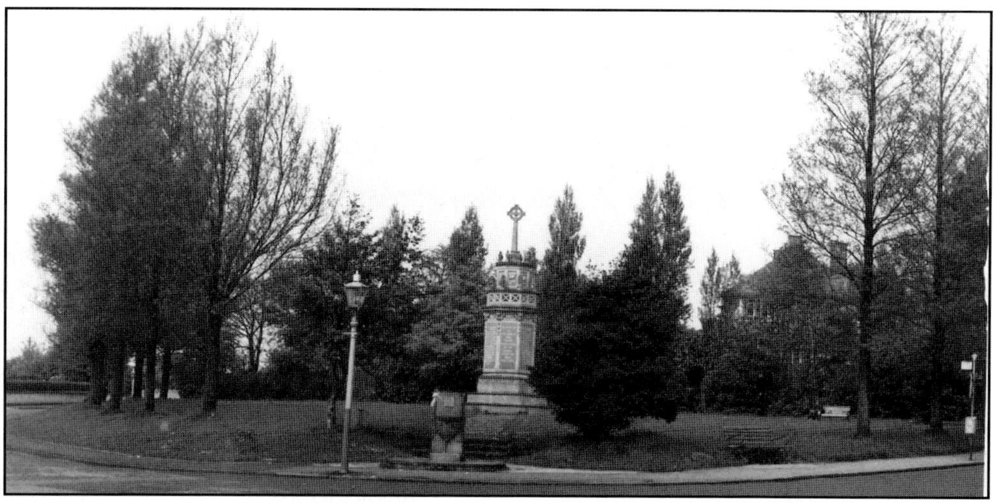

Left:- Prenton War Memorial seen from Prenton Lane, with Osmaston Road to the left, was dedicated in 1919. However, it had to be reconstructed following war damage caused by bombing during the 'May Blitz' on 2/3 May 1941. It was later reconstructed and rededicated to include those men of Prenton who lost their lives in action during the Second World War

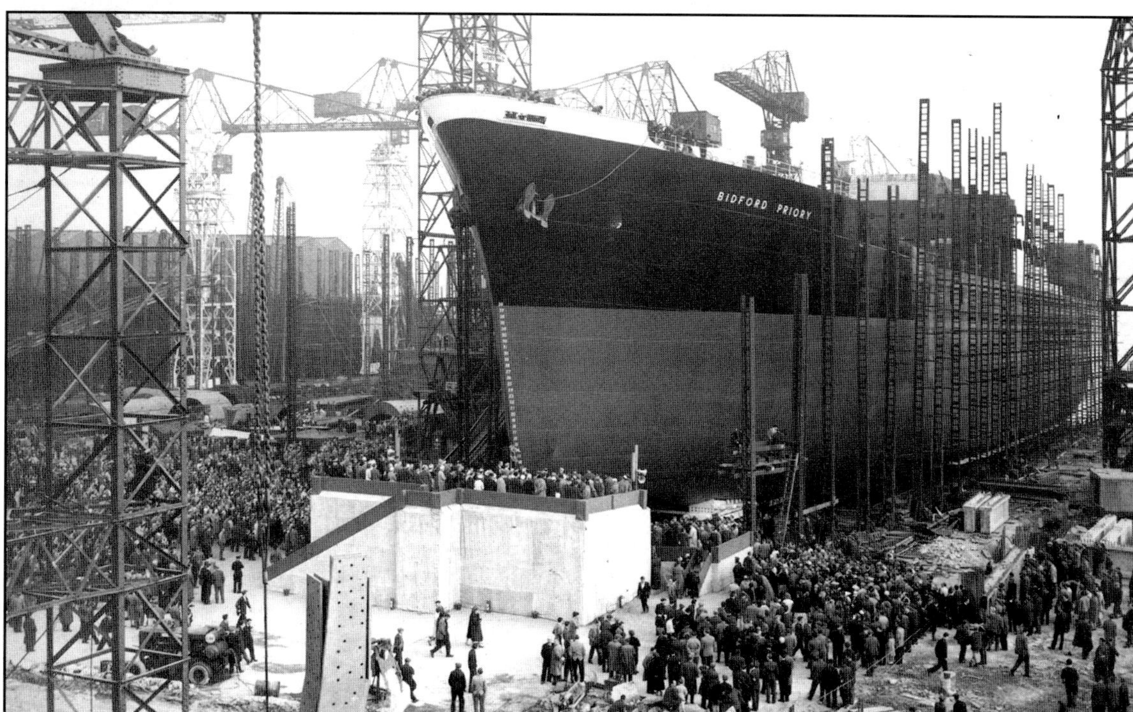

Right: *Workers at Cammell Laird shipyard and invited guests are watching the launch of the ss* Bidford Priory *by Mrs GH Herridge from the launch platform, on 27 April 1960. Chartered to BP, she and her sister ship Brandon Priory (built at Hawthorn Leslie), were 36,000 tons. They were both scrapped in 1975 following the Yom Kippur War, which saw interest in such vessels drastically reduced*

1960 continued

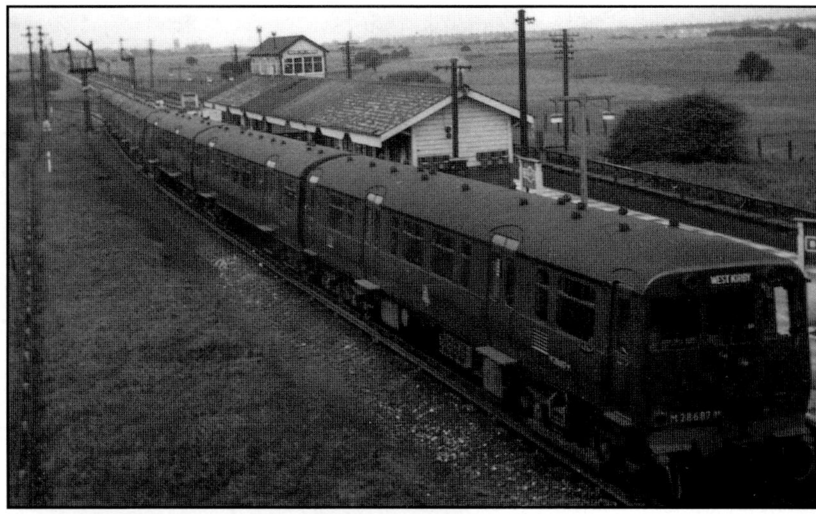

Right: ***Bidston*** *Station was opened in 1866 when the Hoylake Railway connected Hoylake with Birkenhead, extending to West Kirby in 1878. In 1896 Bidston was the junction station which linked Wrexham, Mold and Connahs' Quay Railway and was known as the North Wales and Liverpool Railway*[RSW]

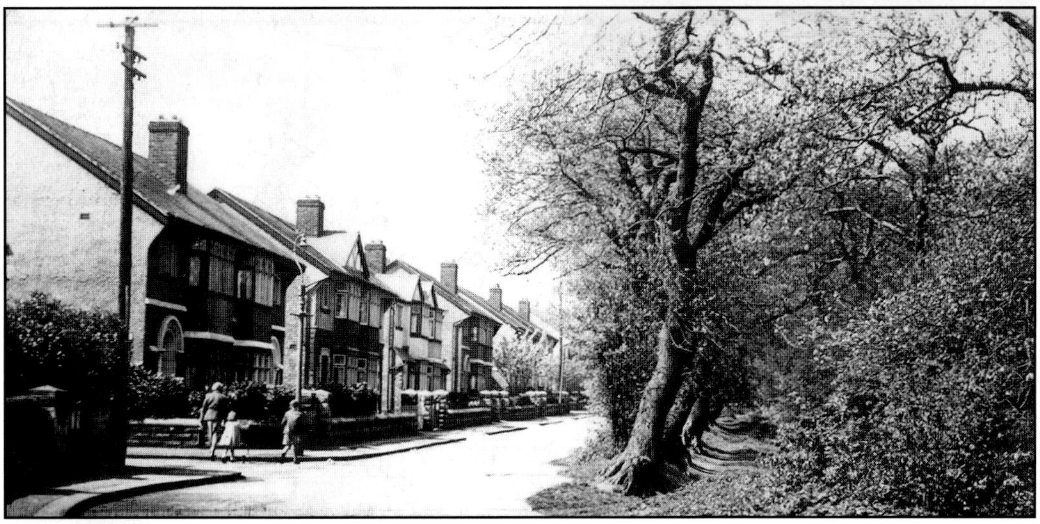

Left: *Looking up Kirket Lane Lower* ***Bebington*** *shows the old and the new - the old Kirket Lane on the right was a path that led from Higher Bebington through to Lower Bebington and when the houses were built, the new road was built parallel to the old. However, some of the trees which formed the original lane survive today and give an idea of the route it took*

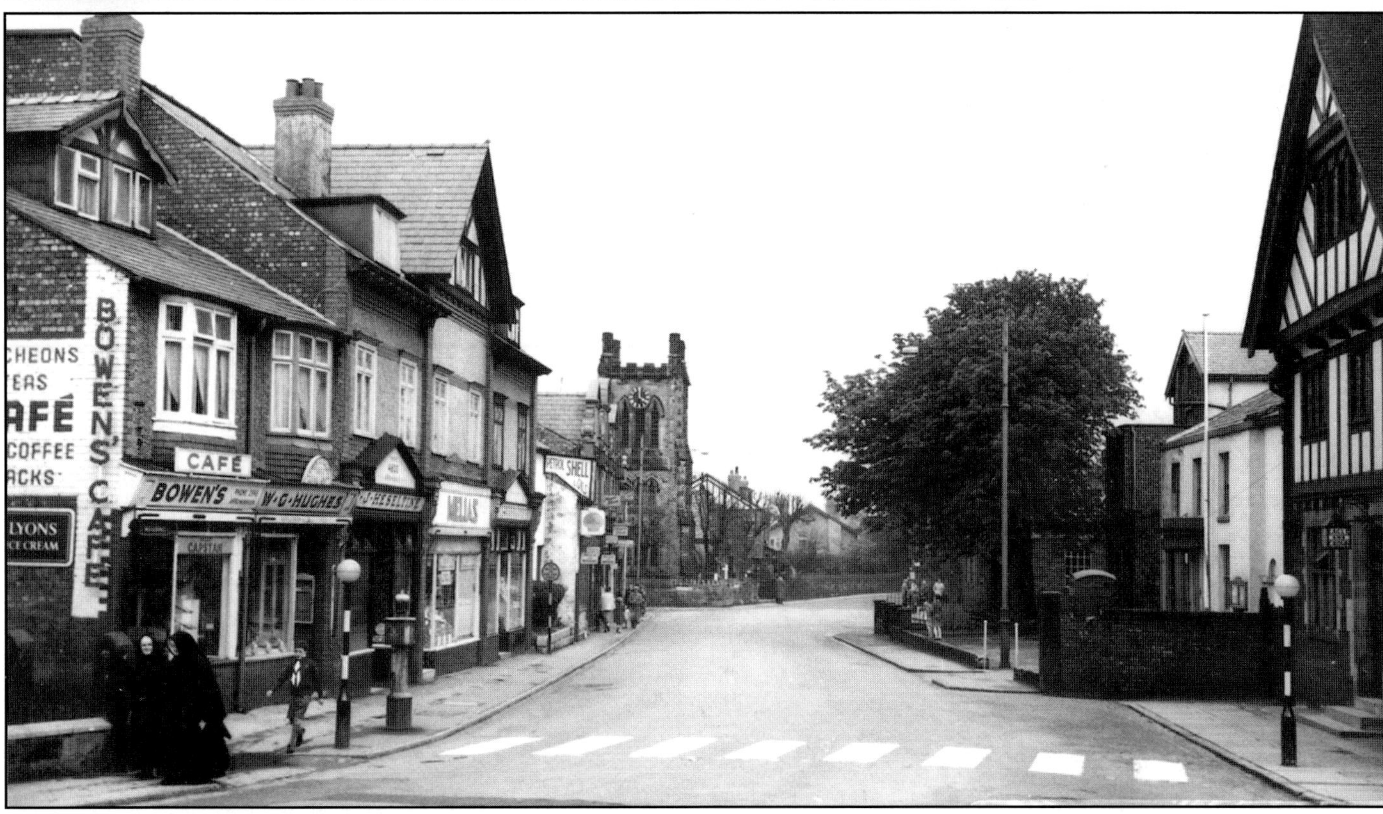

Above: *This postcard view of* ***Upton*** *Village in 1960 was to change over the next few years: the two nuns on the left taught at Upton Convent when most of the teaching staff were nuns - there aren't any today; the Police box by the side of the crossing had a flashing blue light on top to attract the policeman's attention in an emergency and the phone in the box would have direct contact with Police Headquarters; The street sign further down on the left said "No Parking On This Side Today"; Shone's Garage had a Shell sign above the shop and they sold petrol from pumps set back from the pavement and Upton Victory Hall seen on the right was demolished in the 1960s with shops built on the site*

INDEX of PHOTOGRAPHS/GRAPHICS

By the Same Author:

Yesterday's Wirral No 1 – Neston, Parkgate & Heswall
Yesterday's Wirral No 2 – Birkenhead, Prenton & Oxton
Yesterday's Wirral No 3 – West Kirby & Hoylake
Yesterday's Wirral No 4 – Wallasey & New Brighton
Yesterday's Wirral No 5 – Wallasey, New Brighton & Moreton
Yesterday's Wirral No 6 – Neston, Parkgate & Heswall including Thurstaston & Irby
Yesterday's Wirral No 7 – Birkenhead, Oxton & Prenton including Bidston & Upton
Yesterday's Wirral No 8 – Bebington & Mid Wirral Villages
Yesterday's Wirral No 9 – Ellesmere Port to Bromborough
Yesterday's Wirral Pictorial History 1890 to 1953 by Ian & Marilyn Boumphrey
Yesterday's Wirral Port Sunlight 1888 to 1953 by Ian Boumphrey and Gavin Hunter
Yesterday's Liverpool by Ian Boumphrey
Walking , Cycling & Riding Along the Wirral Way & the Story of the Hooton to West Kirby Railway by Ian Boumphrey
Birkenhead at War including Bebington 1939-45 – 84 pages - a War Diary with photographs + list of all those who died by Ian Boumphrey
Wirral on the Home Front 1939-45 – This 128 page book covers all of Wirral during WWII - including adverts & comic postcards of the time - in full colour by Ian Boumphrey

By the Same Publisher:

The Funny Side of Wirral – Cartoons by Bill Stott
Another Funny Side of Wirral – Cartoons by Bill Stott
Liverpool – Cartoons by Bill Stott
Liverpool Home – Cartoons by Bill Stott
Liverpool 3 – Cartoons by Bill Stott
Liverpool - Capital of Culture Cartoons by Bill Stott
The Wirral Country Bus – TB Maund
The Birkenhead Bus – TB Maund
The Wallasey Bus – TB Maund
Shadow to Shadow – History of Bristol Aeroplane Banwell & BAJ – Stephen Parsons
Birkenhead Electric Trams – Charles Rycroft
Railway Stations of Wirral – Mersey Railway History Group
Murder & Mayhem in Birkenhead – David Malcolm
More Murder & Mayhem in Birkenhead inc. Wallasey & New Brighton - David Malcolm & Ian Boumphrey
Walking Through the Blitz in the Birkenhead Area – NHC Tomlinson
The Story of Mariner's Park Wallasey – Robert Currams & Mike Condon
Birkenhead Park Cricket Club 1846-1996 – Chris Elston
Medical Matters in Victorian & Edwardian Wallasey – Dr Richard A Smye
Wallasey at War 1939-45 – Wallasey Historical Society
Helmets, Handcuffs & Hoses - the Story of the Wallasey Police – Noel Smith
Helmets, Handcuffs & Hoses - the Story of the Wallasey Fire Brigade – Noel Smith
Hoylake Racecourse and the beginnings of the Royal Liverpool Golf Club – John Pinfold
Beachcombers, Buttercreams and Smugglers' Caves - New Brighton & Liverpool in the 1950s – Pepe Ruiz